Contents

Counselling Skills and Theory, 4th edition

Counselling ~~Skills~~ Skills and Theory

Fourth Edition

22/23

Margaret Hough

HODDER
EDUCATION
AN HACHETTE UK COMPANY

Photo credits: p.10: © Valua Vitaly – Fotolia.com; p.43: © Darren Baker – Fotolia.com; p.75: © monkeybusinessimages – Thinkstock.com; p.107: © Rob – Fotolia.com; p.142: © Lisa F. Young – Fotolia.com; p.176: © WavebreakmediaMicro – Fotolia.com; p.205: © ideabug – iStockphoto; p.237: © hidesy – iStockphoto; p.273: © paylessimages – Fotolia.com

Orders: please contact Bookpoint Ltd, 130 Milton Park, Abingdon, Oxon OX14 4SB. Telephone: (44) 01235 827720. Fax: (44) 01235 400454. Lines are open from 9.00–5.00, Monday to Saturday, with a 24-hour message answering service. You can also order through our website www.hoddereducation.co.uk.

If you have any comments to make about this, or any of our other titles, please send them to educationenquiries@hodder.co.uk

British Library Cataloguing in Publication Data

A catalogue record for this title is available from the British Library

ISBN: 978 1 471 8 06452

Published 2014

Impression number   10 9 8 7 6 5 4 3 2 1

Year   2017 2016 2015 2014 2014

Cover photo © YAY Media AS/Alamy

Typeset by Datapage India (Pvt.) Ltd.

Printed in Italy

Acknowledgements

I would like to thank the following:

David, for his help and encouragement.

All the students who have contributed so much to discussion during our classes together.

My counselling and teaching colleagues, for their interest and for their helpful and constructive criticism of this fourth edition of *Counselling Skills and Theory*. Psychotherapists Toni Doherty and Marina Sweeney, for their friendship and for their interest in my work.

Former tutors John Redmond and Sue Hamer for their inspirational teaching.

Stephen Halder, Sundus Pasha and Joyce Adjekum at Hodder Education for their support while I worked on this fourth edition of the book.

The European Association for Counselling for information about its work and research.

Sophia von Humboldt for permission to quote from her research paper ('Building Bridges: Person Centred Therapy with Older Adults') published in *The European Journal of Business and Social Sciences*.

Moira Fraser for permission to refer to The Princess Royal Trust for Carers Survey (2011) *Always Concerned, Always on Call: A Survey of the Experiences of Older Carers*, Essex: PRTC.

The British Association for Counselling and Psychotherapy for permission to refer to its *Ethical Framework* 2013.

Jean Gray, Editor in Chief, RCN Publishing Co. LTD. The permission is for an article I cited in Unit 1 and included in the reference list. It is by Manley et al (2011) Person –Centred Care: Principle of Nursing Practice D. Nursing Standard (online) Vol. 25 No. 31 Feb 7th 2011. Pages 35-37.

Permission to use material by Gerald Egan from *The Skilled Helper*, 5E.©1994 South-Western, a part of Cengage Learning, Inc. Reproduced by permission. www.cengage.com/permissions.

Every effort has been made to trace and contact the following copyright holders.

Gwen Clarke for permission to quote from a research article entitled 'Person-Centred Care: Principle of Nursing Practice D' by Manley et al. and published in *Art and Science, Nursing Standard*, April 6 2011, 25, 31.

The publishers will be glad to rectify any errors or omission at the earliest opportunity.

About the author

Margaret Hough is a trained teacher with a degree in English and Education. She is a former registered nurse with extensive experience of health care in the UK and abroad. She has an Advanced Certificate in Counselling from Liverpool University and a Diploma in Counselling and Groupwork from the University of Wales, Bangor. Margaret has taught for many years on both college and university courses; she has experience in many areas of counselling, including general practice, student counselling and private work. She is a writer and consultant trainer in both groupwork and counselling skills. She also facilitates workshops and seminars on a range of relevant topics for students and trained counsellors.

Introduction

In the third edition of this book, published in 2010, I referred to significant developments that were about to take place in counselling and psychotherapy. Perhaps the most important of these initiatives was, and is, Improving Access to Psychological Therapies. This is a government-funded project designed to improve the mental health and general wellbeing of the adult population, through the provision of psychological therapies for depression and anxiety disorders. Such an initiative is particularly relevant in the context of counselling and psychotherapy, since these are the twin disciplines that have traditionally provided support for clients who wish to access talking therapies. However, debate continues apace about the type of therapy best suited to meet the needs of all clients, a debate that is likely to continue for some time into the future. The current focus is still on cognitive behaviour therapy (especially for depression and anxiety) as the approach deemed suitable for clients who wish to avail themselves of talking therapies, although access to a wider range of models is still possible within the Improving Access programme.

My purpose here is not to support any one approach over the others, since I believe they are all potentially effective when used in the context of a good therapeutic relationship between counsellor and client, with the individual client's needs firmly in mind. In this fourth edition of *Counselling Skills and Theory* I wanted to update all the units, with a focus on new developments within individual therapeutic approaches. However, I was concerned to retain all the basic elements contained in the third edition, so I have not substantially altered the contents of the book. One exception to this is the omission, in this fourth edition, of the section on groupwork skills and theory (formerly Unit 9), which dealt with all the theoretical approaches in this context. I am aware that groupwork is a specialised form of counselling that requires additional training, so it made sense to me to omit it from an introductory textbook concerned primarily with basic counsellor training at foundation, certificate and diploma level. It is increasingly the case that many areas of counsellor training (including groupwork) have become more specific in their focus, so require their own particular literature and texts to support them. Having said this, it is worth noting that all the individual theoretical approaches to counselling described in this book can be applied to the group context by counsellors trained to use them in this way.

This fourth edition is intended as a text suitable for students on introductory, certificate and foundation level courses. However, I would like to stress here that each unit is intended as an introduction to the theories described and is meant to stimulate further interest in them, as well as providing impetus for additional research and reading. When I wrote the first edition (1998), I was aware that the students I taught often found it difficult to locate text books that were relatively easy to understand, and which gave them enough information to prompt further research. In revising this fourth edition, my original aim of providing clear and stimulating information on a number of diverse theories remains the same. Each unit in this edition also describes the basic counselling skills that are integral to individual models of counselling. Specific techniques and procedures are discussed. I have tried to do this without using too much jargon, because I know from my own experience of teaching that students value clarity, especially at the beginning of training when they struggle with theories that seem esoteric and are unfamiliar to them.

Throughout the book I have included examples of good practice, and I have drawn on case material from on my own experience of counselling in different contexts, including further and higher education, groupwork, health care and general practice. Any details which could possibly identify individual clients have been omitted. My method of writing case material remains the same and is creative in the sense that it involves selecting a range of issues seen in counselling and placing them in a slightly altered context or background. In addition, clients' names are changed to ensure confidentiality and other details of age, gender and occupation are altered too. The importance of the client–counsellor relationship is highlighted in each unit, and the personal counsellor attributes needed for effective therapy are also addressed. The central place of training and supervision is stressed throughout the book but is more specifically dealt with in the last unit. There are student exercises in each unit, many of which can be used by students working alone, though some are probably more effective when completed with the guidance of trainers. This is because students, especially those starting training, may experience unexpected emotional responses which, if they are to provide insight and learning, need follow-up discussion and support. Experiential learning is invaluable in counsellor training and can only be facilitated within a carefully planned and supportive educational programme.

There are several additional sections in this fourth edition of the book, including (in Unit 5) reference to, and discussion about, the person-centred approach as an effective and compassionate way of helping clients in different contexts, including nursing and other branches of caring. There is a section on bullying in schools and online in Unit 1, along with a case study to illustrate its main points. Units 3 and 4 are also extended to include new sections on countertransference, contemporary object relations theory and the work of Heinz Kohut. In Units 6 and 7 I look at the evolution of both Gestalt and transactional analysis theory and practice; and discuss how new ideas have been developed and assimilated into these two approaches. In Unit 8 I have abbreviated the section on behaviour therapy and extended the second part of the unit, dealing with cognitive behaviour therapy (CBT), to include the work of Aaron Beck and George Kelly. There is an additional section about mindfulness-based cognitive therapy (MBCT), along with consideration of its contribution to the field of CBT. Using the internet to deliver CBT is also discussed in Unit 8, together with an appraisal of this important approach to therapy in health care today. Unit 9 contains a revised section on cultural diversity in counselling, as well as a new section entitled 'Feminism and counselling'. I am very aware that it is impossible to do justice to these very important subject areas in a text book of this kind, but I am also conscious of the need to include them and to suggest specific and extended texts for further study. Finally, I hope students will be sufficiently stimulated by my synopsis of both diversity and feminism to read more about them.

Margaret Hough, 2013

1

Key aspects of counselling

◆ Introduction

What is counselling? How does it differ from other helping activities? These are among the first questions which you may be asked to consider at the start of your training programme. A wide variety of ideas is likely to emerge in response to these questions, because no single answer adequately defines counselling. One way of approaching the problem of definition is to work in small groups and generate as many answers as possible among the participants.

Key aspects of counselling are shown in Figure 1.1.

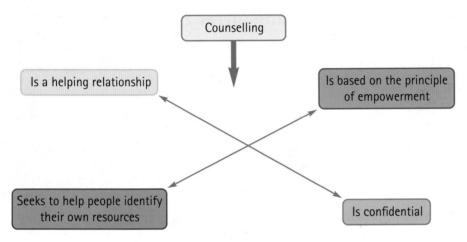

Figure 1.1 Key aspects of counselling

What is counselling?

A typical working group may produce results similar to the following list in answer to the above question. Counselling is:

- a special form of communication with an explicit contract
- a confidential and non-judgmental form of helping
- based on the principle of empowerment
- a relationship in which one person helps another
- an activity that may take place in a group setting, where one person may help several people in a group
- a process that entails a special kind of listening called 'active listening'
- a process which helps people to clarify and address problems

- a process that recognises each person is unique with unique experiences
- guided by theories about the causes of problems, and the methods needed to help
- an activity carried out by trained people.

In this first unit we shall discuss the above responses in turn, along with several other important issues relating to the nature of counselling. These include an examination of the difference between counselling skills and counselling theory, as well as an assessment of the uses of counselling in a wide range of professions. We shall also consider some of the situations in which counselling is used, and the types of problems it addresses. Aspects of counsellor training will be highlighted, although this topic will be taken up and dealt with in more detail in Unit 9.

How does counselling differ from other helping activities?

The above question is also of interest in relation to counselling. Possible answers include the following.

1 Some helping relationships involve giving advice, and counselling doesn't.
2 Other helping relationships may not have the same kind of boundaries.
3 There may be a conflict of interests in other helping relationships.
4 There are some helping relationships in which the helper might be judgmental.
5 Other helpers may offer sympathy rather than empathy.
6 Other helpers may not be objective.
7 There is an absence of mutual expectation in counselling; this means that the counsellor is there to help the client, and does not expect help from the client in return.
8 Counsellors do not impose conditions or expectations upon clients, while other helpers may expect their clients to behave in certain ways.

Awareness and acceptance of counselling

Although these are not exhaustive lists, they do provide enough material for discussion purposes. However, it is worth making the point straight away that counselling is not the mysterious or inscrutable activity which, in the past at least, members of the public sometimes believed it to be. In recent years, consumers have become more aware, and accepting, of the purpose and nature of counselling. There are several reasons for this: in the first place, counselling services are advertised, both in the media and on the internet, and it is now commonplace to hear counselling provisions referred to, following traumatic episodes, in the news or TV programmes. But there are also many people who use counselling skills every day in their work, and yet do not describe themselves as counsellors. Additionally, there are many people who have completed counsellor training, yet do not describe themselves as counsellors either. These are some of the people whose roles and responsibilities we shall discuss later in the unit.

EXERCISE

Responses to questions

Working individually, look at the answers given to the questions: What is counselling? How does it differ from other helping activities?

How many of these answers apply to your own work or professional practice? How many apply to your relationships with family and friends? Afterwards, discuss your ideas and conclusions with other members of your training group.

EXERCISE

Personal expectations

Working in small groups, discuss the characteristics that you would look for in a helper. Do not go into detail about any personal problems or concerns you may have at this stage. Instead, concentrate on listing, in general terms, those attributes and skills that you think an effective helper should possess.

KEY TERMS

Counselling: The process of counselling is very different from the dictionary definition of advice giving. In therapeutic terms it refers to a form of confidential helping which values and seeks to elicit each client's innate internal resources, coping abilities and strengths. Counsellors may help clients with specific problems in the present, but they may also support clients with long-term problems stemming from the past too.

Client: In psychotherapeutic terms, the word client has come to refer to someone who seeks help in counselling. The word 'patient' was traditionally used for anyone accessing psychological support, and some of the older books (those published before 1960) still feature it. In the process of moving away from a purely medical model of helping, however, both counselling and psychotherapy have adopted the term client, which is increasingly used in the hospital context too.

Some definitions

All the responses to the questions raised in this unit are, in fact, correct, though they do need some qualifying comments. Counselling is indeed a relationship, often between two people, but sometimes between a number of people and another person who is designated to act as counsellor for the group. Counselling, therefore, takes place both in individual and group settings, and in the latter context, two counsellors are occasionally present to work with members of the group. Regardless of the setting, however, the counselling relationship is a special form of communication, and this is true for a variety of reasons. One of the factors that make it special is the quality of helper listening, which is developed as a result of training. This listening involves attending to what the client means to say, as well as what he or she is actually saying, and this will be discussed in some detail in the next unit.

Confidentiality is another important component of the counsellor–client relationship that sets it apart from several other helping activities, although it should be noted that most professional helpers also regard it as essential to their work. Nevertheless, there are still some helping activities, like teaching, for example, where confidentiality towards pupils or students cannot be totally guaranteed. On the other hand, absolute confidentiality may not always be possible in counselling either; these and other limitations will be addressed in Unit 9.

Another important aspect of counselling is the concept of client empowerment. In simple terms, this indicates a confidence in the innate potential for self-determination which clients are believed to have. This capacity for self-determination may not always be apparent to the client, and certainly in times of stress or emotional upheaval it may become blocked or temporarily obscured. Counselling can help by enabling clients to look more closely at their experiences and to clarify them. When this is achieved, ways of addressing difficulties can be devised by clients themselves, and strategies for change can be implemented. The non-judgmental and empathic presence of a trained helper facilitates the processes just described, and the fact that counsellors do not expect any reciprocal help from clients (the kind of help friends might expect from each other, for example) means that clients feel valued and respected in a way they may not have experienced before. Nor do counsellors impose conditions or expectations on the clients they help, and even when goals and objectives are an integral part of the counselling contract, these are freely negotiated between client and counsellor.

CASE STUDY

Rosemary

Rosemary, who was aged 26, felt that she was 'stuck' in her life. She had been to university as a mature student, but dropped out after a year. Her boyfriend was unable to commit to a long-term relationship and she was unable to get full-time work, since she had no qualifications and her employment record was erratic.

Rosemary confided in a close girlfriend about her problems and, later on, she talked to her sister and to her mother.

When people are searching for answers they often talk to a number of people in this way. In doing so, they hope to find the right person who will help them make sense of their difficulties. Talking to different people also facilitates the process of thinking aloud, and thinking aloud helps to clarify the problem. However, for the process to work it is important to find the right listener or listeners. Rosemary described her experience in the following way:

My mother's response was to give me a telling off for lacking what she referred to as 'staying power'. I know that as a mother she was worried about me, but her worry made her unable to listen to and support me. My sister really tried, but she just couldn't help being judgmental about my poor work record. She has never been out of work herself, so this was something she couldn't understand. When I confided in my girlfriend she started to give me advice straight away. Though I appreciated her genuine effort to help, I knew that she was encouraging me in a course of action that wasn't right for me. But she did suggest that I talk to a life coach, and she helped me find someone who was trained in this area. The life coach (Becky) was trained in interpersonal skills too, and was therefore able to listen without judging me. She was also concerned with helping me identify what it was that I really wanted to do with my life.

Comment This case study highlights some of the difficulties inherent in direct advice giving. This is a subject we shall look at again in this unit. The importance of a non-judgmental approach in counselling is picked up and discussed in Unit 5. It should be stressed here that life coaching (which helped Rosemary) is not the same as therapeutic counselling. However, life coaches, like many other professionals, often undertake counselling skills training too. The next section offers a definition of therapeutic counselling.

Therapeutic counselling and counselling skills

Therapeutic counselling is an activity undertaken by people who are specifically trained in this field. It differs from many other occupations and areas of work that are often described as 'counselling' but, strictly speaking, are not. These other areas include, for example, career counselling, financial counselling, sports counselling and style counselling. In fact, there is a growing tendency to describe any occupation in which advice is given as 'counselling'. Therapeutic counselling does not include advice giving in its repertoire of skills, although it should be added that clients cannot fail to be influenced by a counsellor's attitudes, even when these are not explicitly stated.

In therapeutic counselling, the relationship between helper and client is especially significant and based on the principle of equality. Vulnerable clients may not always feel equal, but it is a principle that all counsellors need to respect and uphold. There is, moreover, no obvious conflict of interest in the relationship, and this is just one of the factors that sets it apart from other working relationships. Teachers may, for example, need to discipline pupils, while nurses and social workers often give advice to the people they help. However, a distinction should be made here between the use of therapeutic counselling with clients, and the use of counselling skills by other professionals in a variety of work situations. As we noted earlier, there are many people who now undertake counsellor training, because they believe the skills they gain will prove useful in the work they do. As a result of the training they receive, those people are well aware that they are not acting 'as counsellors' in their professional roles. Instead, they are using the interpersonal skills they have developed and refined within their counsellor training. A range of interpersonal or counselling skills will also be discussed in Unit 2 and in subsequent units throughout the book. Before looking at the differences between theory and skills, however, it is useful to consider the ways in which counselling has been defined by organisations that are directly linked to it. The following is a definition offered by the British Association for Counselling and Psychotherapy:

Counselling and Psychotherapy are umbrella terms that cover a range of talking therapies. They are delivered by trained practitioners who work with people over a short or long term to help them bring about effective change or enhance their wellbeing.

British Association for Counselling and Psychotherapy (2013).

KEY TERMS

Psychotherapy: The terms **counselling** and **psychotherapy** are often taken to denote the same process, and in many instances it is difficult to identify any appreciable differences between them. Traditionally psychotherapy training differed in length from that of counselling and tended to take longer. Psychotherapists use all the skills of counselling, but may have additional specific training, and may be concerned with life patterns relating to the past and its influence on the present.

Helping relationships

Working in groups of three or four, compile a list of the ways in which the counselling relationship differs from other helping relationships. These other relationships might include nursing, social work, medicine and church ministry, though there are probably others you can think of. What conflicts of interest could exist within any of these other relationships? How may counselling skills training help people in these professional roles?

Counselling skills and counselling theory

It is important to make a distinction between theory and skills in the context of counsellor training. At a basic level, the word 'skills' refers to the interpersonal tools counsellors need to possess or acquire, in order to communicate effectively with clients. These essential tools or skills include those of:

- listening and attending
- paraphrasing
- summarising
- asking questions
- encouraging clients to be specific
- reflecting their feelings
- helping them to clarify their thoughts
- encouraging them to focus on key issues
- offering forms of challenge when needed.

Implicit in the skills listed here are certain counsellor attitudes as well. These include:

- acceptance of, and respect for, clients
- recognition of each client's personal values, cultural background and resources.

However, in addition to the skills and counsellor attitudes listed, other skills are applicable to the actual organisation of counselling sessions. These basic skills will be discussed in some detail in Unit 2, along with examples of the way they are used with clients.

Counselling theory, on the other hand, deals with assumptions and hypotheses about the process of human development. The problems and difficulties that can arise at various stages throughout our lifespan, as a result of environmental or other influences, are also considered under the heading of counselling theory. The ways in which different forms of therapy and counselling approach these problems, as well as their individual methods of helping clients, have evolved alongside theories about human development and the acquisition of helpful and unhelpful behaviours. A summary of the three main approaches to counselling theory will be given in Unit 2. Individual theories will be described in more detail in subsequent units.

People who use counselling skills in their work

We have already noted that many people, including doctors, nurses, ministers of religion and teachers, use some counselling skills as part of their work. Doctors, for example, listen to their patients, and they usually try to understand the complex messages people in distress often wish to convey. There is a growing emphasis on the need for interpersonal skills training among health professionals, but, even when this is undertaken, doctors and others cannot devote the necessary listening time to individual patients. In addition to this, doctors frequently tell their patients what to do, and the central focus in doctor–patient encounters tends towards the factual rather than the emotional aspects of problems presented. Smith and Norton highlight this dimension of doctor–patient interaction when they state that doctors are trained in 'transmitting information' (1999:15). This transmission of information is usually factual in nature and may, as a result, neglect affective or emotional aspects of communication. This last point is applicable to people working in other areas of health care too. Despite the limitations just described, however, it is still the case that many health professionals, carers and others use what have come to be known as counselling skills in their daily work. A list of professionals in this category would include the following:

- psychologists
- welfare workers
- career counsellors
- teachers
- nurses, health visitors and midwives
- occupational therapists and speech therapists
- social workers
- physiotherapists
- ministers of religion
- voluntary and youth workers.

This represents only a selection of the many areas of work in which some counselling skills form an integral part of the professional's role. All of these people are likely to benefit from further training. The reason for this is that even when their interpersonal skills are quite well developed, professional people gain a great deal from further skills training and the process of self-development, which is a fundamental part of counsellor training. These counsellor skills and attributes will be developed in Unit 2.

CASE STUDY

Mrs Feltmann

Mrs Feltmann was a 68-year-old patient, who attended her central GP surgery suffering from chest pains. She had a history of chronic obstructive pulmonary disease (COPD), as well as a history of anxiety, which had worsened over the previous six months. This heightened anxiety was associated with her recent move to the area, and was further exacerbated by the experience of chest pains and profound worries about her health generally. Mrs Feltmann's doctor ensured that all aspects of her physical problems were investigated and treated. He referred her to a consultant chest physician, who suggested that she may benefit from stress counselling, or some other form of psychological assistance.

Mrs Feltmann tended to become tearful during visits to her GP and, although he was sympathetic and attentive, he could not give her the time and the quality of support she obviously needed. When the subject of counselling was raised, Mrs Feltmann agreed to it and an appointment was made with the practice counsellor.

During her first session with the counsellor, Mrs Feltmann talked at length about her health worries and the sequence of events that had led to her state of anxiety. She also cried a great deal and seemed relieved to express the pent-up emotions she had tried to ignore in the past.

CLIENT: I never really wanted to move here. It was my husband's idea. He always wanted to come here. I just went along with it and never said how I really feel.

COUNSELLOR: You didn't state your true feelings . . .

CLIENT: He never gave me a chance . . . him and the kids. Every time I went to say something they just took the line . . . 'Oh you'll love it. It's a lovely place, and it will help your chest.'

COUNSELLOR: So you felt you were never properly consulted . . . that nobody really listened.

CLIENT: That's right. Now I'm here and I don't know a soul. I feel trapped.

COUNSELLOR: Not able to talk to the family . . . nor to anyone else either.

CLIENT: The neighbours are not friendly. I have tried to be sociable, but the fact that I can't get out much . . . I can't drive and my chest is bad . . . means that I'm isolated. This is the first real talk I've had with anyone.

CASE STUDY Cont...

COUNSELLOR: The first time you have been able to say what you really feel.

CLIENT: Yes.

Comment: One reason for including this case study is that it highlights the difficulties that exist for many professionals in relation to their patients or clients. Mrs Feltmann's GP, for example, understood that she needed more time than he could possibly give her. He had other patients to see, though he was aware of her emotional needs and suggested counselling to address these. Under the current UK-wide programme for Improving Access to Psychological Therapies (IAPT), it is likely that increasing numbers of patients will be offered counselling in this way.

Another reason for describing Mrs Feltmann's problems is that it illustrates the close link between physical and emotional conditions. In her case the link was quite marked, and she seemed aware of this herself, since she readily agreed to counselling when it was suggested to her. This last point is an important one, because clients who feel under pressure to accept counselling seldom achieve a great deal as a result of it. In other words, counselling should be an option which clients are free to accept or decline, according to their individual needs and wishes. In Unit 2 we shall look at other case studies which illustrate the use of various counselling skills. However, an important point to make here is that the counsellor who helped Mrs Feltmann was able to give her time, something which the doctor could not offer because of his other commitments. Lack of time may also be an inhibiting factor in many of the other professional roles mentioned earlier. Nevertheless, there are some professional roles in which the time factor is a built-in consideration, and health visiting is an example of this. Health visitors who work closely with young mothers are very aware of the potential emotional problems which can affect their clients, so they ensure that sufficient time is devoted to the exploration of these problems. The following exchange between a young mother, named Louise, and her health visitor, named Lesley, illustrates this point:

LOUISE: I get a bit uptight about housework . . . I really worry about it.

LESLEY: All the new commitments you have now, especially the baby . . . that's a very new experience and responsibility.

LOUISE: [starting to cry] It seems endless . . . and I'm so tired. Sometimes I can hardly get out of bed.

LESLEY: Sit down for a moment and let's talk about this. Just tell me exactly the way you feel.

Lesley, the health visitor, was concerned to help Louise express her feelings and gave her sufficient time to do so. As part of her work, Lesley used a range of counselling skills including listening, paraphrasing, reflecting back feelings, and the skill of asking relevant questions. However, Lesley's job also included giving advice, which was entirely appropriate and necessary in this instance, since Louise needed it in order to identify and seek help for the post-natal depression she suffered. Advice giving would not be appropriate in therapeutic counselling though, because the focus there is on helping clients to identify what it is they want and need.

Problems of advice giving

In discussing the limits of advice giving, Rollo May makes the point that it is not 'an adequate counselling function because it violates the autonomy of the personality' (May, 1993: 117). Even before Rollo May expressed his reservations in this way, Freud (1920) had cautioned against giving direct advice, for it was his view that people should be helped to identify their own conclusions without pressure from a therapist. However, many clients seek counselling in the hope that they will be told what to do. Others hope for advice about the best ways to tackle their personal problems. Nevertheless, advice is not given in therapeutic counselling, and there are many reasons (including those highlighted by Freud and May) for withholding it. Perhaps one of the most important reasons is one which Amada (1995) identifies. He refers to the experiences of young children who are given frequent and copious advice, and who harbour deep feelings of resentment on account of it. These feelings do not disappear, but are carried into adult life and operate at an unconscious level thereafter. Advice, therefore, is not always valued in the way that advisers would like to believe. Nevertheless, there are some people who may be quite willing to follow any advice in a slavish and uncritical way. These people tend to view all helpers as experts, but in the context of therapeutic counselling they can be helped to look more closely at this aspect of their thinking and identify the reasons such expectations exist. If a client in therapy is willing to believe and follow everything a counsellor says, it is likely that he responds in a similar way to other significant people in his life. These ways of responding should be discussed between counsellor and client: if they are not, the client will have gained little as a result of therapy.

Clients who habitually invite or expect the control of others, or those who acquiesce to the views of other people, are in danger of losing sight of their own capabilities and resources. Counsellors can help their clients to locate and identify these resources, but in order to do this they need to be honest in relation to the subject of advice and its distorting influence. Clients are helped much more when they gain some understanding of the insecurities that impel them to seek advice in the first place. When clients develop greater understanding of their emotional problems, they tend to become more self-directed as a consequence, and the opinions and views of others are considered in a more detached way. This represents a real shift towards personal development and empowerment.

Advice or information?

We have seen that advice is a necessary component of some helping relationships. Patients expect and need advice from their doctors, for example, and practical help is often given too. Psychological and emotional conflicts cannot be approached in this utilitarian way, however, since it is only clients themselves who are aware of the complex dimensions of their own problems. The ways in which counsellors can help clients to identify and clarify their problems will be discussed in subsequent units. Meanwhile, an important caveat should be added in this section about advice: this concerns certain emergency situations in which clients seem incapable of acting in autonomous ways to protect themselves against harm or danger. In these situations, the counsellor may find it necessary to intervene by suggesting alternative courses of action. A client who is deeply depressed or suicidal, for example, may lack the psychological strength to make a constructive or informed decision about effective and available treatments that could be of benefit. Giving information to clients is, of course, not quite the same thing as giving advice, although a distinction between the two is sometimes hard to detect. The skill of information giving will be discussed in Unit 2.

Issues which bring people to counselling

People seek counselling for a wide variety of reasons. Sometimes they have specific problems that have become unmanageable, while at other times they may feel dissatisfied or unhappy with life in general. People frequently find themselves locked in repeated self-destructive relationships, and just as often fail to anticipate the consequences of the actions they take. Clients in counselling will often say that they don't really know why they behave in certain ways. This means that in spite of a genuine desire to change and to engage in more satisfying relationships, it is difficult for them to do so. There are many reasons for this inability to change, and perhaps the most significant is lack of self-awareness and personal insight. Other people seek counselling when they are troubled by physical symptoms that fail to respond to medical investigation or remedy. Psychosomatic problems may include skin problems, tension headaches, sleep disorders, tiredness, stomach problems and many other equally debilitating symptoms. Sometimes people are propelled towards counselling when they lack motivation or direction. Academic under-achievement, difficulties at work, lack of assertiveness and low self-esteem are also reasons that prompt people to ask for help through counselling. Addictions and phobias are problematic for many people, while others are troubled with anxiety, feelings of worthlessness, and often the conviction that they will fall apart or break down if help is not obtained. Figure 1.2 is an outline of some of the reasons that may prompt clients to seek counselling.

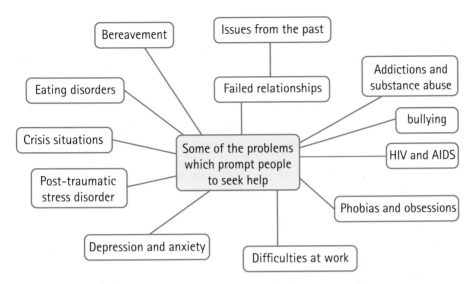

Figure 1.2 Some problems which prompt people to seek help

Repetition of problem relationships

Relationship problems are high on the list of factors that prompt clients to seek counselling. People are often perplexed by their own behaviour and their inability to establish and maintain enjoyable and healthy relationships. This does not imply that counsellors are relationship experts, since clearly this is not the case. Counsellors, like everyone else, experience difficulties in their private lives, although with a background of proper training they should be aware, at least, of the importance of getting help. Clients who attempt to solve their own relationship problems often find themselves unable to do so. This is because of the unconscious element that frequently operates to sabotage all conscious efforts. The units dealing with psychodynamic counselling in this book provide more information about unconscious motivation, and the ways in which it is manifest. With the aid of a trained person (in this case the counsellor), clients can be helped to identify those factors which disturb their relationships.

Crisis situations

The word 'crisis' can be used to describe a variety of situations that seem overwhelming at the time they are experienced. What is perceived as a crisis by one person may not be viewed as such by someone else. On the other hand, there are certain situations including sudden bereavement, assault, the discovery of serious illness, suicidal feelings, loss of employment and divorce, which are likely to constitute a crisis for the majority of people. A sudden crisis may serve to reactivate long-forgotten traumas or emotional problems from the past. These may be factors that bring people into counselling for the first time. Telephone counselling is another context in which crisis situations are addressed. Both Childline and the Samaritans offer listening services for people in crisis, although these two services differ in the sense that Childline also offers practical, sometimes interventionist advice. Volunteers who work for the Samaritans do not describe themselves as counsellors, but nevertheless use counselling skills in their work. Like Cruse, both Childline and the Samaritans provide their own training for volunteers, though some do complete other general training programmes too.

Bereavement

Bereavement is an experience that often brings people into counselling and is also one which everyone is likely to have at some stage in life. Although many bereaved people would, in the past, have received help in the community, from family, or friends, or both, this is not automatically the case today. However, even when bereaved people are supported by family and friends, there remain certain situations for which counselling has added benefits; this is especially true when several members of a family have suffered the same loss. Counselling is also applicable in crisis bereavement, or in circumstances that are complicated in other ways. Children who have lost a parent or parents are especially vulnerable and often need the added support counselling can give. Contrary to many people's beliefs, children experience loss as adults do, though their responses are different in significant ways. For example, small children often don't know how to acknowledge or express strong feelings like anger or sadness. It follows, therefore, that counselling support for children is a specialised area and one that requires its own specific training.

Parents and relatives of children who experience bereavement often complain of poor resources and support in this area. In their report published by the Joseph Rowntree Foundation, McCarthy and McCarthy (2005) express concern about the lack of research in the UK on the subject of bereavement. This lack of research is especially significant when we consider the numbers of young people who lose a parent or sibling (between four and seven per cent) before they are 16 years old. In addition, early bereavement is often a factor when young people commit offences, develop mental problems, or encounter difficulties at school. These findings highlight the need for information and counselling provision for bereaved children. The Rowntree report recommends that more specialist services be developed for young people. It also suggests that teachers and schools should address the issues relating to childhood bereavement. This last suggestion is made in recognition of the fact that many young people never talk to anyone about their experiences of bereavement. A range of complex problems is often a direct result of social isolation after bereavement, so it is certainly imperative that more professional adults are available to help young people who need it. Teachers, however, may not feel confident that they possess the skills to support young people who need help after bereavement. Like many other professional groups, teachers are now under pressure to undertake a range of additional duties, many of which require extra time and training. To their great credit, many teachers are increasingly developing counselling skills through training.

Cruse, which offers its own training programme for counsellors, is a national organisation which can direct family members to access help for bereavement. The Child Bereavement Trust also provides links to other organisations as well as to literature. The Childhood Bereavement Network, which is attached to the National Children's Bureau, provides information on available resources. Not all young bereaved people need counselling, however, and those whose relatives can support them usually manage to cope well. It should be remembered that parents and other relatives are likely to be grieving too, and this makes it especially difficult for them to support and nurture grieving children. Circumstances in which bereaved children may benefit from counselling include situations when:

- both parents have died
- a child feels responsible for the rest of the family
- a child is unable to talk about the loss, or to express feelings
- the child does not acknowledge the loss
- the child's parents are divorced when one of them dies
- there is another bereavement within the family
- the child develops behavioural problems at home or at school.

Issues from the past

There are some clients who seek counselling because of problems they experienced in childhood. These include sexual, emotional or physical abuse, or may be related to experiences of loss or abandonment. The difficulties stemming from childhood abuse, in particular, are now better understood and much more openly discussed. We know, for example, that repeated trauma in early life can often lead to emotional numbness, depression or patterns of destructive relationships. At a deeper level, they can lead to feelings of despair, which in turn may prompt patterns of self-mutilation or even suicide. Herman (2001: 108) refers to these 'attacks on the body' and describes them as attempts 'to regulate internal emotional states'. It is easy to see, therefore, why specialist training is often undertaken by counsellors who decide to work with survivors of childhood abuse and trauma. This is not to imply that it is an especially difficult area of counselling. It is, however, recognition that ongoing training is essential for all counsellors, including those who have completed courses at certificate and diploma level. If we are to understand the many problems, including trauma and abuse, which people are increasingly disclosing, we need to commit to education and training as a routine part of the work that we do. In Unit 9 we shall look again at issues relating to education and training for counsellors.

Depression and anxiety

Depression and anxiety are common problems for many people who seek counselling. It is estimated that one in twenty people suffer from depression, with three times as many women suffering as men (Holford, 2003). But there are many more people who experience minor levels of depression, and these people may never actually be diagnosed with the condition. Both anxiety and depression are sufficiently debilitating to disturb those clients who experience them. Depressive conditions often need medical as well as psychological support, and some of the clients who are seen in counselling may be referred by their GPs. Although some anxiety is unavoidable in everyday living, it can become problematic in certain situations and at certain stages of a person's life. Anxiety attacks, or anxiety which cannot be controlled, often prompt clients to ask for help. In the same way, free-floating anxiety or vague anxiety may impel some people to seek help in identifying the underlying cause. Cognitive behaviour therapy, which we shall look at in Unit 8, is now recognised as an effective approach for helping clients with problems of depression or anxiety. This is the form of therapy most likely to be offered in conjunction with medical support, and sometimes medication.

The subject of depression is often featured in health news items, and increasingly interest has been directed towards its causes, especially in an era of austerity which affects so many people. According to professor of psychiatry and medical historian Edward Shorter, however, depression is not one single illness but encompasses various psychological conditions, including melancholia. Professor Shorter regards melancholia (which is the term historically used to describe depression) as amenable to treatment with antidepressants. On the other hand, he believes that many other psychological or even physical symptoms, often classified as depression, are caused by other factors, including tiredness, for example (Shorter, 2013). Professor Shorter does not believe that antidepressant drugs work for people in this second group, but he points to psychological therapies (counselling) and exercise as beneficial. This supports what we already know about the effectiveness of counselling (especially cognitive behaviour therapy) for clients who are anxious, and/or depressed. The inclusion of exercise as an effective adjunct to psychotherapy, though not an entirely new idea, does emphasise a more holistic approach to helping clients generally.

Addictions and substance abuse

Occasionally, clients are prompted to seek counselling because they find themselves unable to deal effectively with their own addictive behaviour. Addictions and substance abuse include the most obvious examples of alcohol, drugs, and gambling, although we now know there are other addictive problems, which are sometimes highlighted in the press. Excessive shopping and addiction to exercise are two examples, and clients are now more likely to identify difficulties in relation to these, and to ask for help in understanding their underlying causes. It is important for clients to address the underlying causes of addictions and substance abuse, and counselling gives them the opportunity to do this. Different institutions offer specialist courses for people who want to work in the area of addiction. In its information about training, the British Association for Counselling and Psychotherapy notes that specialist alcohol, drugs, AIDS, bereavement, cancer and child abuse counselling courses are offered by various institutions. These courses are provided for counsellors working in the relevant fields, or for counsellors who wish to specialise after general training. The BACP goes on to add that 'It is more usual to complete a substantial counselling training followed by a specialisation' (BACP, 2013).

Phobias and obsessions

There is an almost infinite variety of phobias people can suffer from. Perhaps the most common, or at least the best known, are phobias about animals, insects, meeting people, enclosed spaces, germs and flying. It is probably true to say that people can become obsessive about almost anything, and obsessive compulsive disorder (OCD) is a condition that affects many people, especially when they are under stress. Different theoretical approaches to counselling offer varying explanations for the causes and development of obsessions and phobias, and some of these will be discussed in later units of the book.

However, it should be added here that there is currently a focus on cognitive behaviour therapy as the most effective form of counselling for clients with irrational fears, phobias and obsessions. Many relatively short cognitive behaviour programmes are now being offered for clients with these difficulties, though not everyone is convinced that such programmes are effective in the long term. In a reference to cognitive behaviour therapy, Irvin Yalom places it in the category of empirically validated therapy, or EVT. He adds that although it is certainly an empirically validated approach, he is concerned that 'many false assumptions' are made in cognitive behaviour research (Yalom, 2004: 223). Later in the book, we shall look in some detail at behavioural and cognitive approaches to counselling, and we shall discuss some of the concerns relating to these.

Work problems

Many relationship problems are experienced in the context of work, and employment stress or burn-out are often symptoms of the underlying difficulties clients bring to counselling. Some companies now offer stress counselling to employees who need it, and even those who do not are increasingly aware of the importance of counselling support. People need to understand how they themselves contribute to the stress they experience, and a focus of counselling is this identification of individual factors in stress maintenance. Clients are often surprised to discover that they sometimes collude in punishing themselves when they agree to every single request, no matter how unreasonable it seems.

Stress counselling is effective in helping people to examine their own behaviour in the workplace and to adjust it when necessary. The subject of bullying in the workplace is now routinely reported in the media, and increasingly clients are seeking counselling for its effects. Bullying is probably a phenomenon that was always present among groups of people working together. However, our approach to bullying is now different, and we are less tolerant of its insidious and destructive effects. This means that people who are exposed to bullying behaviour at work are becoming more likely to ask for help through counselling.

Bullying in schools and online

Perhaps one of the most insidious developments in modern times is the pervasiveness of bullying behaviour among teenagers and children. It could, of course, be argued that bullying has always been present in society generally, and that it is no more prevalent now than it was in the past. However, it is only in the twenty-first century that bullying has become a topic of general public concern; one reason for this is the link between bullying and suicide in young people. The fact that bullying behaviour is often identified as a cause of suicide means that counselling support is increasingly available to victims in schools.

We now know that bullying is often hard to detect and may be quite widespread in schools before, and if, it is uncovered. Even when anti-bullying policies are in place, most children experience bullying (which may be physical, emotional or rumour spreading) at some stage in their school years. Cyber bullying may take place outside school, but it is something that school counsellors often have to address. In addition, bullying frequently involves groups of young people, in which case the problem needs to be addressed in the context of the group. This is much easier said than done, as the next case study shows. It also has implications for counsellors working in schools, in the sense that additional training in groupwork skills is clearly indicated.

The British Association for Counselling and Psychotherapy offers guidelines (2011) for counsellor practitioners who work within schools; these counsellors are now seeing increasingly more young people who are subjected to bullying behaviour. As we have seen, school counselling is a specialist area of work, which deserves extra training in that particular context.

CASE STUDY

The school group

Grace, who was a counsellor at a high school for girls, was asked by the principal to talk to a group of 15–16 year olds about some disturbance she (the principal) sensed in the group. There were no overt signs of bullying, and no one had complained, but other teachers had also sensed that something was wrong. Grace had trained in groupwork skills and agreed to facilitate the group, but away from the classroom, where the pupils could sit in a circle in an uninterrupted environment. When the girls arrived at the appointed time it was clear they saw the situation as something of a novelty. Initially, there was a lot of barely suppressed giggling and some whispering, which subsided when Grace introduced herself and asked if the girls would take turns to introduce themselves by name. These introductions started slowly, but gradually the atmosphere became more relaxed. Grace formed a contract with the group, which consisted of basic ground rules. These rules included observing confidentiality about issues discussed within the group, listening without interruption when individual members spoke, and showing respect for other people's views.

One girl started by saying that she had no idea why they were there. Grace asked if anyone would like to add anything to that, and several pupils shook their heads. This was followed by a fairly long silence, and then a member of the group (Eva) pointed towards another pupil and said: 'I think it's something to do with her.'

The girl being pointed at started to cry. Her name was Lynn and she had started attending the school just three months earlier. After a while, she regained composure and revealed that her mother had died six months ago, and that she and her father had moved to the area to be near to relatives. There was a general gasp of surprise from the group, and everyone agreed that they had no idea her mother had died. Lynn's response to this was that no one had asked. The mood in the group became softer, and the class began to focus on Lynn in an attentive and caring way. She was given an opportunity to talk freely about her experience of being ostracised and made fun of from her first day in school. She was never accepted by the others, and she often heard them commenting about her appearance in a negative way.

Grace could see that Lynn's experiences had a huge effect on the group. They seemed subdued, and one girl asked if the group could meet again. This second meeting was arranged by Grace so that other issues arising from the first session could be further processed.

Comment: This is a compressed version of the dynamics and processes that took place with the class group. It is meant to highlight the point that bullying itself is usually a group process in schools, and therefore needs to be addressed within the group. It illustrates also that victims of bullying are often (like Lynn) lonely and lacking in self-esteem. Bereavement can be isolating unless support is available, and loneliness often leads to loss of self-esteem and confidence.

Personal growth

Sometimes people decide to seek counselling in order to assist the process of personal growth and development. This is now regarded as a legitimate quest for anyone interested in dealing effectively with life challenges, especially those arising at key ages or stages throughout life. In the past, such people might have turned to ministers of religion, or even neighbours and friends for help and enlightenment. Now, because of changing patterns of church attendance and the secularisation of society generally, people are less likely to automatically seek help from ministers and priests. In addition, most people have become aware of the difference between help supplied by friends and neighbours and that given in a professional context through confidential counselling. With the best will in the world, friends and neighbours might not keep confidences, or they might want to talk about themselves. This is not to denigrate the support that close-knit communities do supply; instead, it is meant to emphasise the points already touched on at the beginning of this unit, where we discussed the difference between counselling and other helping activities.

Today, personal growth and development are much more acceptable aspirations than in the past. There are many reasons for this, including freedom from relentless physical labour and the attendant focus on health and general wellbeing. Along with this is the current emphasis on self-expression, as well as the confessional style of much radio and television content. Social media, too, exemplifies this desire to be heard.

Eating disorders

Counselling for eating disorders, like other specialist areas of counselling, is often undertaken by practitioners who pursue further training in this specialism once they have completed their general training. Health professionals, working in hospitals, may specialise in supporting clients with eating disorders, and often the therapy takes place in groups.

Anorexia, bulimia and compulsive eating are all problems that sometimes impel clients to seek counselling. Often clients are referred by their GPs, but occasionally they come into counselling for other reasons, such as depression, which are linked to eating disorders. Anorexia and other eating disorders are on the increase, a phenomenon which Orbach (1994) has highlighted in her research and writing. Although eating disorders may be difficult to overcome, experts in the field acknowledge the importance of psychological support (often long term) for those people who suffer from them. A focus of counselling is to help clients identify the underlying cause (or causes) of conflict in relation to food. Many clients benefit from a feminist perspective in counselling. This is because of the sociological factors that are often implicated in eating conditions.

HIV and AIDS

HIV and AIDS is another specialist field of counselling and one that tends to attract people who are especially interested in it. Practitioners may have had the experience of HIV or AIDS themselves, and this may prompt them to undertake counselling training in order to help others. When counsellors are motivated through personal experience, they tend to be deeply empathic towards their clients. However, there are other practitioners who work effectively with clients even when they have no personal experience of HIV or AIDS. In either case, specialist training is important and increasingly accessed by practitioners who wish to work in this field.

People who are concerned about their health in relation to HIV and AIDS include the relatives or partners of clients who have been tested as HIV positive, as well as clients who have actually developed AIDS. This means that people who come for counselling do so with a range of different problems and concerns. In later units we shall look at some approaches that may be appropriate in helping people with diverse needs such as these.

Trauma and disaster

In recent years we have seen a marked increase in the availability of counselling provision for survivors of large-scale trauma or disaster. This provision of counselling support is now so marked that people are routinely given advice about how to access it in the aftermath of a trauma. Not everyone is convinced that such intervention is effective, however. Writing in *One Nation Under Therapy,* Satel and Sommers (2005) argue that therapy tends to undermine each person's innate ability to cope with stress, even stress on a large scale. After September 11th, New York citizens were, it seems, encouraged to seek counselling through Project Liberty, a government initiative created in response to the attacks. In the event, less than one-tenth of New Yorkers came forward for help. Those who didn't seek help appear to have coped with the trauma in their own individual ways. Satel and Sommers (who have conducted other studies in the field of grief and trauma counselling) conclude that grief is, in fact, self-limiting. This implies that people have the capacity to heal themselves over time, even in very extreme circumstances. Joseph (2011) also believes that grief after a trauma may be self-limiting and that response to it is similar to that of bereavement, making it a natural reaction to devastating or exceptional events. He argues that such events make some people stronger in the end, though counselling is often accessed by them in the short term. This is a much more positive assessment of the effects of trauma, and highlights the point that a diagnosis of post-traumatic stress disorder may have a negative impact on some people so that recovery and progress are impeded. Professor Joseph, who is the co-director of the Centre for Trauma Resilience and Growth, has conducted research into why it is that some people struggle after a trauma, while others are more resilient and may even experience personal growth as a result of it. His conclusion is that symptoms of post-traumatic stress do not just go away, but can, with help, be managed. Cyrulnik (2007), too, speaks of resilience, even in children deeply traumatised within the family.

While it may be true that some people survive trauma, and even grow as a result of it, there are, nevertheless, others who seek and need help following such an experience. It is for these people that counselling support is increasingly available. This highlights the point that counselling, if it is to be effective, needs to be undertaken voluntarily by clients. It is not something that people should be pressurised to undertake if they don't feel they need it. An NHS helpline was set up after the July 2005 London bombings; this initiative, the first of its kind, offered counselling to victims of the bombings, along with support for bereaved relatives or witnesses to the traumatic events. This helpline project was clearly the beginning of many similar initiatives, including those by Cruse and the Samaritans, for helping people to deal with trauma and crisis. Provision of this kind of support is important, and means that people have the option to seek further counselling if they choose.

Other reasons for seeking counselling

Today people seek counselling for a wide variety of problems. The BACP website shows seven specialist divisions, including a new one, 'Coaching', which was added in 2010. There is also a large number of counselling agencies nationwide, indicating that counselling is available for numerous psychological, physical, social and behavioural issues. A general summary of reasons for seeking counselling, other than those already described, includes the following:

- chronic illness
- problems experienced by carers
- unresolved or complicated grief after bereavement
- developmental crisis
- social problems
- issues associated with sexual orientation or identity
- job loss, redundancy and problems related to retirement
- problems relating to poverty and financial distress
- issues relating to parenting, stepfamilies and childlessness
- gambling
- addiction to online pornography
- violence and assault.

Different settings

In addition to the reasons for counselling, there is, as we have seen, a wide range of specific contexts in which counselling and therapy are actually used. Discussing the diversity of settings in which counselling is delivered, the British Association for Counselling and Psychotherapy (BACP, 2013) includes counsellors working in private practice, those working in voluntary agencies, and counsellors working in schools, youth work and General Practice.

These are just a few of the many contexts in which counselling provision is now located. Group counselling, another specific setting for counselling practitioners, will be discussed in more detail in Unit 9.

The following is a list of diverse modes and settings in which counselling and psychotherapy are currently provided:

- couples counselling
- family therapy
- group counselling
- telephone counselling
- online counselling
- schools, colleges and university
- voluntary work
- health centre or general practice
- hospitals and hospices
- private practice
- the workplace.

Most of these areas require their own specific training, and are usually undertaken by counsellors who have a special interest in them. A hospital nurse may, for example, have a special interest in caring for patients or clients who have had breast surgery. In this instance, the nurse is likely to undertake training in this particular area of counselling, often within the hospital itself. Increasingly, health practitioners provide counselling support for clients with body image changes as a result of illness or surgery.

EXERCISE

Common problems

Working in small groups, identify the most common problems which clients (in your area of work) tend to have. Afterwards, discuss your findings with members of the training group generally. What were the outstanding problems identified overall?

EXERCISE

Debate about counselling

In pairs, look at the following statement and discuss it. Spend about 15 minutes on this exercise, and afterwards discuss it with other members of your group.

There are certain situations in which some people do not benefit from or even need counselling support. Whether or not people benefit from counselling depends on their prior life experience and their support systems of family and friends.

Don't worry about getting right or wrong answers in discussing these statements. Their purpose is to stimulate debate as to whether counselling is appropriate for everyone involved in traumatic or stressful events.

Self-development and self-awareness in counsellor training

One of the things you will become aware of quite early on in your training is that learning about counselling is not an entirely theoretical exercise. On the contrary, there is a substantial element of personal development that is integral to all training programmes. What this means in practice is that a great deal of what you learn throughout the course will be 'experiential' in nature. From the very beginning you will probably think much more about yourself, the experiences you have had, the opinions you hold, the prejudices of which you were previously unaware, your past and present relationships and, indeed, any other significant factors of your personal and professional life. This experience is both rewarding and challenging, and no doubt your trainer or trainers will discuss it with the group. Your teacher or trainer may also establish a contract or working agreement with group members, and when this is the case a number of important 'ground rules' may form part of it. These ground rules obviously vary from one training establishment to another, but certain areas are common to most of them. Once these rules have been discussed and agreed upon, group members tend to acquire a much clearer view of course structure and objectives. Areas that are usually discussed at the beginning of each course include the following:

- administrative details, course structure and dates of course breaks
- details about placements and supervision
- methods of teaching, learning and assessment criteria
- the role of the trainer or teacher
- guidelines relating to confidentiality
- guidelines about the use of personal experience for skills practice and discussion
- attendance and timekeeping
- keeping a diary or journal
- the importance of listening to what others say
- the need to respect views expressed by other group members.

Timekeeping

Attendance and timekeeping are central issues in counsellor training, especially at the level of introductory and foundation courses. It is sometimes difficult for trainees to understand the link between their behaviour on the course and their behaviour and expectations in relation to the clients they work with (or hope to work with). It is useful to consider the word 'boundaries' in this context, since it refers to the parameters or guidelines governing the working relationship between counsellor and client. Clients need to know that counsellors are reliable, and reliability encompasses such areas as punctuality and good timekeeping. If students are unable to come to training sessions on time, or if they frequently feel obliged to leave before sessions end, it is unlikely that a miraculous transformation of behaviour will occur late on. Another relevant point to make is that other students in a training group tend to resent the disruptive effect created when people arrive or depart at different times. Last, but not least, poor timekeeping means that whole areas of both theoretical and practical experience are missed, and are never properly regained throughout training.

Counselling practice and supervision

Other important issues central to counsellor training include experience of working with clients and supervision. The British Association for Counselling and Psychotherapy states that 'there is a general obligation for all counsellors, psychotherapists, supervisors and trainees to receive supervision/consultative support independently of any managerial relationships' (BACP, 2013). Students on BACP-accredited courses are required to have one hour of supervision for every eight hours of practice work with clients. In addition, there should be a minimum of one-and-a-half hours per month. This supervision for accredited course placements should take place at least fortnightly. For shorter skills-training courses, experience in placement is not usually required, though some specialist agencies have their own placement and supervision arrangements.

The subject of supervised placement should be discussed with you prior to enrolling for the course, and the requirements for the course generally should have been clarified for you. There is an increasing emphasis on providing top-quality training courses, with more uniformity in content and design, so colleges and other course providers are motivated to seek out the best supervised practice for their students. Finding good-quality placements is not easy, however, and training staff are there to help you negotiate with those agencies willing to provide suitable placements for learners. In order to facilitate this process, agencies are likely to receive general information about the course from your training establishment, including details about course structure and design. Agencies may also be asked to complete an 'expression of interest' form, asking whether they are willing to help place students. Agencies willing to provide training opportunities for students also need clear guidelines about placement aims and objectives. This is because close liaison between the training establishment and the placement agency is central to a good experience for students.

Well-organised and supervised placements constitute a core component in full counsellor training. They ensure that the client–student-counsellor relationship is conducted as safely as possible, and that theory and practice are integrated in a paradigm suitable for client needs and welfare. Student members of BACP can access a database of trainee placements. This information is located in the Members area of the website.

Enlisting supervisors who are willing to work with students is another challenge facing many training establishments. A student in placement will need a mentor within the practice agency itself, as well as an external counselling supervisor working in conjunction with college staff. In addition, clear (and often substantial) documentation is needed to support and record the various elements that are integral to practice-based counsellor training. This documentation may include an agency–trainee-counsellor contract, a supervision contract, a log book to record student–client hours, a record of mentor assessment of the student and written trainee–counsellor–individual client contracts. Obviously, this documentation will vary somewhat from one training establishment to another, but the basic elements of contractual arrangements are similar on all generalist courses.

Keeping a journal

Some educational institutions require students to keep an ongoing journal throughout the training course. This record may be either written or verbal (recorded on tape), and its purpose is to enable trainees to reflect on the experiences they have and the personal development they have achieved, as a result of both professional practice and training. Keeping a journal is a valuable aid to self-exploration, and you should make a point of keeping entries up to date. One way of doing this is to ensure you make an entry as soon as possible after each training session. In this way, you are less likely to forget the relevant areas of theory and practice that have been covered each time. Some course trainers require their students to submit these diaries at the end of the course, while others regard them as confidential and for the student's use only. It is a good idea to record the number and dates of sessions at the beginning of each entry, and it is also useful to present the journal in loose-leaf format. A file with individual loose-leaf pockets works well; when journals are used for assessment purposes, relevant sections can be extracted as required. The structure of the journal should be clear, with sufficient space allowed for tutor comments, if applicable. You need to show some evidence of reflection and thought, and this can, of course, prove difficult, especially at the beginning of a course when you are learning about a new subject. The following is a guide to recording sessions:

1 Record the content of the session.
2 What skills were practised?
3 What topics were discussed?
4 How were practice sessions organised?
5 How did you respond to the work being done?
6 How did other people in the group respond?
7 Record any feedback you received from other trainees.
8 Record any significant group discussion which followed each session.
9 Write an entry even when you were absent for a session. Say why you were absent, and how you felt about this. What areas of work were covered when you were away?

10 Record any connections you have made between work covered in sessions, and the experience of the client–counsellor relationship. Has anything happened, or has anything been discussed, which sheds some light on how clients might feel in certain situations, for example?

11 Say something about your reactions to particular theories discussed.

12 Record any connections you might have made between theory and practice.

13 Record any significant insights you have gained.

14 Refer to any relevant newspaper articles or books you have read.

15 Refer to lecture handouts and say how useful or otherwise these have been.

This may seem like a fairly extensive list, but it is meant as a guide only. Most trainers discuss the content of journals with their students, and requirements are often clearly set out. The most important point to remember about journals is that they should indicate evidence of developing self-awareness. They should also show that you are increasingly aware of the way other people think and feel. Both these areas of awareness (self-awareness and awareness of others) need then to be linked to the counselling context. Writing a journal throughout training is a valuable aid to self-understanding, and has some similarity with the therapeutic effects gained through talking in counselling. As Storr (1997: 123) points out, both these activities are similar in the sense that they help to 'increase insight', although it should be added that keeping a diary or journal does not provide the feeling of acceptance that is so important for clients in counselling. A well-kept journal also demonstrates your ability to record information, to collate material, and to present this material in a logical and clear form. It further demonstrates your ability to use skills gained on the course, in your personal and professional life. You may be required to submit your journal for assessment purposes and, when this is the case, it will be regarded as confidential between you, your course tutor and the moderator.

In a later unit (Unit 9) we shall look at the importance of research in counselling, and we shall consider why it is relevant, even at this early stage, to all students in training.

Skills training

Throughout your training you will probably be asked to work with other trainees in groups. Some courses incorporate personal development groups (PDG) into their training programmes. These groups give students the opportunity to work closely together and to explore personal issues and relationships in a safe and supportive environment. Counselling skills practice is another integral part of most training courses, and this is designed to give students the chance to demonstrate the use of a range of basic skills in an ongoing way throughout training. Skills practice may take the form of role play, or it may take the form of peer counselling. In fact, both these methods of training may be used within the same course. Skills practice, whether role played or authentic, has many advantages for students in training. An outstanding advantage is that you can develop counselling skills without harming clients, and when these skills are developed, you can then integrate them into your personal and professional life. One disadvantage is that some trainees may be so lacking in confidence and basic skills to start with that they are unable to conduct these exercises without causing distress to others. However, teachers and trainers are aware of the difficulties that can arise in these practice sessions and are usually vigilant in the way they monitor and observe students work. The following descriptions highlight the advantages and disadvantages of both role play and experiential counselling in skills training.

Role play

Role play, as a method of practice in counselling, is used on some courses, and has the advantage of being a relatively safe way for students to learn basic skills. This approach requires participants to simulate a counselling situation and to assume the roles of client and counsellor. Working through role play means that you are unlikely to 'hurt' a colleague who is playing the part of client, and it has the added advantage of allowing you to explore emotions and feelings in a non-threatening context. Trainers often provide their students with specific scenarios or problems, which are then used in the role-play situation. The following exercise gives an example of a role play brief.

There is, of course, a very wide variety of possible problem situations that can be used for role play purposes. Besides the advantages already mentioned, role play also allows you to stop at any stage throughout the session, in order to discuss your progress and the skills being used. On the other hand, role play makes it difficult for participants to become involved on a personal level, and it is also surprisingly difficult to be 'real' when problems discussed are hypothetical. The core condition of empathy (described in Unit 5) is almost impossible to develop when two people are engaged in a simulated exchange. In contrast, there are substantial advantages to being a real client during skills training.

EXERCISE

Role play

A middle-aged woman has been referred by her doctor for counselling. Her two grown-up children have left home, and she feels lonely and isolated since their departure. She would like to be more socially involved, but lacks the confidence to initiate any real contacts.

Using your own problems

When you use your own problems in skills sessions, you will experience exactly what it is like to be a client in counselling. You will also gain valuable insights into your own attitudes, feelings and areas of personal vulnerability. The learning that takes place at this level is probably more important than anything you can read in books, and highlights the experiential aspect of counsellor training, which we noted earlier in this unit. In addition to gaining insight and identifying areas of vulnerability, being a real client during skills training also allows you to develop trust and sharing among your colleagues, and this is certainly important in any training group. However, time is usually limited in practice sessions, and this can cause problems for trainees who are inexperienced as counsellors. Some trainee counsellors may not possess, or have had time to develop, sufficient competence to conduct the sessions within safe limits. There is sometimes a tendency to push the 'client' too far so that what looked like a simple problem on the surface leads to deeper issues, which neither student is able to deal with. Students who are working as clients may also be tempted to use training sessions as a means of dealing with outstanding or unresolved personal problems. This is, of course, unfair to colleagues who are, after all, in a learning situation too. Once again, your trainer will be aware of potential problems, and will endeavour to ensure that training programmes are conducted in the safest possible way.

Personal therapy

Many professional bodies now ask students on counselling courses to undertake personal therapy if they wish to work towards accreditation. A one-year full-time or two-year part-time course may involve 50 hours or more of personal therapy for students. Short-term courses tend not to have this requirement; an introduction to interpersonal or counselling skills, for example, will not normally include personal therapy as a mandatory component. However, you are probably aware of all the relevant details in relation to your own course.

The inclusion of personal therapy in counsellor training is important for several reasons. Perhaps the most important is that it encourages you to explore your emotional life. This exploration will focus on personal prejudices, relationships, past and present, and reasons (often unacknowledged) for choosing to undertake counsellor training. Personal therapy also forms a link between the theory learned on the course and the actual practice of counselling. The experience of being a client leads to a deeper understanding of the many and varied feelings clients experience in therapy. These feelings may include apprehension, shame, vulnerability, dependency, trust and hope, to name just a few.

Being a client in therapy also provides an opportunity to *see* and *observe* the counsellor at work. It provides, too, some valuable insights into the nature of the counselling relationship itself. It sometimes comes as a surprise to students to learn that feelings towards a helper can be negative as well as positive, for example. In Unit 3 we shall look in more detail at these aspects of the relationship between counsellor and client. Other benefits of personal therapy include a deepening awareness of the stages of counselling, right through from the beginning to the end. Another important aspect of personal therapy, and one linked to the exploration mentioned above, is that it should help you to identify clearly your own problems and conflicts. This identifying process is essential because it means that you become more self-aware generally. It also means that you can take ownership of your emotional experiences and thus are less likely to confuse them with the experiences of potential clients.

Having pointed out the benefits of personal therapy in training, however, it would be unfair to leave it there without mentioning some of the disadvantages too. Chief among these is the fact that a compulsory training component does not allow for personal choice. Since client personal choice is a central principle of counselling and psychotherapy, it is difficult to see how a mandatory requirement for personal therapy in training can be reconciled with this. Additionally, personal therapy is likely to be expensive for students, although the potential benefits of it far outweigh financial outlay. From my own experience of teaching students, I am convinced that the importance of personal therapy lies in the fact that it fosters a greater awareness of self and a deeper understanding of the experience clients have in counselling.

SUMMARY

In this unit we looked at some of the basic questions which are often asked in relation to counselling. These include questions concerning the nature and function of counselling and the ways in which this form of helping differs from several others, including, for example, nursing and social work. Some definitions of counselling were suggested, and the British Association for Counselling and Psychotherapy definition (2013) was also quoted. We looked at a range of occupations which are often described as 'counselling', even though they have little in common with 'therapeutic' counselling. A distinction was made between skills and theory, and we discussed the ways in which counselling skills are used by people who work as health professionals.

The subject of advice and information giving was addressed in the context of the ways in which health professionals and others help their patients and clients. We saw that advice is not normally given in therapeutic counselling, though we considered some emergency situations in which advice and information may become almost synonymous. Aspects of counsellor training were outlined in this unit: these included timekeeping, the use of journals, establishing a training contract, skills training, practice and supervision, personal therapy and role play. The problems which bring people to counselling were highlighted, as were the specific contexts in which counselling is used. In this edition of the book, we have extended the section dealing with trauma and disaster to include references to recent research, and added a new section on the subject of bullying in schools and online.

In Unit 2 we shall also consider the individual skills used in counselling. An overview of the main historical and theoretical approaches to therapy and counselling will also be outlined.

References

Amada, G. (1995) *A Guide to Psychotherapy*. New York: Ballantine Books.

British Association for Counselling and Psychotherapy (2013) *Careers in Counselling*. London: BACP.

British Association for Counselling and Psychotherapy (2010) *Divisions and Forums*. London: BACP.

British Association for Counselling and Psychotherapy (2013) *Counsellor Courses and Training*. London: BACP.

British Association for Counselling and Psychotherapy (2013) *What is Counselling?* London: BACP.

British Association for Counselling and Psychotherapy (2013) *Supervision and Personal Therapy*. London: BACP.

Cyrulnik, B. (2007) *Talking of Love on the Edge of a Precipice*. London: Penguin.

Freud, S. (1920) *A General Introduction to Psychoanalysis*. New York: Horace Liveright.

Herman, J. L. (2001) *Trauma and Recovery*. London: Pandora.

Holford, P. (2003) *Optimum Nutrition for the Mind*. London: Piatkus.

Jenkins, P. & McGinnis, S. (2011) *Good Practice for Counselling in Schools* (4th edn). London: BACP.

Joseph, S. (2011) *What Doesn't Kill Us: The New Psychology of Posttraumatic Growth*. London: Hachett Digital.

May, R. (1993) *The Art of Counselling*. London: Souvenir Press Ltd.

McCarthy, J. R. & McCarthy, J. J. (2005) *Young People, Bereavement and Loss: Disruptive Transitions?* York: The Joseph Rowntree Trust.

Orbach, S. (1994) 'Hunger Strike' in Orbach, S. *What's Really Going on Here?* London: Virago Press.

Satel, S. & Sommers, C. H. (2005) *One Nation under Therapy*. New York: St Martin's Press.

Smith, S. & Norton, K. (1999) *Counselling Skills for Doctors*. Buckingham: Open University Press.

Shorter, E. (2013) *How Everyone became Depressed: The Rise and Fall of the Nervous Breakdown*. New York: Oxford University Press.

Storr, A. (1997) 'Sigmund Freud' in Storr, A. *Feet of Clay: A Study of Gurus*. London: Harper Collins.

Yalom, I. D. (2004) *The Gift of Therapy*. London: Piatkus.

Further reading

Aveline, M. (1990) 'The training and supervision of individual therapists', in Dryden, W. (ed.) *Handbook of Individual Therapy*. Milton Keynes: Open University Press.

Bennett, M. (2005) *The Purpose of Counselling and Psychotherapy*. London: Palgrave Macmillan.

Bor, R. & Watts, M. (2006) *The Trainee Handbook: A Guide for Counselling and Psychotherapy Trainees* (2nd edn). London: Sage Publications.

Burnard, P. (1994) *Counselling Skills for Professional People*. London: Chapman Hall.

Department of Health (2012) *Improving Access to Psychological Therapies* (IAPT). Available at: http://www.iapt.nhs.uk/about.

Dryden, W. & Thorne, B. (1991) 'Key Issues in the Training of Counsellors', in Dryden, W. and Thorne, B. (eds.) *Training and Supervision for Counselling in Action*. London: Sage Publications.

Feltham, C. & Dryden, W. (2004) *Dictionary of Counselling* (2nd edn). London: Whurr Publications.

Nelson Jones, R. (2011) *Basic Counselling Skills: A Helpers Manual* (3rd edn). London: Sage Publications.

Resources

Websites

www.bacp.co.uk
The British Association for Counselling and Psychotherapy.
www.iapt.nhs.uk
The Improving Access to Psychological Therapies Programme.
www.org.uk
National Institute for Health and Clinical Excellence.
www.therapytoday.net
The online magazine for counsellors and psychotherapists.

2

Skills and Approaches

◆ Introduction

This unit is about interpersonal communication skills and their use within a structure, or framework, designed to help clients in counselling. Skills are the abilities helpers need to have, in order to work effectively with people. They are also central to the theoretical approaches to counselling described in subsequent units of this book. Different approaches to counselling place differing emphasis on the use of individual skills – but all, including the three main schools we shall outline in this unit, highlight such basic skills as listening as part of their repertoire.

Counselling skills, which are essentially good interpersonal, or communication skills, can be divided into several components, verbal and non-verbal.

In addition to the verbal and non-verbal skills, however, there are other aspects of communication that have special significance when applied to counselling. These are skills that relate to the actual organisation of sessions with clients and include, among other things, opening and closing interviews, pacing and timing, establishing confidentiality, making contracts, setting targets and referring clients when necessary. Some of these skills will be addressed in this unit. The subjects of confidentiality, making contracts and referring clients will be considered in more detail in Unit 9.

The structure of counselling

Counselling is a process that requires a coherent framework or structure. This framework is necessary as a guide for both counsellor and client; although it is not always rigidly followed, it serves as a map or reference point in the practice of counselling. Egan (1994) offers a structural model of counselling that divides the process into three main components, as follows:

Stage one	Review of the present situation
Stage two	Development of a new or preferred scenario
Stage three	Moving into action

(Egan, 1994: 23)

Within each of these stages, Egan describes a number of skills that are commonly used. These are the skills we shall consider throughout this unit. Before doing so, however, it is useful to look more closely at Egan's stages, in order to identify the processes that occur in each. Stage one of the model refers to the initial phase of counselling, when clients are encouraged to explore their problems so that they may develop a deeper understanding of them. Stage two refers to the process of helping clients to identify what it is they want and need, in order to deal more effectively with problems. Stage three is the phase of action, during which clients devise ways of actually dealing with problems. This stage may encompass a range of practical activities geared towards achieving results.

Egan divides his three stages into a series of sub-sections, all of which are discussed in his book *The Skilled Helper* (1994). However, another model of the stages of counselling may usefully look at what happens before clients even meet counsellors. The following example illustrates such a model:

Stage one	Pre-contemplation: the client thinks about getting help
Stage two	Establishment of contact: the client either contacts a counsellor or is referred to one
Stage three	Imagining the relationship: the client forms a picture of the counsellor and of the relationship that will be formed
Stage four	Client and counsellor meet: a range of pressing issues is discussed where emotions surface and catharsis may occur
Stage five	Clarity and focus: problem situations become clearer to the client, who experiences a diminution of tension and a feeling of being understood
Stage six	Other issues: related problems from the past may surface and need to be addressed
Stage seven	Management and change: ways of addressing problems are discussed and considered
Stage eight	Apprehension about change: fears are expressed about the effect of change; these are discussed between client and counsellor
Stage nine	Achievement: the client moves into action and achieves some changes
Stage ten	Ending: the relationship between counsellor and client comes to an end; the client is more autonomous and is able to cope alone

It is possible to add yet another stage to those already listed, because many clients remember the counselling process long after it is over. This memory then serves as a guide or template for future reference so that similar problems, when they occur, may seem less daunting and are approached more confidently by clients. The relationship a client forms with a counsellor is also significant in this respect and even if further meetings never take place, the client is aware that he or she is capable of sustaining similar bonds.

KEY TERM

Structural model: Regardless of the theoretical approach, counselling needs a framework in order to provide structure for the process. This framework begins with a contract between counsellor and client, but is more extensive than this and includes consideration of the various stages of counselling and the skills and processes which are relevant to them.

Although not all client experiences are identical in counselling, it is important to recognise that certain stages of development are likely to occur.

Most clients experience a beginning phase, where they seek to make sense of their problems, a middle phase, during which they consider what to do, and a later stage, where they start to act.

On the other hand, some clients come into counselling only briefly, and leave once they have been given the opportunity to explore their problems in the presence of someone who really listens. Such clients frequently identify ways of coping with problems early on and, when they have made this kind of identification, feel able to formulate and implement courses of action fairly quickly.

However, the following case study is an example of one client who progressed through a number of different stages in the process of counselling.

CASE STUDY

Bethan

Bethan, who suffered from anxiety and panic attacks, was referred to counselling by her GP. She was in her mid-30s, and worked as a manager in a factory outlet. This was a responsible job, which demanded a high level of commitment. Bethan, who described herself as a 'perfectionist', became increasingly anxious about meeting customers and dealing with junior staff.

Bethan asked her GP about the possibility of counselling, so she had obviously contemplated this course of action for some time. However, before her first appointment she was tempted to cancel it, because her imagined view of the counselling relationship had gradually become a negative one. She believed the counsellor may be 'bossy' and tell her what to do, and this idea increased her anxiety considerably. Bethan had experienced problems with her mother in early life, and she later realised that there might be a connection between this fact and her concerns about control by a counsellor.

When she actually met the counsellor, however, Bethan talked at length about her vague feelings of anxiety and the panic attacks she had been having recently. While she talked, Bethan also expressed a great deal of emotion and afterwards felt relieved that she had been able to unburden herself in this way. In later sessions, she was concerned to identify the causes of her anxiety and feelings of panic. She was also able to make important connections between some aspects of her childhood experience and her current situation as a manager at work. Bethan's family had been poor, and she was often sent out to collect money from neighbours who had bought items from her mother's catalogue. These neighbours were frequently offensive or verbally abusive towards her, and when she returned home without the money, her mother also became angry and rejected any explanations she gave.

At work, customers were sometimes hostile, too, especially when they owed money to the firm and were unable to pay it. Any confrontations with customers, or even the thought of such confrontations, were the basis of intense anxiety and sometimes panic for Bethan.

Once she had established these connections between past and present, however, she felt more in control of her feelings generally. With the help of the counsellor, Bethan was able to devise ways of adjusting her thinking in relation to customers,

CASE STUDY Cont...

and though she was fearful of changing her approach, she did, in fact, manage to do so. Bethan withdrew from counselling once she felt sufficiently confident to deal with her problems.

Comment: Many of the stages highlighted in the model described earlier are apparent in this case study. Bethan did, in fact, experience a pre-contemplation phase, and her fantasy about the nature of counselling almost prevented her from attending the first session. She experienced both emotional relief and greater clarity, as a result of talking through her problems. Afterwards, she was able to identify important links between past and present, and these served to increase understanding, diminish tension and offer some possibilities for management and change. Bethan's view of her work with customers was changed as a result of counselling, and she felt more in control of her responses generally. Both Bethan and the counsellor had worked through a contract of six sessions and, when these were over, Bethan withdrew from counselling, sufficiently confident that she could manage her problems alone.

Theoretical approaches in counselling

Later on in this book, we shall consider some of the theoretical approaches to counselling that are especially helpful for clients who, like Bethan, experience emotional problems when communicating with other people. At this stage, however, it is useful to look at the three main approaches, from which all the others have evolved. These are as follows:

- psychodynamic approach
- behavioural/cognitive behavioural approach
- humanistic/person–centred approach.

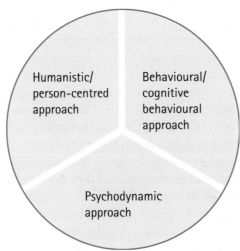

Figure 2.1 Three main approaches to counselling

Theoretical approach: Each model of helping is informed by a set of theories about human development and personality. These theories underpin the skills and techniques used by practitioners of the model, and they also determine the kind of training needed to qualify in that approach.

The psychodynamic approach

The psychodynamic approach to counselling stems from the work of Sigmund Freud (1856–1939). Freud's theories will be discussed in much more detail in Unit 3. In the meantime, it is important to highlight the fact that almost all contemporary approaches to therapy owe at least something to Freud's pioneering work. Ideas which are central to psychodynamic theory include those of unconscious motivation, psychosexual stages of development, innate sexual and aggressive drives, links between childhood and present behaviour, and the nature of defence mechanisms and their use.

All contemporary theoretical approaches acknowledge the influence of the past on the present, and all are aware of the various ways in which people seek to defend themselves against unpleasant experience. In addition, all contemporary approaches are concerned to help clients identify the often hidden (or unconscious) factors that can influence behaviour. Relationship difficulties are also highlighted in diverse current theories, and links between childhood and present experience are explored when, and if, clients request such a focus. The degree to which these factors are considered important varies within each school, as we shall see in the following units.

The behavioural /cognitive behavioural approach

This approach to counselling is based on the work of a group of behavioural psychologists who were interested in the nature of human learning. It is concerned with the observation of human behaviour and the way in which behaviour is perpetuated throughout life by the process of 'reinforcement'. Important behavioural psychologists include Pavlov (1849–1946), Watson (1878–1958) and Skinner (1904–1990). The behavioural approach views human personality as a collection of learned behaviours. This means, in effect, that when we are rewarded for certain types of behaviour, we tend to repeat them. When we are not rewarded, however, the behaviour tends to diminish. Maladaptive behaviour can be perpetuated through reinforcement, so a focus of behaviour therapy (or behaviour modification, as it is sometimes called) is identification of the ways in which problem behaviour is maintained. When this identification is made, techniques can be used to change the problematic stimulus–response pattern.

There is some similarity between the psychodynamic approach and the behavioural, since both emphasise the importance of conditioning in early life. However, behaviourism, unlike the psychodynamic approach, is concerned with observable behaviour. Techniques used in behaviour modification are also quite different, and some of these have been adapted for use within other approaches too. Behaviour therapy has, like psychodynamic theory, been influential in the way its skills and techniques have been taken up by other theoretical schools.

We noted in Unit 1 that cognitive behaviour therapy is an empirically validated approach to counselling (Yalom, 2004). This means that the approach has been extensively researched and shown to be effective in dealing with a range of personal problems. The cognitive behavioural approach is, as its title implies, concerned with a person's thinking and the way in which it affects his or her behaviour. Thus, it extends and enhances the purely behavioural approach, which was almost exclusively concerned with learned behaviours and the observation of behaviour. Within the health service, in particular, the cognitive behavioural approach is now seen as an effective form of talking therapy. This is largely due to the fact that cognitive behavioural therapy (CBT) has been shown to help a wide range of psychological problems, including anxiety disorders and depression, as well as other health problems outlined by Cooper (2008).

In Unit 8 we shall look in some detail at both the behavioural and the cognitive behavioural approaches to counselling.

The humanistic approach

In many ways, the humanistic approach is diametrically opposed (in terms of ideology) to both the psychodynamic and behavioural traditions. This is because the humanistic view emphasises the innate potential every person is believed to possess. It also highlights what is known as the drive towards self-actualisation (Maslow, 1970; Rogers, 1991). Personality is seen as unique to the individual, and problems are set in the context of each person's unique experience. Important names in the humanistic tradition include Carl Rogers (1902–1987), Abraham Maslow (1908–1970) and Fritz Perls (1893–1970). The influences of these theorists will be discussed in greater detail in subsequent units.

Gerald Egan, whose structural model we have referred to in this unit, was also influenced by the philosophy of humanism and, more specifically, by the work of Rogers. Some of Rogers' ideas have been incorporated into Egan's systematic approach, which is described in *The Skilled Helper* (1994). Rogers and Maslow believed that human behaviour is determined by conscious, as opposed to unconscious processes, a view which is vastly different from the Freudian position. The behavioural approach is also different, since it focuses on learned behaviours that operate in a fairly mechanistic way. In addition, this approach indicates that human behaviour is best understood when it is viewed objectively, from a purely external point of view.

This belief is at odds with the philosophy of humanism, where the central focus for understanding human behaviour is on subjective and individual experience. The humanistic movement in therapy has exerted significant influence in other areas, including education and the helping professions.

EXERCISE

Theoretical differences

Working individually, consider the three main theories that have been outlined. What, in your view, are their strengths and weaknesses in their assessments of human behaviour and potential? Discuss your ideas with other members of the training group, and indicate ways in which all of these theories may contribute towards our understanding of clients.

Counselling skills

Having considered the three main branches of counselling theory, we can now look at the skills and counselling abilities common to all. Counselling skills can be divided into the two principal components of verbal and non-verbal communication. In this first section on skills, we shall discuss the significance of non-verbal aspects of communication in counselling, with special reference to the substantial influence that non-verbal behaviour exerts in the therapeutic environment.

Listening

Active listening is a term commonly used in relation to counselling. Egan (1994) lists several factors that are necessary for complete listening, and these include the observation of clients' non-verbal behaviour, as well as understanding verbal content and meaning. It goes without saying that the 'way' something is said is just as important as the actual words spoken. This last point is especially relevant in the counselling context, for clients often have difficulty in finding exactly the right words to express the way they feel. In these circumstances, accompanying non-verbal cues sometimes speak much more eloquently than words. Listening and attending are, therefore, skills that always go together in counselling. This is because it is not possible for counsellors to give clients their full attention without actively listening to them.

Attending to clients incorporates many of the non-verbal skills listed at the beginning of this unit. It is not just client non-verbal behaviour that we need to consider therefore. The counsellor also communicates to the client, and much of this communication is conveyed without words. Active listening is probably the most effective form of communication a counsellor uses, but it is also frequently underestimated by many people. Listening is commonly regarded as a passive rather than an active skill, and you will probably be surprised to discover just how much effort is required to develop it. An outline of some of the distracting factors that impede active listening is shown below.

Obvious external factors	Examples include noise, interruption and physical discomfort.
Response rehearsal	This happens when we become preoccupied with what we would like to say in reply.
Fact finding	This refers to the practice of searching for details and facts, instead of listening to the overall message the client wishes to convey.
Being judgmental	Some listeners are concerned to make mental judgments about the speaker's behaviour.
Problem solving	You may find that when you first practise listening skills, you are tempted to solve the client's problem in your own head. This is something which precludes real listening.
Imposing a personal view	This happens when the listener fails to hear the central feeling a client is seeking to express.

CASE STUDY

Christine

A middle-aged woman, called Christine, wanted to talk about some of the problems she had experienced just before her mother's death. At first she talked to her sister and later to a minister of religion, who was also trained in counselling skills. In the following exchange with her sister, she broaches the subject of her mother's apparent rejection of her.

CHRISTINE: I know I seem to go over this again and again, but I simply can't come to terms with the fact that she told me not to kiss her when she was dying. It is something I can never forget.

SISTER: Well you know she was never a tactile person. She was not one for showing physical affection.

The next exchange took place between Christine and a minister of the church she had attended.

CHRISTINE: I think about it again and again. Just at the end she turned away from me and rejected the affection I wanted to show her.

PRIEST: Causing you real distress and sorrow . . .

CHRISTINE: Yes.

Comment: In the first example, the response given ignored the central feeling of distress the client was trying to convey. In addition to ignoring the feelings expressed, the listener also imposed her own view or interpretation of events and, in doing so, seemed to discount what her sister was saying. The second example, however, shows how the client's feeling were immediately picked up and acknowledged, much to her relief.

Other factors that inhibit listening

There are many other factors that work against active listening, including over-identification with the client or the client's problems. Once again, this highlights the importance of self-awareness for counsellors, since it is only through awareness of our own areas of vulnerability and prejudice that we can hope to avoid this kind of over-identification (which often includes sympathy). The essential differences between sympathy and empathy will be highlighted in Unit 5, but it should be noted here that sympathy is not appropriate in therapeutic counselling. This is because it is an attitude that tends to be superficial, requiring very little effort to demonstrate. It is also fairly easy to simulate and is often extended in an unthinking or perfunctory way when people are distressed.

Listening is by far the most important skill in counselling. It is never easy and requires enormous discipline, self-control and an attitude of heightened receptivity. Active listening assures clients they are heard and that what they say matters a great deal. When we don't listen to people we fail to make any real emotional connection with them.

Many clients who seek counselling have never really been listened to. Their parents may have failed them in this respect, and later on at school, or in the work situation, they may not have been heard either. It is sometimes the case that people hide a painful secret for many years which, as Weinberg (1996: 175) says, 'may seem commonplace to us' but is monumental to the owner. Such people are given the courage to reappraise the problem, providing someone gives time, attention and the skill of active listening to help them do so.

EXERCISE

Appropriate responses

Working individually, look at the responses (A to D) to each of the following five statements. Can you identify responses that seem appropriate and those which do not? Afterwards, discuss your findings with other members of your training group.

1 My father was often away from home when I was a child, so I never really got to know him.

  A That must have been very hard for you.

  B It happened to a lot of people at that time.

EXERCISE Cont...

    C He was almost a stranger to you.

    D It wasn't your fault though.

2 A year ago my husband had an affair with another woman.

    A When did it begin?

    B It reminds me of something that happened to my friend.

    C You must have been devastated.

    D Would you like to talk about it some more?

3 My sister had to go into a hospice in the end because we couldn't look after her.

    A That must have been awful for you.

    B She was too sick to be cared for at home.

    C She will have been cared for really well in the hospice.

    D Most relatives are relieved when that happens.

4 When I had the accident with the car, everyone assumed it was my fault.

    A Nobody listened to you.

    B Were you insured?

    C You poor thing.

    D How will you manage without the car in the meantime?

5 I'm trying to balance my studies with a full-time job. The kids are at an awkward stage, and they don't help much in the house. My husband is exhausted when he gets home.

    A It feels as if everything is down to you.

    B Could you do a rota so that everyone has to chip in?

    C Why not give up the studies until later?

    D I think you are trying to do too much.

EXERCISE

Blocks to listening

Working individually, look at the following list of factors that could affect counsellors, and consider their possible effects on their ability to listen. Factors may include:

◆ tiredness and stress

◆ personal problems

◆ minor illness or pain

◆ similar experiences to those described by the client

◆ total dissimilarity of experience to that described by the client

◆ cultural, religious or social differences.

Non-verbal communication as an aid to listening

Egan (1994: 91) describes what he refers to as 'microskills', which helpers can use when working with clients. These skills are summarised by Egan in the acronym SOLER. This acronym should help you to remember those aspects of non-verbal behaviour which encourage active listening, and it is used in the following way:

S   Sit facing the client **Squarely**. This assures the client that she or he has your attention.

O   Be **Open** in your posture. Do not close yourself off by rigidly crossing arms and legs.

L   **Lean** slightly towards the client in an attitude of interest.

E   **Establish Eye** contact with the client, but avoid staring.

R   **Relax** and don't fidget. Try to adopt a natural posture in relation to the client.

(Egan, 1994: 91–2)

It is obviously difficult to be totally relaxed and unselfconscious, especially at the beginning of skills training. In addition, a position you consider to be relaxed and comfortable may not be exactly the same as that described above. Some people feel more comfortable when sitting slightly to the client's side. This kind of seating arrangement has the advantage of conveying strong subliminal messages of support to the client. In other words, it is one way of saying 'I am on your side'. However, it may be more difficult to maintain eye contact in this position.

The important thing to remember is that your attention should remain with the client, and whatever seating arrangement facilitates this is the right one to use. Obvious barriers such as desks and tables should not intrude between client and counsellor, and the overall atmosphere of the setting in which counselling takes places should be comfortable, uninterrupted, and private.

EXERCISE

Social listening

One way of developing your listening ability is to practise in social situations. Concentrate on what people are saying, paying special attention to accompanying gestures and tone of voice, facial expression and any periods of silence in the speaker's delivery.

Note also the speaker's effect on those listening. Do people appear interested or do they seem bored, for example; and, if so, why might this be. How do you listen when others speak to you? How do other people seem to listen when you speak to them?

CASE STUDY

Really listening

Helena lived with her partner in the country and often socialised with a group of friends from work. Members of the group would take turns to cook meals and invite the others round. One friend (Emma), who lived alone, started to call on Helena unexpectedly, and often stayed late into the evening to talk. Because Helena was busy in the evenings, she only 'half' listened to what Emma was saying, but she was aware that her friend talked a lot, often without seeming to pause for breath.

Emma's husband had left her for another woman; she was now alone and regretful that she had not left her husband first, since the relationship had been dysfunctional for years. Though Helena did not give her full attention to what her friend was saying, she was aware that Emma was angry, depressed and desperate for support.

Finally, one evening when Emma called, Helena (who was not a trained counsellor) decided to set her evening's work aside and really listen to her friend. This attention and listening had an instant effect on Emma, who began to speak in a more focused and thoughtful way. She described her feelings again, this time making links between her current situation and memories of the trauma she had experienced aged six when her father left home.

Helena, in turn, became more interested in Emma's personal story and felt closer to her as a result. She suggested that Emma seek help for her depression and counselling support, via her GP practice. The two friends remained in contact and Emma was able to get the support she needed.

Comment: This case study illustrates the importance of active listening. When Helena decided to listen with interest to her friend, Emma sensed this and felt calmer as a result. She was able to recount and clarify her story in a way that opened up the possibility of seeking the help she needed. Even though Helena was not a counsellor, she was aware at an instinctive level that people who talk a great deal are often desperate for someone to listen with real interest.

The importance of active listening in counselling is stressed throughout the remaining units of this book.

Gestures and touch

You will probably feel quite self-conscious when you first start to practise counselling skills. When video practice is used as an aid to training, students are often disconcerted to see the extent to which they use nervous gestures or movements while listening to each other. Although it is not very pleasant to see this at first, it is nevertheless helpful in the long term, since it serves to identify faulty communication styles that can be remedied.

Excessive use of gestures can create uneasiness between client and counsellor, so counsellors need to minimise these as much as possible. Clients may be anxious and restless initially, but when counsellors 'model' attitudes of calm and stillness, clients often become more relaxed as a result.

The issue of touch is problematic in relation to therapeutic counselling, and in most instances touch is considered inappropriate for a variety of reasons. There are, for example, clients who have experienced physical or sexual abuse in the past and they may, as a consequence, be fearful of this kind of contact.

Student counsellors who already work with clients or patients in other settings, like nursing for example, may use touch routinely in their work. However, in these contexts, touch is used impersonally and is unlikely to be misconstrued by the people they help. In contrast, clients in therapeutic counselling may misinterpret any touching that takes place, precisely because it is not, strictly speaking, an essential or integral component of that relationship. This is not to say that some tactile expressions of support are never extended by counsellors. Individual counsellors vary a great deal in the way they use touch and in the ease with which they do so.

Cultural differences are important here, too, since what might feel comfortable for one group of people may be less so for another. All these differences highlight the earlier point that tactile communication needs to be carefully considered before it is used, and when any element of doubt exists it is best avoided altogether.

In discussing non-erotic touch, Cooper (2008: 147–8) makes the point that though research into physical contact is at an early stage, evidence so far suggests that it can be perceived as 'both helpful and unhelpful by clients'. But these client perceptions depend on the context in which touch is used, as well as the way in which it is used. It should be added the British Association of Counselling and Psychotherapy (2013), makes it clear in its *Ethical Framework* that any kind of sexual activity in counselling (and this would include sexual touch) constitutes exploitation of clients and is prohibited.

Silence

In order to listen effectively it is, of course, necessary to be silent. Just being silent is not enough, though, since clients need to know that the counsellor is interested and paying attention to them when they speak. This means that you need to show by your demeanour that you are, in fact, 'with' the clients in everything they say. Silence is another aspect of communication you may feel self-conscious about at first and, when you are uncomfortable in this way, there is always a temptation to fill in the spaces, either through asking questions or finishing the clients' sentences for them. However, you should remember that clients often need periods of silence in order to collect their thoughts, or as a way of experiencing a very strong feeling or emotion. If they are not allowed to do this, they will almost certainly regard any intervention as intrusive and insensitive. Clients communicate a great deal through silence, both to themselves and to counsellors. As well as this, clients frequently refer to silence afterwards and, in doing so, effectively clarify aspects of their problems that may have been obscured in the past.

EXERCISE

Feelings about silence

Working in groups of three (triads), discuss your attitudes to silence. Start by looking at the following statements, then say how you feel about each.

1 Prolonged silence makes me feel uncomfortable.

2 When there is a lull in conversation, I am tempted to say something to fill in the gaps.

3 I often feel tempted to finish other people's sentences.

4 Sometimes when I am silent and on my own I feel relaxed and can think more clearly.

5 Silence is an essential aid to self-listening, and to listening to others.

The counsellor's appearance

Counsellors, like their clients, reveal much more about themselves than they think. Personal values, and even mood, are often discernible in a person's dress and appearance, and someone who appears scruffy and unkempt is unlikely to retain the confidence of clients. On the other hand, an excessively glamorous or suave appearance might inhibit some clients, especially those who experience problems in relation to body image or personal looks.

However, no style of clothing or dress has the same meaning for everyone, which suggests that counsellors should probably dress in whatever way is most comfortable for them personally. There are, moreover, certain areas of counselling in which casual dress seems most appropriate. Counsellors who work with underprivileged groups of people, or with those who have problems in relation to substance abuse, often feel most at ease with their clients when dressed informally.

Probably the only hard-and-fast rule pertaining to counsellor dress and appearance is respect for clients. Counsellors have to be true to themselves, but they also need to dress in ways that inspire some confidence in their ability and competence.

EXERCISE

Designing a room

Working individually, draw a plan of the type of room which, in your view, would be suitable as a counselling base. Pay attention to such aspects as the arrangement of furniture, position of a clock, lighting and window position, and colours.

Afterwards, compare your plan with those drawn by other members of the training group, and discuss why you included or excluded certain items or furnishings in the room. Would it be appropriate to display family photographs, for example? If not, why?

Verbal communication

Reflection

The word 'reflection' refers to the skill of communicating back to clients that their words and feelings have been heard. Carl Rogers (1991) emphasised this particular skill initially, although counsellors and therapists of almost every theoretical school now place a high value on its use. Reporting back to clients what they have said is one way of indicating that we are listening carefully to them. In a sense, the skill of reflection is like holding a mirror in front of clients so that they can see themselves more clearly. Reflection, if it is to be effective, should be done unobtrusively so that the client is hardly aware that it is happening.

The concept of empathy is closely linked to reflection, because effective reflective responses are those which stay within the client's 'internal frame of reference' (Rogers, 1991: 29). To stay within clients' internal frame of reference means listening to and understanding the problem or problems from their point of view or experience. The following is an example:

LIZ: My mother told me that I was adopted when I was 13 years old. After that I went wild for a while . . . running around with a bad crowd . . . I didn't know who I was any more . . . my world fell apart.

COUNSELLOR: You were lost and confused.

LIZ: Yes . . . and it took me ages to get it all on an even keel again. Actually, I haven't . . . got it on an even keel, I mean. I feel dislocated . . . I still feel lost in some ways.

COUNSELLOR: There is still a sense of things not being right for you . . . of missed connections.

LIZ: Parts of the story are missing . . . large parts. I want to meet my natural parents, yet I'm terrified too . . . terrified that they might not want to know me.

COUNSELLOR: The fear of the unknown . . . and of possible rejection . . . these are the things which cause you the most anxiety.

LIZ: Yes, and this fear keeps me from doing anything.

The counsellor's responses to this client were framed in a way that kept the focus of attention on the emotional content of what the client was saying. This meant that the client felt free to express her deepest fears and anxieties, since she was aware that the counsellor respected and validated these. In her responses, the counsellor also focused on 'feeling' words including 'confused', 'fear', 'rejection' and 'anxiety'.

Clients are sometimes afraid to acknowledge strong feelings, in case the listener becomes distressed on hearing them, or they themselves become overwhelmed by them. When strong or negative feelings are validated in counselling, clients often experience great relief. Such relief is frequently the first step towards clarification and management of the problem.

Paraphrasing

The word 'paraphrasing' refers to the rewording of the content of what clients say. Reflection and paraphrasing are very similar; the difference between them being that the former is generally used to describe a rewording of the emotional content, while the latter is mainly concerned with the factual. However, it is certainly not always easy (or necessary) to separate these two activities. Some distinction is necessary though, because the two words are often used interchangeably in counselling literature, and this can occasionally prove confusing for students. When responding to clients, it is obviously best to do so in a way that does not simply repeat verbatim what has just been said. It is helpful to practise the skill of paraphrasing by concentrating on the content first, and later on incorporating the emotional content as well. Two examples are given below.

The first example refers to an exchange between a student and teacher:

STUDENT: I didn't get the work done because my mother fell ill last week. Then she was taken into hospital for tests and I had to look after the two younger ones. I don't feel so well myself either, especially after all the stress and the extra work.

TEACHER: Other things happened at home and you were too busy to write the assignment; as well as that, you've been ill yourself.

In this situation, the teacher picked up the factual content of what the student said. There is no obvious acknowledgement of the emotional content, however. To reflect back both factual and emotional content, the teacher might have worded her response in the following way:

TEACHER: Things have been hectic and stressful at home for you, and there was no way you could think about writing an assignment. And feeling ill, of course, made it worse for you.

Here, the teacher picks up the stress and anxiety the student expresses, and reflects this back in her response. It is likely that such a response will assure the student that her explanation for not doing the work is respected and understood. On the other hand, it should be remembered that the first response might well have had the same effect, depending on the teacher's tone of voice and general demeanour when she delivered it.

The following example highlights a conversation that takes place between a nurse and patient.

PATIENT: I've never been in hospital before. What happens next? When will I know about going home? There was a doctor here a short while ago and he took my case notes away.

NURSE: You've not had this experience before and you want to know all the details.

Here, the nurse concentrates on the factual aspects of the patient's communication. In the next example, she reflects back both content and feeling.

NURSE: You're obviously anxious about everything that's happening, and that's understandable. I'll talk to you about all the details in just a moment.

This last response acknowledges the patient's fears and her general anxiety about being in hospital.

EXERCISE

Paraphrasing

Read the following passages and paraphrase them, concentrating on the factual content only.

1 Since the car accident, I've been nervous driving. I keep thinking someone will drive into the back of me again . . . I'm on the look out all the time, and wondering what will happen next.

2 Yesterday, we went to London for a conference. I didn't want to go . . . What's the point anyway if I'm going to be made redundant? The others were really enjoying themselves, but I couldn't get into the mood of it.

3 When my illness was diagnosed I didn't believe it. I felt the specialist had made a mistake, and I even argued with him about it.

4 My two children are quite different. The younger one never gave a problem, but the elder one was trouble from the very beginning. I have tried not to compare them, but I've got to the stage where I just have to admit that Harry is different.

5 I don't know how to tell my parents that I am gay . . . I just don't know how they will react. They were both quite old when I was born, and they don't talk very openly about intimate issues anyway.

When you have completed the first part of this exercise, read the passages again and reword them, this time reflecting both the factual content and feeling content.

Summarising

The skill of summarising is used when a helper wishes to respond to a series of statements or, in the case of counselling, to a whole session. As with reflecting and paraphrasing, accurate summarising requires empathy and the ability to stay within the client's internal frame of reference. Clients often talk at random, and they are frequently side-tracked into other related (and sometimes unrelated) issues. This can make it difficult to monitor everything they say, and formulating an accurate summary also requires active listening and an ability to draw all the random threads together into a more coherent framework. Egan (1994: 181) refers to summarising as a 'bridging response' that can be used to provide links between counselling sessions and the stages of the three-stage model he describes. The following is an example of summarising at the end of a counselling session.

A client called Alice talked about her experiences:

CLIENT: The area I live in was flooded about two years ago and we lost almost everything. The insurance did cover a lot of things, but there are some things you can't replace. Then, just about that time, I found out about my husband's affair, something that nearly everyone else seemed to know about. It was devastating and I don't think I'll ever recover from it. Everything seems to happen at once because my youngest child developed eczema at about that time, although I suspect myself that it was linked to all the stress going on in the family. I kept going through it all, but then six months ago I became very depressed . . . I couldn't stop thinking about all that had happened and it just came flooding back to me.

The counsellor gave the following summary of what Alice had said:

COUNSELLOR You had all those stressful experiences two years back . . . being flooded, losing important possessions, your husband's affair and your child's illness. It was terrible for you, but you coped. But now you feel the depression linked to it all.

In this summary, the counsellor identified the factual elements of the story. She also highlighted the stressful feelings associated with it, and she used the word 'terrible' to describe the client's experiences. This confirmed for the client that what she had said was understood and validated by the counsellor. Later on, the counsellor also drew attention to the fact that the client had used the word 'flooding' when describing her delayed reaction to the events of the past, which had, in fact, started with a flood.

Through the skill of summarising, the counsellor identified important themes in the client's story. She also clarified the client's experiences and thoughts, and she used the summary as a way of checking her own understanding of what had been said. The client was therefore given an opportunity to add any other details that may have been missed, or to emphasise any aspects of the story the counsellor may have failed to highlight.

Accurate summarising should:

- show understanding of what the client has said
- reflect the client's internal frame of reference
- show accurate selection of important issues and themes
- avoid critical or judgmental statements
- be accurately timed: clients should not be interrupted
- be tentative: clients need to feel free to add to or correct what has been said
- reflect the order of events, so that clients can look again at the story as it unfolds.

Summarising

Working in pairs, take turns to talk about a recent experience you have had. If you are just starting skills training, try to select experiences that were not too problematic or distressing for either of you. While one person talks for about three minutes, the other should listen, concentrating on the factual elements of the story, the order of events and any feelings expressed. Afterwards, summarise what has been said. When you have both completed the exercise, discuss any difficulties you may have experienced in relation to it.

Asking questions

One of the difficulties you may find in listening to others is that your curiosity is aroused, and you are tempted to ask questions in order to get the detail clear in your own head. Most of us probably ask too many questions in our communications with other people, and active listening is often diminished as a result. Questions can be especially problematic in counselling because they tend to be prompted by an external rather than an internal frame of reference. In other words, counsellors sometimes ask questions in order to get the facts straight for themselves, rather than from a desire to understand the client's subjective experience of things. Consider the following example:

HUW: My daughter and I have frequent arguments. They seem to become more frequent as she gets older. This gives me the feeling that we are somehow losing touch.

COUNSELLOR: What age is she?

HUW: 15 . . . almost 16.

COUNSELLOR: And how often do you argue?

This example may seem like an extreme case of stark questioning, but it does serve to highlight several important points. In the first place, the questions do nothing to help the client examine his relationship with his daughter, even though this is clearly a major concern of his. In the second place, it is difficult to see how such questions could possibly aid the counsellor in her understanding of the client, or the problem he is trying to describe. These questions, therefore, work against the client's best interests, and they also place a barrier in the relationship between client and counsellor.

How should the counsellor have responded? The following is one way of responding to the client's first statement:

COUNSELLOR: There are more differences now, and greater distance between you.

CLIENT: Yes . . . I feel very saddened by it.

In this second example the counsellor responded, not with a question but with a reflection of the client's experience and feeling. This response encouraged him to talk in depth about his relationship with his daughter. However, questions do have their place in counselling, though they should be kept to a minimum. When tempted to ask a question, it is useful to consider why you need to do so. Is it to satisfy your own curiosity, or will it facilitate the client in some way? When questions have to be asked they should always be as open as possible; it is certainly best to avoid questions beginning with 'why', as they tend to sound interrogative, and clients frequently respond to them in defensive or resistant ways. Also clients usually don't really know why things are the way they are, and it is often a desire to find out that prompts them to seek counselling in the first place.

Open questions

Open questions encourage clients to explore their problems in greater depth. In contrast to 'closed' questions, they require much more than a simple 'yes' or 'no' answer. They also encourage the expression of feelings and help clients to explore issues that concern them in much more specific ways. The following example should illustrate the points just made:

ETHNE: My sister was sent to a really good school. We lost touch for a long time, and the school I went to was local and had a poor record. My parents always gave the impression that I was sent there because I had no real ability.

COUNSELLOR: The separation from your sister . . . the second rate school . . . how did you feel about all this?

ETHNE: Well, for a long time I really resented her . . . my sister I mean. Later on, I realised, of course, that it wasn't her fault. When we were in our late teens we started to become closer.

COUNSELLOR: So the resentment was less in your teens . . . what was it at that stage which helped you?

ETHNE: We had similar problems then . . . with my parents I mean. We both realised that we had more in common than we thought. Also I was able to talk to her about my feelings of being stupid. She really helped me then and was very supportive. Now I don't have that old resentment towards her.

In addition to closed questions, there are others which are problematic in the counselling context, some of which are set out below.

Multiple questions

Here, several questions are asked at once and the client doesn't know which to reply to. This is especially confusing when people are emotionally upset. For example:

CLIENT: I think I might be pregnant and I'm really scared.

HELPER: Have you spoken to your parents? Maybe you don't want to? What about your doctor?

Leading questions

These are questions which lead the client in a certain direction, usually in the direction of the counsellor's viewpoint. Value judgments are also usually implicit in leading questions, and this is never helpful for clients, who often find themselves under pressure to agree with what has been said. For example:

CLIENT: I feel tired all the time. Sometimes I just want to stay in the house and never go out.

HELPER: Doesn't staying in the house tend to make people feel even more apathetic and tired?

Rhetorical questions

These are questions which do not require any answer. They tend to express the questioner's viewpoint, and if they are used in counselling, clients may feel obliged to accept what the counsellor has said. For example:

COUNSELLOR: How is it that things always seem to happen at once?

CLIENT: Well yes, I suppose they do.

Greeting clients

Many clients find it difficult to get started unless they are asked at least one opening question. It is important to establish contact with clients as soon as possible, and one way of doing this is by asking a brief question. The following are some examples:

- Please sit down. How would you like to start?
- Is there anything, in particular, you would like to begin with?
- My name is (name). Can you tell me about the issues that concern you at the moment?
- How do you see your situation at present?
- Dr (name) referred you to me for . . . is this how you see the situation?
- How have things been with you since you last saw the doctor?

Once contact has been established and the client starts to talk, the counsellor can then use a range of continuation skills to encourage further exploration. For example:

- Yes, I see
- And after that . . .
- You say you were afraid . . .
- Please go on . . .
- Then . . .
- Tell me more about . . .

- So you feel . . .
- And that felt . . .

You will probably find that once you lose your initial nervousness, your own range of responses will develop naturally. In the meantime, it is a good idea to practise opening questions, along with follow-up responses similar to the continuation phrases given above.

Probing questions

Probing questions are meant to encourage clients to enlarge or expand on their initial response. The following are examples:

- Can you say more about that?
- And what happened then?
- Could you describe that?

Focusing questions

Focusing questions encourage clients to look more closely at specific aspects of a problem. Clients are often vague about their problems, and focusing questions are effective in encouraging them to define issues more clearly. For example:

CLIENT: Everybody bullies me . . . I am always bullied.

COUNSELLOR: Could we look at some of the ways you are bullied?

Timing of questions

We have already seen that too many questions can be threatening for clients and may also have the adverse effect of inhibiting communication generally. Timing of questions is also important in counselling. Clients should never be interrupted, no matter how much they seem to talk initially. It is worth remembering that many clients have waited a long time to be heard, and they may have a great deal of information they want to convey. In view of this, counsellors need to keep questions in abeyance until the time is right to ask them. Clients do pause to pick up responses from counsellors, and a counsellor who is truly listening will be in tune with unspoken invitations to speak.

Another important point to remember is that clients should not be questioned when they are emotionally overwhelmed, or when they are clearly too upset to answer. Use of excessively probing questions can also cause a great deal of anxiety, especially when these are poorly timed. Asking too many, or badly timed, questions of clients is one way of avoiding real contact with them. Active listening, on the other hand, is a sure way of establishing real contact and understanding.

EXERCISE

Encouraging clients to be more specific

Working individually, look at the following list of client statements. Spend about 20 minutes formulating appropriate questions in response to these, concentrating on the skill of focusing. When you have finished, compare your list with those completed by other members of the group.

- ◆ I have had a terrible time with both my partners.
- ◆ No matter what I do I can never get it right.
- ◆ People are always picking on me.
- ◆ Everything is so stressful at work.
- ◆ I get panic attacks all the time.
- ◆ Nobody ever listens to me at home.
- ◆ I feel much better about life now.
- ◆ The illness was what caused me to feel useless.
- ◆ My children are so badly behaved.
- ◆ I feel totally lacking in confidence.

Challenging skills

At the beginning of this unit we referred briefly to Egan's three-stage model of counselling, and to the skills that are integral to it. So far we have considered the basic skills of listening, paraphrasing and reflecting, summarising, asking questions, using silence and helping clients to focus on more specific aspects of their stories. These skills are used in the first stage of the model and, indeed, throughout the whole counselling process. However, the second stage of the model requires the use of other skills that will help clients to develop new perspectives about themselves and the problems they experience. During this stage of counselling, which Egan refers to as the 'preferred scenario', clients are encouraged to identify what they need to do in order to change the situation that is causing difficulties for them (Egan, 1994: 23). The skills used in this phase include the following:

- challenging
- immediacy
- counsellor self-disclosure
- identifying patterns and themes
- giving information to clients.

Used in the counselling context, the word 'challenge' refers to the skill of encouraging clients to confront their own behaviour, attitudes or beliefs. It should always be done with sensitivity and should certainly never be rushed. Immediacy, counsellor self-disclosure, information giving and the identification of patterns and themes are all forms of challenge in counselling.

Immediacy

The term 'immediacy' is one Egan (1994: 23) uses to describe the process of discussing what is actually taking place right now in the counselling situation. The following is an example:

CLIENT: I have been to several helpers now, and I don't feel any more hopeful than before.

COUNSELLOR: Perhaps that's something we should talk about now . . . is it that you don't have confidence that I can help you either?

In the example just given, immediacy was used by the counsellor in order to draw attention to the client's feelings about him. This is challenging for the client, because it serves to focus attention on his belief that he is impossible to help.

Counsellor self-disclosure

There are specialised areas of counselling in which counsellor self-disclosure is sometimes used. These include counselling for substance abuse or addiction, and in these contexts self-disclosure is very beneficial for clients, since it serves to encourage them to persevere in overcoming problems. However, self-disclosure is by no means always appropriate. It can worry clients if it is done frequently, and it can have the very unfortunate effect of making the client feel responsible for the counsellor. Writing about counsellor self-disclosure, Yalom stresses that therapists should not reveal themselves 'indiscriminately' but only reveal what is of value to the client (Yalom, 2004: 87). On the other hand, self-disclosure is very effective as a form of challenge, as long as it is correctly timed and carried out with the client's best interest firmly in focus. Another point to remember is that it is important to show interest in clients without in fact *being* interesting. In the next example, a client called Gillian was worried that she would never get over her panic attacks:

GILLIAN: Sometimes I feel that I might as well just stay in the house and at least feel safe there . . .

COUNSELLOR: Yes, I know that feeling . . . but when I pushed myself to get out of the house, things started improving from there.

Through self-disclosure the counselor, in this example, challenged the client's temptation to give up on her problem and just stay in the house.

Giving information to clients

Information giving can also prove challenging for clients, especially when their expectations are clearly unrealistic in some way. In the following example, a client called David wanted to leave his present relationship, in order to establish a new life with his new girlfriend:

DAVID:	I want to leave everything behind . . . I know I can do it, and I can just about afford it.
COUNSELLOR:	Taking into consideration maintenance for the two children?
DAVID:	My wife is financially OK . . . that's one thing; she has never quibbled about money . . .
COUNSELLOR:	On the other hand, there is probably a certain amount you will need to provide from a legal point of view . . .
DAVID:	Yes, I suppose you're right.

In this example, the counsellor directed the client's attention to the financial details he wanted to minimise. She did this by challenging him with the information that there were certain requirements which, in all likelihood, he would need to observe.

Identifying patterns and themes

Sometimes there are recurrent themes or patterns discernible in the problems clients recount. Once a relationship of trust has been established between counsellor and client, it is possible to identify and highlight these patterns so that clients are challenged to consider them more seriously. A client called Rene talked at length about her problems at work:

RENE:	I do seem to get on the wrong side of people . . . the rent people, the Social Services. Why me? Would you believe it . . . but I was even singled out in my last job, and I'm sure that it was because of my personality . . . the fact that I say what I mean.
COUNSELLOR:	I know you've mentioned this several times . . . that you say what you mean. Maybe we should look at that, to see how much it might be contributing to the problems you describe.

In this example, the counsellor focused attention on the client's insistence that she only said what she felt. This identification of a pattern, or theme, enabled the client to look more honestly at the way she communicated with other people, and the problems this seemed to generate. If at all possible, it is always best to encourage clients to confront themselves and, in this case, this is exactly what happened. Since the client had already identified her problem in relation to others, the counsellor's task was simplified as a result.

Clients also tend to respond best when they are challenged to identify their own strengths and coping resources. For example:

COUNSELLOR:	You've said how shy you are, and you lack confidence that people will like you . . . On the other hand, you've been chosen twice to represent your colleagues at conferences.

EXERCISE

Self-challenge

Working individually, consider some of the areas of your life that could benefit from challenge. Are there any patterns of behaviour, for example, which cause some problems for you? In what ways, if any, do you contribute to these problems? The following examples may help to identify some personal problem areas for you:

◆ keeping others waiting

◆ refusing to accept compliments

◆ agreeing to do things you don't want to do

◆ going into action without first thinking about it

◆ being defensive when others disagree with you

◆ not listening when you don't agree with what is being said

◆ procrastinating about work which should be done

◆ looking to others to make decisions for you.

When you have completed the individual exercise, share your ideas with a partner and discuss any difficulties you experienced in challenging yourself.

The action phase

In the third stage of the model Egan (1994) describes, clients are encouraged to act, aided by the new understanding and knowledge they have acquired in the previous two stages. Along with the counsellor, the client explores a variety of ways of achieving goals. A plan of action is discussed and formulated, and throughout this process the counsellor supports the client and helps him to monitor and evaluate any changes proposed. All the skills of stage one and two are used here, along with a new set of skills, including the following:

● goal setting
● choosing programmes
● creative thinking
● giving encouragement
● evaluating.

Goal setting and choosing programmes

Change is difficult for most people, and clients in counselling tend to find it especially difficult. This is because many of them have endured unsatisfactory work, relationship or other problem situations, over long periods of time. No matter how unsatisfactory their lives have been, however, they are at least familiar with the current situation, and any prospect of change is daunting since change always represents a leap into the unknown.

Setting realistic goals in the third stage of counselling is one way of helping clients to plan the changes they need to make. Sometimes clients know, as a result of the work they have done in stage one and stage two, the action they need to take. More often than not, however, they need support and encouragement in order to set and achieve goals. Clients also tend to respond much more positively to goals and programmes they have chosen for themselves, so it is worth remembering that the counsellor's role is a helping one, which does not include offering solutions to problems. On the other hand, counsellors need to help clients to consider a range of options and a number of different ways of achieving goals. Clients may also need to be encouraged to look at their own resources or those within their environment. Realistic goals are dependent on these internal and external resources; when there is a clear discrepancy between goals and resources, adjustments need to be made. The following questions can usefully be asked in relation to any goals that are formulated:

- Are they clear?
- Are they specific?
- How long will they take to achieve?
- How realistic are they?
- Are they measurable?
- Is the client comfortable with them?

Clients can be encouraged to write down their goals in clear and specific terms. This can be done using the following headings:

- What is it I want?
- How can I achieve this?
- Why should I do this?

Creative thinking

Creative thinking may be difficult for clients, and this is especially true when they are emotionally upset, or under great stress. This is why it is important that they should be given sufficient time to talk about and explore their problems before moving into action. When clients are ready to act, however, there are strategies for encouraging creative thinking that often help them to look at new ways of tackling their problems. Some examples are set out as follows.

Idea storming

This is a strategy first devised in 1942 by an advertising executive called Alex Osborn. The exercise was originally called 'Brainstorming', but I have changed this title to 'Idea storming' because I found that some students objected to the first description. The exercise of idea storming is meant to generate as many ideas as possible. Quantity is encouraged and all options are considered.

Initially, ideas generated, no matter how bizarre, are included and criticism is discouraged. The exercise can be used to help individual clients to think more creatively and develop strategies for tackling problems. Afterwards, the client should be supported in appraising the list so that real possibilities are highlighted and totally unrealistic ideas abandoned. The following is a list of ideas drawn up by a student who wanted to look at ways of improving communication with her parents:

- tell them I want to talk
- ask for a time
- take assertiveness lessons
- talk to other students about how they communicate with parents
- decide on a date to start talking
- write them a letter
- leave a message on the answering machine
- bang the table at dinner time
- jump up and down to attract their attention
- speak to my mother first
- ask my sister to speak to them first
- leave home and phone them
- send them an email
- text them.

The student eventually selected three ideas, which she considered to be realistic and workable, from her original list. These were:

- tell them I want to talk
- ask for a time
- take assertiveness lessons to improve my communication skills generally.

It should be added here that not everyone agrees with the effectiveness of idea storming as an aid to creativity. Writing in *The New Yorker* under the heading of 'The Brainstorming Myth' (2012), journalist and author Jonah Lehrer argues that the exercise produces less original ideas than would be generated by people working alone. In addition, he quotes research to support his contention. It is important to remember, though, that Lehrer was referring to the exercise carried out as a group activity. In my experience, idea storming works well with individual clients, especially when carried out in the presence of a supportive helper.

Visualisation and imagery

One of the most obvious ways to formulate an idea is to visualise it. It is through the practice of visualisation and imagery that many athletes achieve high performance in sport. Clients can also be encouraged to use this method to help them look at ways that will lead to success in whatever they choose to do. A client whose ambition was to feel more confident socially was, for example, encouraged to visualise a number of settings in which he wished to feel more at ease. Then the counsellor asked him to imagine how he would think, feel and act in each of these situations. He was also encouraged to visualise himself handling each situation exactly how he would like to.

Sometimes clients achieve better results in this exercise when they have been given some time and help to relax beforehand. In Unit 8 we shall consider various relaxation techniques, which clients can be taught to use.

Giving encouragement

Clients need encouragement when they are deciding on change and setting goals. This is essential if they are to sustain their efforts and reach their chosen goals. The idea of giving up is often attractive to clients, especially when impediments or barriers are encountered. Counsellors need to direct attention to any personal resources and achievement that clients have. Attitudes of defeat or perfectionism can be discussed, and clients can also be encouraged to accept any mistakes they may make without seeing themselves as failures.

Encouragement is not just appropriate in the last stage of counselling, however. On the contrary, giving encouragement to clients is important throughout every stage of counselling. Clients need to feel valued, and to have their efforts acknowledged. Encouragement also expresses trust and confidence in the client's ability, judgment and capacity for self-development.

Evaluation

An ongoing system of evaluation is necessary if clients are to achieve the results they want. Occasionally, the goals set originally prove to be unrealistic, unworkable or just too ambitious; when this is the case, changes need to be made. The appropriateness of any goal or action should be monitored and reviewed through discussion in counselling and, when this is done, clients tend to feel more confident about their progress overall.

Ending sessions

It is important for counsellors to develop the skill of ending individual sessions. Ending sessions is often more difficult than it sounds, especially when clients talk at great length and it seems impossible to stop them without appearing intrusive or insensitive to their needs. One way of dealing with this issue is to address it at the beginning of counselling, so that clients are aware of time boundaries from the outset. Another useful idea is to state the time ten minutes before the session is due to end. This can be done in the following way:

We have just ten minutes left. Maybe we could look at what you've said so far, and highlight any points you would like to talk about further in your next session. Then we can make arrangements for another appointment next week.

In order to end sessions well, closing sentences should be clear. It is important to avoid introducing new subjects at this stage, and if the client introduces a different topic, schedule this for discussion in the next session. A summary of what the client has said in the present session is also helpful and serves as both a natural ending and a review of topics to be discussed at a later date. It is also worth remembering that although counselling sessions usually last 50 minutes, there are times when the client's conversation comes to an end before this. In these instances, there is nothing to be gained by drawing the session out to a full 50 minutes. In Unit 9 we shall discuss endings again, but in the context of ending counselling generally.

EXERCISE

Setting goals

Working in groups of three to four, discuss any goals that individual members of the group have set themselves in the past. What were the factors that helped you to achieve your goals? Identify any factors, either personal or environmental, which hindered you in any way.

SUMMARY

In this unit, we looked at a range of interpersonal or communication skills, both verbal and non-verbal, and identified the ways in which they are used in a structural framework of counselling. Egan's three-stage model of counselling was described, and this was recommended as a paradigm for structuring the counselling process. A case study was included at the beginning of the unit, which illustrated the various stages of counselling. Other case studies were included to highlight counselling skills and their use with clients. In addition, student exercises, meant to encourage student counsellor self-awareness, were incorporated throughout the unit. The three main theoretical approaches – psychodynamic, cognitive behavioural and humanistic – were outlined, and these were linked to the more specific theoretical models, which will be described in later units, with the counselling skills appropriate to them.

References

British Association for Counselling and Psychotherapy (2013) *Ethical Framework*. London: BACP.

Cooper, M. (2008) *Essential Research Findings in Counselling and Psychotherapy*. London: Sage Publications.

Egan, G. (1994) *The Skilled Helper* (5th edn). California: Brooks Cole.

Lehrer, J. (2012) 'The Brainstorming Myth'. *The New Yorker* (online) 13th Jan., P 1. Available at: www.newyorker.com. Accessed April 2013.
Maslow, A. (1970) *Motivation and Personality* (3rd edn). New York: HarperCollins.
Osborn, A. (1942) *Your Creative Power*. London: McGraw-Hill Book Co.
Rogers, C. (1991) *Client Centred Therapy*. London: Constable.
Weinberg, G. (1996) *The Heart of Psychotherapy*. New York: HarperCollins.
Yalom, I. (2004) *The Gift of Therapy*. London: Piatkus.

Further reading

Argyle, M. (ed.) (2013) *Social Skills and Health*. London: Routledge.
Argyle, M. (1988) *Bodily Communication* (2nd edn). London: Methuen.
Dickson, D. & Hargie, O. (2004) *Skilled Interpersonal Communication*. London: Routledge.
Egan, G. (2010) *The Skilled Helper* (9th edn). California: Brooks Cole.
Rosenberg, M. B. (2003) *Nonviolent Communication: A Language for Life* (2nd edn). Encintas, CA: Puddle Dancer Press.
Wosket, V. (2007) *Egan's Skilled Helper Model: Developments.and Applications in Counselling*. London: Routledge.

Resources

Websites

www.basic-counselling-skills.com
Information geared to the needs of counselling students, health care workers and volunteers.
www.bacp.co.uk
The British Association for Counselling and Psychotherapy.
www.counsellortraining.com
General information about training and courses.
www.communicationskills.com
General information about communication skills and courses.
www.nonverbalcommunication.com
General information about non-verbal communication, including resources and research.

3

Psychodynamic counselling

◆ Introduction

In Unit 2 we considered the main approaches to counselling theory and looked at some of the models that derive from these. However, it is probably true to say that all contemporary models of therapy and counselling are indebted – in some degree at least – to the ideas and techniques first described by Freud. In this unit and the next, we shall concentrate on those approaches which have retained many of the characteristic features of the psychoanalytic tradition. In order to understand and appreciate those distinguishing features, it is important to look more closely at Freud's early background and history and to consider the ways in which his ideas were shaped, as well as the ways in which these ideas and techniques have evolved. The counselling skills that are central to the psychodynamic model will also be considered, along with an appraisal of their usefulness, as well as their limitations in relation to some of the problems clients may bring to therapy.

Freud and his background

Psychodynamic counselling is derived from the classical psychoanalytic tradition, which has its origins in the work of Sigmund Freud, who was born in Austria in 1856. Freud studied medicine at the University of Vienna where he received his degree. Later, he took up a research post in neurophysiology and afterwards switched to clinical practice. Through his work and association with two colleagues, Charcot and Breuer, Freud became interested in the psychological processes responsible for producing certain physical symptoms. Both Charcot and Breuer had used hypnosis, in order to help patients with what they referred to as 'hysterical' symptoms, and Freud used it briefly as well. Over a period of time, however, he came to believe that talking was as effective as hypnosis in helping patients to locate the cause of their problems, and this belief in the value of the 'talking cure' was, and still is, central to psychoanalysis and to all theoretical models that derive from it.

Psychodynamic counselling: key concepts

The word 'psychoanalysis' refers to the form of treatment invented by Freud. It is also used to describe his theory of human psychological development and his hypothesis about the structure of the human mind. The word 'psychodynamic', however, is now commonly used to describe those models of therapy which have evolved from classical psychoanalysis. These models have retained many of the skills and techniques that Freud pioneered, as well as most of the concepts derived from his original work. The 'talking cure' is just one aspect of Freud's original work; there are several other important ideas, including the following:

- the role of the unconscious
- the structure of personality
- the psychosexual stages of development
- the importance of the past and childhood experience
- the use of ego defence mechanisms
- transference and the nature of the therapeutic relationship
- the significance of dreams
- free association, or the 'talking cure'
- interpretation.

The role of the unconscious

The role of the unconscious is a fundamental concept of psychodynamic theory. As a result of his clinical experience with patients in hypnosis, Freud (1923) came to see that many of their problems were the result of mental processes that were hidden to them. The idea that problems could be located in an unknown region of the human mind was a novel and challenging one. Long before Freud expressed these views, it was generally accepted that conscious experience was the motivating factor in all human endeavour. Freud was concerned to show that the mind is not, in fact, always clear to itself and that many inaccessible memories, wishes and impulses are often unacceptable to a person's consciousness. Freud's first description of the human mind is sometimes referred to as a 'topographical model' and includes three dimensions: the unconscious, the pre-conscious and the conscious. The pre-conscious is that area containing thoughts and ideas that are available to recall, so in this respect it is quite different from the unconscious, where thoughts, feelings and ideas are repressed and therefore unavailable to recall in the ordinary sense. In the 1920s Freud changed from his topographical to a structural model of personality, in which he renamed the unconscious the ID, and the conscious the EGO. A new and important addition appeared in this new model, which Freud referred to as the SUPEREGO. (Freud, 1923: 631)

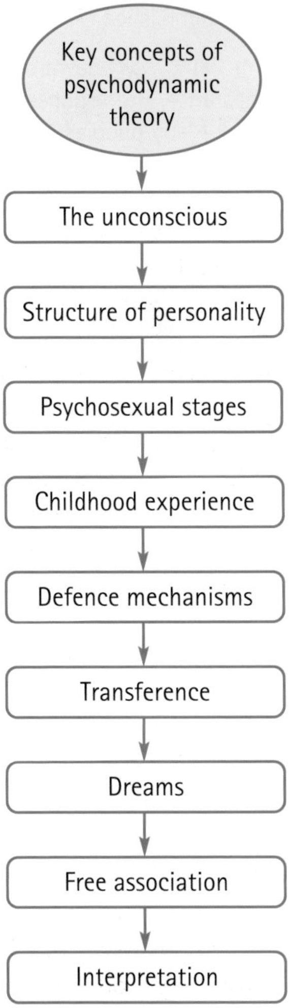

Figure 3.1 Key concepts of psychodynamic theory

The flowchart contains:
- Key concepts of psychodynamic theory
- The unconscious
- Structure of personality
- Psychosexual stages
- Childhood experience
- Defence mechanisms
- Transference
- Dreams
- Free association
- Interpretation

Unconscious meaning

A 55-year-old man was very upset by what he described as 'sloppiness in dress or appearance'. He became especially irritated when he saw someone wearing a jacket or coat casually over the shoulders. In his view, coats should be worn properly with the arms inserted in the sleeves. Like many personal eccentric views, his opinion did not constitute a major problem for him or his relatives. On one occasion, however, he upbraided his wife for wearing her coat in this fashion. In response to this, she suggested that he should try to remember when he first started to think in this way since, after all, the problem was clearly his and not hers. Several days later he mentioned to her in surprise that he remembered an old man who lived in the neighbourhood where he grew up. This man was a frightening local character, who had lost an arm in the war, and frequently shouted at children in the street. Because of his injury, he always wore his coat draped over his shoulders. Once this association had been made by the client, his preoccupation with appearance diminished.

Comment: It can be seen from this account that the client, Mr Cater, was unaware at first of the origin of his strong feelings about dress and appearance. His response to his wife's style of dress was irrational, as he readily admitted. Many phobias are similar to this, and clients are seldom able to identify the factors which triggered them. With help and encouragement, however, it is possible for clients to locate the original (usually traumatic) event that prompted the fearful response. Mr Cater's wife was interested enough to encourage him to look for the cause of his irritation. The cause was, in fact, repressed and buried in his unconscious mind. Through effort, application and interest, he was successful in recalling this childhood event of the old man in the street who frightened him. Material which is repressed in this way is often of a frightening or disturbing nature, and this is exactly why it is repressed in the first place. However, as Mr Cater's example illustrates, the fact that experiences are consigned to the unconscious does not mean that they will cease to cause problems.

Unconscious motivation: As the term implies, unconscious motivation refers to a process outside conscious awareness. However, some motives have both conscious and unconscious components and occasionally a motive is discernible in distorted or disguised form.

Psychoanalysis: This term refers to two aspects of Freud's work. First, it denotes his theory of human development and behaviour, and secondly it describes the related therapy which he used to help patients gain access to mental conflicts. Among the techniques used in psychoanalysis are *free association*, *interpretation*, and the analysis of *resistance* and *transference*.

Psychodynamic: In the context of psychotherapy and counselling, the word 'psychodynamic' refers to an approach which originates in Freudian theory. The term is derived from two words, *psyche* (meaning mind) and *dynamic* (meaning active or alive), both of which are Greek in origin. Put together these two words describe the activity of the human mind, both conscious and unconscious.

Unconscious processes

In groups of two or three, discuss the following short case studies and consider the unconscious processes which may be at work in each.

1 Bill is often invited next door for dinner. He likes his neighbours and enjoys these visits. However, on each occasion he spills wine on the tablecloth, even though he is normally well coordinated and certainly does not drink too much. His neighbours are very gracious about this and always invite him back. They are well off and enjoy Bill's company.

2 Phyllis is 36 years old and has to stay overnight in hospital for a minor procedure. The night before she goes into hospital, she packs a small overnight case, which includes a soap bag containing a wash cloth and some cosmetics. As she does this, she is suddenly overcome with feelings of sadness and loss. The smell of the soap reminds her of an earlier stay in hospital when she was a child of five. She always felt she had coped very well with this at the time, and her parents had commented on her bravery and stoicism.

3 Sarah has recently applied for promotion. She wants to get ahead, but is not totally convinced that management is the job for her. The night before her interview she dreams that she is in the driver seat of a large lorry. She is trying desperately to operate the gears, but is unable to do so. After a while she gets out and goes over to a small car. She gets into this and drives away quite happily.

The structure of personality

Freud (1923) came to believe that human personality is made up of three connecting systems: the Id, the Ego and the Superego. These three areas of personality constantly interact with one another as a means of regulating an individual's behaviour.

The **Id**, which is the most primitive part of the system, is present from birth and is derived from Freud's concept of the unconscious. The Id can be seen, therefore, as the repository for everything that is fixed, instinctual and inherited in a person's make up. The Id is also, according to Freud, the repository of all our impulses, especially those relating to sex and aggression. These impulses are constantly demanding attention and expression, but because of the constraints placed on us by society and the need for civilised behaviour, immediate gratification of instinctual urges is not always possible or desirable. The Id, which is governed by the pleasure principle, needs, therefore, to be modified or regulated, and this function is fulfilled by the Ego, the second part of Freud's system.

The **Ego** is sometimes described as the arbiter, the manger or the executive, of the total personality system, since its function is to deal with the demands of the Id in a realistic way. The Ego is governed by the reality principle – which means that it must devise ways of satisfying the demands of the Id, while simultaneously deciding what behaviour and actions are appropriate at any given time. At about the age of one to two, children begin to learn that they must wait for certain things and that very often it is a good idea to ask. This second part of personality is rational, logical and incorporates problem-solving abilities, memory and perception too. Skills such as talking, planning, negotiating and explaining are important dimensions of the conscious Ego; and, whereas the Id is concerned with subjective needs and internal reality, the Ego is concerned with things as they exist in the real world.

The **Superego**, or morality principle, is the third psychological process which Freud included in his model of human personality. This develops at around the age of three and is composed of internalised values, ideals and moral precepts, all of which derive from parental and other authority figures. The Superego is that part of personality which is concerned with right and wrong and is capable of generating guilt when people transgress their own, or society's moral code. When children develop this aspect of personality they become effective, over a period of time, in regulating their own behaviour. Before this mature stage is reached, however, parents and teachers socialise the child through a system of rewards and punishments. Once society's standards have been incorporated, any infringement of them is likely to produce anxiety or guilt. For some people, the Superego can develop as excessively punishing so that attitudes of perfectionism are fostered, which can, in turn, lead to depression and other psychological problems. The task for the Ego is to maintain a balance or equilibrium between the demands of the Id, on the one hand, and the strictures of the Superego, on the other. Integrated behaviour is dependent on this balance, and on an accurate perception of external reality.

The psychosexual stages of development

Along with his theories of the unconscious and the structure of personality, Freud's three essays on the theory of sexuality (Freud, 1924) make it quite clear what he considered to be the most significant aspects of mental life. It is difficult for us today to realise just how revolutionary his ideas must have seemed at the end of the nineteenth century and the beginning of the twentieth. Although Freud was living and working in Vienna, his was nevertheless a Victorian and sexually repressive era. One of his most outstanding achievements was to focus on childhood experience and, in doing so, to consider the ways in which children develop to sexual maturity and the stages through which they pass in order to achieve this. The subject of sexuality in children had been neglected and even absent before Freud, so his descriptions of infantile sensations and experience were startling and certainly controversial. Freud himself pointed out that previous opinion had inclined to the view that sexual instinct only awakens at puberty (Freud, 1924). He was concerned to show that events take place much earlier and that sexuality evolves through a series of stages, which are commonly referred to as the 'psychosexual stages of development'. The following is an outline of the theoretical framework Freud proposed.

The oral stage: birth to 1 year approximately

This is the first phase of a child's life – from birth until about 18 months – when pleasure is concentrated on the mouth with the experiences of feeding and sucking. In fact, it is probably true to say that the mouth is the centre of existence at this stage, since survival is dependent on taking in nourishment. The word 'Libido', which Freud uses to describe this energy, is a broad term. It does not refer to sexual feelings in a narrow sense; instead, it denotes a comprehensive force or vitality, which is bound up with feelings of pleasure, comfort and the need to survive (Freud 1924: 285–286).

There are two phases during this stage of development: the first is the sucking phase when only fluids are taken, and the second is the biting phase, which is linked to weaning and eating. Weaning can be traumatic for babies, especially if it is introduced abruptly or without sensitivity to emotional needs, and problems associated with either the earlier or later oral stages can be carried over into later life. Food and love are closely linked in infancy, and when early feeding experiences are negative, this link between food, love and security may persist into adult life and become manifest through eating disorders, alcohol or drug addition and smoking. Sarcasm and gossip, which stem from aggressive impulses, are also sometimes associated with problems arising at the weaning oral stage. If weaning is delayed, difficult or emotionally traumatic, for example, the natural activities of chewing and biting may not be given adequate expression and may then seek expression in destructive ways later on. Adult problem behaviours, linked to either of the stages of weaning, tend to become more pronounced at times of stress or unhappiness.

The anal stage: age 1 to 3 years approximately

This is the second important stage of a child's development; during this time the young child is beginning to understand what is expected by parents and society generally. The Ego is beginning to emerge, and the reality principle is replacing the Id or pleasure principle. At this time also, a toddler is subjected to a major socialising process in the form of toilet training.

Conflict can and does arise between the wishes of parents and the impulses of the child. These areas of conflict concern issues of power and control. On the one hand, the child derives pleasure from both withholding and expelling faeces, while on the other hand, there is the desire to please parents and to establish the kind of routine they demand. The issue of hygiene is an important one too; so several major learning experiences are undertaken in a short space of time. Parents often reward small children for using the toilet at specific times. This teaches children about the need to defer gratification. Parents may also seem disapproving when mistakes are made, and these parental attitudes are linked to the emergence of the Superego in the child.

Attitudes to cleanliness and order are fostered at this stage; if these are punishing, problems can develop in adult life, leading to habits of compulsive cleanliness and order. On the other hand, there are those people who tend to spread disorder and mess wherever they go, habits which may have begun at the anal stage when toilet training was not rigorous enough. In psychodynamic literature, faeces and money are often associated. This means that faeces are regarded as a young child's first possession and, in later life, this unconscious association remains with the adult (Freud, 1908). Attitudes to money can, according to Freudian theory, shed some light on an individual's toilet training experiences. If we consider some of the expressions commonly used in relation to money and its possession, we can see the unconscious connection with toilet training more clearly. These expressions include 'filthy rich', 'stinking rich' and 'rolling in the stuff', to name just a few. As we shall see in the next unit, however, contemporary psychodynamic theory offers some interesting and quite different views about human characteristics generally.

The phallic stage: age 3 to 6 years approximately

During the phallic stage, a child's interest becomes focused on the genital area; in psychodynamic theory this applies to both sexes. The Oedipus complex – which is integral to this phase of development – is also applicable to both boys and girls, and represents a family drama in which individual roles within the group become clearer to the child. In formulating his theory, Freud was influenced by the Greek tragedy *Oedipus Rex*, in which Oedipus kills his father and marries his mother. However, Freud was also influenced by personal experience, because in 1896 his father died. During the next three years Freud became preoccupied with self-analysis. He came to see that he had repressed feelings of anger and resentment towards his father. In addition, he experienced shame and impotence at this time, which he linked to early childhood experience. Freud was convinced that as a small boy he had been in love with his mother and jealous of his father. This personal scenario was to underpin his subsequent theory of early sexual development.

According to classical Freudian theory, boys at the Oedipal stage become very interested in their mothers and envious of their fathers. Father is, after all, the person who is closest to mother, and to a small boy this represents an impediment to his own – often explicitly stated – ambition to own or 'marry' mother. Since these aspirations cause anxiety to the child – father might become angry and punish him – the situation is resolved through a process of identification. The identification occurs when the child begins to emulate and adopt his father's mannerisms, style, goals, interests and ambitions. Such a response solves the Oedipal problem and serves a dual purpose: on the one hand, the child has established a male role model for himself, while, on the other hand, he is beginning to learn about the structure of society, in general, and his own place within it. The family, as a microcosm of society, is the setting in which this important learning experience takes place. The onset of genital sexual feelings at the phallic stage also prompts an interest in sex roles, as well as an interest in reproduction and birth.

The Oedipal drama is one aspect of psychodynamic theory which students frequently misinterpret. Often it is taken to mean sexual interest in the opposite-sex parent only. In fact, it is a much broader concept than this and incorporates those personal and sociological elements already mentioned. Girls are considered to experience a similar constellation of impulses, except of course that in their case the mother is seen as the rival and the father as the object of desire. The concept of 'penis envy' is linked to this stage of development in girls, for according to Freudian theory small girls blame their mothers for the fact that they are anatomically different from boys. The punishment which a boy fears from his father (castration) cannot happen to a girl; what she fears, therefore, is that it has already taken place. The situation is resolved for her through eventual identification with her mother. Needless to say, this is a much disputed theory, and in the next unit we shall look at some post-Freudian theories and consider the very different ways in which they interpret female development and the role of girls within the family.

The latency period: age 6 to 12 years approximately

During latency all available energy is directed towards the development of social and intellectual skills. Friendships, especially those with members of the same sex, become very important and recreational activities, including hobbies and sport, are a central focus of this stage. The sexual feelings, which are repressed during latency, will, however, return at the next (genital) stage of development.

The genital stage: age 12 years to adulthood

The hormonal changes which take place at this stage encourage a resumption of sexual interest generally. This interest is, however, much less auto-erotic than it was in the Oedipal stage and has the added purpose of establishing romantic, loving and intimate bonds with other people. The main focus of concern, according to Freud, is in forming heterosexual relationships with a view to lasting commitment and marriage. From a strictly Freudian viewpoint, therefore, mature adult sexuality with a member of the opposite sex is the outcome of successful progression through all the earlier stages. Gay members of any student group are frequently concerned to question this theory and to discuss the ways in which it may have contributed to present homophobic attitudes. This is a topic worth discussing (and, unfortunately, often avoided) but it should be pointed out that Freud's views on homosexuality are complex and thoughtful, and he certainly did not believe that therapy should seek to change a person's sexual orientation. It is a fact, however, that in the history of psychoanalysis, the idea that everyone is constitutionally heterosexual has been a dominant theme.

For those students who would like to do some further reading on this subject, Freud's *Three Essays on the Theory of Sexuality* (1924) is a useful starting point. It is also important to consider contemporary psychodynamic views on the matter and to look at the ways in which ideas concerning the nature of sexuality have been revised and updated, as a result of research and changing attitudes. An overall survey of these latter ideas is contained in *Freud and Beyond* (Mitchell and Black, 1995).

The importance of the past and childhood experience

One of the most important contributions to the psychodynamic approach is its focus on childhood experience and the way this experience can influence adult life. In the latter part of the nineteenth century, Freud (1896) decided that many adult problems originated from early childhood abuse. His theory provoked disbelief and hostility and, in fact, this reaction was so pronounced that Freud felt obliged to abandon his original idea. Later on he suggested that his patients may have been mistaken in the memories they recounted. Perhaps what they thought were memories were, in fact, really unconscious fantasies and wishes? This second idea led to Freud's theory of the Oedipus complex (Freud, 1900) and to his conviction that many of the experiences people discuss in therapy are indicative of unconscious conflicts and wishes. Freud was effective, therefore, in drawing attention to the significance of early experience, even though he did seem to abandon his early, and we now know, probably correct, conclusion. It is clear that many children do indeed suffer sexual and other forms of abuse in childhood. Freud's original discovery proved to be prophetic in a sense, and by focusing on childhood experience he succeeded in bringing the subject to public awareness in a way never achieved before. It is probably true to say that Freud started something, although he certainly did not finish it. Ideas about child development and experience continue to evolve. In the next unit we shall consider some of the contemporary ideas relating to childhood experience. It would be a mistake, however, to assume that it is only sexual trauma or other child abuse that is significant in psychodynamic theory. Children encounter numerous problems while growing up, and many of these can also cause difficulties in adult life.

Childhood experience

Working individually, spend about 20 minutes recalling aspects of your childhood experience. At this early stage, focus on positive rather than negative aspects. Consider the following questions to help you get started:

1 What is your earliest pleasant memory of childhood?

2 How have early pleasant experiences helped to form your adult personality?

3 Can you recall any childhood feelings of rivalry towards one of your parents or carers?

4 What positive aspects of your childhood do you most value today?

The use of ego defence mechanisms

We have already seen that human personality (from a Freudian viewpoint) is made up of three components – the Id, the Ego and the Superego. The Ego, which is governed by the reality principle, has the task of coping with the demands of the Id, while constantly appraising external reality and making decisions about the kind of behaviour that is appropriate at any given time. The threat of punishment from the Superego is another factor to be considered, and the combined pressure from these forces (Id and Superego) has the effect of generating anxiety for the individual.

Psychological processes

The conflict that occurs between a person's wishes and external reality is dealt with by the use of defence mechanisms. These are psychological processes people use, in order to protect themselves against extreme discomfort and tension. They are also effective in maintaining mental composure and self-esteem in a variety of what might otherwise be very painful situations. Defence mechanisms operate at an unconscious level, and all of us use them occasionally. However, prolonged and persistent use of them is counter-productive, because such defences serve to distort reality and falsify experience. They also require a great deal of energy and vigilance, which, if liberated, could be used in much more creative ways. The following is a summary of the main defences.

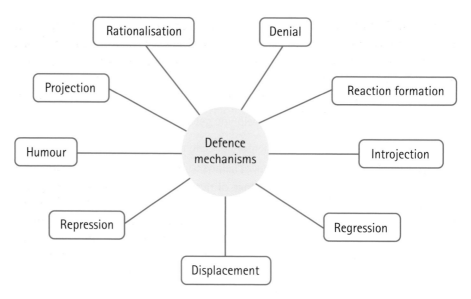

Figure 3.2 Ego defence mechanisms

Repression

Repression is a process whereby traumatic or painful experiences are forgotten, or pushed out of consciousness. This is the most fundamental of all the defence mechanisms and, like the others, is operated unconsciously. A child might, for example, repress a truly threatening experience like abandonment or loss, since this may be the child's only method of coping at the time. Repressed material does not go away, however, but continues to exist in the unconscious (Freud, 1909). Occasionally, disguised signals break through into consciousness, and these may take the form of physical symptoms. Repressed material may also surface in dreams, or at times of stress or illness. Certain major life events may prompt the re-emergence of repressed material. The following short case study illustrates this last point.

CASE STUDY

Repression

An 18-year-old student left home to attend university. During this time she became involved with a boyfriend and fell in love with him. This was her first serious involvement, and it brought into consciousness a painful memory from early childhood. The memory concerned an occasion when she had seen her father being physically abusive towards her mother. The student had forgotten the traumatic incident, but details of it began to surface once she found herself getting close to her boyfriend. She then realised that she had been very reluctant (in her early teenage years) to become involved with boys. This inhibition with the opposite sex stemmed from her fear of involvement and from her wish to avoid her mother's experience. Her first serious encounter served as a catalyst to release the repressed and painful memories from childhood. During a subsequent period of counselling, she was helped to uncover the memory more fully and to understand its effect on her.

A great deal of mental energy is needed in order to ensure that repressed material does not surface into consciousness. However, the force that prevents unconscious material from becoming conscious is particularly strong and is known as **resistance**. Like repression, resistance is unconsciously motivated and used as a means of avoiding the anxiety awareness of repressed material would entail (Freud, 1909).

Denial

Denial is used as a defence mechanism when reality is unpleasant, or disturbing in some way. A person with a serious illness might, for example, deny the condition. This denial may serve a useful purpose initially, since it helps to protect the person against anxiety and high levels of stress. In the long term, though, its use will distort reality and prevent the adjustment and acceptance that are important at such a time. Denial is also used frequently by people who have been bereaved. In this context, it also works effectively in the short term but can lead to complicated grief reactions in the long term.

Rationalisation

Rationalisation is a face-saving defence, which people often use to explain away personal failures, vices or inadequacies. Instead of accepting that failure has taken place, 'rational' explanations are given, and these explanations are sometimes partly true. A parent may say that a particular child is 'difficult', for example, and this label may then be used to excuse parental aggression towards that child.

Projection

The defence mechanism of projection ensures that internal anxiety or discomfort is directed outwards towards other people. It is a way of attributing our own faults to others. A person with a tendency to be hypocritical may, for example, suspect or even accuse other people of hypocrisy. In a similar way, someone who is aggressive or domineering may see these characteristics in others, but fail to recognise and own them personally.

Displacement

Unacceptable impulses and desires are often aimed at the wrong person. This is most likely to happen when the real target is seen as too threatening to confront. Thus, a man who has had problems with his boss at work might be tempted to take it out on someone else – his wife or children, for example. Strong feelings are also sometimes displaced towards authority figures in public life. A person who has had a difficult relationship with a parent may develop hostile attitudes towards the police, judges or even the Pope.

Reaction formation

Reaction formation is a defence in which the conscious feeling or thought is exactly opposite to the unconscious one. An example of this is the person who expresses strong views against liberal sex attitudes, while at the same time fighting to control personal sexual impulses. Reaction formation is evident in many areas and may be implicit in a variety of attitudes. People who claim to dislike lateness may have a tendency in that direction, while those who deplore bad manners may well lack social confidence themselves. It is probably true to say that when strongly held views are evident there is some likelihood that the opposite impulse is present. The degree of emotional investment in the view expressed is a fairly reliable indicator of this particular defence.

Introjection

This describes the process of taking in the views and attitudes expressed by other people. This can work in either a positive or a negative way. One example of positive use is the process whereby children incorporate the values and standards of parents and teachers. Introjection is problematic when less healthy experiences are taken in and held as part of the self. An extreme example of this is the person who has been kidnapped and, in order to survive mentally, identifies with the captors and their cause. A less dramatic, though equally problematic, use of the defence is evident when abused children absorb their experiences and then pass them on to the next generation. With regard to the last point, however, it is important to remember that not all abused children become abusing adults in this way.

Making assumptions about people and attaching labels to them is a mistake that people who work in a caring capacity are liable to make. Counsellors are no exception in this respect, and this is why regular supervision is an essential component of their work.

Regression

People often retreat to an earlier stage of development in the face of threat or failure. Regression is a defence that hospital nurses are familiar with: patients often revert to less adult forms of behaviour once they find themselves in hospital. This defence works well for people in many situations, since it ensures that care and attention are elicited from others. It works well for victims of trauma, who certainly need the added care and attention. Regression is a problem when it is used habitually as a way of being noticed.

Humour

Some people use humour as a shield or barrier against painful experience and trauma. It is interesting that many comedians have suffered from depression, which would seem to indicate a close link between humour and sadness. Humour is, of course, not always used as a defence mechanism; it is quite possible to be funny without any underlying agenda. Freud refers to the 'high yield of pleasure', which people derive from humour (Freud, 1907: 437). However, clients sometimes use humour as a way of avoiding serious and reflective consideration of their problems. Humour may have become an habitual defence with them, and one that is difficult to relinquish.

The concept of anxiety

Anxiety is an important concept in psychodynamic theory and, in Freudian terms, is seen as the catalyst that signals impending danger to the Ego. Defence mechanisms are used in order to reduce anxiety. Danger situations include fear of losing another person's love, the fear of punishment (by others, or by the Superego) and the fear of abandonment (Freud, 1932).

EXERCISE

Looking at defences

Working individually, identify any defences you have used in the past at times of anxiety or stress. How did the defences help, or hinder, you at the time?

Transference and the nature of the therapeutic relationship

Transference is a term which – in psychodynamic literature – refers to the client's emotional response to the counsellor. Clients' emotional responses are, of course, highlighted in all the theoretical approaches, but the concept of transference is especially significant in the psychodynamic model. Freud was the first person to identify the phenomenon; while working with his colleague Breuer, he witnessed it at first hand and later described it both in lectures and in his writing (Freud, 1909).

Transfer of feelings from client to counsellor

Clients may 'transfer' to counsellors feelings that are either positive or negative. These feelings stem from childhood emotional responses to parents and other important adults and are, therefore, not based on any real relation between counsellor and client. Transference feelings operate at an unconscious level, so the client is unaware that responses to the counsellor may be inappropriate, or out of date. Evidence of the client's early emotional life is, therefore, often clearly seen in the counselling relationship. When transference feelings are positive, a client may regard the counsellor as helpful and understanding, but when transference feelings are negative, the client may see the counsellor as unhelpful, perhaps rejecting or even hostile. Both these attitudes are potentially helpful for the client. By looking more closely at them, the client (with help from the counsellor) should be able to link current relationship styles with earlier relationships that may have been problematic. The case study (Transference) included in this section illustrates this last point. In *Five Lectures on Psychoanalysis* (1909), Freud emphasises that therapy does not create transference, but 'merely reveals it to consciousness' (Freud, 1909: 84). He adds that when transference is revealed in this way, the client is empowered to gain control over it.

It is important to make clear that transference is not a mysterious occurrence only seen in counselling and therapy. People may experience strong emotional responses in a variety of 'helping' situations. These situations include patient – doctor and nurse – patient relationships and, indeed, any other context where one person is depending on another for assistance or support. Nurses, doctors, social workers and ministers of religion are aware that the people they help often respond in inappropriate emotional ways. Problems often arise because helpers do not understand the reasons for such feelings and may, in fact, be flattered to receive them. This is especially true when the feelings transferred are loving, idealising, admiring or erotic. Abuse of clients can arise in these circumstances, so the underlying dynamic of transference needs to be understood and the central role of supervision for counsellors recognised.

Another important point made by Freud concerns the universality of transference and its importance in determining the outcome of any helping relationship. In his autobiographical study (1925) he stresses that therapy is an 'impossibility' when there is no transference of emotion in the relationship (Freud, 1925: 26). Freud's writings are the clearest exposition of psychoanalysis and psychodynamic theory; and they are the most rewarding to read on any aspect of his work. However, as we shall see in later units of this book, other approaches have developed their own theoretical models of transference. Some of these stem from Freud's original work, but others, while acknowledging the importance of the therapeutic relationship, place a different emphasis on it.

CASE STUDY

Transference

A 26-year-old client became angry because his counsellor had gone into hospital for a minor operation. The client (Colin) had been told in advance that the counsellor would be away for a week, but this notice did little to reassure him. During a subsequent counselling session he discussed his reaction with the counsellor. At first he was puzzled by the strength of his own reaction, but he later identified some earlier experiences that had some bearing on his heightened emotional response to the counsellor's absence. Colin's parents had divorced when he was five years old, and shortly afterwards his father had been ill with allergy problems. No one had taken time to talk to the small child, nor had he been taken to visit his father in hospital. One consequence of this was that, for many years, Colin blamed himself for his father's illness and departure. Once he was able to explore all these issues, Colin understood why he became angry and frustrated when the counsellor left to go into hospital. The feelings he had transferred to the counsellor were really feelings stemming from the past and his relationship with his parents. In exploring them, however, he was able to look more realistically at his childhood experience of loss and at the burden of blame he had carried for so many years.

Countertransference

The word 'countertransference' refers to the counsellor's emotional response to the client. Counsellors are also capable of displacing feelings from the past into the present situation with the client. If Colin's counsellor (see the case study above) had taken his attitude personally, such a response would have been inappropriate in the therapeutic context and would not have helped the client in any way. The counsellor needed to understand that the client was not angry with her personally. Colin's reactions – which were unrealistic in the present context – were used by the counsellor in order to help him achieve deeper understanding of his problems.

However, counsellors, since they are human, may never be wholly objective in their response to clients. Counsellors have life histories which can colour or affect their reactions, and these areas of personal bias are defined as countertransference. Once again, this highlights the importance of supervision for counsellors, since it is only through supervision that they can identify and deal with their countertransference reactions.

Some forms of countertransference are more common than others. Seeing clients as helpless, or as victims, is one form. When this attitude is pronounced, over-protection or even advice may be offered by the counsellor. This kind of over-protectiveness says a great deal about the counsellor's need to be in control, and it will certainly inhibit the client's self-development and autonomy. Countertransference responses may also appear in the counsellor's inability to confront, or disagree with a client. This may stem from a fear of being disliked, or of being seen as incompetent. Counsellors may also feel themselves to be in competition with particular clients, or to feel envious of them. These responses may be related to childhood problems with siblings and parents. Whatever the reason, it is essential that counsellors monitor their countertransference feelings and discuss them in supervision. Issues concerning supervision will be dealt with in Unit 9.

On the subject of countertransference, however, it is important to remember that every imaginable human prejudice or bias may present itself in this form, and when such bias is left unexamined, it will ultimately distort the therapeutic relationship and work against clients. It is also possible for counsellors to have biased feelings towards certain people, or groups of people. One example of this is the kind of partiality which may be extended to specific groups such as women, minority groups or people seen as disadvantaged in some way. The crucial point to make here is that individual clients are entitled to be treated as individuals and not as stereotypes.

CASE STUDY

Countertransference

Elliot, who was a qualified psychiatric nurse, completed counsellor training to diploma level. Afterwards he worked for an agency that specialised in addiction counselling. Although he received regular supervision, Elliot was surprised by the strength of his responses to one of his clients.

When he was a child, Elliot's parents were neglectful and dependent on alcohol, and, as a teenager, he experimented with drugs and alcohol too. From an early age he had learned to fend for himself; he often took care of his parents, cooking for them and shopping when there was some money to do so. After his turbulent teenage addictive phase, he decided to make something of himself, studied at night class and then went into nurse training.

One of Elliot's clients was a middle-aged man, who had been addicted to alcohol for many years. As soon as he met him, Elliot sensed some characteristics in the man which reminded him of his own father. Supervision provided an opportunity for him to discuss his feelings about his client; nevertheless, on several occasions Elliot found himself 'taking care of' his client in ways that were inappropriate. He had, for example, worried about his client and had more than once given him direct advice. In addition, Elliot wanted his client to like and approve of him. At other times, he felt strong negative feelings towards the man and, although he was careful to conceal these, they were sufficiently disturbing to prompt Elliot to seek extra supervision.

Comment: This case study illustrates some of the points already made about countertransference. It indicates the importance of past experience in determining the way counsellors may respond to certain clients. Elliot did not react like this to every client he had, but this particular man resembled his father in certain ways. These similarities were not directly obvious, but they triggered something in the relationship between counsellor and client that was reminiscent of Elliot's early relationship with his father. This meant that Elliot was relating to the client as he would have to his own father. It is not difficult to see how unhelpful this would be for the client, who was not seen as a separate individual in his own right. The case study also highlights the importance of regular supervision for counsellors. It is only through supervision that these often complicated countertransference feelings can be identified and seen for what they are.

Projective identification and countertransference

The term 'projective identification' was first used by Melanie Klein (1932), whose theories we shall consider in more detail in the next unit. It is important to consider the concept of projective identification in this section because it is a form of countertransference, though its manifestations are often complex and more difficult to define. Klein originally used the term to describe an infant's ability to split off uncomfortable or 'bad' parts of 'self' and project these into the mother (Solomon, 1995: 4). We looked at the defence mechanism of projection earlier in this unit and saw that it is a way of ascribing unacceptable aspects of ourselves to others. However, other people are not usually aware of what is being projected onto them, unless, of course, a verbal accusation accompanies the projection. Projective identification, on the other hand, is actually felt by its recipient in the same way that an attentive mother will feel aspects of an infant's distress or discomfort. The mother is thus identified with her child who, at this stage, is unable to express basic needs verbally.

In the context of therapy, projective identification is manifest in a particular way, though its underlying motivation is unconscious. A client may, for example, project onto the counsellor a feeling, or constellation of feelings that cannot be expressed through language because they occurred at a primitive developmental stage of life. Furthermore, these client experiences originate from a time when boundaries between self and others were not discernible, but blurred. As a result, the counsellor will experience the projected aspects of the client, and may even feel a sense of being 'controlled' by the client.

What then are the feelings a counsellor may experience in relation to a client when projective identification is a prominent dynamic in the relationship? In fact, these feelings encompass an infinite variety, but may include the following:

- sadness
- fatigue
- disinterest
- dullness
- confusion
- anger.

The next case study illustrates one counsellor's experience of projective identification.

Kylie

Kylie, who was having difficulty with her coursework, came to see the college counsellor. During their sessions together the counsellor felt increasingly and unusually tired. Kylie's mother had died when she was a baby, so Kylie had very little memory of her. Her father remarried and Kylie was later sent to boarding school. During holiday periods Kylie felt awkward on going home; she didn't get on particularly with her stepmother, though there was no outright animosity between them. It was just, she said, that she hardly knew her stepmother, so they were more like strangers when they met.

During counselling sessions, Kylie smiled a lot and said she believed in being upbeat and confident. It was just that she was having difficulty in concentrating on her college work. The counsellor (Aisling) was puzzled by her own feelings of fatigue, which she thought were incongruous considering Kylie's cheerful demeanour. In supervision, Aisling discussed her experience, and the supervisor advised her to stay with the feeling of tiredness, in order to identify its meaning. Aisling followed this advice, and in a later session Kylie fleetingly mentioned her mother and then changed the subject. After a while, Aisling referred back to the subject of Kylie's early bereavement and her mother's death. For the first time, Kylie looked deeply sad but began to talk at length about her mother. She expressed her sorrow about the loss of her mother and about being sent to boarding school, which, to her, represented a rejection by her father. As she spoke, her body language changed: she sat hunched up in her chair and all of the pent-up feelings she had withheld came pouring out. She remarked how exhausting it had all been to deal with. Afterwards, she returned for further counselling sessions and covered many of the issues she had previously avoided.

In supervision, Aisling was able to identify exactly when the debilitating feeling of tiredness left her. It was during Kylie's cathartic reminiscences about the early traumatic events she had endured. The counsellor had been able to hold on to the extreme tiredness until the client brought it into conscious awareness and experienced it. Projective identification is therefore a special form of communication, in which aspects of the client's inner world are actually 'felt' by the counsellor.

Student self-assessment

Working in pairs, identify some of the countertransference feelings you have experienced in relation to the people you help. How did you deal with these feelings, and what, if anything, did they tell you about yourself? Take turns to discuss your individual experiences.

The significance of dreams

Freud regarded dreams as 'the royal road to a knowledge of the unconscious activities of the mind' (Freud, 1909: 47). It follows, therefore, that in classical psychoanalysis, dream interpretation is a central component of therapy. Dream interpretation is important in all other psychodynamic models of therapy and counselling too. The difference here is that whereas in the past psychoanalysts might have devoted long periods of time in the analysis of just one dream, psychodynamic counsellors and therapists focus on them only when clients request or understand such a focus. The point to be made is that not all clients are regularly in touch with their unconscious and dream life, although it's probably true to say that any client who requests psychodynamic counselling is aware of the importance given to dreams and to dream interpretation. Such interpretation is, of course, entirely subjective; only the client can say what the dream means for him or her personally, though counsellors who work from a psychodynamic perspective can help clients to examine the symbolism contained in dreams and to discuss what they mean. It is important to add here that dream interpretation through the use of standardised symbols found in popular self-help texts is not useful for clients. This is because dreams are unique to the individual dreamer. Later in this unit, we shall look at some of the skills that can be used to help clients interpret their dreams.

Free association or 'the talking cure'

All theoretical models of counselling are based on the premise that clients need to talk through their problems, in order to make sense of them. The term 'free association' was first used by Freud to describe the process of encouraging his patients to say whatever they liked, on the grounds that whatever occurred to them would be relevant and revealing (Freud, 1909: 46).

In psychodynamic counselling, clients are encouraged to talk at their own pace and to express their feelings and thoughts, no matter how insignificant these may appear to be. What clients wish to say is obviously important to them in any case, and it is never the counsellor's task to decide what should be voiced by clients during sessions. What is important is that counsellors listen carefully to clients, respond appropriately and at the right time.

Free association also forms the basis of dream interpretation. When clients use this technique in relation to their own dreams, significant links are often made so that apparently disconnected symbols come together and form a more coherent picture.

Skills used in psychodynamic counselling

All the basis skills described in previous units are applicable to the psychodynamic approach. In addition to these skills a number of others are used, which have evolved from the original Freudian psychoanalytic model. Psychodynamic counselling is obviously very different from psychoanalysis, however, so the techniques, methods and skills of psychoanalysis have been adapted to suit the approach and to facilitate the client's needs. The following is a list of skills that are central to the psychodynamic approach:

- establishing a contract
- listening
- observing
- clarifying
- giving reflective responses
- linking
- interpreting
- attending to transference
- looking at defences and resistance
- drawing parallels between past and present
- looking at dreams.

The importance of structure: contracts

We have already seen that counselling takes place in sessions that last for 50 minutes. Clients need to know the basic details of counsellor–client contracts well in advance of sessions, if possible, so that structure and stability are an integral part of the relationship. It is essential to establish clear boundaries with clients, a practice that is not, of course, exclusive to the psychodynamic approach. However, the difference is that in psychodynamic counselling the client's response to such a contract has special significance. A client who misses sessions, for example, or who arrives late, is clearly expressing something that is not being said in words. Clients can, of course, arrive later for sessions or miss them occasionally because of transport or other problems. But when poor timekeeping is habitual, there is always the possibility that some form of resistance is operating within the client. Such resistance is usually unconscious, or outside the client's awareness.

In a situation like this, the counsellor's task is to encourage the client to look closely at the underlying meaning of the behaviour and to place it in the context of any other problems, or difficulties, the client is experiencing. It may be that the client is avoiding some painful subject, or it may be that he or she feels unable to disagree with the counsellor, or to express negative or angry feelings. Even though clients come into counselling with the intention of sorting out and understanding their problems, the exploration this involves is often so difficult for them that the temptation to resist further self-scrutiny is often hard to overcome. The following case study is an example of this last point.

CASE STUDY

Lydia

Lydia, who was 30 years old, wanted to talk to a counsellor about her relationship with her grandmother, who had died. She attended three counselling sessions and seemed to be keen to understand why she continued to feel depressed, even though two years had passed since her grandmother's death. In the third session, Lydia referred to the fact that she had gone to live with her grandparents after her parents split up. This was a difficult subject for her to talk about and it gradually became apparent to the counsellor that Lydia wanted to avoid it altogether. In addition to the fact that she obviously wanted to avoid the subject, she also decided to leave early, and on the next occasion arrived late for her session. The counsellor offered a tentative interpretation of Lydia's behaviour in the following way:

COUNSELLOR: You talked a little about living with your gran and grandad last time we met. Then I sensed that it was difficult for you, and that you wanted to leave it.

CLIENT: It's not difficult really . . . [pause] . . . I usually don't mind talking about it. I loved staying with them, although I was sad about my parents.

COUNSELLOR: The sadness about your parents, tell me about that.

CLIENT: [long pause] I suppose I never really allowed myself to think about it. I felt I had to be strong for Gareth [her brother].

COUNSELLOR: Not thinking about it and being strong for Gareth; all that meant that you could never get a chance to grieve for the upheaval in your life.

CLIENT: I think in a way my depression is linked to that . . .

COUNSELLOR: To your parents splitting up . . .

CLIENT: Yes, for ages I thought it was to do with my gran's death. Maybe it has more to do with other things.

COUNSELLOR: Things you thought you had best avoid.

CLIENT: Yes. But then the depression doesn't go away . . .

COUNSELLOR: The depression stays with you as long as you don't let yourself remember how it felt when the break-up happened.

Comment: It can be seen from Lydia's exchange with the counsellor and her previous actions and behaviour that she wanted to avoid the anxiety that awareness of repressed material would entail. The counsellor used the skills of listening, observing, clarifying, linking, interpreting, giving reflective responses and drawing attention to past events and present behaviour, in order to help the client become conscious of experiences she had previously avoided. In making

CASE STUDY Cont...

these responses, the counsellor was precise though respectful in the way she framed them. If the client had not sensed the counsellor's respect for her defence against deep feelings of anxiety, it is unlikely that she would have been willing to continue in counselling. The client, Lydia, was sufficiently reflective, thoughtful and courageous to benefit from psychodynamic counselling. She was also capable of insight and self-awareness, so the interpretations and links the counsellor made were carefully considered by her before she either accepted or rejected them. Clients are free to accept or reject interpretations, because what is said must make sense to the client and should, moreover, 'feel' right and appropriate if they are to be helpful.

Students often ask about the similarities between confrontation and interpretation. On the surface it may seem that they are very alike, and in some ways they are. Successful interpretation does contain some degree of challenge and confrontation. Moreover, it is quite possible to use the skill of interpretation in a challenging way with clients. A client who is indirectly expressing suicidal thoughts, for example, could benefit from this kind of interpretative approach. The following case study is an example.

CASE STUDY

Confrontation and interpretation

A middle-aged man was referred for counselling because he suffered from panic attacks following his redundancy. He had some ongoing problems in his marriage as well, and six months earlier financial difficulties had also featured prominently in his life. During counselling sessions he often referred to the fact that many young people were out of work, so why should he, a middle-aged man, feel entitled to a job? He spoke of his life as if it was already over and, though he denied feeling depressed, the counsellor sensed that he was masking some deep presentiments of despair.

COUNSELLOR: You mentioned several times that other people are more entitled to things than you are; that maybe you are not entitled to hope for much now?

CLIENT: I do feel like that sometimes, yes.

COUNSELLOR: Is that something you feel about your own life . . . that you are not entitled to it either?

CLIENT: [slowly] I had not thought about it in those words. I suppose I have been that despairing.

The counsellor's interpretation here was effective in making the client aware of something which had previously been outside his awareness. He had not consciously thought about suicide, but it was, nevertheless, a recurrent though disguised motif in his communication.

Cooper (2008: 136) points to research that supports the skill of interpretation used in psychodynamic counselling. However, he adds that when interpretations are used, their effectiveness and value depend on several factors including accuracy, tentative wording and the establishment of a 'strong therapeutic alliance'. It should be added that this client also received medical help for his depression and continued to see the counsellor on a weekly basis. It is important to mention here that counselling is limited in its application and usefulness. Many clients require other forms of help, and one of the counsellor's essential skills is the ability to identify those areas which need extra attention and support.

In Unit 1 we looked at the people who use counselling skills and saw that many are professionals who are qualified in other areas. This makes a great deal of difference as far as counselling is concerned, because a sound professional foundation also means that a fairly comprehensive knowledge base is already in place. This knowledge base should ensure that potentially serious medical conditions can be identified, and further help is enlisted for the client when needed. If a counsellor is also a qualified nurse, occupational therapist or social worker, for example, then it is reasonable to assume that sufficient knowledge will have been acquired in the course of training to ensure this kind of competence. On the other hand, it would be wrong to suppose that people without this kind of training are never in a position to function effectively when extra help is required. What is important is a willingness to pursue further and specialised training, as and when necessary, and to remain aware of personal and professional limitations at all times. Supervision helps in this respect and is an essential component of counsellor training and practice, a fact that cannot be stated often enough.

EXERCISE

Identifying skills

Read the following passage and identify the counselling skills you could use to help the client. Identify the basic skills (for example, listening, asking questions) as well as the psychodynamic skills that may be applicable in this instance. Discuss your ideas with a partner, highlighting any helpful techniques you think a psychodynamic counsellor could use.

Lynda, who is 30 years old, has a history of relationship problems. Her first boyfriend was addicted to drugs and was emotionally abusive towards her. A later boyfriend left her when he met someone else, and shortly afterwards she joined a dating agency in the hope that she would meet someone more reliable. Although she met several interesting people through the agency, Lynda was unable to form a lasting commitment with anyone. In counselling she talked about her childhood and her father, who was distant and emotionally uninvolved with her. She is confused about her present situation, since she feels that she is 'full of affection' and has a lot to offer in a relationship.

Attending to transference

We have already looked at different aspects of transference and the way these may be manifest in the counselling relationship. Attention to transference is, therefore, an important aspect of psychodynamic counselling. Transference is, after all, the mirror in which the client's past is reflected in the present. Clients bring all their early experiences with them into counselling, and these experiences are frequently demonstrated in the relationship the client forms with the counsellor. Because they know very little about the private lives of the counsellors who help them, clients use imagination to fill in the gaps, and the imagined figure that emerges from this process may bear little resemblance to the real person. In order to form a picture of the counsellor, the client will draw on past experience, especially on earlier relationships with important figures like parents. This process is carried out at an unconscious level, so clients are unaware that the information they are using is unrealistic and outdated. From a psychodynamic viewpoint, counsellors can help clients to use this information in a way that will help them to understand some of the problems they may have. A client may treat the counsellor as a mother or father, for example, and, depending on the nature of the relationship the client had with the parent, respond to the counsellor in either a positive or a negative way. The following is an example.

CASE STUDY

Attending to transference

A middle-aged woman, who was completing a course at college, attended counselling sessions because of problems she was having with her elderly parents. Her parents were controlling and demanding, and the client (Sylvia) felt that they constantly criticised her. In particular, they accused her of being 'dependent' and lacking in initiative. Sylvia did, in fact, live with her parents and she was financially dependent on them. In her relationship with the counsellor, who was a woman, she was timid and sometimes ingratiating. It was clear that she desperately wanted to please and be a 'good' client. The counsellor drew attention to this attitude of wanting to please, but she did this only after she had established a trusting relationship with the client.

COUNSELLOR: You mentioned yesterday that it was sometimes difficult to know if you were getting it right, that you were worried about getting it right with me.

CLIENT: Yes I do worry about it. It's hard to say why, but I feel I would like to be more myself.

COUNSELLOR: You would like to be more yourself with me and not feel concerned with pleasing me in the way you try to please your parents?

CLIENT: I'm always trying to please them and I suppose that's what I'm doing with you. Yes, I probably do it with everyone, come to think of it.

Many factors can cause transference reactions to occur in counselling. These include the counsellor's physical or behavioural characteristics, voice sound and accent, similarity in dress and, indeed, any characteristic that acts as an unconscious reminder of significant people in the client's past. Once the transference reaction is brought into the open, it serves as an important vehicle for learning, and clients can identify from its faulty patterns within their own behaviour in relation to others. Counsellors are not always automatically aware of transference reactions from clients, and occasionally it is experienced or 'felt' by the counsellor before it comes into consciousness. The counsellor's own countertransference response acts as an indicator of its presence, and once the counsellor is fully aware of the transference it is possible to use this knowledge for the client's benefit.

Attending to countertransference

Unit 9 discusses the importance of countertransference issues and supervision in counselling, in addition to the importance of continuing professional development (CPD) and education for counsellors. All of these areas have either a direct or indirect bearing on a counsellor's ability to function at an optimum professional level with clients.

Looking at dreams

We have already considered the importance of dreams in the psychodynamic approach to counselling, and the point has been made that only clients themselves can interpret their dreams accurately. However, counsellors can encourage clients to become more interested in the contents of their dreams and to record them as an aid to self-knowledge and greater awareness. Some clients are keener than others to do this, and there is no doubt that certain clients have an intuitive or innate knowledge of symbolism and the language of the unconscious. The following case study is an example.

CASE STUDY

Dreams

A 40-year-old woman recounted two dreams she had before she came for counselling. Both dreams convinced her that she needed to talk to someone. The counsellor encouraged her to recount these dreams in the present tense, a technique which gives immediacy and vividness to the experiences of the dream.

'I am going on a journey, on a train or a bus. It is a double-decker vehicle. An old woman directs me on to the lower section. I have a small child with me and I feel very responsible for her. We travel along and eventually get out at a large area of wasteland. There are bars all around this area, like a prison.

In the next dream I am due to see a therapist, who is a well-known person or celebrity. She lives in London, and I find myself there. I have a child with me in a pram. I climb the steps to the therapist's house, taking the pram with me. The therapist is sitting in a room which is too big. It is uncomfortable, too open and there are too many people around. The therapist is not really interested; she gets up, and then comes back with a book. Meanwhile, the child has gone.'

CASE STUDY Cont...

During counselling this client was able to identify several important key elements in both dreams.

COUNSELLOR: And the old woman and child in the dreams?

CLIENT: I think they are two aspects of me; one is the old worn out me, the other is the new beginning which I would like to develop.

COUNSELLOR: The journey . . . what you have just come through, your mother's death and the changes you have had to make.

CLIENT: Yes. And those I still have to make.

COUNSELLOR: So the challenge is between staying with the old (and with the wasteland), or getting onto the top deck, which might be harder to get to but where you can see more?

Comment: These two dreams are very rich in symbolism and meaning, and the client was able to learn a great deal from them. Before she came for counselling there were many futile attempts to enlist help from others, but none were successful. The client could see clearly that the therapist in the dream, for example, represented her hopes and her frustration at not getting help.

EXERCISE

Looking at dreams

Think about any dream you have had recently. Try to recall as much detail as possible, and then write it out in the present tense. Then complete the following:

1 Give the dream a name.

2 Describe, in one word, the emotional atmosphere of the dream.

3 Describe, in one word, the location of the dream.

4 Describe, in one word, any aspect of time in the dream, for example time of day, time of year, time of life.

5 List the various elements of the dream.

6 Start with the most recognisable element and free associate to it, for example say whatever comes into your head in relation to it.

7 Put yourself in the position of each element in the dream and say what you are doing in the dream. If a door features in your dream, for example, pretend to be the door, describe yourself and explain your presence.

EXERCISE Cont...

8 Consider the ways in which the dream has any relevance to current issues or problems in your life.

9 Circle any key words in the dream.

10 Circle any key people in the dream.

When you have completed this exercise you should have some idea of what the dream means to you. This is an individual exercise, which you don't have to share with anyone else, unless you wish to. Dreams are, by their nature, private, and it is often the case that dream interpretation reveals intimate information about ourselves. If you are interested in your own dreams you should keep a record of them. Working with dreams takes time and dedication, but unless we are aware of our own inner lives it is presumptuous to expect clients to be familiar with theirs. Finally, this is not an exercise designed for use with clients: it is meant as a student exercise.

Clients who benefit from this approach

Though we may not agree with all of it, Freudian theory has taught us a great deal about human personality and motivation. We know, for example, that influences from the past are frequently implicated in current problems. Knowledge of Freudian concepts is very important, therefore, in our understanding of people, and in this respect all clients should benefit – if only indirectly – from this approach. The concepts of transference and countertransference are central to Freudian theory, and this is another area of knowledge that is essential for every counsellor – regardless of the theoretical approach used.

There are many other examples of Freudian theory which have contributed a great deal towards our understanding of clients. Psychodynamic counselling is appropriate for clients who are interested in looking at past experience in relation to current difficulties. This would include clients who have experienced trauma in the past and people who feel compelled to repeat destructive patterns of behaviour, or relationships. It is also suitable for some health-related problems and anorexia nervosa. Short-term psychodynamic counselling is suitable, too, for clients with depression and, according to Cooper's analysis of research, for some forms of addiction, particularly opiate addiction (Cooper, 2008). Clients who are interested in personal growth and increased self-awareness are also likely to benefit from psychodynamic therapy.

Some limitations

The psychodynamic approach is adaptable for use with many clients providing, of course, that counsellors who use it are adequately trained in terms of both theory and practice. Short-term counselling is available in many areas now, and there are numerous counsellors who incorporate aspects of psychodynamic theory in other theoretical approaches. An exclusively psychodynamic approach is probably not suitable for clients in crisis (crisis intervention), or for those who are recently bereaved. People in this last category will probably benefit more from bereavement counselling, or from participation in a support group with others who share their experiences. Clients who are addicted to certain drugs or to alcohol are unlikely to benefit from a purely psychodynamic approach. This is because they may be extremely anxious, disorientated or uncommitted to the change needed to overcome addiction. People who have problems of addiction may also need extra support and back-up services. In relation to mental illness, some clients do benefit from psychodynamic therapy, though they are more likely to do so when there is medical support, and hospitalisation when required.

SUMMARY

In this unit we considered the basic principles of psychodynamic theory. These have evolved from the work of Sigmund Freud and from classical psychoanalysis. Freudian theory is based on the assumption that much of what we think, feel and do is determined by unconscious motivation. There is an emphasis on sexual and aggressive drives, and on key stages of development from childhood until adolescence. The Freudian structure of personality (Id, Ego and Superego) was discussed, along with the defences people use to guard against anxiety. The importance of childhood experience was highlighted, and this was linked to the ways in which people transfer emotional experience from the past into the present. Clients' experiences in counselling were described, along with the key concepts of transference, countertransference and projective identification. We looked at dreams and considered their significance in psychodynamic theory. Psychodynamic counselling skills were also described, and examples of these were given. The usefulness of these approaches was also discussed, along with consideration of some of their limitations.

In the next unit we shall look at the way in which psychodynamic theory has evolved over time, and we shall discuss the effectiveness of these approaches for different client groups.

References

Cooper, M. (2008) *Essential Research Findings in Counselling and Psychotherapy*. London: Sage Publications.

Freud, S. (1896) 'The Aetiology of Hysteria' in Gay, P. (ed.) (1989) *The Freud Reader*. London: Penguin Books.

Freud, S. (1900) *The Interpretation of Dreams*. London: Penguin Books. 1991.

Freud, S. (1907) 'Creative Writers and Daydreaming', in Gay, P. (ed.) (1989) *The Freud Reader*. London: Penguin Books.

Freud, S. (1908) 'Character and Anal Eroticism', in Gay, P. (ed.) (1989) *The Freud Reader*. London: Penguin Books.

Freud, S. (1909) *Five Lectures on Psychoanalysis*. London: Penguin Books 1995.

Freud, S. (1923) 'The Ego and the Id' in Gay, P. (ed.) (1989) *The Freud Reader*. London: Penguin Books.

Freud, S. (1924) 'Three Essays on the Theory of Sexuality' in Gay, P. (ed.) (1989) *The Freud Reader*. London: Penguin Books.

Freud, S. (1925) 'An Autobiographical Study', in Gay, P. (ed.) (1989) *The Freud Reader*. London: Penguin Books.

Freud, S. (1932) 'Anxiety and Instinctual Life', in Gay, P. (ed.) (1989) *The Freud Reader*. London: Penguin Books.

Klein, M. (1932) *The Psychoanalysis of Children*. London: Hogarth Press.

Mitchell, S. A. and Black, M. J. (1995) *Freud and Beyond: A History of Modern Psychoanalytic Thought*. New York: Basic Books.

Solomon, I. (1995) *A Primer of Kleinian Therapy*. New Jersey: Jason Aronson INC.

Further reading

Berry, R. (2005) Freud: *A Beginners Guide*. London: Hodder & Stoughton.

Easthope, A. (1999) *The Unconscious*. London: Routledge.

Grosz, S. (2013) *The Examined Life: How We Lose and Find Ourselves*. London: Chatto & Windus.

Higdon, J. (2004) *From Counselling Skills to Counsellor: A Psychodynamic Approach*. London: Palgrave Macmillan.

Howard, S. (2006) *Psychodynamic Counselling in a Nutshell*. London: Sage Publications.

Jacobs, M. (2006) *The Presenting Past: The Core of Psychodynamic Counselling and Therapy*. Berkshire: Open University Press.

Mander, G. (2000) *A Psychodynamic Approach to Brief Therapy*. London: Sage Publications.

Spurling, L. (2004) *An Introduction to Psychodynamic Counselling*. London: Palgrave Macmillan.

Resources

Websites

www.psychotherapy.org.uk
The United Kingdom for Psychotherapy.
www.bps.org.uk
The British Psychological Society.
www.psychoanalysis.org.uk
The British Psychoanalytical Society.
www.psychoanalytic-council.org
An association of training, professional and accrediting bodies.

Journals

Online Journal of Psychodynamic Practice: Individuals, Groups and Organisations. London: Routledge.

4

Post-Freudian psychodynamic counselling

◆ Introduction

Freud attracted a number of talented people who were interested in psychoanalysis, and who wished to be associated with the work he was doing. However, not all of them agreed with him on every aspect of **psychoanalytic** theory. Two of the earliest revisionists were Adler and Jung, both of whom disagreed with Freud's emphasis on the central role of sexual instincts in human behaviour. The Oedipus complex was another key concept that caused disagreement among some of Freud's early and later colleagues.

Many of these followers developed theoretical frameworks that differed in many respects from Freudian theory. Therefore, Freudian theory began to evolve and expand at a very early stage, and it continues to develop and expand today. This unit is concerned with those revised ideas and the theoretical concepts that have developed from the work of Freud.

Alfred Adler (1870–1937)

Individual psychology

Alfred Adler was a qualified doctor, who practised for a time in ophthalmology. Later he qualified as a psychiatrist and, in 1902, joined Freud's circle of admirers and friends. By 1911, however, Adler's theoretical views were becoming more divergent, and he criticised many aspects of Freudian orthodoxy. These differences of opinion forced Adler to resign as President of the Vienna Psychoanalytic Society; and in 1912 he formed the Society for Individual Psychology.

Adler disagreed with Freud's emphasis on the sexual instincts and biological determinism as the basis for human behaviour. In contrast to this, he believed in social determinism and in the influence of family and environmental factors in shaping the individual's behaviour. The following is a summary of the main areas in which Adler has made significant contributions:

- the development of personality and family position
- the inferiority complex
- style of life
- social interest.

KEY TERM

Complex: The word 'complex' is used in both Freudian and Adlerian theory. The *Oedipus complex* is a Freudian term, while the *inferiority complex* stems from the work of Adler. In both cases the term complex denotes a cluster of interrelated conscious and unconscious feelings and ideas, which affect a person's behaviour.

The development of personality and family position

An important departure from traditional Freudian theory concerned Adler's emphasis on the relationship between children and parents and his focus on sibling relationships and ordinal position within the family. Freud did address the parent–child relationship, but only in as far as it affected the development of sexuality and the resolution (or otherwise) of the Oedipus complex. Adler's focus was much more comprehensive and encompassed other variables, including family size and the way in which parents relate to individual children. Adler's interpretation of what he termed the 'so-called Oedipus complex' is that it occurs when the family is too insular and lacking in healthy relationships outside the home (Adler, 1931: 56). In other words, victims of the Oedipus complex are, in Adler's view, people who have been constrained by the family in a way that inhibits the development of maturity and social skills. The Oedipus complex is, therefore, adapted by Adler to explain certain kinds of anti-social and selfish behaviour; it is this shift away from the original and much more specifically sexual definition, which marks the difference between Freud's views and the ideas expressed by Adler. Certain experiences within the family and the position of each member within the group could produce, according to Adler, unique problems for the individual. Distorted goals and life styles can also result from the influence of these factors. Adler described several formative childhood influences, which he believed were important in determining later adult behaviour, including illness and physical disadvantage, neglect, lack of affection and overindulgence.

EXERCISE

Family position

In groups of three to four, discuss your individual family positions and say how you think these positions have affected you. Are there any differences, for example, between those who are first, second or only children?

CASE STUDY

Tony

Tony, by his own admission, had never wanted for anything in his life. Then, at 53 years of age he found himself widowed, alone and unable to cope. He was the only child of older parents, who had never believed they would actually have a child; he had received a great deal of attention throughout his childhood, much of it pleasant but some of it oppressive too. When his wife died, Tony felt that he would not be able to manage and he became resentful that other people were unwilling to help him more. Tony's wife had continued where his parents left off, so his home life had been comfortable, even indulged. It took some time, and a great deal of support, before he was able to function in an autonomous way. Tony's experiences in childhood had not prepared him for certain aspects of adult responsibility. He received counselling and, over a period of time, was able to

CASE STUDY Cont...

see that he would, in fact, be capable of coping, once the acute trauma of his bereavement had diminished. This realisation was not achieved without a lot of effort on Tony's part. One of the factors that helped him was an interest in his own past experience and an ability to look critically at outdated assumptions and beliefs. It should be added that the Adlerian approach may not be suitable for all bereaved clients, a factor which is discussed at the end of this unit.

The inferiority complex

In Adlerian terms, sexual impulses are not accorded the central position they hold in Freudian theory. As far as Adler was concerned, sexual problems represent another aspect of what he called the 'inferiority complex' (Adler, 1931: 56–7). People who confine themselves to the family, with little or no outside contact, are bound to lack healthy sexual and relationship interests. A sense of inferiority follows, therefore, and in adult life such people tend to strive for superiority through attachment to others they can dominate. Adler described many other factors in family life that can produce feelings of inferiority for the individual. A belief that one is not intellectually inclined could, for example, lead to feelings of inferiority, and a person whose home environment is impoverished in any way is also liable to feel inferior. Indeed, Adler believed that inferiority feelings are inevitable in childhood, since children are small, weak and subject to adults and their whims. It was the ways in which people deal with feelings of inferiority that interested Adler. Compensation is the term he used to describe the mechanism whereby people strive for recognition or superiority (Adler, 1927: 70–71). The desire to compensate is seen as a healthy one, since it motivates people to achieve their potential. When people are unable to develop successful compensation, an inferiority complex follows. Adler believed that all of us strive for superiority in some area of our lives, and it is this striving that moves us towards achievement and perfection.

Style of life

Adler believed that each person develops a strategy for living; and this 'life style', as he called it, is firmly established by about the age of five years (Adler, 1931: 45). The strategy each person adopts is designed to cope with feelings of inferiority and may take the form of artistic or intellectual achievement, for example. Other, less positive, strategies are also sometimes used, however. One example is the kind of superiority that some people achieve through bullying or domination of others. Others may seek superiority through illness, an approach which serves two purposes – on the one hand, the child who is ill receives a great deal of attention, while on the other hand the illness can be used as a weapon to control others. The idea of life styles is one which features in other theoretical approaches to counselling; transactional analysis, which we shall consider in Unit 7, is one example.

Life style

Working individually, try to remember when you first decided what it was you were good at and wanted to do. What were the factors that prompted you to choose a particular life style in the Adlerian sense? Then discuss your recollections with other group members.

Social interest

The concept of social interest is an important one in Adlerian theory. The foundation for social interest is nurtured within the family; it encompasses an interest in and a feeling for others. Again, we see the contrast with Freudian theory, which pays little attention to this human predisposition and need. Altruism is another way of describing this specific Adlerian concept, and it indicates a radical shift in perspective from the orthodox psychoanalytic position. People are, according to Adler, much more than a mass of conflicting biological needs. There are people, however, who because of early experiences do not develop social interests, and the price they pay for their isolation is unhappiness and emotional problems. Adler's view about social interest and involvement is, in fact, a very pertinent one today. We are increasingly aware of the problems isolated people have, and social workers, nurses and care workers, generally, are constantly in touch with many of these people. The elderly population is a good example of one section of society that is acutely affected by this problem. Many of the people who seek counselling are also frequently isolated and lonely.

The position of women

We have seen that Adler did not give sexual impulses a central role in his theory of human development. The experiences of men and women were, however, of great interest to him; he used the term 'masculine protest' to describe an attitude he felt was manifest in many aspects of male and female behaviour. This attitude takes the form of chauvinism and macho behaviour in men, while it may be seen in aggressive and resentful behaviour in women. Adler did not subscribe to the notion that men are in any way inherently superior, and he was concerned to point out that most relationship problems were, in fact, caused by this very attitude. To Adler, male dominance was not a 'natural thing' (Adler, 1927: 106); in this respect, his work anticipated many later psychodynamic theories.

Counselling skills

The work of Adler is important because it sheds light on the social factors which contribute to a person's development. It is probably true to say, though, that his ideas are significant because of their *influence* on psychotherapy and counselling generally. Counsellors who are interested in the work of Adler will use all the skills described in Unit 2. These include the skills of listening, attending, reflecting content and meaning, asking questions and helping clients to set goals. The following is a summary of other skills and attitudes that are highlighted in the Adlerian approach:

1 The counsellor–client relationship is a collaborative one, in which both people work towards agreed objectives and goals.
2 The major goal of therapy – for the client – is the achievement of insight. (The major goal for Freud was also client, or patient, insight.)
3 The counsellor is concerned to understand the client's individual experience or subjective reality.
4 The counsellor's role is a teaching one. There is an emphasis on helping clients to identify self-defeating behaviour.
5 There is a corresponding emphasis on helping clients to re-educate themselves for positive change.
6 The Adlerian approach encourages clients to become more socially involved – relationship problems are identified, and clients are encouraged to relate more effectively to others.
7 Interpretation is used in the approach and is specifically meant to help clients to identify faulty attitudes and motivation.
8 Confrontation and encouragement are used in the approach; these are set within the framework of an empathic relationship.
9 Clients are encouraged to pay attention to dreams, to record them and use them as a means of gaining further insight.
10 Transference, while acknowledged, is not regarded as a problem in Adlerian counselling, because the relationship between counsellor and client is seen as one that is based on equality.

Clients who benefit from the approach

There is a wide spectrum of clients who would probably benefit from this approach. These include people with relationship difficulties, those with problems of addiction or substance abuse, and clients who specifically need marriage and family counselling. It can also be used to help older people who – like the client, Tony, mentioned earlier – have reached a stage in life where change is imperative. Adlerian counselling is applicable to groupwork; in fact, Adler and his colleagues used groupwork extensively, especially when he worked in the field of child guidance. Groupwork is the ideal medium for this approach, since the educative or learning aspects of it are reinforced in a groupwork setting. When there are a number of people present to give feedback and encouragement – two important elements in the Adlerian approach – participants are more likely to gain positive results from the experience.

Some limitations

An Adlerian approach may not be suitable for some clients. A person who is in the middle of a crisis situation, for example, will want immediate help and may be unwilling to engage in the process of looking at the past and the influence of family position and relationships. Another potential limitation is concerned with cultural expectations. People from different cultural backgrounds will have different views about family relationships and, indeed, may not wish to discuss them as a part of counselling. Although the Adlerian approach is phenomenological in the way that the person-centred approach is, the former is nevertheless more directly educative in a way that may not suit everyone. Clients who are in deep distress, or those who are grief-stricken, will probably not benefit (initially at least) from this approach. This is not to say that they might not benefit later on, because in many instances they could well do so.

Carl Jung (1875–1961)

Analytical psychology

Jung was another admirer and one-time associate of Freud. He, too, became disenchanted with several aspects of Freudian psychoanalysis and broke away from the original school in 1913. The main point of difference between the two men was Freud's definition of sexuality and libido. Although Jung conceded the importance of the sexual instinct, he considered Freud's view of it to be imbalanced. He pointed out, for example, that there are societies and cultures in which the instinct for food and survival must take precedence over sexual interest (Jung, 1957). In addition to this, Jung's theory of libido is more wide-ranging than Freud's and is invested with spiritual, mystical and, above all, creative meaning. His theory of personality has a much wider base and, in this sense, his approach to psychoanalysis is quite different from the orthodox position. Another important difference between Freud and Jung is the type of clinical experience they both had. Freud had worked with patients who suffered from neurosis, whereas Jung's experience was mostly with people who suffered from schizophrenia. Jung may have developed his interest in symbolism as a result of his work in this area, although he probably drew on other sources including archaeology, religion, astrology and Eastern philosophy. Like Adler, Jung was a qualified doctor and psychiatrist. His branch of psychoanalysis is called analytical psychology. The following is a summary of his most important contributions:

- personality structure
- archetypes
- ego orientations or personality types
- symbolism and dreams.

Personality structure

Jung formulated his own version of personality structure and divided it into three basic components: the ego, the personal unconscious and the collective unconscious. The ego is the conscious part of the self and is made up of thoughts and feelings, perceptions and memories. In this sense, the ego is the centre of awareness and is similar to Freud's Ego. In contrast to this, the personal unconscious is that area of personality which contains forgotten and repressed material that can, however, be made conscious without great difficulty. The third part of Jung's personality structure, the idea of collective unconscious, is the most radical and innovative in terms of theory and sets Jung apart from any other thinker in the field. In Jung's view, the collective unconscious is common to all of us and is the foundation of what people in ancient times referred to as the 'sympathy of all things' (Jung, 1961, p.160). By this, Jung appeared to mean that each person has an area of mental functioning that is shared by all of humankind. The collective unconscious is, therefore, impersonal in a sense and contains universal elements that are of significance to all of us. Every society has, according to Jung, collective convictions and problems that affect each person in the group (Jung, 1957). The cumulative experience of our ancestors is contained within the collective unconscious and dates back millions of years in time. This knowledge acts as a guide and is essential for our survival.

Archetypes

Archetypes are primordial images that form the structural elements of the collective unconscious. These images present themselves in symbolic form and, though there are many of them, Jung described just four in detail. They are as follows: the persona, the anima and animus, the shadow and the self. The word 'persona' describes that part of ourselves we present outwards to society. This is an image of how we think we should appear, and it is based on convention and defined largely by the way other people expect us to be. There are certain accepted images of individuals, or groups of people, which are almost universally familiar. In many ways, this is similar to stereotyping, but it does serve a purpose in that it gives us a blueprint, or formula, for viewing people and interpreting their behaviour. Problems arise when we identify too closely with our persona. When we do this, we hide behind the mask and fail to acknowledge the existence of our true selves.

The 'anima' describes the collective image of woman in the male psyche, while the 'animus' describes the image of man in the female. These images have arisen over millions of years and are derived from contact with, and observation of, the opposite sex. A symbolic anima image might, for example, take the form of goddess, witch, prostitute or seductress, while the animus might take the form of hero, adventurer or villain.

The 'shadow' is the base, evil or sadistic side of our personality and accounts for the cruelties people have inflicted on each other since the beginning of time. In religious terms, the shadow is symbolised by Satan, and in fiction the shadow is seen in many guises. Faust, who made a pact with the devil, is one example, while Dr Jeckyll, who is turned into the evil Mr Hyde, is another (Fontana, 1993).

The 'self' is that image of perfection that prompts us to search for meaning, unity, wholeness and harmony in our lives. According to Jung, religion is one aspect of this search for integration, although there are others (Jung, 1964: 58). Full integration is impossible to achieve before middle age, however, but when it is achieved the individual becomes more balanced, more whole and more in tune with all aspects of the personality.

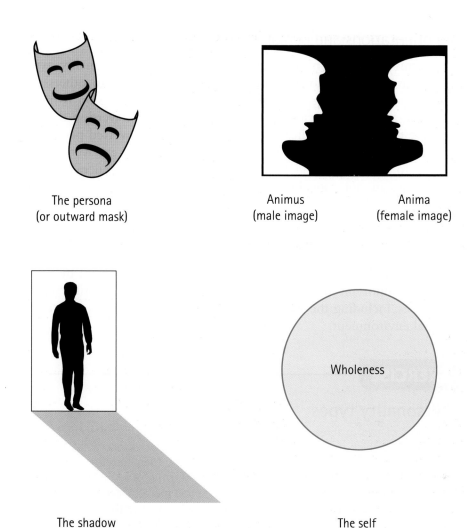

The persona
(or outward mask)

Animus
(male image)

Anima
(female image)

The shadow

Wholeness

The self

Figure 4.1 Archetypes of the collective unconscious

CASE STUDY

Carol

Carol was a middle-aged woman, whose children had grown up and left home. She was going through the menopause and had suffered several physical and psychological symptoms as a result. In addition to her health problems, Carol felt strongly that she lacked a sense of purpose and self-fulfilment. Once her menopausal symptoms were under control, she decided to ask for careers guidance at her local college. As a result of this, she was able to go into full-time education and train for the kind of work she wanted to do. During this time, she had a series of dreams in which she was swimming strongly, although in reality she couldn't swim at all. Carol was able to interpret her dreams without too much difficulty and could see that they reflected, in symbolic form, the success and harmony she felt she was currently achieving in her life.

Ego orientations and personality types

The terms 'introversion' and 'extraversion' refer to personality types and are used by Jung to describe the way people relate to others and their surroundings (Jung, 1961: 414–5). The word introversion is meant to denote a subjective orientation, while the word extraversion denotes an interest in external reality, or the outer world. Introverted people are more inclined to be reserved and interested in ideas. The extravert person is likely to be sociable and more involved with others generally. These orientations are not static, however, and may change with life experience. It is also possible that a natural introvert may, for example, live life as an extravert in order to fit in with the expectations of others. The same is true, of course, for extraverts. One reason personality types are of interest to counsellors is that they highlight the importance of clients' subjective experience and the way other people and reality are perceived by them. It is also important that counsellors know as much as possible about themselves, including the ways in which they relate to others and to the external environment.

EXERCISE

Personality types

In groups of two to three, discuss the two ego orientations just described. Say whether you think they help us in our understanding of clients, and whether they also help us in our understanding of ourselves. Then consider your own individual preferences and share these ideas with the group. Are you interested in thoughts, feelings, ideas and imagination, or are you more concerned with your surroundings and with other people? Remember, when you do this exercise, that imagination is just as real and valid as external reality. Jung himself pointed out that much of what exists in the outside world existed in someone's imagination first (Jung, 1957).

Symbols and dreams

Jung was interested in symbols, and he believed that they represent complex ideas that cannot be described in any other way, since these ideas defy reason (Jung, 1957). Symbols are the language of dreams and often give us clues about important issues in our lives. The following dream illustrates this last point.

CASE STUDY

Mrs Edwards

An elderly woman, called Mrs Edwards, was very ill in hospital and recounted this dream to one of the nurses:

In the dream I am near the sea, and I suddenly realise that the water is coming over the sand beneath my feet. I am not worried about this, just mildly excited. At the same time I am filling my old car at a petrol pump, which is just there on the sand. There is something about the amount of petrol: I don't seem to need as much as I thought.

The nurse who took care of Mrs Edwards was a student on a counselling skills course. She was interested in the patient's dream and discussed it with her. Mrs Edwards was aware that she was dying and could, therefore, make sense of the symbolism in her dream. She could see that the car represented her now-almost-complete journey through life, while the sea represented the next stage of experience. It should be emphasised that the nurse listened carefully to the patient's account of her dream, and did not at any stage try to impose her own interpretation on it. As a result of her dream, Mrs Edwards was less frightened about the prospect of dying.

EXERCISE

Symbols

Working individually, take a large sheet of paper and divide it into six squares. Draw a symbol in each square to represent the following: life, love, food, rebirth, mother, loss. When you have finished, discuss your images with other members of the group. Are there any which are common to all of you? Where do you think these images came from?

It has often been pointed out that Jung's theories are not 'scientific' and cannot be tested or proven in any way. In spite of this, however, his ideas have had a substantial impact on various theoretical approaches to therapy, including the person-centred approach and the work of Abraham Maslow. Jung was also interested in the whole of a person's lifespan and, in this sense, he differs from Freud. This is not to say that Freud was actively disinterested, but he certainly did not focus extensively on the middle or later years of life. Jung's emphasis on the spiritual dimension is also important, and his description of the process of '-individuation' is significant in this respect. This concept is roughly equivalent to Rogers' actualising tendency (to be discussed in the next unit) and to Maslow's description of self-actualisation needs. In Jungian terms, individuation is a process of psychic development that culminates in the achievement of wholeness or selfhood. He likens it to an evolutionary process, similar to that which takes place biologically in the body (Jung, 1957: 206).

Individuation

Individuation is a gradual and lifelong development of one's unique personality. It is a complicated and often difficult journey of self-discovery and is likely to become more marked during and after middle age.

Working in pairs, discuss the kinds of changes which commonly affect people at midlife or later.

Skills used in Jungian therapy

Although there are Jungian therapists who train exclusively in this approach, it is a model that tends to influence rather than dominate the work of some counsellors. All the basic skills of counselling are used in this approach, along with others listed as follows:

- assessment and the establishment of a contract
- free association: the client speaks at his or her own pace
- interpretation, including interpretation of dreams and of transference
- interpretation, by the therapist, of personal counter-transference feelings: this is seen as an invaluable aid to understanding the client.

Jungian therapeutic techniques do vary, but the general aim of therapy is to help clients or patients to become more reflective, self-aware and more in harmony with their internal world without losing touch with the realities of the external world. The relationship between client and therapist is a cooperative one. A central goal of therapy is the integration of all aspects of the personality, including the shadow and the anima or animus. Spiritual awareness and problems of later life are also a focus. Clients may be asked to fulfil certain tasks, including reading books, doing homework or drawing to illustrate dreams ('active imagination'). The issue of transference is discussed when it arises. In Jungian therapy, the concept of transference has special meaning, since it is understood that clients project onto the therapist archetypal images, as well as images derived from important early figures, like parents.

Clients who benefit from this approach

Clients who are sufficiently interested in a Jungian approach would certainly benefit from it. In its purest form, analytical psychology is time-consuming and requires some dedication and commitment. Some therapists see clients once or twice a week; others may see them as many as five times. Time and cost are important considerations, therefore, for clients. In Jungian terms, therapy is a spiritual quest with the aim of achieving individuation for the client.

People who feel alienated or psychologically 'stuck' will probably benefit from the approach. Those who have reached a certain stage of maturity, the middle years for example, may also find it helpful, and problems related to meaninglessness or 'dis'-ease in life are addressed in Jungian therapy. Because of its emphasis on creativity as a medium for healing, Jungian therapy tends to attract people who are involved in the arts.

CASE STUDY

Mr Richards

Mr Richards was 70 years old and had recently been widowed. Prior to his wife's death he had been involved in a wide range of activities and interests, but after her death he lost interest in most things and became deeply depressed. He had worked as a teacher until his retirement, and after he left full-time employment he studied for a wide range of courses, including a higher degree. In addition to his academic studies, Mr Richards was interested in spirituality and comparative religions. When his wife died he experienced what he described as a 'chasm or void' opening up all around him. The things he had been interested in before seemed pointless to him now.

Mr Richards saw his GP, who prescribed medication for him. This helped in the short term, but when he started to feel better Mr Richards decided he would find someone who could help him make sense of the new and frightening life phase he seemed to have entered. He was able to locate a Jungian psychotherapist in the city where he lived and, in the course of his work with the therapist, was helped to look at the overall pattern of his life. The therapist also encouraged him to examine his progress and psychological adaptation following his wife's death. Mr Richards was able to identify connections and links between all the significant events of his life.

Throughout, he was encouraged to record his dreams and to analyse these. In the initial stages of therapy, Mr Richards experienced a great deal of emotional upheaval and catharsis; at a later stage he looked back on his early relationships and discussed these. He also discussed his transference responses to the therapist, and then began the longer phase of self-education. Mr Richards became familiar with the concepts of personal and collective unconscious and with his own protective façade or persona. He also came to see that denial of his shadow had caused him to project many of his less pleasant characteristics onto other people, including his late wife. This gradual self-realisation was difficult for Mr Richards, and though he was now seeing the therapist less often, he continued with therapy until he felt sufficiently independent to continue the process of individuation alone.

Some limitations

Although trained counsellors often use ideas borrowed from Jungian therapy, there are some limitations in terms of the way it can be used with certain clients. In common with Freudian psychodynamic counselling, it is not suitable for clients in acute crisis situations with presenting and pressing problems that need to be addressed fairly quickly. Although the client (Mr Richards) in the above case study had been bereaved, he was not in the initial acute stage of grief, and he was interested in Jungian therapy as an aid to self-realisation and individuation. The approach may be too intellectual for some clients, and others may not be able to give the time and commitment needed for a course of therapy. It is true that shorter forms of therapy are available in some areas, but not all potential clients have access to these. However, developments in the theory and practice of Jungian psychotherapy continue worldwide, which suggests that many people value the approach and benefit from it.

Ego psychology and object relations theory

Ego psychology and object relations theory represent two important extensions of Freudian psychology. To some degree, both Adler and Jung had focused attention on certain aspects of both these schools. Adler had, for example, looked at the central role of relationships in shaping personality; and human relationships, especially those which are formed in infancy and childhood, are a fundamental consideration in object relations theory. Although Jung gave special emphasis to the collective unconscious, he is also noted for his descriptions of personality types or ego orientations. In this sense, it could be said that he gave a greater role to the ego, a role that is extended and highlighted in the work of the ego psychologists.

Ego psychology

Heinz Hartmann (1894–1970)

Heinz Hartmann, an American doctor and psychiatrist, is generally considered to be the father of ego psychology. Hartmann did not believe that the ego is simply a mediator in conflicts among id and superego. On the contrary, he took the view that the ego is responsible for many important functions, including perception, language development, attention, planning and learning (Hartmann, 1958). To Hartmann, therefore, the ego is capable of interaction with the external world, and is much more autonomous than Freud's definition of it. Hartmann was influenced by the work of Darwin (as was Freud) and he believed that humans, like animals, are designed to fit into their environment. This ability to fit into the environment is reflected in each person's physical and psychological make up. An important point of difference between Hartmann and Freud is that the latter was preoccupied with the physiology and biology of human nature – what Guntrip refers to as the 'the workings of human experience' (Guntrip, 1971: 5). Hartmann, on the other hand, shifts attention to the essential quality of the ego and identifies it as the core of human selfhood.

Anna Freud (1895–1982)

In Britain, Anna Freud was the leading proponent of ego psychology. She continued the work of her father, Sigmund Freud, and became a pioneer of child analysis. Her most important work was, however, devoted to the subject of ego defence mechanisms, and in 1936 she wrote *The Ego and the Mechanisms of Defence*. Like Hartmann, Anna Freud attached more importance to the ego or conscious mind. What interested her most was the way in which the ego seeks to defend itself against external as well as internal forces, and she was especially concerned with the ways in which children deal with threats from the external environment. She also stressed the role of environmental conditions and their critical influence on human development. Her work is important because of its focus on the ego rather than on the id. This represents a significant shift of emphasis, as well as a departure from her father's insistence on the supremacy of the id. Although Anna Freud did not abandon interest in the unconscious and in human sexuality, she did, nevertheless, give a greater role to the ego and, in doing so, paved the way for further developments in ego psychology and object relations theory.

Erik Erikson (1902–1994)

Erik Erikson has a unique place among ego psychologists, because his theory of psychosocial development, first described in 1950, directs attention to difficulties people experience not just in early life, but throughout the total lifespan. Erikson, who trained as a teacher to begin with, met both Freud and his daughter, Anna, and became interested in psychoanalysis. He completed his training and afterwards became a member of the Vienna Psychoanalytic Institute. Erikson, who was Jewish, was forced to emigrate to the United States when Hitler rose to power; and in 1950 he published his book *Childhood and Society,* which laid out his theory of psychosocial development. The following is a summary of these stages.

Erikson's psychosocial stages of development	
Trust versus mistrust:	From birth to 1 year
Autonomy versus shame and doubt:	1 to 3 years
Initiative versus guilt:	3 to 6 years
Industry versus inferiority:	6 to 12 years
Identity versus role confusion:	12 to 20 years
Intimacy versus isolation:	20 to 35 years
Generativity versus stagnation:	35 to 65 years
Ego integrity versus despair:	65 years until death

(Adapted from Erikson, 1995)

Erikson asserted that Freud's stages of psychological development are paralleled by psychosocial stages. At each of these stages the individual is presented with a crisis, and the way in which this is dealt with will determine the person's capacity to cope successfully with the next stage. Although Erikson, like Freud, highlights the concept of stages, there are some vital differences. In the first place, Erikson places more emphasis on the social aspects. There is also more focus on problems of adolescence, adulthood and old age. This has implications for people who work with the elderly, for example, and, indeed, for counselling where the concerns of the elderly have not always been adequately addressed. Helpers who work with the elderly, whether in a residential or hospital setting, should be encouraged to read Erikson's work. His theoretical approach will illuminate some of the special difficulties elderly people have.

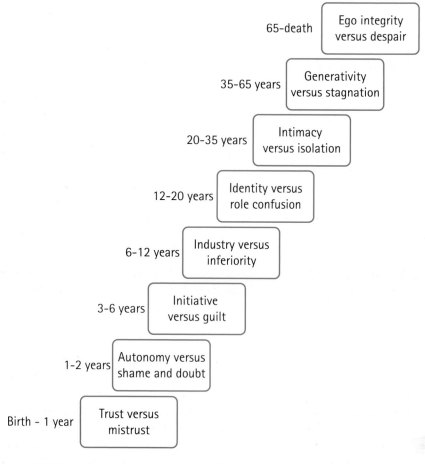

Figure 4.2 Erikson's psychosocial stages of development

Environmental factors

Working in groups of three to four, identify any environmental factors that could have adverse effects on growing children. What are the coping strategies children may use in adverse circumstances? How do children deal with loss, pain, abandonment or threats, for example? Which defence mechanisms are they likely to use?

Implications for counselling

Most ego psychologists subscribe to the belief that the ego is present from birth and capable of developing independently of the id. In their view, the ego is able to deal with the demands of the environment and is concerned to make sense of experience. Cognitive processes are emphasised in this approach; these include learning, perception, thinking and memory. The importance of the id and biological drives have not been totally rejected by ego psychologists, but the balance has been redressed in favour of a more comprehensive and less mechanistic view of human development and motivation. People are seen as independent and autonomous in a way which conflicts with the orthodox Freudian model. This has implications for counsellors – and for people who work in a helping capacity with others generally – since it emphasises cognitive and thinking processes, as well as emotional experience. If each person has an autonomous ego which is concerned to make sense of experience, then each person is also capable of change, adjustment and control of the environment when necessary. In simple terms, this means that people have the resources to deal with problems, even if they need some help initially in order to identify these resources.

Another important contribution of the ego psychologists – especially in the work of Hartmann – is the idea that pleasure does not depend solely on the satisfaction of instinctual impulses but is, to some extent, dependent on the quality of a person's external environment and the amount of pleasurable experience it provides.

In common with orthodox Freudian theorists, most ego psychologists have concentrated their interest on childhood experience. Erik Erikson, who is sometimes referred to as a self-psychologist, is the exception here, since he describes a sequence of developmental stages occurring throughout the total lifespan. However, in ego psychology, generally, there is particular and frequent reference to the anxieties and challenges of early childhood and to the potential problems these can produce. In ego psychology, too, the ego is regarded as a representation of the 'self', and, in this respect, the approach has some affinity with object relations theory, which we shall now consider.

Object: In object relations theory the word 'object' refers to another person to whom emotional energy, including love and desire, is directed by the subject. An object may also be a part of a person, or a symbolic representation of either a person or part of a person. Additionally, an object may be external, or it may be an internal image derived from an actual external relationship.

Psychosocial: This is a term used to describe Erikson's stages of human development. The first part of the word 'psych' refers to the mind, while the second part 'social' refers to one's place within society and our relationships with others. Erikson's stages, therefore, describe mental and social development throughout the lifespan.

Object relations theory

Object relations theory is concerned with human relationships and the way these are imagined and represented mentally by each individual. This is quite different from a theory of interpersonal relationships where, for example, the focus is on the dynamics of an external relationship, rather than on each person's experience of it. In classical Freudian theory, the word 'object' refers to a person or thing, towards which an individual's emotional or libidinal drive is directed.

In object relations theory, the objects referred to are mental representations of significant people in an individual's life. The word 'subject' is frequently used to describe the individual whose mental representations we are concerned to discuss. Object relations theory may also involve consideration of the way in which parts of other people are represented mentally by the subject. Objects (or part objects, as they are called) include anatomical divisions of others, such as hands, voices, breasts, hair, and so on. Human relationships theory is another, and more straightforward, way of describing this particular psychodynamic approach, although it should be added that the term 'object relations' is probably more precise, since it does not denote interpersonal relationships in the way that the former tends to. However, the point to be emphasised here is that object relations theory does highlight the importance of relationships in human development and motivation. In this respect, it differs quite significantly from the Freudian approach, with its stress on the gratification of sexual and aggressive drives as the prime motivating forces of all human endeavour. Object relations theory is associated with several important names in psychodynamic theory, including the following:

- Melanie Klein
- Donald Winnicott
- W.R.D. Fairbairn
- Harry Guntrip
- John Bowlby
- Heinz Kohut.

Melanie Klein (1882–1960)

Melanie Klein, born in Vienna and the youngest of four children, is generally regarded as the most significant figure in the context of object relations theory. She was a contemporary of Freud and trained as a psychoanalyst, after which she developed a special interest in working with children. During the 1920s and 1930s many prominent analysts, including Freud, left Germany and settled in either England or America. Melanie Klein moved to London, where she became acquainted with Anna Freud and other members of the British Psychoanalytical Society. Many in the society came to regard Klein's work as heresy, although Klein herself claimed that she was fundamentally orthodox in the Freudian sense.

In spite of her claim, however, there are certain important points of difference in her work. Perhaps the most striking of her contributions is the emphasis on early infancy, and the primitive phantasies, or unconscious mental images, which a small baby experiences in relation to the mother. Although Freud had certainly been interested in family relationships – especially in the context of the Oedipal drama – he had not focused attention on the mother–infant bond to the extent that Klein eventually did. While continuing to use Freudian terminology and many of his concepts (for example, the structural scheme of id, ego and superego), Klein succeeded in opening up the realm of psychodynamic thinking, so that her work has become an evolution as well as a departure from Freudian theory. It is worth mentioning here that Freud never worked directly with children, whereas Klein did. Freud's experience of children was limited, in the main, to adult recollections, including his own, of early childhood. Klein also pioneered a method of analysing children using play therapy as the basis of her work, which enabled her to communicate directly with them. The most significant contributions of Kleinian theory include the following:

1 The belief that an infant has, even before birth, some innate, unconscious knowledge of the mother. As Cashdan (1988) points out, this is similar to Jung's concept of the collective unconscious.
2 The belief in a destructive inner force or death instinct. Klein suggested that the infant is caught up in a struggle between the forces of life and death. Another way of saying this is that human beings are, from the very beginning, striving to deal with feelings of goodness and badness.
3 The concept of positions, as opposed to developmental stages, in the early life of the infant. Klein agreed with Freud's emphasis on oral, anal and genital preoccupation in early childhood, but she suggested that movement from one to the other is not rigid or definite. The positions Klein describes are the paranoid–schizoid position and the depressive position.

The paranoid–schizoid position

The paranoid–schizoid position spans the first three or four months of life. After the trauma of birth and the loss of security in the womb, the baby feels persecuted and distressed. The word 'paranoid' is appropriate in this respect, since the idea of attack or imminent attack is very real. During this time the baby encounters its first 'object', which is the mother's breast. According to Klein (1932), this presents an opportunity to vent the strong aggressive feelings she believes the child to have. Aggression, then, is directed towards the mother's breast, which is also the source of sustenance and comfort. Positive feelings are also experienced in relation to the breast, but these are less powerful than those which are disturbing, frightening and destructive.

One way of dealing with the intense and conflicting sensations, and also of making them more manageable, is to 'split' or separate the images one from the other. The baby's inner world is thus divided into good and bad experiences, which are kept rigidly apart. This 'splitting' is necessary from the infant's point of view, since it serves to identify the nature of 'goodness' and 'badness' – a distinction that is important if parents and others are to be trusted. Later on, these good and bad sensations become, according to Kleinian theory, the very foundation of feelings about oneself. An infant who is subjected to neglect or cruelty, for example, is likely to introject or 'take in' negative images about 'self' and these will persist into adult life. It would be impossible, however, to eliminate all frustrating experiences in early life, and fortunately most of these experiences do not cause lasting damage. Episodes of frustration are usually balanced by the love and attention the mother frequently provides. Problems arise when strong feelings of worthlessness are absorbed early on, with no modifying influence to temper these. A client called Alan recounted the following experience.

CASE STUDY

Alan

I can remember several times in my life when I became very depressed when things did not go the way I wanted them to go. The depression was usually out of all proportion to the incident that triggered it, and I can honestly say that I never really understood why my reactions were so marked and so illogical. I remember once when I entered a drawing competition and failed to make the grade, I became depressed for a very long time and felt that I was 'no good' and a failure. Even when I became successful in art, I still felt hopeless when I thought about that early rejection. Another time I got depressed for a long period, when a girl I really liked wouldn't go out with me. Again, the depression lasted for ages, and even though – on one level – I knew we weren't really suitable for each other, I felt intensely rejected and worthless.

Alan was unaware of the origin of his depression, but he did identify it as illogical though very real. One possible reason for his feelings concerns his early experience (which he could not remember but believed may have had a detrimental effect on the way he regarded himself). He had been neglected and abandoned by his mother, though he was adopted by parents who loved him a great deal. It is important to remember that experiences like these are recorded by the child at an early stage, even before language has developed. This explains why it is impossible for some clients to put into words the nature of their experience, or the reasons for the feelings they have in relation to these. In Alan's case, he was baffled by the intensity of his depression, though he knew it was out of proportion to his disappointments. It is quite likely that his exaggerated reactions were prompted by feelings about himself he had absorbed in early infancy. In his view, he was never good enough or likeable enough to make the grade with other people. Fortunately, he was interested enough to seek help in finding out why he should feel like this.

The depressive position

The second position – the depressive – begins at around four months and continues until the end of the first year. During this time, the baby begins to perceive the mother as a whole and separate object, in whom both good and bad are simultaneously embodied. This dawning realisation that mother is fallible is a significant step in terms of development and maturity. It does, however, present other problems for the baby at this stage. The intense and aggressive feelings that were first experienced in relation to the mother are now a source of guilt, sadness and anxiety. The person, for whom both love and hostility were felt, is now identified as mother. This necessitates some form of reparation for the imagined damage and hate that have been directed against her (Klein, 1932). The outcome of this crisis is important for later development, and people who suffer depressive problems in adulthood are said to be fixated at this point. Other problems, related to both positions, include difficulties in forming relationships, low self-esteem and inability to make commitments, or trust others. In addition, small babies do not possess language, so distress is often registered at a physical level, which may lead to psychosomatic conditions in later life.

Some difficulties

Several aspects of Kleinian theory are often the focus of controversy when students discuss the subject. It is often pointed out that not all babies are breast fed, for example, and, of course, this is true. However, both object relations theory and psychoanalytic theory use symbolic language and metaphor, in order to illustrate complex ideas. A bottle-fed baby cannot make the distinction between a bottle as object and the breast as object. At that early stage, both serve the same function. It is important also to remember that the mental activity Klein referred to is taking place at an unconscious level, and the Kleinian concept of 'phantasy' is relevant here. Phantasy describes a different, more primitive kind of mental activity, composed of vague, often frightening images and sensations present long before the development of language. This term is used very specifically in object relations theory and differs from the word 'fantasy', which usually refers to conscious mental activity. The word 'projection' is also significant in relation to Kleinian theory and describes the way in which the infant disowns everything he or she experiences as 'bad'. These disowned parts of the 'self' are then attributed to the 'other'. 'Introjection' is another term Klein used more specifically than Freud and refers to the process of internalising external material – especially external material relating to the mother. Aspects of the mother are monitored and metabolised in this way (Klein 1932).

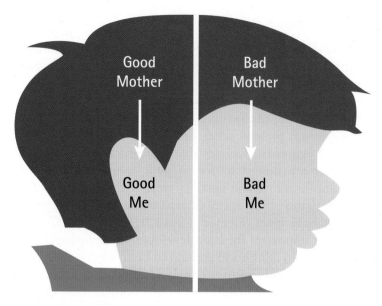

Figure 4.3 Transformation of maternal images into images of 'self'

KEY TERM

Introjection: This is the process whereby objects (or other people) are internalised and become mental representations. The mental structure resulting from this is referred to as an *internal object* or an *introjected object*. These internal objects then form the subject's values, beliefs and attitudes and are the basis of the superego.

Donald Winnicott (1896–1971)

Winnicott was a paediatrician, as well as a psychoanalyst. He worked closely with mothers and babies and was in a very good position to observe infant–mother interaction first hand. One of Winnicott's most important contributions concerns the concept of 'transitional objects' (Winnicott, 1991). These transitional objects include dummies, pieces of cloth, teddy bears, blankets or clothing, all of which are invested with emotional significance by small children. The purpose of these intimate possessions is that they provide comfort and security when a child's mother is absent. Winnicott also highlighted the need for continuity of care in childhood, and stressed the importance of a mother being there when she is needed. He elaborated on this, however, by saying that it was equally important for a mother to give a child space by receding into the background when she is not needed. The position of the father is emphasised, too, especially in relation to the necessary and supportive family environment he needs to help create.

Transitional objects

Many adults retain their childhood transitional objects, including teddy bears or other toys. Work with a partner and discuss the range of objects which children value in early life. Did you have a transitional object and, if so, what was it? Can you remember what it represented to you and how long you kept it?

Loss of a transitional object

A 25-year-old client recalled the loss of a blanket which she had valued highly as a small child.

CLIENT:	I can't remember what age I was at the time, but I must have been very small. My mother was in hospital and an aunt came to stay. She burned the blanket; she said it was smelly.
COUNSELLOR:	She took it from you and burned it?
CLIENT:	Yes. She did tell me she was going to do it, but in a way which didn't give me any choice.
COUNSELLOR:	So this possession, which was valuable to you . . . she couldn't see that.
CLIENT:	No, and the thing is that it was smelly. It smelt of my mother. That is why I liked it.
COUNSELLOR:	It was a link to your mother who was in hospital, when you couldn't see her.
CLIENT:	Not see her, or even know where she was.
COUNSELLOR:	And that would have made the blanket very important to you. And it was taken away, too, when you needed it most.
CLIENT:	I've never cried about it until now. In fact, I've never known why it should have been so important. A bit of old blanket, after all. But yes, it was my mother I was trying to hold on to at the time.

EXERCISE

Adult transitional objects

Many adults also have 'substitute' transitional objects which are very important to them. These include the following:

- photographs
- items of jewellery
- special items of clothing
- books
- cars
- furnishings.

Can you add anything to this list and say what you think these possessions mean to people? There are other, less healthy transitional objects which people become attached to in adult life. Look at the following list and say what you think these may represent to the people who use, or abuse, them:

- cigarettes
- alcohol
- drugs
- food
- mobile phones.

Other views

W.R.D. Fairbairn (1899–1964)

The other object relationists, including Fairbairn, Guntrip, Bowlby and Kohut added their individual ideas to this theoretical approach. Fairbairn, for example, published a series of papers in the 1940s in which he stated that human behaviour is motivated towards the establishment of meaningful human relations. He reformulated the Freudian concept of libido and defined it as object seeking, rather than pleasure seeking. Human development in the early years is not, according to Fairbairn, prompted by erotic impulses. On the contrary, the desire for relatedness is an evolutionary imperative, necessary for human survival. Fairbairn does not dismiss the erotic element in human development, but sets it in context as a key part of object seeking and the desire for intimate relationships.

Fairbairn (1954) also emphasised the importance of the mother–child bond, with special reference to the nature of dependency. He focused on three phases through, which he believed each child would pass. The first stage is early infantile dependency, in which the child is psychologically fused with the mother. In the second and last stages the child becomes gradually more independent, while still remaining (maturely) dependent on the mother. Fairbairn also addresses the subject of ego 'splitting' and divides the infant's inner world into good and bad objects. Extremes of splitting in the very early stages of development could, according to Fairbairn, lead to abnormal behaviour in later life.

Harry Guntrip (1901–1975)

Guntrip wrote extensively about the work of Fairbairn and Winnicott and was, in fact, analysed over a long period of time by both these men. Guntrip's childhood relationship with his mother had been distant and unhappy, a situation that led in later life to periods of depression and various psychosomatic problems. In addition, Guntrip had vivid childhood memories of the death of his younger brother, and this became a trauma which haunted him for the rest of his life. As a psychoanalyst, Guntrip drew on his childhood experience to formulate and describe his unique contribution to object relations theory. Besides interpreting and explaining the contributions made by Fairbairn and Winnicott, Guntrip also focused on a particular aspect of Klein's original object relations theory and set out to extend and explain it.

In the section about Melanie Klein, we described the two important infant experiences, which she identified as the paranoid–schizoid position and the depressive position. Guntrip was particularly interested in Klein's thesis on the paranoid–schizoid position; though he noted that in her original work she spoke exclusively of the 'paranoid' position and only later added the term 'schizoid' (Guntrip, 1971: 61). To Guntrip, however, the term schizoid represented a third and separate position and one in which the infant is withdrawn from any relationship with its primary carer. This, according to him, is in direct contrast to the paranoid position in which the infant is in a relationship, but feels persecuted by it. Guntrip's extension of object relations theory led to his later interest in patients with schizoid problems; he described these problems as stemming from impoverished early relationships, and he included 'feeling of not belonging' and alienation among the experiences his patients expressed (Guntrip, 1971: 148). As a result of his work, Guntrip came to believe that the early relationship deficit suffered by his patients could only be ameliorated by a form of psychotherapy, in which the psychotherapist replaces the missing parent, who, in infancy, is essential for growth, development and a sense of self.

John Bowlby (1907–1990)

Bowlby also argued that human nature is orientated towards relationships with other people. Like Winnicott and Fairbairn, Bowlby did not subscribe to the Kleinian view that aggression is innate. On the contrary, he believed that human beings only become aggressive when they need to defend themselves against threat. It is on the subject of deprivation, however, that

Bowlby has proved to be most controversial. In his view, the infant needs a continuous bond with the mother during the first two years of life. Bowlby believed that the infant–mother bond – or infant–mother substitute bond – is different from all other relationships. Change from one mother figure to another during the first three or four years would, in his opinion, result in emotional problems for young children (Bowlby, 1990). Even though these views have been disputed by other child care experts, they have, nevertheless, had an influence on child care practice generally. This is especially true in areas like social work, where it became usual to keep children at home, if possible, rather than have numerous other people care for them. Hospitals also developed more flexible attitudes to visiting in mother and baby units, and maternity hospitals stopped separating babies from their mothers. Feminists have not been entirely happy with Bowlby's views, since they place enormous pressure on women to supply the continuous and uninterrupted care, which he felt was necessary. There is resentment, too, that women are almost invariably blamed when children do develop emotional problems.

Heinz Kohut (1913–1981)

Heinz Kohut, who was Jewish, emigrated to England in 1939 and later to America to escape the deteriorating situation in Austria, as Hitler rose to power. In America, Kohut studied psychiatry and psychoanalysis and worked mainly at the University of Chicago. His theoretical and practical approach to psychoanalysis was Freudian to begin with, but over time he evolved his own ideas about the way humans develop a sense of 'self' from infancy onwards. A central tenet of Kohut's work is that humans are motivated by the need for relationships; this is in contrast to Freud's 'Drive' theory, according to which we are motivated by our (mainly sexual) instincts. Kohut's two most important books are: *The Analysis of the Self* (1971) and *The Restoration of the Self* (1977), though he wrote numerous papers delineating his theories, as well.

Kohut is referred to as a self-psychologist, but his work has discernible links with object relations theory, since it, too, is concerned with the way we internalise aspects of significant people, in order to develop a secure sense of self. Because of his early allegiance to Freudian theory, Kohut initially subscribed to the classical definition of 'narcissism', a term used by Freud (1900: 355) to denote a particular way of relating to other people. In Freudian terms, 'primary narcissism' refers to the way in which an infant directs all libidinal energy or love towards self. At this stage, the infant is believed to be unaware that anyone else exists as a separate person, but later realises that others are needed to gratify his or her personal needs. The infant then turns to others for gratification of these needs. In Freudian terms, therefore, love of self is seen to precede an ability to reach out to and love other people.

Through his extensive work with patients suffering from personality disorders, Kohut came to formulate his own theories about early childhood experience. In Kohut's view, the developing infant is destined from the very beginning to establish close relationships, in order to fulfil basic psychological and other needs. It is only through this kind of interaction with parents or carers that the child is able to develop a sense of self. 'Selfobjects' is the term Kohut (1977: 275) uses to denote significant adults in the child's life. These Selfobjects are gradually absorbed into the psyche of the developing child and become, in turn, the very essence of the child's being. Kohut did believe that the developing child is basically narcissistic; by this, he meant that each child naturally prefers good or rewarding experience, in order to develop a positive sense of self. Additionally, each small child seeks to be admired and praised, in order to believe in the reality of their own intrinsic goodness. Kohut also suggested that another fundamental need is the child's desire to incorporate an idealised image of a parent (usually the mother) into his or her own representational world. When these needs are neglected through lack of parental empathy or unreliable care giving, the child grows into adulthood without a proper sense of self. This can then lead to the condition known as narcissistic personality disorder (NPD), which is manifest as an inflated or grandiose self, along with a lack of empathy for others and a need for constant admiration. Kohut worked with many such patients, and he came to see that there were frequent problems in the transference with them. Many were unable to detach from early narcissistic internalisations, which meant they often feared yet more relationship failure, this time with the analyst. Many were also grandiose or superior and expected admiration from the analyst. Others left therapy early, which Kohut saw as a failure of understanding on his part. As a result of his honesty and insight, Kohut came to believe that the most effective way of understanding his patients' own unique experiences was through empathic listening. This approach has obvious links with person-centred therapy, which we shall consider in a later unit. Kohut discovered that if he set aside all assumptions about his patients and listened empathetically instead, he would understand their experiences from their point of view, without any clinical assumptions on his part. Empathy, therefore, became a central concept in Kohut's approach to understanding the internal world of people whose early relationships were inadequate or dysfunctional. In one reference to empathy, he describes it as 'an irreplaceable tool in depth psychology' which actually 'defines the field of depth psychology' (Kohut 1977: 305).

Contemporary object relations theory

Object relations theory and practice continues to develop and evolve. However, it is impossible, within the scope of this section, to consider all the contributions to this very important field of psychodynamic theory. Some significant names within the evolving sphere of object relations include the following:

Otto Kernberg (1928–)

Otto Kernberg, who is an American psychoanalyst and professor of psychiatry, is best known for his integrative work, especially in relation to Klein's object relations theories and those of ego psychology. Like Kohut, Kernberg is also interested in pathological conditions including narcissistic disorders and borderline personality disorders.

Hanna Segal (1918–2011)

Hanna Segal was a British psychoanalyst, who was born in Poland. She, too, was a follower of Melanie Klein and has written extensively on the subjects of envy and narcissism. Her specific area of interest was in symbols and symbolism. However, she was also deeply interested in the meaning of creativity and dreaming. Another area of interest was conflict and war, with particular reference to the symbolic and psychological factors attendant upon the events of September 11 and the subsequent war in Iraq.

Eric Brenman (1920–2012)

Eric Brenman trained in medicine and psychiatry and then psychoanalysis. He became senior training analyst and supervisor in the British Psychoanalytic Society. Brenman was a follower of Klein and wrote a collection of papers on aspects of object relations theory. He was concerned about the usefulness, or otherwise, of interpretation when used in therapy and emphasised that it could only be meaningful in the context of a close relationship between analyst and patient.

Integration of object relations theory

In Unit 6 we shall look at some of the ways in which aspects of object relations theory is being integrated with Gestalt therapy. This has been achieved by Delisle (2013), clinical psychologist and Associate Professor of Psychology at the University of Sherbrooke. The work of Delisle and colleagues is on the integration of Gestalt theory with other theoretical approaches, with special reference to the work of Fairbairn. Other theoretical approaches have incorporated aspects of object relations theory into their work and practice, and there is currently a selection of books available dedicated to the theme of integration in general.

Object relations theory and its influence on therapy and counselling

Object relations theory has had an enormous influence on the therapy movement generally. This is largely because of its specific focus on the early mother–child relationship, which is seen as a template for future relationships throughout life. We can see from the work of Klein and the other object relationists that the development of an individual's sense of self is a central concern in all their deliberations. There are, of course, some differences in their individual theories, but what is striking are the similarities between them. All, for example, redefine the earliest human impulses as object seeking, rather than pleasure seeking, and all place greater emphasis on this dynamic than on any other. Many counsellors now integrate aspects of object relations theory into their work with clients. This is because counselling is a relationship, too, and has the potential to mirror or reflect aspects of early client experience. The emphasis on human relationships and their central importance for everyone means that transference and countertransference are especially significant in the counselling context. Countertransference (described in Unit 3), which is the emotional response of the counsellor to the client, will probably provide some indicators about the client's interpersonal problems in other relationships. The following case study illustrates aspects of transference and countertransference in the counselling context.

CASE STUDY

Veronica

Veronica came into counselling because of the eating problems she had suffered for many years. She had difficulty in expressing her feelings and, in many ways, could hardly identify what her feelings were. Veronica's mother had been depressed for as long as she could remember. Each time she expressed any negative feeling as a child, Veronica's mother became upset and anxious. When her mother was 'down', however, Veronica had to console her. This pattern meant that the client had difficulty in separating herself from her mother, and, indeed, she had no clear idea who her 'self' was. The anorexia, which had plagued her for so long, was an attempt to regain some control of her relationship with her mother. She described it as a form of control herself and added that it was one way of getting her mother to notice her and show concern. During sessions, Veronica seemed concerned to please the counsellor at all costs, and this was something which the counsellor was able to sense and experience at an emotional level. The task for the counsellor was to highlight the client's relationship style and then help her to establish a firmer sense of who she was. This was done over time and involved encouraging the client to identify and express her feelings and needs in a supportive and accepting environment.

The therapeutic relationship

Bowlby (1990) took the view that therapy could provide the kind of secure corrective experience clients may have lacked in childhood. It is probably true to say that any successful relationship established in later life has the potential to ameliorate early dysfunctional experience. However, in therapy clients are given the opportunity, time and support to explore less problematic ways of relating to people. The therapist becomes another, though temporary, attachment figure, who should prove to be more reliable, more consistent and certainly more reliable than parents were in the past. There is a definite switch of focus in object relations theory, from the father to the mother, and this is both problematic and reassuring from a feminist viewpoint, since it stresses the role of the mother, while highlighting the problems that can arise in relation to maternal provision.

EXERCISE

Infant experience

Working individually, try to imagine that you are a newborn baby. Write down all your sensations for a day, concentrating on your sensory experience and emotional needs. Discuss your experience of the exercise with other members of the group.

Skills essential to the theoretical approaches outlined

The theoretical approaches described in this unit are important because of the way they increase our knowledge of human development and the problems that can arise at different stages of life. All the basic counselling skills, including listening, reflecting and asking questions are used by counsellors who are familiar with, and influenced by, any of these theories. However, the relationship between client and counsellor is perhaps more important than anything else, since it is relationships that are generally highlighted by all these theories. This is referred to in the previous section (The therapeutic relationship) within this unit and Unit 3, where we defined the concepts of transference and countertransference. A central area of therapy is to help clients become more aware of their inner emotional world in the hope that their capacity to relate to others will improve as a result. The skill of interpretation is especially important when helping clients to connect the past to the present, but it should be used gradually and sparingly, and always accompanied by the empathy Kohut valued so highly.

Clients who benefit from these approaches

Because of the emphasis on early development (central to all these theories) and the focus on problems that can arise in later life (implicit in psychosocial theory), the approaches are certainly applicable to clients who experience relationship problems. Many people have the experience of repeated difficulty in relating to others, and attempts to resolve these problems alone are often doomed to failure. This is because of the unconscious components, which frequently operate in the perpetuation of interpersonal problems. In such instances, outside help may be needed, in order to locate the source of current difficulties. Disturbed relationships in childhood are often re-enacted in the present, and clients who become aware of this repetition are likely to benefit from these approaches. Clients who experience crises at different life stages are also likely to be helped by a therapist who is familiar with (among others)

Erikson's psychosocial stages of development. People who feel stuck and unable to make sense of their lives may also benefit through working from this perspective. It should be added, however, that it is not enough for a counsellor or therapist – or indeed any other helper – to be well versed in theory. Practical experience of working with people in a caring capacity is essential too.

Clients who have been ill, or who suffer from disability, are also increasingly helped by a psychodynamic, or an object relations, approach in therapy. Many chronic illnesses result in psychological as well as physical difficulties. Research carried out by Mikolajczyk and Bateman (2012) into the psychological effects of stroke measured responses to psychodynamic therapy among 15 patients who had suffered this condition. High levels of anxiety, depression, grief and recurring themes of loss and attachment dependency, were just some of the after-effects they identified in those patients who had suffered a stroke. Many of the issues addressed in counselling related to some aspect of loss, including loss of a significant family member, retirement, and loss of mobility. Difficult family relationships were also identified, including previous relationship break-up and divorce. Mikolajczyk and Bateman make the point that an understanding of unconscious object relations is important in the work they were doing, because 'in relation to stroke, the lost object may be part of the self' (Mikolajczyk and Bateman, 2012: 17). This can lead to lack of confidence in many areas, including lack of confidence in one's own body, which is likely to have changed as a result of stroke.

It is probably true to say that a psychodynamic approach is likely to help clients who have suffered a range of physical or disabling illnesses. Most serious physical illness has the potential to create deep anxiety and to precipitate difficulties in close relationships. The following short case history illustrates this dynamic.

CASE STUDY

Tess

Tess had been diagnosed with cancer and was told she had only months to live. She was cared for at home by her husband and daughter and a number of professionals, who came to help as part of a 'care package' designed to support the family. Tess was reluctant to take some of the medication prescribed for her, and this refusal caused deep anxiety for her husband and daughter, who, having no experience in caring, were 'at sea' in this new situation. Tess misread their anxiety as reluctance to care for her and became deeply depressed and anxious, in return. She talked to a visiting social worker, who arranged for her to receive some respite care in a Macmillan unit of the local hospital. While in the hospital, Tess received counselling from one of the nurses trained to give this kind of support. During counselling, Tess was able to talk about her relationships at home and the difficulties she experienced in relation to her own parents when she was younger. As a result of having someone listen to her feelings of anger, resentment and loss, Tess was helped to accept the reality of her impending death and to forgive herself and family for relationship failures, past and present. Because of the continuing problems at home, she was admitted to the hospital and cared for there until her death.

Some limitations

Clients, who are in an immediate crisis situation, including sudden bereavement, may not wish to examine relationships straightaway. Once the crisis is over, however, a focus on family or other relationships will probably be beneficial for them. Clients who are in the acute stage of addiction are unlikely to benefit either, although they, too, may benefit later. Through a focus on object relations, especially in childhood, such clients may come to a deeper understanding of their problem and may, in fact, be helped to identify the underlying cause of their addiction. Working with problems that stem from the past requires commitment, as well as a capacity for reflection and self-awareness. Clients who are deeply depressed may benefit from a different approach to begin with, for example cognitive behaviour therapy. Later on, though, they may wish to consider their relationships (past and present) from a psychodynamic perspective. However, therapy of any kind may be financially unavailable for some clients, unless it is provided for them within the health service. Long-term psychodynamic therapy may be expensive and unobtainable in some areas, though short-term counselling is increasingly offered by counsellors who are trained in these approaches. Other counsellors may integrate their knowledge of object relations theory and practice into their work with clients.

Since it is an interpersonal approach, object relations counselling can also be used with clients in family or couples therapy. However, one criticism of this approach centres on the fact that object relations is specific to family members or partners (past and present), but it may not take into account the cultural and social structures in which a particular family lives. These structures will invariably impinge, either positively or negatively, on individuals and families. In addition, there are many other figures in any person's life; all of them affecting (directly or indirectly) that person's development. On the other hand, practitioners of object relations therapy are not oblivious to these considerations and increasingly take them into account.

SUMMARY

In this unit we considered the psychodynamic theories which have evolved from the Freudian approach. These include the work of Adler, Jung, the ego psychologists, the object relationists and the psychosocial stages described by Erik Erikson. The counselling skills that are central to these approaches were also discussed, with special reference to the importance of the therapeutic relationship in all of them. We considered the influence of different theories on counselling and stressed the need for adequate training – both practical and theoretical – for students who wish to develop their skills in these areas. The usefulness of each theoretical model was discussed, along with consideration of their limitations for certain clients.

References

Adler, A. (1931) *What Life Could Mean to You*. Oxford: Oneworld Books (1992).

Adler, A. (1927) *Understanding Human Nature*. Oxford: Oneworld Books (1992).

Bowlby, J. (1990) *Child Care and the Growth of Love*. London: Penguin.

Brenman, E. (2010) *Recovery of the Lost Good Object*. London: Routledge.

Cashdan, S. (1988) *Object Relations Therapy: Using the Relationship*. New York: W. W. Norton & Co.

Delisle, G. (2013) *Object Relations in Gestalt Therapy*. London: Karnac Books.

Erikson, E. (1995) *Childhood and Society*. London: Vintage.

Fairbairn, W.R.D. (1954) *An Object Relations Theory of Personality*. New York: Basic Books.

Fontana, D. (1993) *The Secret Language of Symbols*. London: Pavillion.

Freud, A. (1936) *The Ego and the Mechanisms of Defence*. London: Hogarth Press (1937).

Freud, S. (1900) *The Interpretation of Dreams*. London: Penguin Books (1991).

Guntrip, H. (1971) *Psychoanalytic Theory, Therapy and the Self*. London: Basic Books.

Hartmann, H. (1958) *Ego Psychology and the Problem of Adaption*. New York: International Universities Press.

Jung, C.G. (1961) *Memories, Dreams, Reflections*. (ed. Jaff, A.) London: Fontana Press (1995).

Jung, C.G. (1957) *C.G. Jung Speaking: Interviews and Encounters*. (eds. McGuire, W. & Hull, R. F. C. London: Picador (1980).

Jung, C.G. (1964) *Man and His Symbols*. London: Picador.

Kernberg, O. (1976) *Object Relations Theory and Clinical Psychoanalysis*. New York: Jason Aronson.

Klein, M. (1932) *The Psychoanalysis of Children*. London: Hogarth Press.

Kohut, H. (1971) *The Analysis of the Self*. London: The University of Chicago Press.

Kohut, H. (1977) *The Restoration of the Self*. London: The University of Chicago Press.

Mikolajczyk, A. & Bateman, A. (2012) 'Psychodynamic Counselling after Stroke: A Pilot Service Development Project and Evaluation in Advances in Clinical Neuroscience' (online) 12, 4,16–20 Mere, Wiltshire: Whitehouse Publishing. Available at: www.acnr.co.uk. Accessed May 2013.

Segal, H. (2007) *Yesterday, Today and Tomorrow*. London: Routledge. Published in Association with the Institute of Psychoanalysis. London.

Singer, J. (1995) *Boundaries of the Soul*. Dorchester, Dorset: Prism Press.

Winnicott, D. W. (1991) *Playing and Reality*. London: Routledge.

Further reading

Altschuler, J. (2012) *Counselling and Psychotherapy for Families in Times of Illness and Death*. (2nd edn). London: Palgrave Macmillan.

Berry, R. (2000) *Jung, A Beginner's Guide*. London: Hodder & Stoughton.

Black, M. J & Mitchell, S.A. (1995) *Freud and Beyond: A History of Modern Psychoanalytic Thought*. New York: Basic Books.

Charles, R. (2004) *Intuition in Psychotherapy and Counselling*. London: Whurr Publications.

Erikson, E. (1969) *Identity, Youth and Crisis*. New York: Norton.

Erikson, E. (1995) *Childhood and Society*. London: Vintage.

Erikson, E. (1998) *The Life Cycle Completed*. New York: Norton.

Hayman, R. (1999) *A Life of Jung*. London: Bloomsbury.

Hughes, J.M. (1990) *Reshaping the Psychoanalytic Domain*. Berkeley, CA: University of California Press.

Jacobs, M. (1998) *The Presenting Past: The core of psychodynamic counselling and therapy* (2nd edn). Maidenhead: Open University Press. McGraw-Hill Education.

Lapworth, P. (2010) *Integration in Counselling and Psychotherapy* (2nd edn). London: Sage Publications.

Mitchell, J. (1987) *The Selected Melanie Klein*. New York: The Free Press.

Segal, J. (2004) *Melanie Klein* (2nd edn). London: Sage Publications.

Resources

Websites

www.adleriansociety.co.uk

Based in London, this is the Adlerian Society (UK) and the Institute of Individual Psychology. Offers residential courses, lectures and group discussions.

www.adleriansummerschools.org.uk

Offers courses for trainees and qualified counsellors.

www.jungiananalysis.org

The Society of Analytical Psychology and a provider of training in Jungian therapy. Also offers supervision courses.

www.jungiananalysts.org.uk

This is the Association of Jungian Analysts.

www.object–relations.com

This is the object relations home page. Provides information about object relations theory and practice.

www.orinyc.org

Object relations Institute for Psychotherapy.

www.selfpsychology.com

Dedicated to discussion and information about Heinz Kohut.

www.simplepsychology.org
Designed to help psychology students on academic courses, with links to other sites and information about Erik Erikson and others.

Journals

The Journal of Analytical Psychology.
Published on behalf of the Society of Analytical Psychology, UK. Wiley Online Library.
www.psypress.com

5

Phenomenological and humanistic approaches

◆ Introduction

The attitude enshrined in humanism is essentially positive: it identifies and upholds the basic goodness of each individual, while at the same time recognising the adverse circumstances that may obscure these qualities at various stages throughout life. This is in sharp contrast to the theory of personality described by Freud, which stresses drives, instincts, impulses and urges as motivating factors in human behaviour. In Freudian terms, people are governed by powerful forces originating in the unconscious, and it is those forces which compel them to act in certain ways.

Both Adler and Jung moved away from this deterministic position and, in doing so, highlighted other aspects of experience they felt could explain human development and behaviour. In Jung's paradigm, however, unconscious forces are still very much in evidence, although his overall view of people is more extensive, with a focus on adult dilemmas not found in Freudian theory.

The work of the ego psychologists indicates another fairly radical shift of emphasis, with their focus on thinking and other cognitive processes they believed to be present at an early stage of life.

In this and the next unit we shall discuss those models of counselling which have been directly influenced by phenomenology and humanism; we shall also consider the concepts and skills integral to each theoretical approach. The following theories and counselling models are dealt with in this unit:

- Rogers and the person-centred approach
- Maslow and humanism
- the existential approach.

The meaning of phenomenology in relation to counselling

The word 'phenomenology' stems from philosophy and refers to the way in which individuals perceive and interpret events. Another way of stating this is to say that it is not the actual events that cause people to behave in certain ways; instead, it is each person's unique perception of those events which determines their responses. The recognition that each individual is influenced by his or her own phenomenal field is important in the counselling context, since it underlines the need to discover clients' individual perceptions if we are to be effective in helping them. It is not enough for counsellors to simply assume that clients will respond in specific ways to certain situations or events. On the contrary, counsellors need to be aware of the vast spectrum of individual difference that has to be taken into consideration in relation to the experiences clients describe. The following example gives some idea of the way in which two people, who appear to have exactly the same experience, record entirely different perceptions of it.

CASE STUDY

Recalling an accident

A client called Rosaleen came into counselling because she had been in a car accident and had suffered post-traumatic shock as a result of it. Her sister had also been in the accident, and though neither of them sustained physical injury, both had taken time off work in order to recover. The difference between the two sisters' responses lay in the fact that whereas Rosaleen felt immensely traumatised by it, her sister seemed relatively unaffected by events, although she did concede that it had been frightening initially. Rosaleen's sister took some time off work on the advice of her doctor, but she was anxious to get back to the office just as soon as she could. The resilience of her sister caused some difficulty for Rosaleen, because it made her feel guilty about her own response. She discussed her feelings with the counsellor.

CLIENT: I worry that people might think I'm putting it on. Jean [her sister] never seemed to look back. I'm sure people must think it's all in my mind.

COUNSELLOR: That's obviously something that concerns you a great deal . . . the idea that people will think badly of you.

CLIENT: Well yes . . . Because of the way she is. There is such a contrast in our reactions.

COUNSELLOR: Yet people do react in very different ways . . . to a whole lot of situations.

CLIENT: People can't be the same in the way they see things . . . I suppose I'm . . . maybe weaker in some ways. But it's hard to believe we were both in the same car.

COUNSELLOR: With a different experience of the accident . . .

CLIENT: Yes, and different reactions, too.

COUNSELLOR: In the way that people tend to respond quite differently to things.

Comment: The counsellor who worked with Rosaleen was concerned to help her explore all the circumstances of the accident. She also wanted to show the client that her individual response to the accident was a perfectly valid one, even though it differed from her sister's response. To do this the counsellor listened carefully to the client's story, and encouraged her to voice all the worries she felt in relation to

CASE STUDY Cont...

other people's views. It might have been tempting for the counsellor to reassure the client that she was not, in fact, weaker than her sister, but such reassurance would have been misplaced. From a purely person-centred perspective, it is important to remember that clients' feelings are real to them, and the counsellor's task is to stay within the client's internal frame of reference – a concept we shall discuss later in this unit.

However, several other points are significant in relation to this client's experience and the counselling she received. The first point concerns the two quite different responses to the car accident, a difference that can be explained in various ways. In the first place, no two people are ever entirely the same, even when they are sisters. In the second place, Rosaleen's life experience just prior to the accident was very different from her sister's. It emerged in the course of counselling that the client had recently been ill with glandular fever, a fact that compounded the trauma of the accident. Rosaleen's relationship with her parents was different too. She had never felt as close to them as her sister seemed to be, and just before the car accident she had argued with her father. All these factors combined to influence the client's unique response to the accident, but once she identified them she felt less guilty about any differences in relation to her sister.

KEY TERM

Person-centred: This refers to an attitude which counsellors, or ideally any person in the helping professions, should have. It means paying attention to the real person of the client and identifying their individual experiences and needs, which are quite separate from anyone else's.

Rogers and the person-centred approach

Carl Rogers (1902–1987) is the psychologist whose name is synonymous with the person-centred approach to counselling. Rogers, who was born in Illinois, studied theology, but later switched to psychology and received his Ph.D. in 1931. During this time he worked at a child guidance clinic in New York, and published *The Clinical Treatment of the Problem Child* in 1939. After this, he was invited to become a member of the Psychology department at Ohio State University. However, it was not until 1945 that Rogers' counselling theory and practice began to make an impact. Throughout his academic career he also gained a great deal of experience as a therapist and continued to write books, including *Client-Centred Therapy* (1951) and *On*

Becoming a Person (1961). The emphasis in all of Rogers' later writing is on the importance of each person as the architect of their individual destiny. Rogers firmly believed that everyone has sufficient innate resources to deal effectively with life and the various problems living entails. These innate resources are, according to the person-centred approach, sometimes obscured, forgotten or even denied, but they are, nevertheless, always present with the potential for development and growth (Rogers, 1951). The impact of Rogers' work is best understood when we contrast it with the world of therapy that had existed before he contributed to it. Freudian theory and practice was in the ascendant, especially in America where many prominent psychoanalysts had been forced to emigrate from Europe. The other major influence that had dominated North American psychology was the behaviourist school (which we shall discuss in a later unit), with its emphasis on learned behaviour as the basis of human personality development. Against the background of these major influences, Rogers' insistence on the uniqueness of the individual, and the individual's innate tendency towards growth and wholeness, certainly seemed to represent a much more optimistic and positive viewpoint.

Rogers' concept of 'self'

Rogers believed that people will, if given the right conditions and opportunities, move towards autonomy and self-direction (Rogers, 1961). The concept of 'self' is important here, and refers to the 'I' or the 'me' part of each person. According to Rogers, personality development can be viewed in terms of self-concept development, which, in turn, depends on the individual's interaction with other people and the environment. Rogers did not describe stages or phases of development in the way that Freud, Klein or Erikson did, for example. Instead, he concentrated on the individual's perception of self, as well as the ways in which these perceptions are coloured by other people's evaluations and expectations. From a very early age, children seek to please their parents or carers who are, after all, the most important people in the world to them. Each person's self-concept is acquired in this way and is continually reinforced throughout life, as a result of ongoing interaction with others. The small child sees him or herself reflected in the attitudes expressed by parents and other important people. When very little love and a great deal of criticism are received, a negative self-concept is bound to follow.

The real or organismic self

No matter how traumatic or negative the environment, however, there remains within each person a core or inner self, which is never entirely obliterated. Each person's innate tendency towards growth is always present and, with the right conditions, will emerge and flourish. Clients in counselling often refer to their 'real' selves; they often do so with regret and sadness, especially when they have never before been given the opportunity to identify and express their authentic needs and feelings. The following client had such an experience.

CASE STUDY

Identification of needs

A 65-year-old woman received counselling while in hospital suffering from cancer. She talked to a nurse who was specially trained to help people in her position. During their exchanges she referred to her early years as a mother bringing up a large family.

MRS COOPER: I did most of it without too much thought . . . I certainly didn't have much time to think about myself!

NURSE: You were just too busy attending to everyone else . . .

MRS COOPER: It's a funny thing [pause] . . . when I was younger . . . As a child, I didn't get time to think of myself either. It probably sounds like self-pity, but it's only now that I'm ill . . . that I've thought about it seriously.

NURSE: So it feels like self-pity because you've never had anyone else ask you or seem interested before.

MRS COOPER: That's it. I even feel guilty talking to you . . . that I might be wasting your time.

NURSE: You are not wasting my time. I am interested in what you say, and it's your time too.

MRS COOPER: Well I would . . . [hesitates] I would like to start some studies . . . if it's not too late.

NURSE: It's not too late to do that. Maybe we could talk about what it is you would like to do?

MRS COOPER: Well when I was in my teens, I loved poetry and literature . . . Then I just got away from all that . . . and then marriage and the family intervened [laughs]. The thing is, my husband will think I've gone crackers.

NURSE: But you don't think you're crackers.

MRS COOPER: No.

NURSE: So now, you're really sure of what you really want to do, and that's a very important start.

MRS COOPER: It is, I don't think I would be happy at this late stage . . . if I didn't try to do something for myself . . . for the real me.

It is often very difficult for people to identify the real self. Many people go through life convinced that the outer self, or self-concept, is the only reality they have. It sometimes takes a crisis to highlight the 'falseness' of the image someone presents to the world. At times like this, a person may finally get in touch with the feelings, needs and ambitions that had previously been obscured. The fact that people do frequently alter their lifestyles in the wake of a crisis illustrates this last point. Clients also come into counselling in the aftermath of a crisis, or indeed even in the middle of one. At such times, they often sense some intimation of disquiet or regret that prompts them to pursue the idea of change. When there is a vast difference between a person's self-concept and the real self, problems of identity will certainly arise at some stage of life.

The case study (identification of needs) highlights another important point, which is that elderly people are rarely given sufficient opportunity to talk about their unique life experiences. In Mrs Cooper's case, it was different because she was diagnosed with cancer and being cared for by a specialist nurse, who was trained to listen to her. In her book *Growing Old: A Journey of Self-Discovery*, Danielle Quinodoz explains that in her work as a psychoanalyst she had often observed elderly people who were surprised to discover that they had lived their lives as if the script had been written by someone else. She then points out that these clients still had time to change things, to make the 'imaginative leap' so that their experiences became their own and 'nobody else's' (Quinodoz, 2010: 131). To achieve this, however, elderly clients need to be heard, so that they can identify the 'real self' as distinct from the 'outer self', which they may have presented to the world over a very long period of time. Person-centred counselling can facilitate this change of focus, a change that is possible regardless of how old a person actually is.

KEY TERM

Organismic self: The real inner life of the person which is present from birth and gravitates towards self-actualisation, integration and harmony.

The actualising tendency

The term 'self actualisation' is one Rogers (1951) uses to describe the human urge to grow, to develop and to reach maximum potential (Rogers, 1951: 488). The actualising tendency is responsible for every aspect of human endeavour and achievement. In some ways it resembles the Freudian concept of libido or life force. The actualising tendency is present from birth onwards and is not just concerned with achievement in a narrow sense. On the contrary, it has a much broader meaning and describes the holistic development of all aspects of the person, including the spiritual, emotional, physical and creative dimensions. The concept of the actualising tendency is important in the counselling context, since it underlines the idea that clients have the necessary resources for dealing effectively with their own problems. If counsellors truly believe this, they are likely to value and respect the people they help. It is sometimes the case that a client's actualising tendency is, for whatever reason, temporarily stultified. But when the right conditions are present in counselling there is a strong possibility that the client's inner resources will be located.

KEY TERMS

Actualising tendency: A propensity described by both Rogers and Maslow. It refers to the human urge to grow, develop and reach maximum potential.

Self-concept: This is a person's view of self which is acquired in early childhood, and developed through life experience. It is reinforced by the reflected appraisals of other people, especially parents, and other important figures in a person's life.

The core conditions

Rogers identified certain core conditions he believed to be necessary if clients are to make progress in counselling. These conditions really describe counsellor qualities and attitudes, which, if present, will facilitate change and growth within the client. Among the most important of these attitudes is the counsellor's ability to understand the client's feelings. Another is respect for the client, while a third is described as counsellor congruence or genuineness. In summary then, the Rogerian core conditions are as follows:

- empathy
- unconditional positive regard
- congruence or genuineness.

(Rogers, 1957: 95–103)

Empathy

The word 'empathy' describes the counsellor's ability to understand the client at a deep level. This is, of course, much easier said than done, since it involves awareness of what it is the client is actually experiencing. Earlier in this unit we discussed the word 'phenomenology' and looked at the different ways in which people experience reality. Rogers refers to the 'internal frame of reference' to denote the client's unique experience of personal problems (Rogers, 1951: 29). The task for the counsellor is to get inside the client's frame of reference. If this is not achieved, then no real point of contact is made between counsellor and client.

Rogers further uses the term 'external frame of reference' to describe this lack of understanding and contact (Rogers, 1951:47). When a counsellor perceives the client from an external frame of reference, there is little chance that the client's view will be clearly heard. It is important for clients (if they are to benefit from counselling) to sense that their individual experience of 'self' and reality is appreciated by the helper. However, this does not mean that counsellors should experience the emotions a client experiences. In fact, it would be counter-productive for the counsellor to become emotionally involved in this way; it would certainly upset the balance of the relationship between client and counsellor. In order to stay within the client's internal frame of reference, it is necessary for the counsellor to listen carefully to what is being conveyed (both verbally and non-verbally) at every stage of counselling. The counsellor needs to imagine and appreciate what it is actually like to be the client, and this appreciation of the client's experience then needs to be conveyed to him or her.

EXERCISE

Sympathy and empathy

In groups of three to four, discuss the words 'sympathy' and 'empathy' and say what you think the differences are between them. Are there any circumstances (outside counselling) when it may be appropriate to use sympathy? What skills are necessary in order to convey empathy to clients?

EXERCISE

My own thoughts and feelings

To develop awareness of other people's feelings, we must first become aware of our own. One way of tuning into our own feelings is to set aside some time each day to listen to ourselves. Start now by spending ten minutes in silence. Identify your thoughts and feelings during this time, and then write them down. It doesn't matter how mundane or banal these feelings and thoughts may be; they are all relevant to the exercise. The point here is to gain practice in becoming more self-aware and ultimately more aware of others in the process.

EXERCISE

Identifying feelings

We often express our feelings inaccurately by using vague or general terms, rather than words that express specific emotions. For example, we may say we feel 'let down' when someone fails to turn up, when we really mean that we feel rejected. In order to develop true awareness of feelings, it helps to make lists of 'feeling' words that express emotions more precisely.

Working individually, make lists of all the words that express the following:

- grief
- disappointment
- sadness
- happiness
- sorrow
- excitement
- relief
- embarrassment.

Unconditional positive regard

The need for positive regard is present in all human beings from infancy onwards. This need is so imperative that small children will do almost anything in order to achieve it. People need love, acceptance, respect and warmth from others, but unfortunately these attitudes and feelings are often only given conditionally. Parents may say, or imply, that their love is given on condition that certain criteria are met. When this happens it is impossible for children to feel valued for themselves alone. Many people who come into counselling have experienced such parental attitudes, which are often reinforced throughout life. Rogers believed that counsellors should convey unconditional positive regard or warmth towards clients if they are to feel understood and accepted. This means that clients are valued without any conditions attached, even when they experience themselves as negative, bad, frightened or abnormal (Rogers, 1996).

Acceptance implies a non-judgmental approach by counselors; it also means caring in a non-possessive way. Rogers refers to a counsellor attitude of positive regard, which clearly acknowledges the client as a separate person, one who is entitled to his or her own feelings and experiences (Rogers, 1996). When attitudes of warmth and acceptance are present in counselling, clients are likely to accept themselves and become more confident in their own abilities to cope. However, acceptance of clients does not mean that counsellors must like or approve of everything they do. What is important is that counsellors are able to separate their own views from those of clients. The values and views held by clients may differ quite dramatically from those held by individual counselors. But even in these circumstances, clients deserve (and should receive) respect and positive regard from the people in whom they confide.

EXERCISE

Conveying warmth

Working individually, think of a time in your life when you received warmth and positive regard from someone who helped you. How did this person convey these attitudes to you? What were the circumstances in which you needed help? How did these attitudes help you at the time?

Congruence or genuineness

The words 'congruence' and 'genuineness' describe another quality which Rogers believed counsellors should possess. This quality is one of sincerity, authenticity and honesty within the counselling relationship. In order to be congruent with clients, counsellors need to be themselves, without any pretence or façade (Rogers, 1996). This means, of course, that counsellors need to know themselves first. In the absence of self-knowledge, it would be totally impossible to develop attitudes of openness and honesty in relation to clients. Honesty and openness do not imply uninhibited frankness; however, when empathy and positive respect are also present in the relationship, uninhibited frankness is unlikely to be a problem. A very important aspect of counsellor genuineness is that it acts as a model for those clients who may find it difficult to be open and genuine themselves. Appropriate and genuine responses to clients are always prompted by real concern for them. The following exchange between counsellor and client illustrates this point.

CASE STUDY

Being open

CLIENT: My boyfriend has been really nasty at times . . . Sometimes, well last week he did go over the top and lashed out.

COUNSELLOR: He hit you . . .

CLIENT: Well maybe I asked for it [smiles] . . . we both have tempers. He's OK really.

COUNSELLOR: I'm a bit puzzled by what you've just said . . . and the way you said it. You smiled when you mentioned that he hit you.

CLIENT: It's just that I don't want to make too much of it . . . or blame him for everything.

COUNSELLOR: But still the situation makes you tense and nervous?

CLIENT: It does. I want to understand it . . . him I mean. He wasn't always like that. He used to be so kind to me [starts to cry].

Comment: During this exchange with the client, the counsellor identified what she regarded as a discrepancy between what the client said and the way that she said it. The counsellor was confused by this discrepancy so she referred to it, in order to clarify things for herself. However, she was also concerned to encourage the client to look more closely at her own feelings, including those feelings she had expressed and those which were unexpressed. Being open with the client was the counsellor's way of indicating that she wanted to understand her more fully. This openness also helped the client to understand herself at a deeper level.

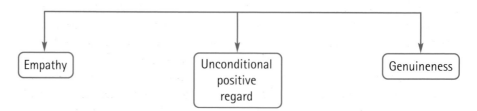

Figure 5.1 Rogers' core conditions

The counselling relationship

We have already seen that the person-centred counselling relationship is based on respect for the client, the establishment of an empathic bond and a willingness on the counsellor's part to be open and genuine with the client. In addition to these qualities, however, there is also an emphasis on facilitating each client's growth or self-actualisation. It is only when the core conditions, described above, are present in the relationship that self-actualisation can be achieved. The counselling skills discussed at the beginning of this book are used in the person-centred approach and are necessary for the development of a therapeutic relationship between counsellor and client. These skills include:

- active listening
- responding to clients through reflection of feeling and content
- paraphrasing and summarising
- asking open questions
- responding appropriately to silence and client non-verbal communication.

Helpers who are interested in the person-centred approach must be prepared to encounter clients on a basis of equality and to work with them in a non-directive way. In many respects, the person-centred approach is characterised more by what the counsellor does not do, rather than what he or she does. Offering psychodynamic-style interpretation, for example, is avoided and the main focus of therapy is on clarification of the client's feelings so that identification of the 'real' self is facilitated. In conclusion, the essence of person-centred counselling lies in the attitudes and values of the helper and this, of course, necessitates proper training and adequate supervision for those counsellors who wish to use it.

Transference

Although the possibility of transference reactions is acknowledged in the person-centred approach, these reactions are never highlighted or encouraged by the counsellor. A basic aim of the model is to help clients achieve independence and autonomy, so the projection of dependent feelings on to the counsellor would be viewed as a hindrance to this. The attitude of the counsellor to the client should indicate acceptance and equality from the outset and this, in turn, will lessen the possibility that transference reactions are sustained. Rogers does concede that transference attitudes do exist 'in varying degrees' in clients who undertake person-centred therapy (Rogers, 1951: 200). He specifically refers to clients who may be dependent, or expect to be dependent, and to clients who may fear the therapist as an authority figure. Of course, these fears are likely to be a reflection of apprehension towards all authority figures, especially parents. However, Rogers goes on to point out that it is what happens to these clients' expectations that matters. In Freudian psychoanalysis, transference attitudes tended to develop into an intense emotional relationship, whereas in the person-centred approach this is unlikely to happen because of the basic equality of the relationship (Rogers, 1951).

It should be added that unconscious motivation is also acknowledged in the person-centred approach, but counsellors do not focus specifically on it, nor do they usually ask clients to work with dreams. Since the model is person-centred, however, clients who wish to look at dreams or the unconscious are at liberty to do so. In a similar way, counsellors accept and understand any transference feelings expressed by clients towards them. It is this very acceptance of the client's experience that tends to foster equality in the relationship.

Clients who benefit from this approach

The person-centred approach has wide application within the helping professions, the voluntary sector, human relations training, groupwork, education and institutional settings, where the goals are to foster good interpersonal skills and respect for others. This last group would include, among others, churches, businesses, youth organisations and crisis centres. In the context of therapy and counselling, the person-centred approach is suitable for use with clients in the first stages of crisis. Later on, however, clients in crisis may need a more directive approach to help them cope with the practical and long-term aspects of their problems.

From a feminist viewpoint, person-centred counselling has significant advantages over some of the other models. This is because it encourages clients to consider and identify their own feelings and needs, something which many women (especially those who have spent a lifetime caring for others) may never have been able to do before. Clients who have been bereaved should also benefit from the person-centred approach, since one of the things bereaved people appear to need most of all is validation of their individual responses to loss. However, as Cooper (2008: 45) indicates, counselling for bereavement has become 'controversial' in recent years. Grieving is certainly a natural process that cannot be 'cured' by counselling, regardless of the theoretical approach being used. When grief is complicated though, many clients do seek counselling and benefit from it. If the core conditions Rogers describes are present in counselling, clients are more likely to explore any difficulties that impede their ability to cope with loss. People with relationship difficulties should also derive some advantage from working with a counsellor who gives them respect, understanding and openness, which they may not have experienced in everyday life.

The principles of the person-centred approach have been applied to a variety of therapeutic situations including marriage counselling and family therapy. Many support groups work by extending the core conditions to its members. Alcoholics Anonymous is a case in point and is a good example of the therapeutic effects of respect, understanding and openness for people who want to change. Telephone counselling is another therapeutic medium through which Rogerian attitudes can be extended to clients, especially to those who are in deep distress or crisis.

Perhaps one of the greatest strengths of the person-centred approach is that it is often the training of choice for health professionals and others who are affiliated to hospitals, health centres and other organisations where people work together to help clients and patients. However, other models can be used in these settings too.

The person-centred approach in other contexts

The person-centred approach to counselling is suitable for use with elderly clients, a group whose needs are often diverse and sometimes overlooked. It is worth elaborating on the needs of this particular client group. We know that old age is associated with many real or potential problems and that elderly people face possible deterioration in physical, as well as psychological, health. In their research paper 'Building Bridges: Person-Centred Therapy with Older Adults' (2012), Humboldt and Leal enumerate some of the problems that may beset people as they grow older. They include declining physical health, loss of independence, loneliness, depression, bereavement issues, disability, feelings of worthlessness and regret for past failures. In an approach to helping elderly clients, Humboldt and Leal highlight the Rogerian concept of empathy, and emphasise its effectiveness in interpersonal communication with older adults. When the core condition of empathy is used by helpers, older clients are more likely to feel understood; this is especially true when they have been bereaved or have experienced other losses. Humboldt and Leal also stress the importance of helpers (including therapists) to free themselves from any ageist stereotypes they might have about older people. These ageist stereotypes and negative attitudes are prevalent in society as a whole, so it is not far fetched to speculate that they could affect (at least unconsciously) those within the helping professions too. A more thoughtful approach to supporting the elderly to live fuller and more meaningful lives is an objective to which we should all subscribe. Use of Rogers' core conditions of empathy, unconditional positive regard and genuineness would certainly go a long way towards helping us to see older people and their individual needs more clearly. Another important point to make here is that when older people are helped to identify and express their real needs, they tend to become more confident as a result. This, in turn, leads to a greater capacity for self-help and willingness to access sources of support in a more confident manner.

Experiences of older carers

There is a particular group of older people whose needs have, until fairly recently, been almost entirely ignored. In 2011, the Princess Royal Trust for Carers published the results of a survey, which indicated that people near, or over, retirement age undertook a high proportion of caring. This commitment to caring comes at a time when retired people would normally expect to wind down, or perhaps spend more time with grandchildren. The idea of pursuing leisure activities or enjoying retirement is not an option for older people who find themselves cast in a caring role, a responsibility which frequently arises when carers themselves are in poor or declining health. The person being cared for is often a spouse or partner, which means that the relationship itself is fundamentally altered. This change is likely to produce stress, which has the potential to exacerbate any health problems a carer may already have. The survey carried out by The Princess Royal Trust for Carers and entitled *Always on Call, Always Concerned* lists a number of key findings. These include the fact that two-thirds of older carers have health problems or a disability. Because of the demands of looking after another person, many carers cancel their own medical appointments, or abandon planned operations or procedures. Many carers never get a break or a holiday and many have financial problems and worry about the future. The report makes a number of recommendations, including the importance of training in carer awareness for health and social care professionals. In addition, it suggests that 'effective methods of promoting mental wellbeing' should be developed for older carers so that the risk of depression is minimised, or treated if already present (2011: 18–22).

Although there are a number of carers' support groups in existence, it is often the case that carers cannot get the time, or opportunity, to attend these. Individual counselling sessions are probably equally inaccessible when the demands of caring take precedence. One way of supporting older carers, however, is by concentrating on training for health and social care professionals as the report suggests. A person-centred approach to training, where the core conditions of empathy, positive regard and congruence are highlighted, is one way of helping professionals to develop the skills necessary to communicate effectively with carers. Many carers feel frustrated when they are not consulted by professionals, or when they are not involved as full partners in care. This deficit in communication means that carers do not feel heard, or understood, and their confidence is undermined as a result. There are numerous areas in which the difficulties experienced by carers could be ameliorated; but better communication through a person-centred approach to their needs is surely the most important one to address.

Person-centred care and nursing

Training in person-centred communication skills would help health and social care professionals to relate more effectively to the people they care for. However, this is not an entirely new idea. Several writers including McCormac and McCance (2010) have described its theory and practice. As far back as 2006, Innes et al. conducted an investigation into the role of health and social care workers delivering person-centred care to older people, disabled people and people from minority groups. They highlight (among other findings) the importance of overcoming bureaucratic obstacles before implementing person-centred care (Innes et al., 2006).

In 'Person-centred care: Principle of Nursing Practice D' (2011), Manley et al. discuss the person-centred approach to caring and make the point that organisations and health care teams often subscribe to the ideal of person-centred caring. However, actually delivering the philosophy is more challenging, since it requires 'specific knowledge, skills and ways of working', as well as organisational support and a culture that is accepted throughout the workplace (Manley et al. 2011: 35). The writers enumerate those nursing situations which are particularly problematic because of the transient nature of contact between patient and health care worker. These include, for example, nurses who work in theatre, where the skill of making rapid rapport with patients is essential. On the other hand, rapid rapport is not inconsistent with person-centred caring, and Manley et al. are clear about this. They discuss the ways in which a person-centred philosophy can be beneficial to patients and nursing staff. These include an emphasis on compassion, dignity and respect for human rights. In particular, they stress a need for greater understanding of the experiences of minority groups, their communication and cultural styles, and their perceptions of personalised care. A person-centred approach in nursing would also ensure that patient needs and aspirations are identified, patients are helped to make informed choices and shared decision-making between patients and staff is facilitated. Providing information to patients so that they understand procedures and technical information and supporting them in their own choices are also key elements discussed by Manley et al. (2011).

In order to establish good relationships with patients, nursing staff need to have self-awareness and good interpersonal skills to begin with. Training for staff is of vital importance, therefore, and not just at ward level but throughout the hospital system. Person-centred values need to be modelled by clinical leadership so that junior staff feel valued too. In all the criticism recently levelled against nurses and the nursing profession generally, this point is seldom made. It is difficult to see how nurses can embrace person-centred caring for patients, if they themselves feel undervalued.

Carl Rogers, who founded the person-centred approach, described it in the title of his book as *A Way of Being*, by which he meant that it is not just a method of communicating reserved for special occasions (Rogers, 1980). Rather, it is a psychological mindset, which we can all learn to develop in our relationships with other people. Such a mindset includes sincerely felt attitudes of acceptance and respect for everyone, including clients in counselling, patients in hospital, carers at home and vulnerable elderly people in residential care.

Some limitations

Person-centred counselling is an approach that is suitable for most clients, though some with deeply repressed traumas and conflicts may benefit from a more psychodynamic perspective. However, the core conditions Rogers described would certainly work effectively if combined with appropriate skills from the psychodynamic model. People with depression, addiction, phobias or eating disorders are also likely to derive more help from other models, and some of these will be discussed in later units. Clients with alcohol problems may need more support than can be offered through individual counselling. Even when the core conditions are present in a one-to-one therapeutic situation, they may not be enough to sustain change for clients with some addictive problems. Another important factor to remember here is that deeply distressed and addicted clients (providing they are committed to change) may respond more positively in the presence of others with similar problems. Clients with repetitive thoughts and obsessions will probably gain more from a cognitive behavioural approach to counselling; there is no doubt that certain clients benefit from a more directive and structured approach generally. Cultural difference can also influence the way clients perceive those who help them; person-centred counsellors may sometimes be seen as passive, or lacking in initiative, by people who value advice or other more directive forms of intervention.

EXERCISE

The core conditions

Working in pairs, look at the following relationships. How could Rogers' core conditions facilitate the work of the helper or manager in each case? Discuss a range of issues that may crop up in these relationships.

- nurse–patient
- doctor–patient
- lecturer–student
- social worker–client
- priest–parishioner
- manager–worker
- mother–child
- health visitor–new mother
- elderly resident–care assistant
- youth worker–teenager.

Maslow and humanism

Implicit in Carl Rogers' person-centred theory is the idea that people have free choice and the ability to exercise control over their destinies. This is essentially an optimistic view of human nature, since the emphasis is on each person's creativity and strengths, rather than on weaknesses or failings. Such ideas are common currency in phenomenology and humanism, and it is this latter concept that has come to be associated with the work of Abraham Maslow.

Maslow (1908–1970) was born in Brooklyn, New York, where, as the only Jewish boy in the neighbourhood, he had a difficult and lonely childhood. His parents were keen that he should become a lawyer, but Maslow studied psychology instead and obtained his Ph.D. in 1934 from the University of Wisconsin. Maslow's first interest was in behavioural psychology, but over a period of time he became dissatisfied with this approach since it did not, in his view, adequately explain what it is that motivates people and gives meaning and purpose to human life.

Although he did acknowledge the existence of evil and destructiveness in the world, Maslow's primary focus of interest was in the more positive aspects of human experience. His views about aggression and hostility in children clearly show him as an advocate of humanism, since he highlights the fact that although children have been represented in a negative way throughout the history of psychoanalysis and psychology, there is a remarkable lack of scientific evidence to support this view (Maslow, 1970). Maslow refers to the selfishness and innate destructiveness of which children have been accused, and proposes instead that other, more positive, qualities are just as evident, especially in those children who are loved and respected by parents. This last point is important, because it stresses the central role of parents in the child's psychological development.

In addition to this, Maslow's focus on the formative influence of parents and on the need for positive emotional experiences in childhood links his ideas to those of several other theorists, whose work we have already considered. Relationships, and the need to be valued by others, is a central theme of Maslow's work; in this respect, it echoes the approaches described by Adler, the ego psychologists and, of course, the work of the object relationists. Although Maslow did not set up his own specific school of therapy or counselling, his influence on all contemporary approaches is considerable. In addition to this, he was certainly interested in ideas connected with therapy generally, and he was concerned to offer his own views about the helping process and the factors which facilitate or hinder it. The following is an outline of some of the contributions Maslow has made to our understanding of human motivation, personality and the nature of the helping relationship:

- the hierarchy of needs
- self-actualisation

- self-actualising people
- psychotherapy and other helping relationships.

(Maslow, 1970)

The hierarchy of needs

Maslow formulated a theory of human motivation and outlined a series of innate needs, which, he believed, gave purpose, satisfaction and meaning to life. These are arranged in a hierarchy and include physiological, safety, relationship, esteem and finally self-actualisation needs (see Figure 5.2). Obviously, those needs which are lowest in the hierarchy (hunger, thirst, and so on) must be satisfied before any of the higher needs can be pursued. People living in circumstances of extreme poverty and privation, for example in certain third world countries, are unlikely to be concerned about self-actualisation needs when they are preoccupied with basic survival instead. This is not to say that people in these situations do not have the higher order needs that Maslow refers to. Indeed, their self-actualisation needs may simply take a different form. To produce healthy children and to live on through one's family is one example of a self-actualisation variant, which might well be applicable to different cultural groups. Maslow was, however, concerned to describe what he perceived to be the needs of people in America and other western cultures. In any case, the point he wished to make was that satisfaction of basic needs is generally important if people are to be motivated to achieve those higher up.

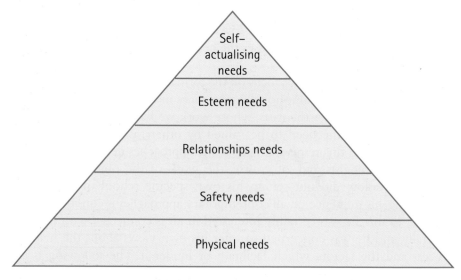

Figure 5.2 Maslow's hierarchy of needs
(Maslow, 1970: 15–45)

Needs

Working in groups of two or three, discuss Maslow's hierarchy and say how you think a deficit in any of these needs could affect others in the hierarchy. What are the possible effects on those children whose safety and relationship needs are neglected, for example? How do neglected relationship needs affect an individual's chances of achieving full potential, educationally or otherwise?

Self-actualisation

A significant point of difference between the work of Maslow and most of the other theorists we have discussed in this book (apart from Rogers) concerns the emphasis Maslow places on psychological health and wellbeing. Many of the others, including Freud, were preoccupied with illness or pathology. This switch of attention from illness to health is evident in Maslow's concept of self-actualisation. A truly healthy person is one who is capable of developing innate talents and achieving maximum potential. In Maslow's opinion, it is impossible to understand human motivation if we look at it purely from a psychotherapist's viewpoint (Maslow, 1970). Any motivational theory, he believed, must consider the ultimate potential of healthy people, as well as looking at the problems and neurosis of those who are ill or debilitated. True understanding of human development and motivation is only achieved through a more comprehensive and holistic appraisal of humanity generally.

These ideas, expressed by Maslow, are similar to those articulated by Rogers and, indeed, the self-actualisation concept is common to both of them. This is not surprising, since both men worked together and, in 1962, helped to found the Association for Humanistic Psychology, along with other colleagues (including Rollo May, whose ideas we shall consider later in this unit). Maslow's definition of self-actualisation is that it is a process whereby each person strives to become what they are actually intended to be. People with specific talents like art or music, for example, must develop those abilities in order to be psychologically healthy and at peace with themselves. The need to self-actualise may, of course, take various forms. These include excellence in sport, success in parenting or caring for others, or indeed achievement in any other personal area that has meaning and importance for the individual. One difficulty clients often express in counselling is that they are unable (for various reasons) to develop the skills and natural talents they feel they possess. This inability to fulfil potential can cause a great deal of suffering. Some aspects of this problem have been discussed earlier in this unit in the section dealing with Rogers' concept of self-actualisation.

Self-actualising people

Maslow studied a group of healthy people, in order to identify their characteristics and to show how they differed from other, less fulfilled, individuals. Maslow described his work as 'a study of psychological health' (Maslow, 1970: 125) and selected his subjects from his personal acquaintances and friends. However, he also included a selection of public and historical figures that he studied through biography. Among these were the philosopher Spinoza, Aldous Huxley, Eleanor Roosevelt, Abraham Lincoln and Thomas Jefferson. Maslow's study points to several significant characteristics his selected group of people seemed to share. These include the following:

- the ability to perceive reality clearly; this includes the ability to judge people and situations accurately
- acceptance of self and of others; this includes acceptance of one's own human nature, without too much concern about personal shortcomings
- spontaneity in thinking and behaviour, as well as a sense of humour
- the capacity to be problem-centred rather than ego-centred; this means the ability to look outside oneself to the problems of the wider world
- a quality of detachment and an ability to be self-contained when alone
- the ability to resist cultural pressure without being deliberately unconventional
- the capacity to appreciate the good things of life, including everyday experience
- the capacity for heightened or transcendent experience
- interest in social issues and the welfare of other people
- the ability to form deep and satisfying relationships, although these may not be as numerous as those of other people
- originality and creativity and a willingness to experiment with new ideas
- the ability to tolerate uncertainty.

The significance of Maslow's work in relation to counselling

Maslow is at pains to point out that the self-actualising people he describes are, in fact, also imperfect in many ways. Many of these people are, he says, sometimes 'boring, irritating, petulant, selfish, angry or depressed' (Maslow, 1970: 147). These qualifications are helpful, since they indicate that Maslow's self-actualising people are, after all, human. Without these qualifications it would be impossible to look at the qualities listed without feeling slightly intimidated by them. However, what Maslow proposes is that there are people who are capable of developing their potential to a very high level, while at the same time remaining essentially human. This, of course, highlights the point that a great many people never achieve this kind of development, and there are others whose innate potential is inhibited for a variety of reasons.

There are many reasons for this kind of inhibition; clients who come into counselling frequently exhibit some, if not all, of them. If we look at the list again, it becomes clear that the qualities Maslow describes are strikingly absent when people are distressed or emotionally upset, as clients often are. Distressed people find it very difficult to tolerate uncertainty, for example, and they frequently lack spontaneity, creativity and a sense of humour. Perceptions of reality may be very distorted, while acceptance of self and others may be lacking too. Autonomy and self-reliance are easily impaired when problems seem insurmountable, and relationships with other people, if not actually the cause of difficulties, may well suffer as a result of them. Appreciation of life experience is often diminished, and there may be no interest whatever in wider social issues. Transcendent or heightened experiences, which are in any case associated with psychological wellbeing, may be non-existent during a time of crisis or emotional upheaval. However, implicit in the work of both Maslow and Rogers is the belief that people can be helped to overcome their problems, so that some measure of self-actualisation can then be achieved.

One way of helping people to realise their potential is through a truly therapeutic relationship, although this is by no means the only route to self-actualisation. In the next section, we shall look at some of the experiences and relationships Maslow believed could help people to achieve maximum development and fulfillment.

Psychotherapy and other helping relationships

Maslow points out that 'psychotherapy has always existed' in one form or another (Maslow, 1970: 94); these forms of helping include shamanic healing, religion, the physician and the wise man or woman within communities. Common to all is the ability to help people heal themselves, and Maslow outlines what he believes to be the therapeutic characteristics of such relationships. He also highlights the point that many people are helped by untrained workers, who are, nevertheless, often effective in the work they do. These untrained therapists may include nurses, teachers, social workers, psychology graduates, and so on. This is not to suggest that counselling and therapy training is superfluous; on the contrary, it should encourage us to look more closely at those skills and natural abilities which effective helpers do possess. We have already considered some of these qualities in Unit 1, but it is worth reflecting on Maslow's views in this context. In Maslow's opinion, clients appear to make more progress when the following factors are present in the helping relationship:

- the helper shows real interest in the client, and a willingness to listen
- there is obvious concern for the client
- the helper's efforts are clear to the client, which assures the client that he is worthwhile as a person
- the client feels safe and protected, and feelings of vulnerability and anxiety are diminished
- there is an absence of judgmentalism on the helper's part
- the helper is accepting
- the helper is frank and encouraging

- the helper is kind
- the client perceives that the helper is on his or her side
- the client feels the helper's respect.

(Maslow 1970: 96–97)

EXERCISE

Maslow's helping factors

Working individually, look at Maslow's list of helping factors. In the light of what you have learned so far about counselling, are there any other helping skills or conditions that you would add to this? Discuss with other members of your group.

The helper's attitude

Maslow makes the further point that it is not what is said or done by the helper that seems to make the difference. Rather, it is the presence of certain helper attitudes, unconsciously transmitted, which appear to encourage clients in the process of therapy. There is a close similarity between attitudes discussed by Maslow and those proposed by Carl Rogers in the person-centred approach. If we analyse Maslow's attitudes, we can see that he refers to Rogerian-type conditions, which are implicit in terms such as interest, frankness, accepting, respect, concern and absence of judgmentalism. Furthermore, the idea that the helper's partiality should be perceived by the client is one that clearly echoes the Rogerian concepts of unconditional positive regard and empathy.

The only skill mentioned by Maslow is that of listening. This also ties in with Rogers' (1951) view that therapeutic progress results from the relationship between client and counsellor and may have little to do with any verbal exchanges between them. There are clear implications here for counselling and counsellor training, since it illustrates the importance of self-development and self-awareness as prerequisites for admission to, and progress through, any training programme. Counselling skills can certainly be learned, but personal characteristics are much more difficult to acquire and sustain.

Therapeutic life experience

It is worth pointing out once again that therapy and counselling are not the only helping activities that facilitate change when people are in crisis or emotional distress. Maslow reminds us that helpers from diverse backgrounds are also effective in these situations, some of which have been mentioned in this section. As well as the helping relationships discussed, however, Maslow also points to the fact that certain life experiences are in themselves therapeutic. Among these are 'good human relationships', education, job satisfaction, creative activities, family security and 'loving and being loved' (Maslow, 1970: 97–8). However, Maslow concedes that certain clients, especially those who suffer from long-term and intractable problems, need the kind of help which can only be given by trained therapists or counsellors. Furthermore, he is concerned to point out that it should be possible to extend such training to those untrained professionals who already work effectively with clients. This is, in fact, what is currently happening in many areas like social work, nursing, occupational therapy, teaching and church ministry.

CASE STUDY

Shirley

In the space of six months both my elderly parents died. At the time I was also changing jobs, and my partner, who was abroad, had his work contract extended. This meant he wouldn't get home for another three months, so along with the stress of my new job and the double bereavement, I felt, mistakenly as it turned out, that I would have to cope with all this on my own. However, I am really fortunate to have good friends, two of whom are particularly close, and they supported me and listened to me when I was at my lowest ebb. This helped me enormously, and when my partner returned he was supportive as well. I don't think I could have survived all those stresses without the help of my friends, my partner and members of my family. Later on though, I went for bereavement counselling because I was troubled by some aspects of my relationship with my mother. I knew I couldn't confide in family or friends about these worries, as they were too private and personal.

Comment: This case study, recounted by Shirley, illustrates a point made by Maslow. His research led him to conclude that there are other forms of helping aside from psychotherapy. Maslow suggests that the experience of friendship and secure relationships are in themselves therapeutic. However, he did concede that there may be a conflict of interests in some close relationships, and this is a point that we also highlighted in Unit 1. Shirley was helped and supported by her family and friends, but she reached a point later on when she needed to talk to someone who was not emotionally involved with her or her family.

The existential approach

The existential approach is one which, more than any other, stresses the individual's capacity for freedom and choice. Earlier in this unit we noted that psychology had, until the middle of the twentieth century, been dominated by two major ideological traditions. The first tradition was that of scientific behaviourism, while the second was Freudian psychoanalysis. Gradually, however, a new tradition began to emerge, whose adherents, including Maslow and Rogers, were convinced of the limitations of behaviourism and psychoanalysis. Behaviourism, with its view that freedom is restricted by social and cultural conditioning was, in their opinion, a limiting one. By the same token, the psychodynamic explanation that unconscious forces also restrict the ability to make free and informed choices seemed limiting too. Behaviourism and psychoanalysis did not, as far as Rogers and Maslow were concerned, acknowledge important human qualities like creativity, self-actualisation, self-awareness, love, choice and freedom. By 1950 they had established a new force in psychology, which they called humanistic psychology; this later became known as the third force. Many of the ideas expressed by Rogers and his colleagues are similar to those enshrined in the existential approach to therapy. These include the qualities already mentioned, as well as an emphasis on the need to value the unique and subjective world of the individual.

Further background information

Existential psychotherapy is influenced by the philosophy of existentialism. This philosophical tradition is, in turn, associated with the work of Kierkegaard, Nietzsche, Heidegger and Sartre. These philosophers were concerned with the meaning of human existence and with the concepts of free will, subjectivity and the nature of individual experience. It can be seen, therefore, that humanism and existentialism are closely allied.

In the context of psychotherapy, the existential tradition was established first in Europe, and later emerged as a theoretical approach among certain psychologists in America. In both countries, however, existentialism and psychotherapy were seen to have much in common. Rollo May (1986) makes the point that both these concepts are concerned with people in crisis. Important figures in the European therapy movement include Luwig Binswanger and Medard Boss, while those within the American tradition include Rollo May, Otto Rank, Karen Horney, Erich Fromm and Irvin Yalom. Within the European therapy framework, the emphasis has always been on the need to face anxiety, uncertainty and the prospect of death. In contrast to this, the humanistic–existential approach in America tended to be more concerned with the development of human potential, self-awareness, a holistic view of the person, the importance of meaningful relationships and the possibility of transcendent experience. Irvin Yalom points out that many of the humanistic and anti-intellectual trends in America were effective in causing a split between humanistic psychology and members of the academic community who were interested in existential issues (Yalom, 1980). Although the humanistic and existential approaches in therapy are now identified as separate, they still have much in common, and humanistic psychologists like Rogers and Maslow retain their association with existential concerns.

The British existential psychiatrist R.D. Laing was another significant contributor to this field, although his focus was somewhat different in the sense that his special interest was schizophrenia. Laing's views were controversial and include, among other things, the belief that people who suffer from severe mental illness may have a clearer grasp of reality than those who do not (Laing and Esterson, 1990). Orthodox psychiatry takes the contrasting view that schizophrenia sufferers are at odds with reality.

The existential view of the person

In contrast to Freudian theory, which is based on the premise that human behaviour is determined by unconscious forces and past events, the existential approach assumes that people are free and responsible for their own choices and behaviour. According to the theory, human beings cannot, therefore, escape the necessity of dealing with, and making sense of, existence. The unconscious is certainly acknowledged in existential psychotherapy, but it is not viewed as a repository of culturally unacceptable impulses and desires. On the contrary, it is seen as an often neglected area of human potential which, according to Rollo May, is sometimes difficult for people to actualise (May, 1986). From an existential perspective, fear and anxiety result from an individual's awareness, albeit at an unconscious level that such potential exists and is being neglected. Anxiety or angst is an important concept in existentialism; it refers to feelings of dread that are associated with extreme threat. Perhaps the greatest threat of all is contained in the knowledge that we are indeed free, and if this is true then it follows that we are entirely responsible for how we act and what we do. The first principle of existentialism, in the words of Jean-Paul Sartre, is that 'man is nothing else but that which he makes of himself' (Sartre, 1987: 221). This may seem like a bleak proposition, but it is a fundamental idea in existentialism.

Application to clients

A central goal of the existential approach to therapy is to help clients become more personally authentic. Authenticity is a prominent theme in the approach; it refers to the individual's ability to define who they are and what they feel. The person who is not authentic accepts, without question, that it is others, including family, culture and religion that are responsible for this important definition. Alienation is seen as a direct result of allowing oneself to become separated or detached from personal experience.

The four dimensions of human experience are the physical, the social, the psychological and the spiritual (Avery, 1996). Physical experiences include our relationship with all our basic needs and with the world around us. Our social experience encompasses our relationships with other people, while our psychological experience is concerned with the way we feel about ourselves and our personal identity. Finally, experience of spirituality describes the individual's relationship with the transcendent, the mysterious or the unknown.

It can be seen from these descriptions that clients do indeed have frequent problems in relation to them. Many clients recount experiences of alienation in relation to themselves and others, while some may feel despair and loss of purpose in life. Isolation and meaninglessness are further problems described by some clients, and these are among the themes highlighted in the existential approach to therapy. Certain significant life stages may also precipitate crises which prompt clients to seek help through psychotherapy and counselling. These include adolescence, mid-life and old age. Other experiences, including bereavement, redundancy or divorce may also act as catalysts for change or a search for meaning. The following case study illustrates this last point.

CASE STUDY

Searching for meaning

Mrs Jackson, who was in her early 50s, took early retirement to care for her elderly mother, who was dying. Her relationship with her mother had not been good in childhood, and she hoped to redress the balance by forming a more positive bond before her mother died. Mrs Jackson had spent her life caring for other people. Although she was an intelligent woman she had not gained any satisfactory educational qualifications. She lived with her husband, who had separate interests, while their three children, who were now adults, had left home. Mrs Jackson found the task of nursing her mother much more difficult than she had expected, and the relationship between them did not improve. After her mother's death, Mrs Jackson moved house with her husband, and six months later their new home was burgled. She described her experiences to the counsellor.

CLIENT: About two days after the break-in I started to cry and couldn't stop. It was just as if I could take no more . . . first my mother . . . then the move, and now this.

COUNSELLOR: It all seemed like too much . . . and in such a short space of time.

CLIENT: Yes that's right. And then . . . and then to make it all the more frightening, I found that I didn't believe in anything any more.

COUNSELLOR: You lost your faith.

CLIENT: I always relied on my faith in God's will. But how can God have willed this? [starts to cry]

COUNSELLOR: That is a frightening thought for you . . . To have lost so much, and now to feel that you have lost your faith too.

CLIENT: It's terrifying . . . I can't tell you what it's like. It's as if the ground has opened up beneath my feet. I don't know where I am any more.

COUNSELLOR: Nothing makes sense to you any more . . .

Counselling skills

The counsellor worked with this client, in order to help her explore her feelings in relation to her mother's death. Mrs Jackson experienced despair and outrage following the break-in at her new home, and these feelings were also discussed in counselling. After several sessions it became clear that other disturbing issues were causing concern for the client; she was preoccupied with ideas of her own mortality and with her inability to accept her mother's uncaring attitude towards her when she was a child. She also felt guilty that she had not helped her mother more and blamed her husband for his inability to support her emotionally after her mother's death. The counsellor was concerned to understand the client's subjective experience or internal frame of reference, and, in this respect, the existential approach is similar to Rogers' person-centred view of the helper's role in therapy.

In order to achieve these goals, the counsellor used the skills of active listening, clarification of content and meaning, asking relevant and open questions, and encouraging the client to look more closely at all her beliefs, both past and present, so that she could identify her own inner feelings in relation to these. Throughout her whole life, Mrs Jackson had behaved in a way she thought would please her mother. In fact, this had never worked; and now that her mother was dead, Mrs Jackson realised that she was free to be herself. This realisation of freedom was, in itself, frightening, and this fear presented her with the greatest challenge for the future. A fundamental task for the counsellor was to encourage the client to listen to herself, an exercise that many clients find difficult to undertake. There are no specific techniques in existential therapy, but counsellors who are interested in it need to be skilled in a wide variety of techniques that may be used in other approaches. Existential psychotherapy is often referred to as an intellectual approach, so knowledge of philosophy, psychology and literature are prerequisites for anyone wishing to undertake training in it. The person of the therapist is important as well; and in this approach, more than in any other, self-knowledge is essential.

EXERCISE

Ultimate concerns

In existential therapy certain important human concerns are highlighted. Yalom (1980: 8–10) lists four 'ultimate concerns', which, according to him, underlie all existential conflict. These four major concerns are as follows:

1 Death

2 Freedom

3 Isolation

4 Meaninglessness.

(Yalom, 1980)

Working in groups of three to four, discuss these concerns, focusing on the ways in which each of them may cause tension and conflict at different stages of life. How may a helper's inability to confront these issues at a personal level affect the therapeutic relationship?

EXERCISE

Individual freedom

We tend to think of freedom as a wholly positive concept. However, in the existential sense, freedom has a different meaning and refers to the absence of external structure or security. Working individually, consider the ways in which freedom of choice can cause problems for clients in counselling. What are the factors which inhibit the individual's ability to choose? Afterwards, discuss your views with members of the class group.

Relationship between counsellor and client

The therapeutic relationship is the most important factor in the existential approach. It is much more significant than skills or techniques; although this probably applies to any theoretical model, it is certainly emphasised by practitioners of existential therapy. Irvin Yalom, for example, in referring to the relationship between client and counsellor, observes that a positive encounter is 'positively related to therapy outcome' (Yalom, 1980: 401). From both the client's and counsellor's point of view, therefore, the relationship should be real and genuine, which means that the counsellor should concentrate on the quality of the encounter, rather than on the application of techniques designed to help solve specific problems. In order to establish this kind of rapport with the client, the counsellor must first be interested in him or her, and in the story he or she wishes to communicate. This means being receptive and sensitive to all aspects of the client's communication, both verbal and non-verbal.

Rigid theoretical views tend to work against this kind of receptiveness and interest, since they frequently inhibit real person-to-person contact. The experience of true human contact and understanding is what benefits clients most; this experience often convinces them that they are indeed valuable and capable of sustaining not just this relationship, but others as well.

The concept of transference is addressed within the existential approach, but any preoccupation with it, or specific focus on it, is viewed as an impediment to an authentic person-to-person encounter. According to Yalom, 'a singular focus on transference impedes therapy' and shifts attention away from the here-and-now relationship between client and therapist. It also encourages a preoccupation with the client's relationships from the past and minimises the importance of working fully in the present (Yalom, 1980: 413).

Clients who benefit from this approach

The existential approach to therapy is appropriate for clients who are concerned about meaning, or loss of meaning, in their own lives. Attitudes to personal freedom and to isolation and loneliness are also addressed from this theoretical perspective. There are a great many clients who do, in fact, suffer from feelings of isolation and alienation, some of whom would probably benefit from this approach. The experience of isolation and separateness arouses immense anxiety, and such experience may indeed be what Eric Fromm calls the 'source of all anxiety' (Fromm, 1995: 7). If clients are to benefit from the approach, however, they need to be committed to it. The aim of existential therapy is not to change people, but to help them accept themselves and to face, with courage, the major issues which concern them and brought them for help in the first place. Clients who are interested in personal growth and greater self-awareness should also benefit from this perspective. Some of the basic concepts of existential therapy can be integrated with other models and, in this way, problems relating to developmental crises, for example, may be addressed. These include issues which arise at certain times, or at certain stages of life. Adolescence, mid-life, retirement, redundancy, illness, disability and divorce are examples. Existential therapy is also sometimes applicable in brief therapy and in certain crisis situations, once the initial trauma phase is over. It can be used in either individual or groupwork settings and is appropriate for use in family therapy too.

Some limitations

Perhaps the most important point to make about existential therapy is that counsellors who use it should be interested in its concepts and the philosophical tradition from which it stems. Clients who are also interested in existential therapy may seek out practitioners of it. On the other hand, there are clients who are not versed in the theory of existentialism but who benefit anyway. This is because effective counselling and psychotherapy should be tailored to the needs of individual clients, regardless of the theories behind it. It is quite possible for counsellors who are informed by existentialism and its concerns to work with clients in an accessible way. The language of existentialism is fairly esoteric and some clients may not understand it. Existential concepts tend to appeal to people with an intellectual orientation, but this does not mean that it cannot also encompass emotional issues. The types of insights it offers may not be useful to people who are in poverty, dispossessed, homeless or suffering from mental illness. Certain environmental factors may limit personal options, so it may be difficult for people in any of these groups to feel they have the type of choices the existential focus suggests.

Transpersonal psychology

Another significant approach to helping clients has emerged since the early 1970s. This approach, called transpersonal psychology or transpersonal therapy, is also sometimes referred to as a fourth branch of psychology, since it follows on from the Freudian, behavioural and humanistic approaches. In addition, transpersonal counselling and psychotherapy incorporates many elements of humanistic, Jungian and existential psychology. Another important dimension of the transpersonal approach in counselling and psychotherapy is a focus on spirituality (Rowan, 2005). There is an implicit understanding that therapy must facilitate each person's total experience, including different states of consciousness, awareness of a higher or spiritual self, and a connectedness to something transcendent or 'transpersonal'. The word transpersonal means 'beyond the personal' and denotes an acceptance that each person is complex, with many layers of experience, many of which are outside the merely personal or material. There is a close connection here with Jung's concept of the collective unconscious, which points to a layer of human experience shared by everyone.

Consideration of the spiritual dimension is not an entirely new idea in counselling and psychotherapy. All major approaches accept that clients have different levels of experience that are individual to them and should be respected and acknowledged. However, the transpersonal approach is different in that it highlights spiritual experience and openly discusses it. Transpersonal psychology could, therefore, be described as a uniquely metaphysical approach, and one that gives permission to incorporate an aspect of human experience formerly neglected. It should be added that transpersonal psychology is not a specifically religious approach, though it does recognise the transcendent experiences which people of different religions sometimes have.

A central focus of transpersonal counselling and psychotherapy is integration of every aspect of each client's experience. There is an emphasis, too, on self-actualisation and personal empowerment. It can be seen, therefore, that transpersonal therapy has much in common with the person-centred and humanistic approaches of Maslow and Rogers, both of which stress these aspects of client development.

Clients who benefit from this approach

Counsellors and psychotherapists who are informed by the transpersonal approach use the range of skills described in Unit 2. They also use a variety of other techniques with individual clients. These skills and techniques include guided imagery, meditation, creative therapies and working with dreams, to name just a few. Accredited practitioners work with clients in both individual and group settings. Client problems include eating disorders, bereavement, self-harm, relationship difficulties, life-threatening illness and sexual problems.

Some limitations

In common with every other approach to helping clients, transpersonal psychology is not without its critics. The emphasis on a spiritual dimension of human experience is problematic for some people, though it is difficult to see how such a reservation would interfere with any therapist's willingness to work with particular clients. However, the reservation about working with a spiritual perspective is not applicable, obviously, to those counsellors and psychotherapists who specifically choose the transpersonal approach as their preferred way of working with clients. Those students who are interested in learning more about transpersonal psychology and therapy should refer to the list of books for further reading given at the end of this unit, along with relevant websites and other resources.

EXERCISE

Personal experience and spiritual awareness

Working in pairs, discuss your understanding of the term spiritual awareness. Does it have meaning for you and, if so, how is it is shown in your personal experience?

SUMMARY

In this unit we looked at the concepts of phenomenology and humanism in relation to counselling. The person-centred and existential approaches were discussed in some detail, and the work and influence of Maslow was highlighted. In addition, we included a section on transpersonal psychology and therapy, with an emphasis on its transcendent or spiritual focus. Comparisons were made between these models and the psychodynamic approaches dealt with in the previous units. The nature and importance of the therapeutic relationship was highlighted within each approach, and the concept of transference and its various interpretations was also considered. The need for adequate training in all aspects of theory and practice was emphasised, and some of the difficulties in the existential perspective were outlined. We looked at the benefits and limitations of each theoretical model, and considered the counselling situation in which each might work effectively for clients.

In this unit, we also discussed in some detail the effectiveness of person-centred counselling with elderly clients and older people who find themselves in the role of carer for ill or disabled relatives. In addition, a selection of research projects, indicating the importance of person-centred communication in these contexts, was included. The central role of training for health and social care staff was highlighted, along with the difficulties in achieving this without the involvement of staff at all levels. Commitment to the concept of person-centred care was seen as a prerequisite for senior as well as junior staff. The problem of organisational or bureaucratic structures that could impede adequate training was indicated as a possibility in any large organisation.

References

Avery, B. (1996) *Principles of Psychotherapy*. London: Thorsons.

Cooper, M. (2008) *Essential Research Findings in Counselling and Psychotherapy*. London: Sage Publications.

Fromm, E. (1995) *The Art of Loving*. London: Thorsons.

Innes, A., Macpherson, S. & McCabe, L. (2006) *Promoting Person-Centred Care at the Front Line*. York: Joseph Rowntree Foundation.

Laing, R. D. (1990) *The Politics of Experience and The Bird of Paradise*. London: Penguin Books.

Laing, R. D. & Esterson, A. (1990) *Sanity, Madness and the Family*. London: Penguin Books.

Manley, K. et al. (2011) 'Person-centred care: Principle of Nursing Practice D'. *Nursing Standard* (online) 25, 31, 35–37. Available at: http://nursingstandard.rcnpublishing.co.uk/resources/archive. Accessed July 2013.

Maslow, A. (1970) *Motivation and Personality* (3rd edn). New York: HarperCollins.

May, R. (1986) *The Discovery of Being*. New York: W. W. Norton & Co.

McCormack, B. & McCance, T. (2010) *Person-Centred Nursing: Theory and Practice*. Oxford: Wiley-Blackwell.

Quinodoz, D. (2010) *Growing Old: A Journey of Self-Discovery*. London: Routledge.

Rogers, C. (1939) *The Clinical Treatment of the Problem Child*. Boston: Houghton Mifflin Co.

Rogers, C. (1951) *Client Centred Therapy*. London: Constable (1991).

Rogers, C. (1957) 'The Necessary and Sufficient Conditions of Therapeutic Personality Change', *Journal of Consulting Psychology,* 21, 95–103.

Rogers, C. (1961) *On Becoming a Person*. London: Constable (1993).

Rogers, C. (1980) *A Way of Being*. New York: Houghton Mifflin Company.

Rogers, C. (1996) *The Carl Rogers Reader* (ed.) Kirschenbaum, H. & Henderson, V. London: Constable.

Rowan, J. (2005) *The Transpersonal: Spirituality in Psychotherapy and Counselling*. London: Routledge.

Sartre, J. (1987) 'Freedom and Bad Faith', in Hanfling, O. (ed.) *Life and Meaning: A Reader*. Oxford: Blackwell in association with the Open University.

The Princess Royal Trust for Carers (2011) *Always Concerned, Always on Call: A Survey of the Experiences of Older Carers*. Essex: The Princess Royal Trust for Carers.

Von Humboldt, S. & Leal, I. (2012) 'Building Bridges: Person-Centred Therapy with Older Adults'. Instituto Universitario, Portugal: *European Journal of Business and Social Sciences* (online) 12th November, 1, 8, 23–32. Available at: http://www.ejbss.com. Accessed May 2013.

Yalom, I. D. (1980) *Existential Psychotherapy*. New York: Basic Books.

Further reading

Casemore, R. (2011) *Person-Centred Counselling in a Nutshell* (2nd edn). London: Sage Publications.

Cooper, M. (2003) *Existential Therapies*. London: Sage Publications.

Lines, D. (2006) Spirituality in Counselling and Psychotherapy. London: Sage Publications.

Mearns, D. & Thomas, B. (2007) *Person-Centred Counselling in Action* (3rd edn). London: Sage Publications.

O'Farrell, U. (2004) *Considering Counselling: The Person-centred Approach.* Dublin: Veritas.

Portner, M. (2008) *Being Old is Different: Person-Centred Care for Older People.* Ross-on-Wye: PCCS Books.

Rogers, C. (2003) *Client Centred Therapy*. London: Constable.

Thorne, B. (2002) *The Mystical Power of Person-Centred Therapy*. London: Whurr Publishers.

Tudor, K. & Worrall, M. (2006) *Person-Centred Therapy*: A Clinical Philosophy. Hove: Routledge Taylor & Francis Group.

Van Deurzen-Smith, E. (2002) *Existential Counselling and Psychotherapy in Practice* (2nd edn). London: Sage Publications.

Wellings, N. & Wilde McCormick, E. (2004) *Transpersonal Psychotherapy*. London: Sage Publications.

Wilkins, P. (2003) *Person-Centred Therapy in Focus*. London: Sage Publications.

Resources

www.transpersonalcentre.co.uk
The Centre for Transpersonal Psychology. A member of the Humanistic and Integrative Psychology section of the United Kingdom Council for Psychotherapy (UKCP).

www.bapca.org.uk
The British Association for the Person-centred Approach.

www.existential-therapy.com
Links to various sites offering theory and topics for discussion.

www.maslow.com
The official Maslow publications site.

www.carlrogers.net
General information about Carl Rogers.

www.carlrogers.info
Resources for students, researchers and practitioners.

www.psychotherapydvds.com/rogers
Carl Rogers in interview.

6

Gestalt therapy and psychodrama

◆ Introduction

This unit is concerned with two models of therapy, which are often referred to as active and experiential. Although quite different in many respects, both Gestalt therapy and psychodrama share the premise that people come to know themselves best through direct experience. There are other similarities between these two approaches, including the fact that both are commonly practised in groupwork settings, with individual clients receiving individual therapy within the group. In addition, Gestalt therapy and psychodrama are sometimes described as existential models, and both stem from the humanistic tradition, which places a great deal of emphasis on the uniqueness and creative potential of each person.

However, the differences between Gestalt therapy and psychodrama are also quite marked. Perhaps the most significant point of difference between the two models concerns the way in which group members participate, for example in psychodrama, but remain as spectators in Gestalt groupwork. Fritz Perls, one of the founders of Gestalt therapy, highlighted this difference in his book *Gestalt Therapy Verbatim* (1969). Here he referred to the practice of group participation in psychodrama and made it quite clear that this was a faulty method (Perls, 1969). This criticism, together with others, will be discussed in this unit, along with details of the various skills, techniques and underlying philosophies that are peculiar to each model.

KEY TERMS

Gestalt: The word 'gestalt', which is German, means a pattern, shape or configuration. In Gestalt therapy it applies to a person's whole or complete sensory experience which is seen as more important than the parts of that experience in deciding meaning. Gestalt psychology states that *the whole is greater than the sum of its parts*.

Psychodrama: This refers to the exploration of emotions and situations through actions in a supportive therapeutic environment. When emotions are explored in this way feelings tend to surface quickly, and are re-experienced in a way which leads to new learning.

Gestalt therapy: Fritz Perls (1893–1970)

Fritz Perls, a founder of Gestalt therapy, was trained as both psychiatrist and psychoanalyst in pre-war Germany. His wife, Laura, a psychologist, was jointly responsible for developing the work, although Fritz Perls' name is commonly associated with it. Perhaps one of the reasons for this credit imbalance is that Fritz Perls was a charismatic, dynamic and colourful character, who certainly impressed those people who met him. He appears to have cultivated a particular style that blended well with the mood of his time. M. V. Miller, who met him in 1966, describes, in his introduction to *Gestalt Therapy Verbatim*, Perls' style and impact in the way he conducted his seminars (Miller, 1988). From this description, it is quite clear that Perls did not conform to the image of the classical Freudian psychoanalyst, which is, in fact, what he actually was. Perls, who was born in Berlin, completed his psychoanalytic training and was influenced by many of the major figures in psychoanalysis, including Freud, Rank and Jung. Like many other Jewish psychoanalysts, he was forced to leave Germany when the Nazis rose to power; and, in 1933, he went to Johannesburg with his wife Laura. Later, in 1946, he left South Africa and emigrated to New York. From here he made his way to California. Perls was influenced by all the trends of the 1960s, including the peace movement, flower power, drugs, meditation, Zen Buddhism and the cult of the guru. There was no doubt that this was an exciting time for anyone interested in humanistic psychology and therapy, though Perls, who was a colourful character himself, did not subscribe to the idea of therapy 'jazzing' up just for the sake of novelty (Perls, 1969). He was concerned to point out that the Gestalt approach does not rely on quick-fix solutions but is a serious, though different, form of therapy, designed to promote human growth and potential – processes that require time, dedication and skill.

Other influences

In developing Gestalt, Perls was also influenced by his association with Dr Kurt Goldstein, whom he had met in the 1920s. During this time, Perls worked at the Institute for Brain-Damaged Soldiers in Frankfurt, where Goldstein, a neuropsychiatrist had pioneered a 'holistic' approach to caring for people. Fritz Perls' wife, Laura, a Gestalt psychologist, was another significant influence on his work. Perls was further impressed by the achievements of a group of psychologists, including Max Wertheimer, Kurt Koffka and Wolfgang Kohler. These psychologists formed what came to be known as the Gestalt School of Psychology.

Finally, the work pioneered by J.L. Moreno in the 1920s, and which later came to be known as psychodrama, was in some respects a forerunner of Gestalt therapy. This approach is the subject of the second part of this unit, but it should be emphasised that Gestalt terminology owes much to Moreno and his revolutionary work. The term 'here and now', for example, is one which has special meaning in Gestalt therapy, though it is certainly derived from Moreno's reference to the 'now and here' (Zinker, 1978).

Origin of the word 'Gestalt'

The word 'gestalt' is a German one and means pattern, shape, form or configuration. Christian Von Ehrenfels (1859–1932), an Austrian psychologist, was the first person to use the term. He described the pattern or shape that is characteristic of a whole structure, and which is absent in any of its constituent parts. Later on, in 1912, Koffka, Kohler and Wertheimer founded the Gestalt School of Berlin and studied the organisation of mental processes, with special reference to the importance of perception in determining each person's view of reality. As a result of their work, Wertheimer and his colleagues formulated a set of theories that considered the manner in which people organise stimuli into patterns and shapes. According to Gestalt theory, people are concerned to create meaning in their lives, so the whole pattern of each person's sensory experience is seen as more important than the individual elements of that experience in deciding meaning. An illustration of this principle of perceptual organisation is the way in which we see a picture or hear music, for example. When we look at a picture we see it as a coherent whole, rather than as a set of random colours and shapes. Our response to music is the same. We do not hear all the individual notes, which make up the harmony; instead we perceive the totality of the music, or the overall tune. This awareness of structure and form gives meaning to experience and, according to the Gestalt psychologists, all our perceptions are similarly organised.

The Gestalt approach was in many ways a reaction against some of the limitations of other schools. Behaviourism, for example, is concerned to break up complex mental processes into simple conditioned reflexes – a view that is certainly the opposite of Gestalt theory. Perls took up the ideas expressed in Gestalt theory and emphasised the point that each person's experience of reality is dependent on how she or he perceives the world (Perls, 1992). This idea is similar to Rogers' person-centred philosophy and has further echoes in the work of Maslow, for example.

Figure and ground

Perls drew upon the principles of perceptual organisation, first described by the Gestalt psychologists, and incorporated these into Gestalt therapy. The Gestalt psychologists were interested in external perceptions and were especially concerned with the way in which people deal with visual and auditory experience. Perls, on the other hand, was interested in the ways in which people deal with more complex internal experiences and the issue of how each person becomes aware of individual needs in relation to the environment. In this context the environment refers, of course, to other people as well as to things. According to Perls' theory, it is necessary for people to be fully aware of all aspects of themselves, including their defences. If this awareness is not present, psychological growth is impaired and symptoms will appear.

The word 'figure' in Gestalt theory refers to a person's need at any given time. Those needs may be relatively simple ones like hunger and thirst, but they also include emotional, relationship and esteem needs. People obviously experience different needs at different times, but when an individual is functioning well in relation to the total environment, each need is clearly seen against the background or ground of awareness. Needs continually emerge and become figures against the background of awareness, and the individual's task is to deal with the most important need as it emerges. When needs are dealt with in this way, they fade into the background and other pressing needs appear. In Gestalt theory this process is referred to as the formation and destruction of Gestalts. Figure and ground form a pattern or whole, which is known as a Gestalt. A simple example of the way in which needs emerge and are dealt with is outlined in the following scenario.

CASE STUDY

Figure and ground

Marian got up late and went to work without eating breakfast. She had been stressed the night before, because her five-year-old child had a temperature and was clearly unable to attend school. Throughout the morning, at work, Marian felt hungry and slightly unwell. She found it difficult to cope without food and, although she also worried about her daughter, she was constantly aware of the empty and queasy sensation in her stomach. In this situation, Marian's current physical needs controlled her experience, and it wasn't until she managed to eat in the canteen that she was able to address the next most pressing need, which was information about her child. Once she had eaten, she phoned her baby-sitter and got news of her daughter's condition. After that, Marian was in a position to deal with the other pressing needs of the day. If Marian had not bee able to eat when she did, she could not have dealt effectively with other figures or needs that emerged in the course of the day. Her perceptual field would have been cluttered and confusing.

This example explains why it is that people tend to become ineffective when they are caught up in several activities and preoccupations, none of which are ever properly addressed. The same principle applies when needs are more complex, as the next example illustrates.

CASE STUDY

Unfinished business

A patient who attended his GP surgery was referred for counselling because he was depressed. The patient (Simon) had been bereaved two years earlier, when his father died of a heart attack. Since that time, Simon was unable to shake off the depression and had been taking medication for sleeplessness and anxiety. During counselling it emerged that his brother had also died ten years previously, as a result of suicide. His brother was a student at university at the time, and Simon had never been able to accept his death. In fact, he felt a great deal of guilt and responsibility in connection with it. Because of his unresolved grief about his brother, Simon could not adequately address the issue of his father's death either. In addition to this, there were other factors in Simon's life that had never been properly dealt with. His relationships were problematic, largely because (as he said himself) he was difficult and moody to live with. Simon felt drained of energy and confused about which issues he should tackle first, since his job situation was not good either. It was some time before he came to see that the unfinished business of his brother's death needed to be dealt with if the other factors were to be seen in clearer focus. In Simon's case there was a lack of purpose and clarity, which meant that he was unable to separate the important from the unimportant things in his awareness. Figure and ground had become indistinguishable as far as he was concerned.

Working through complex issues like these takes time, and later in this unit we shall look at some skills the Gestalt therapist can use to help clients deal with such problems.

EXERCISE

Becoming aware

Working individually, spend about five minutes becoming aware of your experiences at the present moment. What bodily sensations do you experience, for example? Are there any 'needs' which appear to be more pressing than others? If so, how does the pressing need affect your ability to attend to other factors in your present environment?

EXERCISE

Body awareness

Working in twos, sit silently observing each other for three to four minutes, concentrating on body language and posture. Afterwards, take turns to describe your observations of the other person. What are your feelings about your partner's observation? Is this how you see or experience yourself?

The here and now

The central focus of Gestalt therapy is on the present. Clients' present experiences, including their thoughts, feelings and actions, are – according to this approach – the most important point of interest in therapy. Even the experiences of remembering and planning are seen as present functions, regardless of the fact that they refer to the past and the future (Polster and Polster, 1974). Thus a client may be concerned about an issue from the past, but instead of focusing on a lengthy (and verbal) account of what happened a Gestalt therapist would encourage the client to experience the past in the present. The following is an example of this idea.

CLIENT: It was a very long time ago, but I remember the feeling exactly. My father would expect me to be perfect at everything, and when I wasn't I was humiliated.

COUNSELLOR: The humiliation which you describe . . . can you get in touch with that and feel it now.

CLIENT: [pausing] Yes, I can. I can feel it in my stomach like a dull sensation.

COUNSELLOR: If that sensation could talk to you, what would it say?

CLIENT: [surprised] That it is angry . . . that it wants to be rid of the humiliation for good.

It can be seen from the example that the counsellor's emphasis on present experience enabled the client to access strong feelings that would have remained outside her awareness. Other forms of counselling and therapy encourage clients to talk about their problems; and this, according to Gestalt therapists, can be counter-productive, since it leads clients away from the actual experiences they describe. It is entirely possible to talk at length about something without ever feeling any real emotion in connection with it. It is possible also for people to hang on to past experiences and emotional traumas as a way of avoiding change. This tendency, which Gestalt therapy seeks to overcome, may be encouraged (inadvertently) by other approaches. In Gestalt therapy the emphasis is on experience rather than on the counsellor's or client's interpretation of it.

Intellectualisation has always been regarded with suspicion by practitioners of Gestalt and, indeed, Fritz Perls used very strong language in condemnation of this tendency (Perls, 1969). However, in view of the fact that Gestalt is a holistic approach to the person, there is now greater recognition of intellectual and cognitive experience. Contemporary practitioners of the model are certainly less confrontative, sarcastic and cantankerous than Fritz Perls appears to have been (Miller, 1988). Gestalt therapy is quite different in many ways from some of the other theoretical models described in this book. There is an obvious contrast with the psychodynamic approach, for example, since Gestalt emphasises present experience and the here and now, while the former encourages clients to look at the past and the childhood events that have shaped their lives. Recently, however, new ideas stemming from psychodynamic object relations theory and practice are being incorporated into the Gestalt model of therapy. At the end of this unit we shall look at some of these ideas. We shall also consider other developments in Gestalt theory, which highlight its effectiveness in a range of situations.

Wholeness

The concept of 'wholeness' is an important one in Gestalt therapy; it refers to the client's total experience – physical, sensory, emotional and intellectual. Integration of all these dimensions is a central aim of therapy; and, to this end, clients are encouraged to become more aware of themselves and to work towards a healthy assimilation of all their component parts. The clients' non-verbal communication is often indicative of the real message they seek to convey, not just to the therapist but to themselves as well. Clients may, for example, express one view verbally while clearly indicating by their body language that the opposite is, in fact, the case. The following case study illustrates this point.

CASE STUDY

Eamonn

Eamonn, who was in his early 30s, received stress counselling because of problems at work and the break-up of his marriage. He did not entirely believe in counselling, but decided to try it as a last resort. His friends and relatives were unable to give him the kind of help he needed, so, on the advice of his line manager, he received counselling over a period of six sessions. In spite of his initial reservations, Eamonn found the experience helpful. At first he had some difficulty in expressing his feelings, and the counsellor who worked with him used a Gestalt approach to help him. Eamonn was emphatic that he has recovered from his marriage break-up, but the counsellor noted that his body language was incongruent with this verbally expressed statement.

CLIENT:	I am over the worst of it and I don't have grudges against Siân.
COUNSELLOR:	I would like you to become aware for a moment, of your left hand and what you are doing with it.
CLIENT:	My hand? [slightly disconcerted] I'm holding my neck with it, my throat.
COUNSELLOR:	And what is it you throat wants to express.
CLIENT:	I don't know what it wants to say . . . but I know I had problems with my throat, which the doctor said were due to stress.
COUNSELLOR:	Your throat is you. Say what it is your throat is saying.
CLIENT:	[slowly, and after a pause] I can't swallow it. That's it . . . I have to say . . . I can't swallow it yet. I suppose I've been fooling myself that I could get over something like that so quickly.

It can be seen that this case study is similar to the example given to illustrate the here and now. This is because the body and the way it expresses itself is regarded as the most significant vehicle for true meaning. Gestalt therapists are aware of the fact that people often refer to their own bodies, or parts of their bodies, as if these were in some way alien or separate from them. Thus, a client might speak about parts of himself as 'they' or 'it' and, in doing so, cut himself off from immediate experience and from a vital source of knowledge and information. In his book *Care of the Soul*, Thomas Moore points out that in the body we often see 'the soul presented in its richest and most expressive form' (Moore, 1994: 153). Dress, gesture, movement, facial expression, mannerisms and tics are all indicative of inner psychological processes at work. This is why active listening, which we discussed in the early units of this book, is such an essential counsellor skill. Counsellors need to 'listen' to everything that the client expresses, which means that every form of expression needs to be monitored and observed.

EXERCISE

Language of the body

1 In groups of two to three, discuss the ways in which our inner problems may be reflected by our bodies. Has anyone in the group had personal experience of physical expression of feeling or conflict?

2 Think of your work with clients, and consider any examples of bodily expression of feeling you have observed in them.

3 When you have completed your discussion, look at the following list of physical organs and say what you think are the most obvious emotions or conflicts associated with each:

A heart

B head

C face

D limbs

E stomach

F colon.

The use of language

The way in which clients use language is another important focus of attention in Gestalt therapy. Clients can use language to distance themselves from immediate experience; they may alienate themselves through the use of 'it', 'they', 'you' or 'one' statements, instead of owning their individual feelings through the use of the personal pronouns 'I' or 'me'. A client might say, for example, 'It seemed hot and stuffy', instead of 'I was hot and bothered', when referring to an uncomfortable encounter in the past. In Gestalt therapy such a client would be encouraged to 'own' his feeling by using the personal pronoun 'I' and by bringing the experience alive in the present. For example:

CLIENT: Yes, I was hot and bothered.

COUNSELLOR: Can you experience that feeling now, at this moment?

CLIENT: At the moment? Yes I feel it . . . hot and agitated.

Another example of the Gestalt focus on language is that clients who speak quickly may be asked to repeat slowly what they have said, in order to highlight and emphasise what it is they wish to convey. Clients who speak quietly may be encouraged to become louder, while those who hesitate might be asked to stay with the hesitation to discover its possible meaning. The use of certain words is also significant in the Gestalt approach, and clients may be asked to look more closely at the words they choose. A central tenet of Gestalt therapy is that linguistic habits say a lot more about the client, regardless of what he or she is trying to convey (Polster and Polster, 1974). Communicating through jargon is another way in which people can distance themselves from others and from their own experience. The jargon that clients use in their work may be transferred by them into counselling too. When this happens, no real identification of personal feeling is possible. Some clients talk a great deal and this, in itself, is often a clue that things are carefully hidden, not only from the person who is listening, but also from the client. Language can, after all, act as a smoke-screen behind which important aspects of the real self are carefully guarded. There are many reasons for this type of defence, and in most theoretical approaches counsellors are tentative in the way they respond to these. However, the Gestalt approach is somewhat more challenging in this respect, although, as I have already indicated, contemporary practitioners are also sensitive in their responses to clients' defences.

CASE STUDY

Ria

Ria, who was in her early 50s, came into counselling through referral by her doctor. She had developed rheumatoid arthritis the year before but had never been committed to the treatment programme her doctor prescribed. The counsellor noticed at once that Ria talked about her body as if she didn't really own it.

RIA: The feet are very sore at night, and the hands really seize up in the cold.

COUNSELLOR: Could you think about that for a moment and just change it around using 'my' for your feet and hands?

RIA: My feet are very sore at night. (She pauses) Yes, my feet are agony at times. My feet are agony and my poor hands go dead in the cold.

After this exchange Ria started to cry. She looked at her hands and feet as if seeing them for the first time. During later counselling sessions, she talked about her feelings in relation to her illness and admitted that she had been in denial about its severity. She started to take care of herself more, and accepted help from her doctor and an occupational therapist. She had been very angry when she first became ill, and this led her to despise and disown her body. When she started to take ownership of her body again, she accepted the fact of her illness and gradually made some progress. Her depression and anger decreased, and the constant pain she had previously felt was substantially lessened too.

Shoulds and shouldn'ts

Clients frequently refer to behaviours, thoughts or feelings and use the words 'should and shouldn't' in relation to these. In such instances, clients may simply be repeating outmoded rules and prohibitions that are inherited from childhood. These rules and prohibitions were probably accepted without question so that their suitability, or otherwise, to adult life is never seriously considered. Perls used the terms 'topdog' and 'underdog' to refer to the conflicting parts of human personality (Perls, 1992: 38–39). This concept is analogous to Freud's theory of personality, including Superego, Ego and Id, and the intrapsychic conflict that exists within this system. 'Topdog' is defined by Perls as the righteous part of personality, while 'underdog' is insecure, manipulative, ingratiating and lacking in conviction. Topdog is, according to Perls, a judge and a bully, and people can spend a great deal of time trying to please or placate this internalised 'parent' part of personality. The pressure of always trying to please can have the damaging effect of alienating people from their own feelings. Underdog, on the other hand, is incapable of dealing in a straightforward way with topdog's demands, and frequently resorts to procrastination or rationalisation, in order to evade the strict demands being made. In Gestalt therapy the emphasis is on the integration of these conflicting parts, which means encouraging clients to accept that they are both valid parts of the self. If it is accepted by clients that both of these parts of personality can exist side by side, then pressure and conflict are diminished while insight and integration are increased.

EXERCISE

Topdog and underdog

Working individually, think of the rules (shoulds and shouldn'ts) you have carried with you since childhood. Make a list of these, and consider how many of them still cause conflict within you. When you bring these rules into conscious awareness, you begin to understand their effects upon you in the present. You can also start to look at them in a more critical way and, in doing so, lessen their inhibiting or damaging influences.

Layers of neurosis

Perls referred to the ways in which people avoid awareness of self, and described these as five layers of neurosis (Perls, 1992: 37). These layers include the phony, the phobic, the impasse, the implosive and the explosive. In Perls' view these layers of neurosis need to be stripped away if clients are to achieve psychological growth and maturity.

The first layer – the phony – refers to the clichéd or inauthentic way in which we often relate to others. One example of this inauthenticity is reflected in the social games we play and the daily rituals including small talk and role playing.

The phobic layer is the point at which we resist seeing aspects of ourselves that might cause emotional disturbance or pain. Thus aspects of the real person are denied and self-acceptance is forfeited as a result.

A feeling of nothingness or emptiness is characteristic of the impasse layer and marks an attitude of avoidance, or a sense of being stuck. At the impasse layer people seek to manipulate the environment, including others, instead of acting with maturity and accepting personal responsibility. In Perls' view, however, it is impossible to overcome difficulties by resisting them, and he regarded the impasse layer as a source of many problems in therapy (Perls, 1992: 76).

The implosive layer is activated when we allow ourselves to come into contact with feelings of deadness. Perls describes this layer as the 'death' layer, and he believed that behind it lies the explosive experience, which is, in effect, a connection or link with the 'real' or authentic person. Clients who access this layer of awareness often experience catharsis, through grief, anger, or great joy. Inability to experience appropriate feelings is a fundamental cause of emotional problems for many clients. However, catharsis on its own is not sufficient, and clients need to work through and make sense of this kind of experience. Perls pointed out that the 'growth process' takes time, the aim of Gestalt is to enable clients to become independent and to move from environmental to self-support once the layers he describes have been uncovered by them.

Resistance

In Gestalt terminology the word 'resistance' refers to the defences people use to prevent real or authentic contact with others and with the environment in general. This resistance to real contact prevents us from identifying and mobilising our own innate resources and energy. It also prevents us from utilising our reserves of energy and inhibits healthy participation in the present, or the 'here and now'. Polster and Polster (1974) list five defences, as follows:

- introjection
- projection
- retroflection
- deflection
- confluence.

The word 'introjection' refers to the internalised rules governing our thoughts, feelings and behaviour, which we absorb from parental and other influences from childhood onwards. Perls called this nagging inner voice 'topdog', a concept we discussed earlier.

The second defence, 'projection', can be defined as a process of attributing aspects of ourselves to other people, as a result of which we disown them or fail to recognise them personally. Important aspects of the self are therefore not integrated or acknowledged. One example of this tendency is highlighted when people of either sex refuse to acknowledge the feminine or masculine side of their personalities, yet express negative views about other people who are unafraid to do so (Harris and Phillipson, 1989).

'Retroflection' is a process whereby we do to ourselves what we would like to do to someone else. We may, for example, direct aggression inwards when we are fearful of directing it outwards towards others. This can result in depression or psychosomatic illness. It is also restrictive and stultifying. While

Gestalt theory does not recommend that clients should actively be aggressive towards other people, it does suggest that there are other more positive and creative ways of expressing strong feelings.

The use of deflection as a defence means that contact with others is diminished through a process of distraction. Humour and intellectualisation are two ways of avoiding real intimacy and contact. Asking questions, instead of making statements, is another way in which people can distance themselves, not just from others, but from themselves as well.

'Confluence' describes a style of relating to other people that is based on an absence of conflict, and a conviction that everyone should be in agreement. Those people who are afraid to speak for themselves may use this particular defence and, in doing so, protect against disagreement and the anxiety that might accompany it. This blending with others is negative when it precludes any recognition of one's real or personal feelings; when it is evident in therapy, clients are encouraged to focus on themselves in order to identify and express their own views.

These five defences have much in common with the Freudian defences discussed in Unit 3, although the terminology is in some cases different. However, these similarities are understandable in view of the fact that Perls trained as a psychoanalyst, although he was certainly innovatory in his approach to clients and their problems.

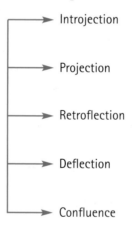

Figure 6.1 Gestalt defences indicating resistance to real contact

Dreams

In Gestalt therapy there is a special emphasis on working with clients' dreams. Perls believed that dreams were the 'royal road to integration', and he regarded dreaming as a spontaneous art form, through which the various fragmented parts of the self are expressed (Perls, 1992: 87). In Perls' view, each element of a dream represents an aspect of the dreamer, so any understanding of the dream must integrate or 'own' these projected parts. One way of doing this is to ask the dreamer to 'become' each part, or element, of the dream. This identification technique differs from techniques used in the psychodynamic model, where various parts of the dream are interpreted, usually by the dreamer, but with assistance from the therapist. In the Gestalt approach the dream is brought back to life by the client in the present. The following case study is an example of this technique.

CASE STUDY

Gestalt dreamwork

A client called Lois recounted her dream.

CLIENT: This is my dream. I am in my own bedroom at home, and I notice that a large hole has opened up around and beneath the wardrobe. I am very anxious about this and I try to draw my husband's attention to it, but he isn't listening.

COUNSELLOR: Become the wardrobe, and say what it is that the wardrobe is saying.

CLIENT: [after a long pause] I am on shaky ground and the floor is opening up beneath me. Michael [the client's husband] is not aware of what is happening.

Almost as soon as she said this the client knew what it meant. She and her husband were planning to move house, but he refused to discuss the fears she had in relation to this. The last time they moved house they had encountered many problems, and this time the client did indeed feel that she was on shaky ground. When the client explored the dream further she identified other relevant details of her relationship with her husband. These included the following:

CLIENT: I am a container for all the clothes, my husband's as well as my own. I am in charge of these and I'm keeping everything together.

The client was, in fact, keeping everything together, since she was the one in charge of the planned move.

The counsellor then asked the client to engage in a dialogue with parts of the dream, and from this exercise she was able to explore her relationship with her husband in greater depth.

COUNSELLOR: Stay as the wardrobe, and now speak to the floor.

CLIENT: You are letting me down . . . I'm sinking. I have no support.

As a result of working through this dream the client realised that she would need to find a more effective way of communicating her needs to her husband. Perls believed that dreams contained important existential messages which, if recognised and assimilated, would provide the knowledge we need to help us understand and deal with problems in our lives.

The empty chair

There are other creative Gestalt approaches that can be used to help clients become acquainted with their dreams. Clients could, for example, use a 'two-chair technique' as a means of addressing separate elements of the dream. This method involves the client sitting in one chair, while addressing a part of the dream that is 'sitting' in the other. The two-chair technique is used quite extensively in Gestalt therapy, and can be used in other contexts apart from dreamwork. A client who has been bereaved, for example, may benefit from speaking to the deceased person, who is present in another chair. This is one way in which clients can be helped to deal with complicated or unfinished grief reactions, including reactions of anger, guilt or resentment.

The client named Simon, referred to in the 'Unfinished business' case study, would probably have benefited from such an approach. Simon could also have conducted the dialogue by 'answering' for his brother who had died. Separate parts or aspects of a person can be addressed and reintegrated by means of the two-chair, or empty-chair technique. Thus a client who claims to be too anxious to socialise could be encouraged to talk to the anxious self in the opposite chair, and so on. The two-chair technique is usually effective and quite often very powerful; it should, of course, only be used by therapists and counsellors who have received adequate training in this particular approach.

It should be pointed out here, though, that this two–chair approach to helping bereaved clients may prove to be too confrontative for some. In addition, there are clients, who for cultural or, perhaps, religious reasons may consider the idea of addressing a deceased person as unacceptable.

Groupwork

Gestalt therapy is often conducted in groups and, in fact, Fritz Perls himself was in favour of groupwork as a medium for therapy. There are many benefits for clients who participate in groupwork: these include the benefits of learning through participation, as well as the practical benefit of reduced cost. However, Gestalt groups tended, in the past at least, to be different from other therapy groups. One reason for this is the way in which therapy was traditionally conducted. One member of the group was usually asked to take centre stage, while the rest of the group looked on. In his writing, Perls outlined the essential tools of groupwork, including a technique called the 'hot seat', where people are invited to sit when they wish to address a personal issue or problem (Perls, 1992: 96). In this situation, the group provides both feedback and support for the person who elects to use the seat. This approach to groupwork is one in which the therapist is placed in a central and quite powerful position. It is a role that obviously suited Fritz Perls, but the role may not be attractive to every Gestalt therapist.

Harris and Philippson (1992) outline a new model of groupwork that is quite different from the 'hot seat' model used by Perls and many others. This new model places the group, rather than the individual, centre stage. Attention is focused on group dynamics, although the experiences of individuals in the group are considered too. Such a model acknowledges the fact that many of the problems which bring people into therapy in the first place are relational or social in origin. People do not function in isolation, and contemporary Gestalt groupwork tends to reflect this fact. The Gestalt principle that the whole is more than the sum of its parts is one that can certainly be applied to therapy groups. Harris and Philippson's book, *Gestalt: Working with Groups* (1992) offers a clear and comprehensive description of their approach and should be of interest to anyone wishing to find out more about developments in Gestalt therapy.

Skills and techniques

The basic counselling skills discussed at the beginning of this book are used in the Gestalt model, as in any other. There are, however, specific creative skills that are used in Gestalt therapy, although these are never slavishly followed. Creativity is a fundamental principle of this approach and therapists usually adapt their ideas to suit the needs of individual clients. Some Gestalt therapists regard the word 'technique' as limiting and would prefer to discuss the different vehicles that can be used (Zinker, 1978). Some of these vehicles, such as dreamwork and the two chairs, have already been discussed in this unit. Others include the following:

- dialogue exercise (between topdog and underdog)
- role playing
- dialogue with opposites (these could be opposite parts of personality)
- staying with feelings (really experiencing a strong feeling which may have been evaded in the past)
- focus on language and the way it is used
- focus on the body, and what it conveys
- reliving unfinished business (incomplete gestalts)
- exaggeration (becoming aware of the obvious through exaggeration, including awareness of gestures, movements and speech)
- changing questions into statements (for example, instead of saying 'what's the time?' the client says 'I am worried about the time')

- being the projection (clients are encouraged to 'own' projected parts of themselves: a speaker who says 'you are dishonest' might be asked to play the role of the person who is supposed to be dishonest, which helps to clarify just exactly where the dishonesty lies)
- taking responsibility for self (clients are asked to take responsibility for statements they make; for example, 'I find it difficult to get here on time, and I take responsibility for it')
- describing the group (group members are asked for a metaphor to describe the group; for example, animal, situation, journey, building or vehicle).

This is just a selection of some of the creative ideas used in Gestalt therapy. There are obviously many others that have worked for individual therapists and their clients and have never been recorded. Certain techniques work for some clients, while others may be quite unsuitable. Creativity and sensitivity to clients needs are essential components of Gestalt work. Counsellors who are interested in this approach need to be flexible, skilled and, above all, well trained to work from this perspective.

EXERCISE

Group metaphor

Working individually, think of a metaphor which describes your training group. Discuss this with other group members and identify any similarities that emerge.

The counselling relationship

Counsellors from a wide spectrum of theoretical backgrounds use Gestalt skills in their work with clients. In order to do this, however, they need to undertake specific training in Gestalt work. They will also realise (as a result of their training) that not all clients respond to this approach. There are, of course, specialist Gestalt therapists who work exclusively from this perspective and, in these instances, clients who seek their help are usually well informed about Gestalt therapy and what it involves. These clients would, therefore, expect a fairly challenging approach and would be prepared to put a great deal of effort into the work. On the other hand, the idea that Gestalt therapy is always confrontative probably does it a disservice. Therapists are well aware of their clients' needs and will tailor the work they do with them accordingly. Clients are viewed as unique individuals who require individual approaches. This is an important point to remember, since clients often have deeply emotional responses to the work done. There is always a danger that techniques may come to dominate therapy, so that the actual relationship between counsellor and client takes second place. Clients should be informed and consulted about techniques used, and a trusting relationship between counsellor and client is certainly a prerequisite for successful therapy. Fritz Perls makes the point (1992) that what clients expect from a therapist can be done just as well by themselves; helping clients to realise this places the relationship on an 'equal' footing and serves to lessen the possibility that transference dependence will hamper therapy.

Clients who benefit from this approach

Gestalt therapy is suitable for clients who suffer from psychosomatic problems, with the proviso, of course, that they understand the approach and wish to get to the root of their problems. These problems may include tension headaches, colitis, nervous stomach reactions, skin irritations, fatigue, breathlessness and, indeed, any other condition which has been medically investigated and found to have no underlying physical cause. People who suffer from inhibiting shyness and those who have unresolved issues relating to bereavement and loss may also benefit from a Gestalt approach. Clients who are out of touch with their emotions can gain a lot from Gestalt therapy, and those who are interested in dream work and self-exploration tend to be attracted to it. An important point to remember is that clients who benefit most from Gestalt therapy tend to be those who understand the approach and feel they can gain help from it. Aspects of Gestalt therapy may be used in both family and marital work and in certain behavioural problems in younger clients and children. Gestalt work is also applicable in training groups, especially those which value experiential learning for participants.

Some limitations

People who are frightened of groups and those who are inhibited about expressing themselves in front of others may not be suitable clients for Gestalt therapy. On the other hand, such clients may gain a great deal if their initial reluctance could be overcome. Clients who do not understand the links between the physical and emotional aspects of themselves are unlikely to benefit from Gestalt work. Some degree of imagination and creativity is necessary if clients are to be helped by this approach, and those who simply cannot express feelings may find Gestalt therapy very threatening. There are cultural limitations, too, in the sense that the Gestalt emphasis on expression of feeling may run counter to what some people consider to be appropriate behaviour. We have already noted, for example, that some clients may have deep reservations about using Gestalt techniques to address issues of bereavement.

The possibility of abuse is also, unfortunately, a consideration. Counsellors who are attracted to the approach but not adequately trained in it may be tempted to use techniques, simply on account of their dramatic and highly charged impact. It cannot be stated often enough that adequate training, both at theoretical and at an experiential level, is an absolute prerequisite for practice in Gestalt work. Regular supervision will act as an inbuilt safeguard too.

Finally, Gestalt therapy has not traditionally been used with deeply disturbed or mentally labile clients. This is because the approach is active and directive in a way that was considered too challenging for this group. However, new developments in Gestalt therapy, as discussed by Joyce (Joyce and Sills 2009), for example, highlight the usefulness of this approach with disturbed clients. Obviously, such work requires specialised training on the part of the therapist, along with specialist supervision and support.

Evolution of Gestalt counselling and psychotherapy

In his study of Gestalt and object relations theory, Delisle (2013), along with his contributing authors, seek to address what they believe to be a deficit in the evolution of Gestalt therapy. This deficit is, in their view, a historical one, and refers to a dearth of printed material about Gestalt theory and practice over the past 50 years. However, Delisle and his contributors make the point that in spite of this deficit, Gestalt therapy is still used extensively and continues to be well regarded as an approach to therapy (Delisle, 2013). The work of Delisle is on the integration of Gestalt theory with other theoretical approaches, but with specific reference to object relations theory and the work of W.R.D. Fairbairn. In Unit 4, we briefly described Fairbairn's contribution to object relations theory, but noted that it deserved greater delineation in order to be fully appreciated. Delisle takes the view that Fairbairn's theory of object relations has been 'underestimated and neglected during several decades'; he goes on to highlight similarities between Fairbairn's approach and those of several Gestalt theorists, referring specifically to their 'positive "ideal" vision of human nature' (Delisle, 2013: 8). In addition to their focus on Gestalt and object relations theory, Delisle and contributors also explore the ways in which emerging research in neuropsychology and neuroscience contributes to a deeper understanding of clients' problems.

Other writers have sought to illustrate the development of Gestalt theory and practice. Joyce (Joyce and Sills 2009), for example, has also considered Gestalt counselling in the light of developments in neuroscience, a subject that we shall look at in Unit 9. Additionally, Joyce considers the usefulness of Gestalt therapy for helping disturbed and disturbing clients, as well as its potential in short-term work within the NHS and primary care.

In *Gestalt Therapy: Therapy of the Situation*, Wollants (2012) revisits and extends Gestalt theory and practice. Using his knowledge of European philosophy and psychology, he examines the various concepts that are central to Gestalt in order to highlight and clarify them. He further uses comments from experts in different areas of Gestalt to provide an overall picture of contemporary theory and practice.

Perhaps one of the most interesting aspects of Gestalt therapy today is the application of its use with clients from diverse cultural, ethnic and religious backgrounds. The Gestalt Institute of New Orleans (2005) has considered such application in its collected papers garnered from various contributors. These writers look at a wide range of issues including gender, religion, ethnicity, immigrant families, and structure within different family groups. They also examine the way that non-verbal expression of language is used by people from different cultures, as well as the way feelings are expressed by those caught up in violence or war. The contributors to this book, entitled *The Bridge: Dialogues Across Cultures,* set out to show that Gestalt therapy is capable of bridging differences across culture, through use of what they term the dialogic-field approach as a means of enhancing meaningful contact and coexistence (Bar-Yoseph, 2005).

EXERCISE

Other theoretical approaches

Consider the other theoretical approaches outlined in this book. Say whether you think aspects of Gestalt therapy could be incorporated into any of them in a way that would be helpful to clients.

Psychodrama and the work of J. L. Moreno (1889–1974)

Jacob Levy Moreno

J. L. Moreno, the founder of psychodrama, was a psychiatrist who worked in Vienna during the first part of the twentieth century. He became interested in the way children engage in play and was especially impressed with their spontaneity and ability to role play various important figures in their lives. Moreno observed the therapeutic effects of this kind of acting, and he could see that children derived enormous emotional benefits from expressing their feelings, anxieties and concerns in this way. Through a process of role reversal, these children could 'become' the important authority figures in their lives; this enabled them to view themselves, and their own behaviour, from a different and more informed perspective.

In 1921 Moreno also founded the Theatre of Spontaneity in Vienna. This was, in fact, quite unlike the usual theatre, where professional actors perform using scripts. Moreno's theatre was meant as a venue for ordinary people who wished to participate and act out, in a spontaneous way, events from everyday life, including news events they had read about in the papers. In 1925 Moreno emigrated to the USA, where he set up the Moreno Institute and continued his work in psychodrama. Although primarily interested in the therapeutic effects of his approach for emotionally disturbed people, Moreno was also concerned to show that psychodrama was a medium through which almost anyone would benefit. It is widely accepted that he coined the term 'group therapy', and he was certainly instrumental in promoting theatre as a medium for exploring emotional problems.

The theory of psychodrama

Moreno rejected the Freudian concept of psychoanalysis as a method of dealing with personal problems. Psychodrama, unlike Freudian therapy, is action based and conducted in a groupwork setting. Moreno opposed the notion of treating individuals in isolation by verbal methods alone. Instead, he proposed that people derive most benefit from experiential treatment conducted in the presence of others who are supportive and understanding. Moreno wished to give clients the opportunity to experience and rework important developmental stages of their lives that might have been problematic for them.

This repetition of past traumatic events, conducted in the safe environment of a supportive group, forms the basis of therapeutic psychodrama. When clients relive past events in this way, new meaning is acquired, which can then be reintegrated in its more positive form. Psychodrama, therefore, allows people to correct original negative experience. It also allows clients to articulate those things which should have been said in the past but never were. In reference to this need to make sense of the past, Dayton (1994) makes the point that although society may not, at times, allow us to speak from the heart and to say what we most need to say, psychodrama does give us this opportunity.

Moreno's psychodramatic stages of development

Moreno described four stages of personality development, related in name to the action roles of psychodrama. These are quoted by Dayton (1994) and placed under the following headings:

- the double
- the mirror
- the auxiliary ego
- role reversal.

(Dayton, 1994: 32)

The first stage of development, the double, is that phase during which the infant is symbiotically fused with the mother or caregiver. In this stage the baby feels at one with the parent, and the parent, in turn, senses the baby's needs. This relationship forms the basis of trust, and when good experiences are repeated often enough the child's development will proceed in a healthy way.

During the mirror stage of development, information from the outside world is conveyed to the child that may not, in fact, be congruent with what he or she actually feels. This process of mirroring helps to adjust a child's perceptions of self, and when it is provided in a supportive and caring environment will give important information about the way others see us from the outside. If the environment is harsh and unsympathetic, however, it becomes difficult for a child to feel located in the world. A sense of dislocation and weakened identity are the result of feeling oneself mirrored in a threatening and judgmental world.

The stage of the auxiliary ego is one in which the developing child is aware that other people exist. Along with this realisation of the existence of other people there is, or should be, a willingness to fit in and be part of society. Through the first two stages of doubling and mirroring, most children will have learned that they are not alone and that the world is a friendly place to live in. If a strong sense of self is in place, then an ability to empathise with other people is likely to follow at the third stage.

The stage of role reversal is reached when the individual is able to stand alone. If this is achieved, it becomes possible to 'take on' the role of another. One example is the way in which adult children take on roles of their own parents, once they themselves become parents. This stage can only be reached when people are sufficiently separate to stand on their own feet.

Roles and role playing

The twin concepts of 'roles' and 'role playing' were used by Moreno (1947) to form the basis of therapeutic psychodrama. The word 'roles' refers to predictable patterns of behaviour, which people use in order to cope with various situations in life. For example, a woman may play many roles, including mother, sister, wife, teacher, nurse and works manager. When people are psychologically healthy they are able to move in and out of roles with some ease. On the other hand, psychological ill health is associated with rigidity and an inability to move out of certain roles. Another danger arises when the role dominates the person, so that spontaneity and a true sense of identity are lost. Psychodrama offers the opportunity to explore a variety of roles in a wide range of situations so that many alternatives and solutions become apparent. Participants in a psychodramatic group take it in turns to role play and to explore their conflicts and difficulties. This is carried out in a controlled and safe groupwork setting, in which all the people in the group are assigned certain roles. The following is a summary of those roles as described by Dayton (1994: 62–6):

- director
- protagonist
- auxiliary ego
- audience.

Another essential component of psychodramatic technique is the stage on which the action takes place.

The director

In psychodrama the director is the therapist, whose task is to supervise the action, direct it and observe from a supportive distance. The therapist–director also selects the protagonist and decides which techniques are appropriate for individual clients. Preparation and planning are carried out by the director, and the selection of problems to be dealt with in sessions is part of this role too. An important aspect of the director's role is to help group participants become psychologically receptive to the work that is about to take place. This usually involves talking to the group about the nature and purpose of psychodrama, or it may take the form of preparatory exercises and techniques. Group members need to know that they are working in a safe environment and the director needs to assure them of this. Additionally, participants should not feel pressured to take part if they don't wish to do so.

The director–therapist monitors all aspects of the psychodrama as it unfolds, clarifies when necessary, summarises at the end, observes the reactions of group members and facilitates group discussion when the work is over. All this requires a high level of skill, specialist training, creativity and substantial experience in working with groups.

The protagonist

The protagonist is a volunteer from the group who selects the issues he or she wishes to explore. These issues may be from the present or the past, and the protagonist's task is to re-enact the chosen scenarios. Both action and words are used by the protagonist in psychodrama. Relevant significant figures from the past are brought to life in the present, and important aspects of relationships are explored in the drama. The director's task is to follow the protagonist through the scenes that are re-enacted and to encourage, when necessary, greater focus on specific situations or events. The therapist–director is the person who, according to Dayton, holds the protagonist's hand with one hand, while 'carrying a flashlight with the other' (Dayton, 1994: 9–10).

The auxiliary egos

The protagonist selects group members who will act as auxiliary egos. The function of the auxiliary egos is to play the parts assigned to them by the protagonist. These roles may include significant people, either alive or dead, in the protagonist's life. The protagonist presents himself, as well as all the other characters in turn, according to his perceptions of them. Corey (1995) lists several functions of the auxiliary egos; these include playing out the perceptions of the protagonist, looking at the interaction between their own roles and those of the protagonist, helping to interpret the various relationships, and acting as facilitators in the development of improved relationships for the protagonist.

The audience

The audience is involved in the action that takes place on stage. Through a process of identification, they can benefit from the psychodrama in progress. Because the atmosphere is heightened, and quite often intense, most people in the audience become absorbed in it. In this way, learning by comparison takes place. Empathic responses, experienced by the audience, are often accompanied by insight and release of feelings. Feedback and support are also provided by the audience, and the protagonist is likely to receive helpful ideas concerning the issues being highlighted. General group discussion following action will provide further clarification, feedback and support.

The stage

The stage is the physical area in which the action takes place. It should be large enough to accommodate some basic furniture, in addition to being comfortable, warm and private. The stage provides a platform from which the protagonist's story can be seen and heard by others.

The double

The double is the person who plays the inner voice of the protagonist. This is an optional role and may be played by the director, or any member of the group. The double's function is to move the action to a deeper level so that material from the protagonist's unconscious is brought into focus. The protagonist thus sees himself portrayed simultaneously by someone else, and this helps to reveal aspects of himself that were outside his awareness.

The stages of psychodrama

Dayton lists the stages of psychodrama and includes the 'warm up' stage, during which the group members are helped to prepare for the action ahead (Dayton, 1994: 108). The purpose of this phase is to enable participants to become connected to the issues they need to work on. The second stage, enactment, is the action phase during which the protagonist's inner problems are structured and enacted before the audience. During the third stage, sharing, the protagonist is supported by the other group members and the director encourages a general sharing of experiences and feelings in the group. The final stage, analysis, takes place later when group members are less emotionally involved. It refers to cognitive appraisal of what has taken place, and it helps members to assess the emotional learning and insight they have gained. It also helps participants to bring into conscious awareness those destructive patterns and compulsions which have been problematic for them.

Skills and techniques of psychodrama

Various techniques are used in psychodrama. These include the following:

- role reversal (where the protagonist assumes the role of someone else in his personal drama)
- self-presentation (the protagonist presents himself and the other characters in the psychodrama)
- soliloquy (the protagonist is encouraged to think out loud and to talk freely about what is going on in his mind at any given time)
- mirror technique (one of the auxiliary egos takes on the role of the protagonist and mirrors his movements and words – the protagonist observes this and sees 'himself' more clearly)
- interview (the director asks the protagonist questions which help to clarify his thoughts and feelings)
- future projection (the protagonist is encouraged to play a future event in order to experience how it feels)
- vignettes (these are small scenes in which an empty chair is often used as an opportunity to express strong feelings like rage and anger)
- behavioural practice (the protagonist is encouraged to experiment with new ways of acting)
- dream presentation (the protagonist acts a dream instead of describing it).

CASE STUDY

Expressing feelings

Annette was a member of a training group, in which participants were given the opportunity to work through a personal issue. During the 'warm-up' phase the course trainer talked to the group about the nature and purpose of psychodrama. Each member of the group was interviewed, in order to clarify any important issues they might want to examine. Annette volunteered to work on a personal issue. She told the group about her difficult relationship with her father and described the conflict she still felt in relation to this. Annette had been bullied at school over a period of some years, but her father refused to take her seriously when she plucked up the courage to tell him. Annette's mother had died when she was young, so she felt isolated, vulnerable and very afraid of bullies. With the help of the director–trainer, she assembled the main players in the drama she wished to re-enact. One member of the group represented Annette's father, another a teacher at her old school, while two other participants became the school bullies.

Throughout the presentation of the psychodrama the director supervised and directed the action. As a result of recreating the original drama, Annette experienced intense disappointment and anger with her father and his failure to protect her. This catharsis of feeling, which is important in psychodrama, is regarded as the first step towards recovery and integration. However, catharsis, if it is to be properly effective, needs to be accompanied by both cognitive and emotional shifts in perspective (Dayton, 1994).

CASE STUDY Cont...

Annette was supported by the other group members and was able to share her feelings and experiences with them. A week later, during another group meeting, participants assessed the events of the previous week and discussed what they had learned and the insights they had gained. The director–trainer highlighted several aspects of the psychodrama and clarified issues raised by some group members.

Clients who benefit from this approach

Because of its emphasis on spontaneity and creativity, psychodrama is suitable for clients who are inhibited in these areas but wish to do something about it. The approach is also useful for people who have experienced childhood traumas that have never been adequately addressed. In this context, psychodrama may prove very helpful for adult children of alcoholic parents. Additionally, it may be used with clients who are addicted to alcohol or other substances, since it provides support and a holding environment for strong feelings that emerge during recovery (Dayton, 1994). The format is highly structured, so participants feel safe and they know they will be listened to. New skills can be learned through interaction with others and feelings of isolation are lessened. For those clients who have difficulty with verbal expression, psychodrama offers an alternative means of communication. Corey (1995) highlights an area in which psychodrama has special application: while working with people who spoke English as a second language, Corey found that emotions came quickly to the surface when clients spoke in their original tongue. This helped them to become more expressive and other group members responded positively to them.

Some limitations

There are clients who could not bear to explore difficulties in front of other people, and there are those for whom the idea of acting in front of other is unthinkable. Although psychodrama is a powerful and effective therapy, it is limited in some respects. Perls (1990) identified at least one of these limitations, which relates to the roles other people play in the protagonist's drama. According to Perls, these auxiliary egos know very little about the protagonist, and they may even introduce their own fantasies and interpretation into the drama. In this way, the client's role is falsified and contaminated by others. Zinker (1978) highlights another limitation when he refers to psychodrama's commitment to a formal structure and to the drama, often at the expense of the process taking place within each. It is also possible for group members to hide behind roles, although this is something which the director–therapist should be able to identify. Psychodrama may be difficult to obtain in many areas, but it's occasionally available within the NHS.

SUMMARY

This unit was concerned with two experiential and action-based models of therapy. We discussed the work of Fritz Perls and the psychology that influenced his approach. The terms 'gestalt', 'figure and ground', 'here and now', and 'wholeness' were also discussed and placed in the context of the Gestalt model of counselling. Defence mechanisms were identified and the importance of dreams in Gestalt work was emphasised. The benefits of groupwork were also described and the skills and techniques used in Gestalt counselling were outlined. Benefits and limitations of the approach were discussed and aspects of the therapeutic relationship were highlighted. At the end of the section on Gestalt therapy we looked at some developments in both theory and practice, including links with object relations theory. We also looked at research into Gestalt and neuropsychology and neuroscience, and the use of the approach in the NHS and primary care. In addition, we referred to American research indicating the usefulness of Gestalt therapy for a diverse range of clients. In the second half of the unit we looked at psychodrama as a method of therapy and placed it in its evolutionary context. The theory of psychodrama was explained, along with Moreno's psychodramatic stages of development. The terms 'role' and 'role playing' were examined, and participants' roles in the psychodrama were described. Stages of psychodrama were also outlined, and the skills and techniques central to it were listed. Finally, we looked at some of the areas of application and identified others where psychodrama may not be appropriate.

References

Bar-Yoseph, T. L. (Ed.) (2005) *The Bridge: Dialogues Across Cultures*. New Orleans: Gestalt Institute Press.

Corey, G. (1995) *Theory and Practice of Group Counselling*. California: Brooks/Cole.

Dayton, T. (1994) *The Drama Within*. Florida: Health Communications Inc.

Delisle, D. (2013) *Object Relations in Gestalt Therapy*. London: Karnac Books.

Harris, J. B. (1989) *Gestalt: An Idiosyncratic Approach*. (2nd edn). Manchester: The Manchester Gestalt Centre.

Harris, J. B. (1992) *Gestalt: Working with Groups* (2nd edn). Manchester: The Manchester Gestalt Centre.

Joyce, P. & Sills, C. (2009) *Skills in Gestalt Counselling and Psychotherapy*. (2nd edn). London: Sage Publications.

Moreno, J. L. (1947) *Theatre of Spontaneity: An Introduction to Psychodrama*. New York: Beacon House.

Moore, T. (1994) *Care of the Soul*. New York: Harper Perennial.

Perls, F. (1992) *Gestalt Therapy Verbatim*. U.S.A.: The Gestalt Journal Press.

Polster, E. & Polster, M. (1974) *Gestalt Therapy Integrated: Contours of Theory and Practice*. New York: Random House. Inc.

Wollants, G. (2012) *Gestalt Therapy: Therapy of the Situation*. London: Sage Publications.

Zinker, K. (1978) *Creative Processes in Gestalt Therapy*. New York: Vintage Books.

Further reading

Baim, C., Burmeister, J. & Maciel, M. (2007) *Psychodrama: Advances in Theory and Practice*. London: Taylor & Francis.

Clarkson, P. (2004) *Gestalt Counselling in Action* (3rd edn). London: Sage Publications.

Desmond, B., Lapworth, P. & Sills, C. (2012) *An Introduction to Gestalt*. London: Sage Publications.

Ginger, S. (2007) *Gestalt Therapy: The Art of Contact*. London: Karnac Books.

Hare, A. P. & Hare, J. R. (1996) *J. L. Moreno*. London: Sage Publications.

Hycner, R. & Jacobs, L. (Eds.) *Relational Approaches to Gestalt Therapy*. London: Routledge.

Houson, G. (2003) *Brief Gestalt Therapy*. London: Sage Publications.

Jones, P. (2007) *Drama as Therapy: Theory, Practice and Research*. London: Routledge.

Mann, D. (2010) *Gestalt Therapy: 100 Key Points and Techniques*. London: Routledge.

Phillipson, P. (2009) *The Emergent Self: An Existential-Gestalt Approach*. London: Karnac Books.

Mackewn, J. (2004) *Developing Gestalt Counselling*. London: Sage Publications.

Perls, F. (1969) *In and Out of the Garbage Pail*. Lafayette, CA: Real People Press.

Perls, F. (1995) *Gestalt Therapy*. London: Souvenir Press.

Sacks, J. M. & Fonseca, J. (2004) *Contemporary Psychodrama: New Approaches to Theory and Technique*. London: Taylor & Francis.

Toman, S. M. & Woldt, A. L. (2005) *Gestalt Therapy: History, Theory and Practice*. London: Sage Publications.

Resources

www.britishgestaltjournal.com
The home of the British Gestalt journal, including subscription information and abstracts.
www.gestaltbodymind.co.uk
Information about psychotherapy, counselling and group therapy.
www.counselling-directory.org.uk
Edinburgh training institute–counselling directory.
www.brianmcminn.co.uk
A one day workshop in the gestalt approach, for continuous professional development.

www.ukagp.org.uk
United Kingdom Association of Gestalt Practitioners.
www.gtpi.org.uk
Gestalt Psychotherapy and Training Institute.
www.gestaltcentre.co.uk
The Gestalt Centre, London. Holds a register of trained psychotherapists.
www.mgc.org.uk
Manchester Gestalt Centre.
www.psychotherapy.org.uk
UK Council for Psychotherapy (UKCP)
www.gaiehouston.co.uk
Provides training and workshops.
www.psychodrama.org.uk
The website of the British Psychodrama Association which was founded in 1984. It has links to The British Association of Drama Therapists.
www.psychodramansp.co.uk
Northern School of Psychodrama which provides training in Psychodrama.
www.birminghampsychodrama.co.uk/training
A new centre for workshops and training in psychodrama.
www.londoncentreforpsychodrama.org
Registered with the British Psychodrama Association (BPA) as an accredited training organisation.

7

Transactional analysis

◆ Introduction

The subject of this unit is transactional analysis and its use in the context of counselling and therapy. Transactional analysis is a psychoanalytically inspired approach that links problem behaviour to early experience. According to the theory, this early experience exerts considerable influence in the present and is discernible in the 'ego states' each person feels and exhibits at any given time. In the course of this unit, we shall define and discuss these ego states and consider a number of other important concepts that are central to the theory of transactional analysis.

The approach also highlights each person's aptitude and capacity for change. This means, for example, that through awareness and insight the events of early childhood can be redefined by the individual and self-defeating patterns of behaviour altered. These ideas are similar to those expressed in psychodynamic theory, where the emphasis is also on childhood experience and the possibility of change through therapeutic intervention in later life.

The goals of psychodynamic counselling and transactional analysis have much in common, since both aim to help clients bring unconscious material into consciousness. In transactional analysis terms this means helping clients to become more autonomous and 'script'-free. A similar view is implicit in the person-centred approach, where the individual's 'actualising tendency' is seen as a powerful force for improvement and change. However, transactional analysis differs greatly from both the psychodynamic and humanistic approaches, since it stresses the importance of social transactions – a dimension not emphasised by the other two.

KEY TERM

Transactional analysis: This refers to the analysis of a person's communications style or 'transactions', which is carried out with the aid of diagrams so that the specific ego states involved are identified.

Eric Berne (1910–1970)

Eric Berne, who was the founder of transactional analysis, completed his medical training in 1935 and later studied psychiatry at Yale University. In the 1940s he trained as a psychoanalyst at the New York Psychoanalytic Institute, and in 1956 applied for membership there. This request was refused, possibly because of Berne's divergence from, and criticism of, traditional Freudian teaching.

Berne was greatly influenced by his father (also a doctor), who died when Eric was 11 years old. This early bereavement had a lasting effect on Berne and, when he came to formulate his own method of helping the patients in his care, he dedicated his most important work to the memory of his father (Berne, 1961). It is worth mentioning this, because it serves to underline a degree of commitment to patients (or clients), which Berne shared with his father, a man who exemplified dedication to the poor and disadvantaged. Berne demonstrated his own concern for the patients in his care through the design and use of transactional analysis. As a method of communication and a psychotherapeutic tool, it was meant to translate complex ideas and concepts into more accessible and user-friendly language that could be understood by ordinary people. In addition to his work with patients, Eric Berne also wrote several very successful books. These include *Transactional Analysis in Psychotherapy* (1961), *Games People Play* (1964), *The Principles of Group Treatment* (1966) and *What Do You Say After You Say Hello?,* which was published in 1972, after his death. The principles of transactional analysis are expressed very clearly in these books, and should be first choice for anyone wishing to specialise in this approach.

Terminology

Already we can see that the terminology used in transactional analysis is quite different from that used in any other approach. This is both a strength and a weakness of the model, because although the language is memorable and accessible, it is also regarded by some critics as simplistic and superficial. Berne was concerned to demystify the esoteric language of psychotherapy so that it could be grasped by anyone. He was especially interested in helping his patients to understand the basic principles of the approach and the origins of the psychological problems they had come to experience. In this respect, Berne was certainly successful, not least because transactional analysis does appear to help clients and patients to participate more fully in their own therapy. Since its inception, however, Berne's model has been extended considerably by different schools and theorists, and new and more complex ideas have been added to it. While the fundamental principles of transactional analysis remain intact, the accessibility, which Berne valued so much, is often obscured.

Apart from these criticisms, however, transactional analysis continues to gain popularity, not only as a theoretical approach to counselling and therapy, but also as a communications skills model that is used extensively in education, management, industry, health care and many of the caring professions. The International Transactional Analysis Association (ITAA) was formed in 1964 as a training and accreditation body, while the European Association for Transactional Analysis (EATA) performs a similar function. Many of the people who become involved in transactional analysis do so because they are interested in it as a communications model. It is important to remember this fact, since it highlights the point that transactional analysis is first and foremost about the development of effective interpersonal skills.

Groupwork

Transactional analysis therapy usually takes place in a group setting. Berne believed that many problems could be addressed more readily in groups, since such a format lends itself to the identification and analysis of faulty social interactions and communication styles. He had gained a great deal of experience of groupwork in the 1940s, while working as a psychiatrist in the United States Army Corps, and he set up the first transactional analysis group in 1954. Invaluable information about the way people relate to each other is readily available when clients work together in groups. Each participant is afforded the opportunity to monitor and perhaps change the interactive styles they habitually use. As we shall see, Berne formulated his user-friendly theory of personality in a way that seems to owe something to Freud's concept of Id, Ego and Superego, although Berne did point out that his concept of personality was different in the sense that his ego states represent 'phenomological realities' (Berne, 1961: 31). In simple terms, this means that the three ego states are real and observable, whereas the parts of personality Freud described were not always clearly seen in this way. Group participants can, therefore, learn about personal styles of social interaction and any problems associated with these, while at the same time becoming aware of the intent behind their ways of relating to others.

Ego states

An idea fundamental to transactional analysis is that of ego states. Berne suggested that human personality is made up of three elements, which he referred to as Parent, Adult and Child. These familiar words were used by him to describe states of 'self' or states of mind, which he believed gave rise to their own individual patterns of behaviour. In transactional analysis, 'Parent', 'Adult' and 'Child' are always spelt with capital letters, in order to distinguish between their usual meaning and that which Berne assigned to them. Ego states are, of course, common to all of us and govern our thoughts, feelings and behaviour. In any given situation an individual will exhibit a certain pattern of behaviour that corresponds to the way that person is actually feeling at the time. As feelings change, so also do the patterns of behaviour the person displays. As a result of his experience with groups, Berne observed that these patterns included noticeable changes in voice, posture, vocabulary and all other aspects of behaviour (Berne, 1964: 23). The principles of transactional analysis are illustrated in diagrammatic form, the most basic of which is the structural diagram illustrated in Figure 7.1.

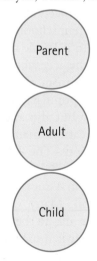

Figure 7.1 Structural diagram of personality

Each of these states, Parent, Adult and Child, is present from early childhood, and all are described by Berne as 'psychological realities' (Berne, 1964: 23). In Figure 7.1 the ego states are separated from each other because they are incompatible and differ considerably.

Parent ego state

The Parent ego state represents a set of thoughts, feelings and behaviour, which are derived from parental figures. According to Berne (1964) the Parent ego state is exhibited in both indirect and direct form. A person may, for example, respond as one of his parents actually responded in a given situation. When this occurs, the ego state is directly shown. When the parental influence is an indirect one, then the person is likely to respond as his parents would have wished him to respond. A distinction between these two forms is important, and explains how people:

- can sometimes 'become' one of their own parents when the Parent ego state is directly active.
- exhibit the kind of response which parents required in the past.

A client called Viv recounted the following experience.

CASE STUDY

Parent ego state

Sometimes I feel that the children are driving me crazy. Most of the time I cope quite well, and my husband is supportive and helpful. At other times, especially when I have just got in from work, I simply don't know where to start. Then I find myself getting into a panic and I start to shout at them. When this happened to me yesterday I suddenly realised that I sounded exactly like my mother. It wasn't just the tone of my voice . . . it was the words as well. I actually used the word 'weary' as she used to do, and later on I used another expression of hers as well. I'm sure I looked like her too, standing there with my hands on my hips glaring at the children. It pulled me up short and made me really think . . . do I want to become old before my time and end up hassled and bad tempered, the way she always seemed to be?

Comment: In the example just given, the client described a situation in which she felt she had 'become' her own mother in her response to her children. Her actions and her state of mind were the same as her mother's used to be in a similar situation. It is important to point out here that the word 'Parent' refers to parental substitutes as well as to actual parents, and could include, for example, teachers and others who exerted influence on a person's early life.

Do as I say: indirect Parent

The second category of Parent Berne identifies actually operates in conjunction with a person's Child ego state. This is, in effect, a dialogue between ego states, and when a person responds in this way, the parental 'influence' is evident. Another way of saying this is that the response shown is one which clearly stems from the instruction 'this is how one should behave' or 'do as I say'. This adaptation to parental influence is evident in the 'adapted Child' ego state, which we shall consider later in this section.

Aspects of socialisation

Whether shown in direct or indirect form, the Parent ego state resembles a compendium of the entire socialisation process each person has received in early life. This early socialisation is passed from parents, teachers and other significant people in childhood, and is usually absorbed without question by the growing child. However, it is not just parental pronouncements and injunctions that are recorded in this way; the example given by parents and other significant people is also relevant here. Both negative and positive influences are recorded in the Parent ego state, and everything that is experienced by the child is internalised to become part of the personality. Once again Berne's psychoanalytic training is evident in his theory, since the idea of parental internalisation is common to all branches of psychodynamic teaching, including object relations theory.

There is an important point of difference, however, between Berne's theory of personality and those described by the various branches of psychodynamic theory. This difference concerns the 'paternal' influence, which, in Berne's formulation, is potentially just as influential as the 'maternal'. If we consider the theories discussed in Units 3 and 4, it is clear that such an equal emphasis is absent from many of the psychodynamic approaches. In transactional analysis, therefore, both parents are believed to impart information explicitly and implicitly to the developing child's Parent ego state.

CASE STUDY

Paternal influence

During bereavement counselling, a client called Kavita remembered her experiences in childhood and her relationship with her father, which she described as follows:

My mother was talkative and outgoing. She was the one who seemed to have an opinion about everything. I can see many aspects of my mother in myself, but I can identify characteristics of my father too. When he came to this country he concentrated on working hard, setting up a business and working virtually non-stop from early morning until late at night. I only really started to think about him after he died, and to appreciate all that he did for the family. Though I can't remember him directly influencing me when I was a child, I know now that his unspoken influence was immense. I have absorbed his attitude to work and to family, and I am very grateful now for the many positive messages he conveyed to me.

Information from the past

Information which is recorded in the Parent ego state enables us to cope with all aspects of living. It also provides all the data necessary to enable people to function as parents themselves and raise their own children.

Another significant aspect of the Parent ego state is that it enables people to respond automatically in many situations, so that many 'routine matters', as Berne describes them, can be dealt with without unnecessary expenditure of energy (Berne, 1964: 27). Problems arise, though, when the Parent ego state is inappropriate or counter-productive in a given situation. One example of this is the bank cashier who adopts a certain 'superior' stance in relation to the account holders she is meant to serve. Her critical parental attitude is likely to stem from a childhood in which attitudes to money (and especially those who borrow it) are fraught with ambiguity and moral disapproval. In the present situation, however, the bank cashier's Parent ego state is liable to cause problems, since it is sure to encourage a 'Child' response from the customer and an end to real, productive communication.

Berne (1972: 75) elaborated on his structural diagram of personality, so that the Parent ego state is now commonly divided into 'Nurturing Parent' and 'Critical' or 'Controlling' Parent – see Figure 7.2. This diagram also illustrates the subdivision of the Child ego state into 'Free' or 'Rebellious' Child, and 'Adapted' Child.

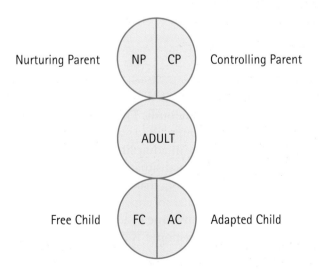

EXERCISE

Parent ego state

Working individually, try to identify as many situations as possible where you respond in a Parent ego state. How do you think, feel and act when you respond in this way? Think carefully about your tone of voice, your gestures, your facial expressions and any other observable features that are manifest in your Parent ego state.

Figure 7.2 Descriptive diagram of personality

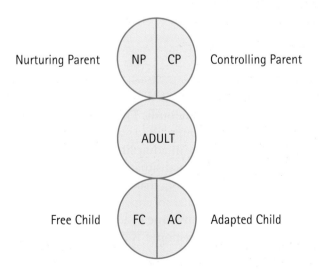

Nurturing Parent and Controlling Parent

The terms 'Nurturing Parent' and 'Controlling Parent' refer to two different sets of influence, which are absorbed in early childhood and are clearly distinguishable from each other when they are manifest. Berne originally used the word 'prejudicial' instead of 'controlling' to describe the second form, in which the Parent ego state is exhibited (Berne, 1961: 48). However, both these words, 'Controlling' and 'Prejudicial', are meant to denote arbitrary and prohibitive attitudes that are borrowed from parental figures and are usually exhibited automatically and without question in certain situations. The example of the bank cashier is a case in point here, and serves to illustrate the way in which some people respond to particular situations exactly as a parent or parents would have done. The 'Nurturing Parent' ego state is shown in a completely different way, and is usually manifest as sympathy or support for others in need or distress. It is important to remember that children are also capable of responding in all three ego states, and when they are in the 'Nurturing Parent' state it tends to be demonstrated as concern for someone or something smaller, weaker and more vulnerable, including toys and dolls.

EXERCISE

Nurturing Parent and Controlling Parent

Working individually, identify any situations where other people responded to you as either 'Controlling Parent' or 'Nurturing Parent'. How did these people sound and look when they responded to you in these two ego states? How did each style of communication affect you, and how did you respond to each?

Child ego state

While information is being recorded in the Parent ego state, another recording is taking place simultaneously. This second recording also derives from the past and represents a young child's actual reactions to what is going on in the environment. Later on, in adult life, the Child ego state is evident when the emotions that the original situation produced are felt once again. Harris (1973) refers to this response, making the point that a child has no vocabulary in the very early years, so experiences are recorded as feelings. These feelings can be evoked at any time in adult life, and often the individual concerned is unaware that the response is an archaic one. The following is an example of this.

CASE STUDY

Child ego state

Gwyneth, who was in her early 40s, received counselling because she was unable to cope at work. Her problems arose when she had to deal with complaints from staff or customers, or when any situation arose in which there was conflict. When things became difficult, Gwyneth felt angry and defensive, or extremely tearful. She was aware that her responses were inappropriate, but was unable to modify the strong feelings certain people and situations evoked. In the course of counselling, she revealed that her parents had been habitually critical so that she reached a point in her childhood where she despaired of ever pleasing them. Her transferential responses to staff and customers were an exact replica of the way she responded to parental criticism in the past. When she understood this, Gwyneth was in a position to alter her responses and access her Adult ego state when conflict or disagreement arose. This was not something she achieved immediately, however. Understanding and practice are necessary before long-established ways of responding are changed in this way. Gwyneth's counsellor taught her the basic principles of transactional analysis and showed her how 'complementary' and 'crossed' transactions work in practice (see also Figures 7.3, 7.4 and 7.5).

Adapted Child and Free Child

We have seen that the Child ego state is preserved from childhood so that a person functioning in this way behaves as she or he did at a very early age. Like the Parent ego state, the Child is demonstrated in speech, stance, demeanour and overall appearance. In addition, Steiner (1974) suggests that these outward signs are accompanied by feelings and thoughts that correspond to the visible indicators. In referring to the Child ego state, Berne stressed that it was not intended to mean 'childish' or 'immature' (Berne, 1964: 24). Berne was aware of the danger that his terminology could be misinterpreted and used in a disparaging way. In his early writings he uses the terms 'Adapted' and 'Natural' Child to describe the two broad manifestations of that particular ego state. The word 'Free' is now often substituted for 'Natural'.

Adapted Child

In the section entitled 'Do as I say' we looked briefly at how people adapt to parental influence, and the way in which this adaptation is revealed through the Child ego state in adult life.

The person who is functioning in Adapted Child will demonstrate behaviour meant to conform to the expectations of parents and parental figures. Different parents have different expectations, however, and behaviours that please one will not necessarily please the other. This means that people learn to respond or adapt to both parents; and in later life, these responses will be triggered in situations that are reminiscent of earlier ones. A young woman who has received poor grades in college assignments, for example, may respond to a male lecturer by becoming silent and withdrawn, since that was the way she responded to her father's disapproval when she was a child. A woman teacher may, on the other hand, evoke a different, perhaps more combative response, which stems from the relationship the student had with her mother. The point to make here is that both these 'adapted' responses are outmoded and archaic, because in each case the student is communicating in the way that she would have done at a much earlier time with the important people in her life. The Adult ego state, which we shall consider later, represents a much more effective way of communicating.

Free Child

The Free Child ego state is the source of strong feelings and can be classified as either positive or negative. Spontaneous expressions of joy, anger, sorrow and a sense of fun are characteristic of Free Child. These are all feelings which have escaped the inhibiting influence of parents, but when they are expressed inappropriately these uncensored impulses can be problematic. On the other hand, positive Free Child ego states are often observed in social situations or contexts where such expressions are permitted. Steiner (1974) lists sports events and parties as examples of structured situations, in which the Free Child ego state is given unlimited opportunity for expression. Apart from aspects of behaviour that can be identified with Free Child, there are also words and phrases like 'super' and 'wow', for example, which are associated with it.

Adult ego state

The Adult ego state denotes the feelings, attitudes and behaviour patterns which belong exclusively to the individual, and which are in touch with current reality and relationships in the present. Once again, it is possible to detect similarities between Berne's description of personality and aspects of psychodynamic theory, since the Adult ego state appears to have much in common with the Freudian concept of the 'Ego'. Like the Ego, the Adult ego state represents reason and common sense. It is that part of the personality which can truly be described as autonomous and free from parental influence, or strong feelings emanating from the Child ego state. The Adult ego state is characterised by objective, logical thinking, and an ability to make independent judgments and decisions in any situation. Experiences gained throughout life are examined and used by the individual when in Adult, so that realistic choices can be freely made. Every so often the material stored in the Adult ego state is reassessed and updated, in order to keep in touch with changing circumstances and needs. Children, too, have an Adult ego state, which represents that part of personality which has absorbed and tested information passed to them from parents and other significant people. The central concern for the Adult ego state is the development of individual autonomy and the ability to make informed and realistic decisions on one's own.

Looking at ego states

Working individually, look at the responses given to the situations described. Say whether you think these responses come from each person's Parent, Adult or Child ego states.

1 Helen has been asked by her manager to work extra hours at the weekend. She asks for some time to consider the situation. Next day, she replies that she has given it some thought and is willing to do the overtime.

2 Bruce has been admitted to hospital for an operation. He is approached by a doctor who wishes to carry out some diagnostic procedures which Bruce does not understand. Instead of asking, however, he keeps silent and worries for the rest of the day.

3 Catherine has just learned that she has not got the promotion she hoped for. She has a confrontation with her boss and finds she becomes angry and tearful.

4 Joanne and Lyn are friends and attend the same university. Joanne has a row with her boyfriend and Lyn responds in the following way:
'He's not worth it. I never thought he was good enough for you. To be quite honest, I thought you were wasting your time.'

5 Phil and Simon are friends who share the same office at work. Phil's girlfriend breaks off their relationship and Simon responds in the following way:
'Look, I know you must be feeling rotten. If you like, I'll clear up those files for you and you could leave a bit early.'

6 Karen's husband asks her to consider changing their next year's holiday plans. They had planned a sightseeing holiday, including visits to the local art galleries and museums. He suggests they need a more relaxing break. Karen responds by pointing out that they had both resolved to improve their knowledge of art and, anyway, she has better things to do than waste time on the beach.

7 Mrs Rae is an 80-year-old resident in a nursing home. One of the attendants asks her if she would like to go out for a walk, since the day is warm and sunny. Mrs Rae is enthusiastic about the suggestion, and adds that she wouldn't mind paddling at the local beach as well.

8 James, who is eight years old, has been told by his parents that he must not play in the sun without wearing sunscreen lotion. He replies that he knows not to do this, because he got burned on holiday last year.

9 Carolyn's mother has asked her to visit home more often. Carolyn, who is 20 and shares an apartment with some friends, replies that her mother needs to get out and about more so that she can have a life of her own.

10 The manager of a small firm is concerned that her secretary is repeatedly late for work. The manager, Mrs Burrows, waits until her irritation is under control, then makes an appointment to speak to her secretary. She expresses her concern and asks for an explanation.

EXERCISE Cont...

Answers

It should be stressed that it is not possible to be totally accurate about the correct answers to this questionnaire. This is because so much depends on the manner and tone of voice of the person responding in each case. However, from the evidence given, the answers are shown at the end of this unit.

Application to counselling

Berne's main objective in formulating transactional analysis was that it should provide a frame of reference for helping clients in therapy. He developed his theories as a result of working directly with patients, whose behavioural changes he observed and then identified in the ego state model. The behavioural changes he noted included alterations in voice tone, gesture, choice of words, facial expression, posture, body movement and even sentence construction. Berne was intrigued by this phenomenon, and observed that people seemed to be governed by different 'inner' personalities, whose influences were manifest at different times and according to circumstances. He also observed that people communicated in a variety of ways, depending on the ego state which dominated the personality at any given time. These 'transactions', as he called them, could be analysed in order to help people identify some of the problems they experienced in communicating with others (Berne, 1964: 28). Transactional analysis, therefore, is meant to help clients gain intellectual insight through analysis of the way they relate to other people. It is concerned with four major areas of analysis:

1 Structural analysis: the analysis of individual personality or ego states
2 Transactional analysis: the analysis of communication styles or social behaviour
3 Game analysis: analysis of the psychological games people play
4 Script analysis: analysis of a complex set of transactions people act out compulsively.

KEY TERMS

Script analysis: This is based on the idea that everyone has a life plan or 'script', which determines behaviour and life choices. Analysis of scripts brings these, largely unconscious, motivations into conscious awareness.

Structural analysis: This refers to a theory of personality based on the study of specific ego states. These ego states are: Adult, Parent and Child.

Transaction: This refers to communication between two or more people in any social situation. This communication can be verbal or non-verbal. Berne used the term 'strokes' to denote the exchanges that people engage in socially (Berne, 1964:14).

Structural analysis

We have considered Berne's structure of personality, which was shown in diagram form (see Figure 7.1). Berne believed that structural analysis should always come before transactional analysis, and can be taught to clients in either group or individual settings (Berne, 1961). It is important for clients to understand the ego state model before they can move on to consider the way they conduct transactions with other people.

Transactions

While structural analysis refers to the individual, analysis of transactions refers to social behaviour. The word 'stroking' is used by Berne to describe the social exchanges that take place between people. Stroking implies recognition of another person and is defined by Berne as 'the fundamental unit of social action' (Berne, 1964:15). Any exchange of strokes is called a 'transaction' and is the basic unit of social interaction. We exchange strokes through verbal greetings, non-verbal recognition, touching, kissing, hugging, and so on. According to Berne, strokes are a necessary and integral part of human interaction, and we all need them even when they are negative. Children will, for example, seek recognition from parental or other important figures; and, when positive recognition is not forthcoming, negative strokes are seen as preferable to none at all. When patterns like this are established in early life, it may take some time for people to change them. Transactional analysis counselling is one way in which clients can learn to change the way they communicate with, and seek approval and recognition from, other people.

Complementary transactions

People communicate with others from the Parent, Adult or Child ego state. The person making the response will also do so from one of the three ego states. A complementary transaction will take place when, for example, one person addresses another from the Adult ego state, and the second person replies from Adult. This is illustrated the following example. (See also Figure 7.3.)

STIMULUS: Have you seen my glasses?
     (Adult to Adult)

RESPONSE: Yes, they're on the dining room table.
     (Adult to Adult)

Berne illustrated his theory of transactional analysis in diagram form, in order to make it easier to understand. He also stressed the point that when transactions remain complementary, communication proceeds indefinitely. Complementary transactions don't just take place between Adult to Adult ego states. Berne (1972: 14) identifies nine possible types of complementary transactions, in which the responses given were those which the question or stimulus intended. Figure 7.4 is an example of one.

STIMULUS: Isn't it dreadful how long it takes to get through these checkouts?
(Parent to Parent)

RESPONSE: Yes, it's disgraceful. They should have more staff.
(Parent to Parent)

The following is another example of a complementary transaction, this time Parent to Child.

STIMULUS: That's twice this week you've kept me waiting.
(Parent to Child)

RESPONSE: I'm sorry to be such a nuisance.
(Child to Parent)

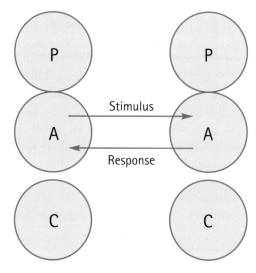

Figure 7.3 Complementary transaction

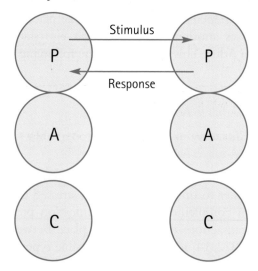

Figure 7.4 Complementary transaction

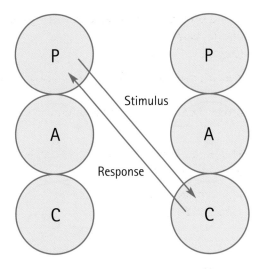

Figure 7.5 Complementary transaction

Crossed transactions

A crossed transaction occurs when the response given is not the one which the stimulus intended. When such a situation arises, communication tends to break down. Figure 7.6 illustrates this.

STIMULUS: Have you seen my glasses?
(Adult to Adult)

RESPONSE: Oh you haven't lost them again!
(Parent to Child)

The response to the question 'Have you seen my glasses' might have been given from a Child ego state as follows:

STIMULUS: Have you seen my glasses?
(Adult to Adult)

RESPONSE: You can't expect me to look after your things.
(Child to Parent)

Once again this is illustrated in diagrammatic form (see Figure 7.7).

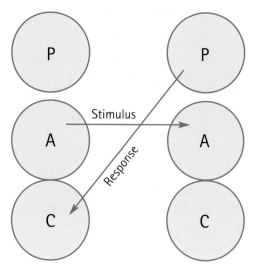

Figure 7.6 Crossed transaction

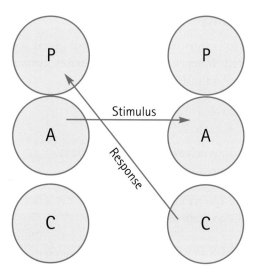

Figure 7.7 Crossed transaction

Ulterior transactions

Both complementary and crossed transactions are relatively simple, and operate on one level. However, Berne describes another, more complicated, transaction that operates on two levels and conveys a double set of messages. These are referred to as 'ulterior' transactions because they contain a hidden agenda. Another way of stating this is to say that one of the messages occurs at a psychological level, while the other takes place at a social level. The psychological aspect of the transaction is conveyed subtly, and is often picked up via non-verbal clues. It is by far the stronger of the two messages and dominates the social message, which is conveyed verbally. Ulterior transactions are frequently contained in exchanges between people who wish to become more intimate and are wary of stating their intentions openly. However, they are also common in many other situations. The following is an example:

PATIENT: My back is less painful, although it does tend to play up when I'm sitting at my desk.
(Adult to Adult)

DOCTOR: Certain situations make it worse for you.
(Adult to Adult)

On the surface this is a straightforward transaction between two people who are discussing a medical condition. At a psychological level, however, the transaction is likely to be more complex, with a subtle testing of responses taking place on both sides. Depending on voice tone, body language and other non-verbal clues, the ulterior message may be as follows:

PATIENT: I'm not ready to go back to work and I need your help.
(Child to Parent)

DOCTOR: I'll take care of you and give you extra time.
(Parent to Child)

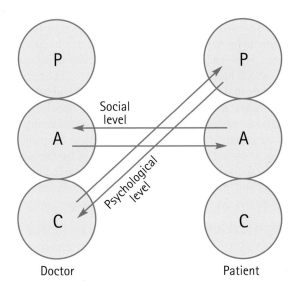

Figure 7.8 Ulterior transaction

Unit 7 Transactional analysis

EXERCISE

Ulterior transactions

Working individually, identify any ulterior transactions you have experienced either at work or at home. Illustrate these in diagram form and discuss the way they work with other members of the training group. Are there some transactions that are common to a number of people in the group?

Game analysis

Berne (1964) defines the psychological games people play as follows:

- They are extensions of ulterior transactions.
- They progress to an expected and definite outcome.
- Superficially, they appear to be straightforward transactions.
- What is said is not what is felt.
- All games have some common elements, including a hidden agenda and a negative payoff.

Berne also makes a useful distinction between an 'operation' – a simple transaction or transactions set in motion for a specific purpose – and a game – a dishonest 'manoeuvre' (Berne, 1964: 44). If someone asks for help and gets it, for example, then that is an operation. If, on the other hand, the person who gives the help is adversely affected in doing so, then that is a game. The following case study is an example of a game.

CASE STUDY

Mr Phillips

Mr Phillips was a 36-year-old man who had been out of work for several years. He had a number of minor health problems, which meant that he had visited his doctor on many occasions. However, his GP had some difficulty in persuading Mr Phillips that he had no serious health problems, an assessment confirmed by the many diagnostic procedures that had been carried out. Mr Phillips had also visited several alternative practitioners, all of whom he described as 'hopeless' and incapable of giving him the help he needed. At a later date, he requested counselling, and during his first sessions informed his counsellor that no one had been able to help him so far. The counsellor observed that Mr Phillips smiled as he described all the failed attempts to understand and assist him. Nevertheless, she worked with him over a period of ten weeks and, during that time, was able to help him identify the game he was playing over and over again, and the payoff he received on each occasion.

Comment: We can see that Mr Phillips was receiving a great deal of attention as a result of his repeated visits to helpers. Gaining attention in this way was a continuation of the strategy he had employed as a small child. However, the kind of attention this client received effectively prevented him from achieving any real intimacy in relation to other people. In transactional analysis terms, games are designed to confirm and support the original decisions people make in early life about the best way to relate to others. As far as Mr Phillips was concerned, real intimacy was fraught with danger. This was a lesson he had learned in childhood, at the hands of neglectful and often abusive parents. In response to these early events, he had devised his own method of gaining the 'strokes' or recognition he desperately needed. As a result, he was also able to experience the familiar, and what Berne (Harris, 1972: 137–139) referred to as 'racket', feelings of hurt and satisfaction associated with his own special game. The fact that he was sabotaging his own best interests did not occur to him. In the units dealing with psychodynamic approaches to counselling, we noted that Freud (and other Freudian theorists) believed that people frequently repeat early patterns of behaviour in an unconscious and repetitive way. This idea is taken up by Berne and is integral to his theory of games and life scripts.

Scripts

The theory of life scripts has a central place in transactional analysis. Berne refers to life scripts as 'complex operations' and goes on to describe a script as 'an extensive unconscious life plan' to which people construct their activities, lives and relationships (Berne, 1961: 23). According to this theory, fundamental decisions about an individual's entire lifespan are formulated at a very early age. Scripts are based on parental conditioning and influence, and they come under two headings: 'Winning' and 'Losing' (Berne, 1972: 203–5). These scripts are closely associated with another transactional analysis concept, the OK positions, described by Harris (1973). OK positions represent a variety of convictions people adopt and adhere to from childhood through life. There are four basic OK positions, from which games and scripts originate. These are as follows:

1 I'm not OK – You're OK.
2 I'm not OK – You're not OK.
3 I'm OK – You're not OK.
4 I'm OK – You're OK.

(Harris, 1973: 42)

What the positions mean

The fourth position is the most positive one; it is based on the conviction that everyone has worth and value. An infant who is loved and cared for is likely to imbibe feelings of goodness which, if the quality of care continues, will last a lifetime. Feelings of goodness about 'self' are then translated into feelings of goodness about other people too. Once again it is possible to detect echoes of psychodynamic theory – in particular, object relations theory – in Berne's ideas. Unfortunately, problems tend to arise in later childhood when the parents and others become more critical and demanding. When this happens, the I'm OK – You're OK position of an earlier era may be questioned, and the original conviction of worth may then be lost.

Some fortunate people retain the I'm OK – You're OK position throughout life, but the majority of others probably fall into the depressive I'm not OK – You're OK group. This is because so much learning has to be done in childhood, and so many obstacles have to be overcome. Parents often give negative feedback and, in extreme cases, they may even be abusive or neglectful.

When this last situation obtains, some children respond by adopting the I'm not OK – You're not OK 'futility' position. Another group of people, those who are arrogant and distrustful of others, will slot into the I'm OK – You're not OK 'paranoid' position. An important point to make in relation to OK positions is that it is possible for all of us to move from one to the other at different stages of life, depending on changing circumstances.

However, a fundamental I'm OK – You're OK position that is established in childhood is never totally obscured, even in the most adverse conditions of life.

Focus on counselling

Achieving the I'm OK – You're OK position often requires a conscious decision (and some effort) in adult life. People who do achieve it tend to respect themselves, and all people with whom they are in contact. In his writing, Berne (1961) makes it quite clear that personal change cannot simply be effected by external circumstances, but must come from within the individual.

An important objective in counselling is to help clients identify and use their own resources so that therapeutic change becomes possible. In transactional analysis people are viewed in a positive way; a basic principle of the approach is that people can be helped to locate their innate (though often neglected) coping abilities. Clients are encouraged to make new decisions about their lives, and alternative ways of behaving are explored in therapy. The OK positions adopted in early childhood can be challenged and changed, and negative life scripts can be reconstructed to become more positive.

Earlier in this unit, we noted that transactional analysis is frequently conducted in groups. The group is, in fact, the ideal medium for clients who wish to become more aware about their personal life scripts and how they originated. Understanding must always precede change, and in transactional analysis groupwork, clients receive feedback from other participants. This practice is of considerable help in increasing self-knowledge for individual clients. The following is a summary of objectives in transactional analysis therapy. Clients:

- should become more autonomous and 'script free'
- work towards the I'm OK – You're OK life position
- learn to state their needs and views clearly without game playing
- take responsibility for their own feelings.

EXERCISE

Life positions

Working either individually or as a group, look at the four life positions listed below and identify any situations in your own life when you experienced each of them. What were the circumstances in each case, and how did you resolve any difficulties you had?

1 I'm not OK – You're OK

2 I'm not OK – You're not OK

3 I'm OK – You're not OK

4 I'm OK – You're OK

Contracts and goals

In transactional analysis, client and counsellor establish a specific and detailed contract, which must be agreed by both. All administrative and business aspects of the counsellor–client relationship are included in a transactional analysis contract, but a much wider agreement on the goals of therapy, and the way these will be achieved is included too. Goals are always stated in positive terms and revised and updated when necessary. This means that attention is directed towards a wide view of personal development and away from a superficial problem-solving approach. However, this does not imply that therapy should always be lengthy. Clients state the specific beliefs and behaviours they wish to change and both client and counsellor work towards these objectives. This joint approach serves to strengthen the equality of the relationship, and encourages clients to experience themselves as active participants in their own therapy. In 1971 Franklin Ernst, a behavioural transactional analysis practitioner, suggested that contracts should be agreed at the end of therapy, as well as the beginning. This end of therapy was meant to solidify the clients' commitment to change. In fact, contracts can be renegotiated at any stage throughout transactional analysis counselling.

The relationship

The relationship itself is based on the concept of equality between the two people involved, and all information, including any notes taken, is shared openly. Clients in transactional analysis counselling are helped to achieve emotional and intellectual insight, but the primary focus of therapy is certainly cognitive. This refers to the understanding we have already mentioned, as a necessary component in the progress towards autonomy and script-free independence. However, creativity and flexibility are further attributes that transactional analysis counsellors need to have.

Clients are also encouraged to become more aware of all aspects of everyday life, and to live with spontaneity in the present. Spontaneous living in the here and now implies freedom from outdated scripts, as well as an ability to choose appropriate responses in personal and social situations. The ability to form relationships without resorting to games or subterfuge is another desired outcome in counselling. Communication between client and counsellor should be clear, and this clarity is facilitated when clients are familiar with the theoretical framework of transactional analysis and its terminology. Clients are encouraged to learn about transactional analysis and to attend courses, if possible. When therapy is taking place in a group context, its aims and objectives are discussed so that all participants are clear about purpose and progress.

Attitudes about the relationship between counsellor and client have changed considerably since Berne first introduced his transactional analysis model of helping. These changes are discussed later in this unit under the heading of 'How transactional analysis has evolved' on page 229.

Permission

In the transactional analysis model of counselling, the concept of 'permissions' has an important place, although, as Stewart (1996) points out, some transactional analysis counsellors now tend to de-emphasise this. The word 'permission' refers to the counsellor's role in encouraging clients to abandon unhealthy or destructive behaviours, in favour of more positive and life-affirming action. Giving permission may take the form of simply telling clients that they need not continue with certain types of behaviour that stem from childhood beliefs still operating at an unconscious level. Many of these beliefs have been passed on from parents and become absorbed into the client's own Parent ego state. The rationale underlining the concept of permission is that it is possible for the counsellor or therapist to switch off the parental recording that is responsible for the client's problems. However, there is another much more important reason for helping clients to become free of negative parental messages. Clients need to learn to trust their own judgment before they can experience true autonomy and freedom from outdated scripts. The following case study highlights the therapeutic effects of permission in counselling.

CASE STUDY

Shelly

Shelly was a middle-aged client, whose mother had died two years before she started counselling. She was now living alone and complained of an inability to enjoy herself, which she described in the following way:

I make plans to go out with Freda [her best friend] and I'm really looking forward to it. Then when I get to the cinema or the restaurant, a black cloud seems to descend on me and something inside me says that I should not enjoy myself. After that I start to feel guilty that I am out on the town, when so many other people can't afford to socialise in that way. I think something bad will happen to me if I enjoy myself.

Comment: The counsellor who helped this client agreed and established a specific contract with her. Background details about Shelly's lifestyle and general health were also discussed, and after this a treatment contract was devised. Shelly stated what it was she wished to achieve through counselling, and later on goals were agreed between client and counsellor. The treatment contract was outlined in positive terms, and Shelly stated that she wished to become more confident about going out. She also wished to be free of the guilt feelings that had plagued her for so long. Her parents had been very religious, and the idea that enjoyment was sinful was accepted in the family when Shelly was a child. These strong messages were stored, therefore, in her Parent ego state, and she was unable to dislodge them without someone to encourage her. The counsellor told Shelly that she need not feel guilty on the next social outing. In order to reinforce this permission, she asked Shelly to picture their present conversation each time pangs of guilt assailed her. This worked very well for the client, who then learned to give herself permission when she needed it. Eventually, even this conscious self-permission was no longer necessary, as Shelly started to feel more independent and free to think for herself.

EXERCISE

Inherited beliefs

Working in groups of three to four, identify any strongly held beliefs (either positive or negative) that you have inherited from your families of origin. Discuss how these beliefs affect you now, and identify any that you now consider to be outdated.

Potency and protection

Offering permission to clients, in the way just described, can only be done when the other important conditions of potency and protection are also present. The word 'potency' refers to the counsellor's strength or conviction, which must be felt by the client if parental injunctions and outdated rules are to be challenged. In other words, the counsellor must, as Berne describes it, feel sufficiently potent to deal with the client's 'Parent'. Furthermore, the client's 'Child' must be convinced that the counsellor is potent enough to give 'protection' against parental anger (Berne, 1972: 371–6). Protection can often take the form of assurance from the counsellor that she is available if the client should need her. This highlights an aspect of transactional analysis that sets it apart from many other models, for although there is an emphasis on client–counsellor equality, there is also recognition that clients frequently need strong support and protection at certain stages of therapy. This means that counsellors need to be aware of their own strength and protective position within the relationship, as well as the need to be directive when necessary. The client is there to receive help, and the counsellor is there to give it. However, clients are not encouraged to become dependent in transactional analysis therapy, and the emphasis throughout is on helping the client to get well and become more autonomous.

Transference

We have considered the concept of transference in the units dealing with psychodynamic approaches to counselling, and it is discussed in Unit 9, alongside other important issues in counselling. Individual approaches to therapy have their own views about transference, but all are aware of its existence, or potential existence, in the counselling relationship. Transactional analysis is no exception. Indeed, Berne (1972) believed that it was a common cause of many problems, both inside and outside therapy. In the context of transactional analysis, the most effective way of illustrating transference (and countertransference) is in diagram form. When clients transfer to counsellors their feelings and attitudes stemming from childhood, then the counsellor is cast in the role of a parent figure. An example is shown in Figure 7.9.

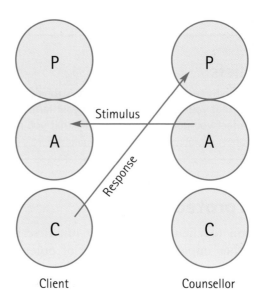

Figure 7.9 Transference (crossed transaction)

The conversation taking place between counsellor and client was as follows:

COUNSELLOR: Last week we talked about the changes you wanted to make . . .
(Adult to Adult)

CLIENT: I'm going to need a lot of help to get started.
(Child to Parent)

Transference dependence on the counsellor is certainly not encouraged in transactional analysis, and the equality of the relationship tends to work against its continuing development in any case.

Countertransference

Countertransference can also be illustrated in diagram form. Figure 7.10 shows the counsellor's Parent response to a statement the client has made.

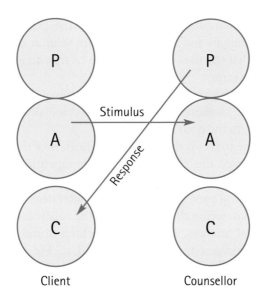

Figure 7.10 Countertransference

The conversation during this exchange was as follows:

CLIENT: I want to refer to one point in the contract we discussed last week.
(Adult to Adult)

COUNSELLOR: Is there something that worries you . . . something I can help you with?
(Parent to Child)

EXERCISE

Transference and countertransference

Using the ego state model described in this unit, illustrate in diagram form any examples of transference or countertransference you can identify from personal experience of helping, or being helped.

How transactional analysis has evolved

Since its inception in the 1960s, transactional analysis has evolved and changed in fundamental ways. Erskine, who refers to transactional analysis as a 'live culture' (Erskine, 2009), enumerates the many and varied developments the approach has undergone, especially within the past ten years (Erskine, 2009: 15). These changes and developments are seen as essential by Erskine and proof to him that the theory and practice of transactional analysis is in a vibrant and healthy state.

In his analysis of the ways in which transactional analysis has absorbed and integrated new methods and theories, Erskine details his 40 years of professional involvement with it.

The first point he makes is that some practitioners of transactional analysis have always emphasised the 'centrality of the therapeutic relationship', but it is only within recent years that the quality of this relationship has become 'paramount' in training programmes and in its literature (Erskine, 2008: 16). Before going on to describe the centrality of the relationship as it exists now within transactional analysis, Erskine enumerates some of the significant developmental milestones that have preceded it. He highlights his own introduction to Berne's original theories, with its emphasis on ego states, analysis of transactions and theory of life scripts, but it was not until he started to treat clients with posttraumatic stress that he came to understand the true nature of games, for example. To Erskine, it was not that clients were simply involved in game playing. On the contrary, games were the clients' attempts to convey unconscious messages they could not convey in any other way. From this point onwards, he details the major advances in transactional analysis theory and practice. Some of these are as follows.

Major advances in transactional analysis theory and practice

Franklin Ernst

Franklin Ernst (1971), who was a behavioural transactional analyst and writer, emphasised the importance of behavioural change as a means of ending outdated script patterns. He introduced the idea of using contracts at the end of therapy and not just the beginning. This end of therapy innovation was meant to solidify the client's commitment to change. In addition, Ernst placed greater stress on the use of strokes with clients. This meant addressing them by name and focusing on areas of their lives that they were proud of. Ernst often worked with prisoners, and his approach with them was positive and affirming.

Behavioural change and short-term therapy

An emphasis on behavioural change began to emerge in transactional analysis, along with a focus on short-term therapy. This era also became synonymous with a more confrontational style. Aspects of these developments are indicated by Karpman (1968), whose illustration of the 'Drama Triangle' was meant to explain the dynamics of game playing, but often encouraged confrontation. Schiff (1975) developed the 'Cathexis' model of transactional analysis, which was designed to help patients in residential care and used the concept of 'reparenting', in order to mend their original dysfunctional relationship with parents. The word 'Cathexis' is derived from psychoanalysis and refers to the psychic energy a person invests in another person, ideas or objects. In the Cathexis model of transactional analysis the Parent ego state develops constantly throughout the life span. If the Parent ego state is not fixed as Schiff suggests, then it follows that a reparenting relationship with a therapist is possible. The Cathexis model was meant to help disturbed clients repair a dysfunctional relationship with an actual parent. Schiff's techniques were also designed to encourage these clients to consider the effects of their behaviour on other people, but Schiff's approach tended to be confrontational as well.

The 'Redecision' school

The 'Redecision' school founded by Mary and Robert Goulding (1979) integrated the theory and practice of transactional analysis with Gestalt therapy and often used confrontation as a prerequisite to change or redecision. Their theory of redecision stresses the possibility of reversing early decisions made in childhood. In order to facilitate this change in clients, the Gouldings encouraged them to return to childhood and the time when inappropriate decisions were made. This approach meant that clients were prompted to go back to the original childhood scenes, and from a Child ego state new decisions could be made. Theoretically, it is then possible, over time and with practice, for clients to gain a new sense of confidence and freedom from outdated injunctions.

Egograms

The egogram is a diagram or graph designed by Jack Dusay (1977) to indicate the relative importance of each ego state within a person's personality. This is based on the premise that we all have different amounts of psychic energy invested in the three ego states. The egogram shows this distribution of energy. It should be possible for a person to chart their own egogram by drawing a graph of their feelings over a period of time, indicating the ego states operating as feelings and behaviour change. Aside from his work with egograms, Dusay's style was also confrontational at this time.

Decrease in confrontational methods in 1980s

The 1980s saw a decrease in confrontational methods within transactional analysis. Many practitioners challenged aspects of the approach to clients and patients in vogue at that time. Erskine (2009) refers to his work with people suffering from post-traumatic stress disorder; sensing their vulnerability he avoided any focus on behaviour change or confrontation. He did not use the transactional analysis methods of interviewing, interpretation or explanation, but focused instead on clients' experiences and feelings. Alongside this, Erskine came to believe that clients most needed attitudes of acceptance rather than confrontation.

Change in theory and practice continued to develop

Change in the theory and practice of transactional analysis continued to develop. At numerous workshops and seminars, practitioners discussed the relative merits of various approaches. Cognitive understanding was a central tenet of transactional analysis, but gradually its pre-eminence began to wane, though it certainly did not disappear. The emphasis on explanation through teaching and the use of diagrams as aids to client understanding were no longer the bedrock on which transactional analysis therapists built their approach to helping. However, these skills are still considered useful in transactional analysis, but they no longer dominate the approach.

Integration of diverse theoretical concepts

Today, transactional analysis integrates diverse theoretical concepts. Erskine (2009: 18) suggests that there may be a 'dozen' different schools of transactional analysis, including 'psychodynamic transactional analysis', 'constructivist transactional analysis', 'relational transactional analysis' and 'body-centred transactional analysis'. In addition to those listed by Erskine, there are now 'cognitive behavioural' transactional analysis practitioners and 'narrative' transactional analysis practitioners. The term 'narrative' used in this context refers to an approach that is client centred and collaborative and seeks to understand the client's story, with an emphasis on what is of interest to the client. Erskine attributes this proliferation of different approaches to the 'flexibility' of transactional analysis, as well as to its lack of strict or unbending dogma.

Quality of therapeutic relationship is central to therapy and healing

The quality of the therapeutic relationship is now regarded as central to the process of therapy and healing. Erskine (2009: 19) describes key aspects of current transactional analysis theory and practice. These include the ability of the therapist to be personally involved in relationship with the client. This does not imply any overlapping of professional boundaries, however. What it does mean is that the focus has moved away from the client's 'internal disturbance alone' to a newer, two-person 'relational psychotherapy', in which the therapist is engaged in an empathetic relationship with the client (Erskine, 2009: 20). The work of Kohut (1977), whose theories we have discussed in Unit 4, was a key influence on Erskine's decision to move from an interpretive approach to one that emphasised validation, presence, empathy and an acknowledgement of the client's unique, phenomenological experience. As we have already seen, this does not mean that the classical concepts of transactional analysis (described in this unit) have been abandoned; what it does mean is that new perspectives, including the focus on the integrative and relational are welcomed and absorbed. These new perspectives ensure that transactional analysis theory and practice continues to grow and develop.

Clients who benefit from this approach

Transactional analysis is a model of counselling that has potential benefit for most clients. Its strength lies in its accessibility as a communications skills model, and it is especially helpful to those clients who have relationship problems (whether at home or in the workplace). In either of these two situations, clients can be helped through the use of the structural and descriptive diagrams of personality, in order to identify the source of their difficulties in communicating effectively with others. Transactional analysis can also encourage clients to abandon outdated ways of relating to others through game playing. The unpleasant feelings like anger, hurt, fear and guilt, associated with games and referred to as 'rackets' by Berne (1972: 137), are highlighted in therapy too. When such feelings are identified in this way, clients are then able to make the changes necessary to become more open and spontaneous in relation to other people.

The concept of scripts is useful, too, since it serves to illuminate the early events and formative influence that tend to govern the course of our lives and behaviour. Clients who experience a compulsion to repeat certain patterns of behaviour, for example, can learn a great deal through transactional analysis, and those clients who are simply interested in personal growth can also benefit from it. The approach has many applications to everyday life, and, since it is often conducted in groups, it has special relevance for clients who experience problems in relation to groups. The group approach tends to make therapy cheaper for clients as well; and because transactional analysis training is well established and thorough, with an emphasis on professionalism and accreditation, clients are likely to get quality service from the counsellors who help them.

Because of its strong 'cognitive' orientation, transactional analysis tends to appeal to people who value a more intellectual approach. As we have already seen, this does not imply an absence of attention to feelings, but it does mean that a thinking and analytical engagement is more prominent in transactional analysis than in some other models. In addition, some people respond well to an approach that is questioning and educational. With its attention to contracts and goals, which can be renegotiated between counsellor and client when necessary, transactional analysis offers a structured and problem-focused psychotherapy that can be either short or long term, depending on the needs of clients. Corey (2009: 32) suggests that transactional analysis has much to offer when applied to multicultural counselling. This is because of its focus on 'family injunctions and the emphasis on early decisions'. Clients from different cultural backgrounds may have received injunctions that bind them to certain restricted work choices, for example, or to limited marital or other choices. Depending on their commitment to autonomy from family injunctions, these clients may welcome the descriptive clarity and structure the theory of transactional analysis offers.

Some limitations

At the beginning of this unit, we noted that the specialised terminology of transactional analysis is both its strength and its weakness. The language of the approach is attractive to many people, but there are others for whom it seems simplistic or contrived. However, it is relevant to point out here that Berne deliberately designed a system that would simplify complex Freudian concepts, thereby making them comprehensible to everyone. The personality structure Berne delineated through his use of Parent, Adult and Child is readily understood by most people, including teenagers and even children. The traditional cognitive emphasis in transactional analysis may limit it for some people, especially those who place more value on the expression of emotion. On the other hand, most transactional analysis therapists are familiar with diverse approaches and integrate aspects of these in their work, where appropriate. In addition, the current emphasis on the client–counsellor relationship means that a more empathic approach to clients is likely within contemporary practice. It is possible that the language of transactional analysis may come to dominate exchanges between therapist and client during sessions, thereby potentially distancing both from true person-to-person contact. There are some situations, including crisis counselling, for example, for which the approach may not be immediately suitable. This is because people in severe crisis often lack the concentration necessary to engage with unfamiliar concepts such as those intrinsic to transactional analysis. On the other hand, clients post-crisis may benefit greatly from transactional analysis, especially if the crisis has led them to seek enlightenment about family and their experiences within it. Corey (2009), whom we quoted in the previous section, also points out that even though transactional analysis has definite strengths in relation to multicultural counselling, it has some limitations in this context too. He states, for example, that 'the terminology may seem foreign to some people', in spite of the fact that it is generally considered easy to understand (Corey, 2009: 34). In addition, there are clients who, because of their culture and background, would consider it anathema to question family traditions in the way that transactional analysis encourages people to do.

SUMMARY

In this unit, we looked at transactional analysis and considered its application to therapeutic counselling. The first part of the unit dealt with some aspects of the specialised terminology used in the approach, and its groupwork format was also discussed. A brief history of Eric Berne was provided, and his ego state model was described in some detail. The four major areas of transactional analysis (structural, transactional, game and script) were outlined. The four basic OK positions were also described, and the way in which games and scripts originate from these was discussed. We looked at the objectives in transactional analysis counselling, the importance of contracts and goals, and the therapeutic relationship between client and counsellor. Transference and countertransference were shown in diagram form, and the dialogue was included to illustrate these concepts. Early and more recent developments in transactional analysis were outlined, along with some discussion about the advantages and disadvantages of the approach in relation to clients.

References

Berne, E. (1961) *Transactional Analysis in Psychotherapy*. London: Souvenir Press.

Berne, E. (1964) *Games People Play*. London: Penguin Books.

Berne, E. (1966) *Principles of Group Treatment*. New York: Grove Press.

Berne, E. (1972) *What Do You Say After You Say Hello?* London: Corgi Books.

Corey, G. (2009) 'Transactional Analysis' (online) Available at: www.acadiau.ca/transactional analysis. Accessed June 2013.

Dusay. J. M. (1977) *Egograms*. New York: Harper and Row.

Erskine, R.G. (2009) 'The Culture of Transactional Analysis: Theory, Methods, and Evolving Patterns.' *Transactional Analysis Journal*. 2009 39: 14. Available at: http://Tax.Sagepub.com/content/ 39/1/14 (accessed June 2013).

Ernst, F. H. (1971) *Getting Well with Transactional Analysis: Get-On-With, Getting Well and Get (to be) Winners*. Vallejo, CA: Set Publications.

Goulding, M. & Goulding, R. (1979) *Changing Lives Through Redecision Therapy*. New York: Brunner Mazel.

Harris, T. A. (1973) *I'm OK- You're OK*, London: Pan Books.

Karpman, S. (1968) 'Fairy Tales and Script Drama Analysis'. *Transactional Analysis Bulletin*, 7 (26) 39–43.

Schiff, J. et al.(1975) *The Cathexis Reader: Transactional Analysis Treatment of Psychosis*. New York: Harper and Row.

Steiner, C. (1974) *Scripts People Live*. New York: Grove Press.

Stewart, I. (1996) *Developing Transactional Analysis Counselling*. London: Sage Publications.

Further reading

Erskine, R.G. (ed.) (2010) *Life Scripts: A Transactional Analysis of Unconscious Relational Patterns.* London: Karnac Books.

Fowlie, H. & Sills C. (eds.) (2011) *Relational Transactional Analysis: Principles in Practice*. London: Karnac Books.

Hargaden, H. (2012) *Transactional Analysis*. Oxford: Taylor & Francis.

Hargaden, H. & Sills, C. (2002) *Transactional Analysis: A Relational Perspective*. London: Routledge.

James, M. & Jongeward, D. (1971) *Born to Win*. London: Signet Penguin.

Klein, M. (2013) *Know Yourself, Know Your Partner: Successful Relationships Using Transactional Analysis*. Plymouth: Zambezi Publishing.

Kohut, H. (1977) *The Restoration of the Self*. Chicago: The University of Chicago Press.

Lapworth, P. & Sills, C. (2011*) An Introduction to Transactional Analysis: Helping People Change*. London: Sage Publications.

Midgley, D. (1998) *New Directions in Transactional Analysis: An Explorer's Handbook*. London: Free Association Books.

Stewart, I. (1992) *Eric Berne: Key Figures in Counselling and Psychotherapy*. London: Sage Publications.

Stewart, I. (2007) *Transactional Analysis Counselling in Action* (3rd edn). London: Sage Publications.

Tudor, K. (2001) *Transactional Analysis Approaches to Brief Therapy: Or, What Do You Say Between Saying Hello And Goodbye?* London: Sage Publications.
Widdowson, M. (2009) *Transactional Analysis: 100 Key Points and Techniques.* London: Routledge.

Resources

Websites

www.itaa-net.org
The International Transactional Analysis Association.
www.ita.org.uk
The Institute of Transactional Analysis. Gives details of education and training.
www.claudsteiner.com
Information about Claude Steiner, Eric Berne and other TA theorists.
www.ericberne.com
The official website for Eric Berne. Includes a detailed history and description of Transactional Analysis.
www.ta-tutor-com
General educational information about Transactional Analysis.
www.eataneews.org
The European Association for Transactional Analysis.
www.usataa.org
The USA. TA Association.
www.tastudent.org.uk
Official professional journal of the International Transactional Analysis Association.

Addresses

Institute of Transactional Analysis
Broadway House
149–151 St Neots Road
Hardwick
Cambridge
CB23 7QJ
Email: admin@ita.org.uk

Answers [from page 218]

1 Adult
2 Adapted Child
3 Free Child (Negative)
4 Controlling Parent
5 Nurturing Parent
6 Controlling Parent
7 Free Child (Positive)
8 Adult
9 Controlling Parent
10 Adult

8

Cognitive behavioural therapy

◆ Introduction

In Unit 2 we identified the major theoretical approaches to counselling, from which all the contemporary models described in this book have evolved. Of the three perspectives – psychodynamic, humanistic and behavioural – only the behavioural and the cognitive behavioural approaches remain to be discussed.

Many of the counselling models we have looked at describe the internal or unseen characteristics said to govern human behaviour. The structure of personality outlined by Freud, and the actualising tendency both Rogers and Maslow upheld, are located firmly within the person. In contrast to this, the cognitive behavioural tradition is concerned with human behaviour and thinking. The behavioural tradition, which originated before the development of cognitive behavioural therapy, stems from the work of a group of psychologists whose findings we shall briefly outline in this unit. The emphasis on observable behaviour alone, which was the hallmark of behaviour therapy, has radically shifted to incorporate the importance of cognition in determining a person's actions and behaviour. In this unit, we shall concentrate on the development and principles of cognitive behavioural therapy, which is now used widely within the NHS and by private practitioners.

KEY TERM

Cognition: The experience of thinking, reasoning, perceiving and remembering. Early behaviour therapy highlighted observable behaviour only, while cognitive behaviour therapy stresses that thinking affects how we feel and what we do.

Evolution of behaviour therapy

Behaviour therapy evolved from theories of human learning that were formulated at the beginning of the twentieth century. The first studies of learning took place in laboratories, and animals, not humans, were used in the experiments. In the following section we shall list some of the main contributors in the field of learning theory.

Ivan Pavlov (1849–1936)

Through his work with dogs, Pavlov formulated the principle of classical conditioning (Pavlov, 1927). The dogs in Pavlov's experiments salivated at the sound of a bell, prior to eating. Eventually, the dogs were seen to salivate when they heard the bell, even when no food followed. This associative learning offers some explanation about the way humans develop phobias.

It highlights the process whereby an event, object or activity becomes associated with a specific response, usually avoidance in the case of a phobia.

J. B. Watson (1878–1958)

Watson contributed to learning theory by frightening a small child who was playing with a pet rat. This was achieved by producing a loud noise each time the boy played with the animal. Eventually, the child's fear extended to all furry toys and even fur coats (Watson, 1928). Watson's work supports the view that human emotional responses, like phobias, are usually the result of conditioning. If we accept this is the case, then it seems logical to suppose that conditioning can be reversed through a process of unconditioning. Such a process is fundamental to many of the methods traditionally used in behaviour therapy.

E. L. Thorndike (1874–1949)

Learning theory was furthered by Thorndike (1911), who also experimented with animals. He formulated the law of effect, which states that when a response to a specific stimulus is followed by a reward, the bond between the stimulus and the response will be strengthened. On the other hand, when the response is followed by a negative outcome, the bond will be weakened. His research enhanced the status of learning in psychology and showed that it is possible to predict behaviour through an understanding of its laws. In simple terms, we could say that a satisfying experience is one that induces movement towards it, while an unsatisfying experience has the opposite effect. Behaviour is therefore dependent on its consequences, which may be either reward or punishment.

B. F. Skinner (1904–1990)

Skinner, whose work was conducted in the 1930s at the University of Minnesota, extended the research of Thorndike. Skinner's experiments on laboratory animals indicated that in order to ensure responses will be repeated, animals need to be rewarded. This, in turn, means that animal behaviour is reinforced. Skinner's laboratory animals learned by trial and error that there is a link between behaviour (pressing a lever) and the reward of food. If a certain type of behaviour leads to discomfort, however, or an expected reward is not forthcoming, then the behaviour becomes less likely in the future. According to Skinner, 'Behaviour is shaped and maintained by its consequences', a maxim which is as relevant to humans as it is to animals (Skinner, 1988: 23).

Albert Bandura (1925–)

Bandura belongs to another group of psychologists, called the social learning theorists, who accept that human learning takes place according to the principles of reinforcement and punishment. However, they go beyond this and suggest that children learn from others, too, through a process of observation and imitation. Children who observe others being disciplined for certain behaviours, for example, are unlikely to engage in that behaviour themselves.

By the same token, behaviour that is clearly rewarded in others is likely to prompt imitation. The social learning theory of Albert Bandura (1977) helps to explain how people acquire complex social behaviours in social settings.

Joseph Wolpe (1915–1997)

Wolpe, a South African psychiatrist, also contributed significantly to the field of behaviour therapy. In 1958 he developed behavioural methods that were effective in relieving a number of psychological problems, including stress, anxiety and irrational fears. He pioneered the use of systematic desensitisation, for the treatment of phobias, and the technique of progressive relaxation training, which is used in conjunction with systematic desensitisation in therapy (Wolpe, 1958).

Hans J. Eysenck (1916–1997)

Eysenck, a psychologist who worked at the Maudsley Hospital in London, contributed to the development of behavioural therapy when he produced a study in 1952 of the effectiveness of psychoanalysis as a treatment for psychological problems. The results of the study are interesting and suggest that psychoanalysis achieved very little. These findings gave a great boost to behaviour therapy as a model for treating people with emotional problems. It also ensured that the work of clinical psychologists who used behaviour therapy techniques gained in popularity, as attention focused on the work they were doing. However, Eysenck's findings have been disputed by various theorists and practitioners over the past 50 years.

Procedures which stem from the behavioural tradition

Behaviourism has within its repertoire a wide range of methods that can be used with clients. Some of the established behavioural techniques that are frequently used in therapy are given below.

> ### KEY TERM
>
> **Behaviourism:** The scientific study of behaviour based on observable actions and reactions. The focus is on analysing the relationship between behaviour and the environment, and the way that stimuli provoke responses.

Relaxation training

Anxiety and stress are common problems for many clients who seek help. In view of this, relaxation training is used extensively for a variety of problems.

Anxiety affects people on three levels – psychological, physiological and behavioural. It tends to increase the heart and breathing rates and may cause other symptoms, including muscle tension, irritability, sleep problems and difficulty in concentrating. Many anxious people breathe in a shallow fashion from the chest. Clients can be taught to change this pattern so that deeper abdominal breathing is learned. This has the effect of increasing oxygen supply to the brain and muscles which, in turn, help to improve concentration, promote calmness and deeper connectedness between mind and body. Clients can be taught to set aside time each day for relaxation, and there are numerous instruction manuals and recordings to facilitate this practice.

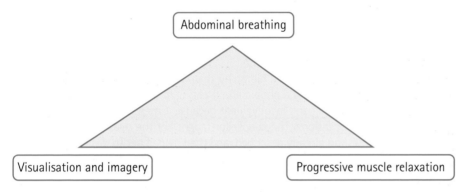

Figure 8.1 Aids to relaxation

EXERCISE

Relaxation

Sit quietly in a chair until you feel still and comfortable. Beginning with your feet, allow all the muscles of your body to relax. Place your hand on your abdomen and breathe in slowly and deeply through your nose. You should feel your abdomen extend as you do this. Now breathe out slowly through your mouth, noting how your abdomen returns to its usual shape. Repeat the breathing exercise for about five minutes, then sit still again and experience your relaxed state. A slight variation of the exercise is to repeat a chosen word, or phrase, each time you breathe out.

Comment: This simple exercise forms the basis of most relaxation techniques. To test its effectiveness, you could ask someone to take your pulse before and after the exercise. Your pulse rate should be slower afterwards, which indicates a more relaxed state.

Systematic desensitisation

This is a technique devised by Wolpe (1958). It is used as a means of helping clients to deal with irrational fears and phobias. It is based on the premise that it is impossible for someone to be anxious and relaxed at the same time.

Since anxiety responses are learned or conditioned, it should be possible to eliminate these responses if the anxious person is helped to relax in the face of the anxiety producing stimulus. The client is, therefore, systematically desensitised to the fearful object, or situation, through a process of exposure to it, while in a relaxed state. Progressive muscle relaxation techniques and deep breathing are integral to this technique, and clients are taught how to reduce anxiety before they confront their fear. Constructing a 'hierarchy' is another important feature of systematic desensitisation and involves a series of situations or scenes relating to the phobia. Each scene in the hierarchy is ranked from mildly to extremely anxiety-provoking.

CASE STUDY

Constructing a hierarchy

The following is an example of a hierarchy that was used to help a 20-year-old client, called Isobel, who had a phobia about eating in front of strangers. Isobel's phobia was embarrassing and inconvenient because it meant that she refused to socialise on many occasions. The counsellor taught her the relaxation procedure and breathing method already described, and then helped her to design and work through the following hierarchy, which she was encouraged to practise on a regular basis.

Visualise:

- asking a close friend to accompany you on a visit to a restaurant
- phoning a restaurant to make a reservation
- getting dressed for your evening out
- doing your hair and putting on make-up
- opening the door to greet your friend
- walking to the restaurant, a short distance away
- meeting people along the way
- passing other cafes and restaurants as you walk along
- arriving at the door of the restaurant
- speaking to the waiter about your reservation
- walking to the table with your friend and the waiter
- placing an order with the waiter
- looking at your food when it arrives
- picking up the knife and fork and starting to eat
- tasting the food and enjoying it
- looking around at other diners
- noting that other people are enjoying themselves
- becoming aware that other people are enjoying themselves
- becoming aware that other people occasionally glance at your table
- continuing your meal and the conversation with your friend.

CASE STUDY Cont...

Comment: Clients need to give a detailed history of the phobia, with special emphasis on those aspects of it which cause the most anxiety. What made this client most anxious was the thought of being observed while eating. For this reason, observation was presented towards the end of the hierarchy, which meant that Isobel could work gradually towards it.

Assertiveness training

Clients who seek counselling often experience difficulties in three key areas. These include:

- expressing their feelings
- asking for what they need or want
- saying no to requests from others.

The most important aspect of assertiveness training is in helping clients to differentiate between submissive, aggressive and assertive styles of communication. When people are submissive they tend to ignore their own rights and needs, and this can result in feelings of depression and anger, which are never really expressed. Aggressive people may be bullying and demanding, characteristics that alienate others. On the other hand, assertive behaviour involves direct person-to-person communication without manipulation, hostility or submissiveness. Assertiveness training is widely available in groups and clients are sometimes referred to them so they can increase their self-awareness and confidence generally.

The cognitive emphasis

As the name suggests, cognitive therapy is concerned with the thinking and reasoning aspects of a person's experience. We have seen that behaviour therapy evolved from the theories of learning first formulated by Pavlov, Watson, Thorndike, Skinner, Wolpe and Eysenck, and from the experiments of Bandura and other psychologists who were interested in the effects of observation on the individual's learning experience. The behavioural approach, widely used in the 1950s, emphasised the importance of visible behaviour and its environmental context. However, this emphasis tended to ignore the thinking and feeling aspects of human behaviour; it was not until several psychologists, including Aaron Beck and Albert Ellis, began to focus on the thoughts and beliefs of disturbed or anxious clients that the cognitive dimension came into being.

The work of these theorists highlights the way in which anxious and depressed clients contribute to their own problems through faulty, or destructive, thought processes and preoccupations. This section looks in some detail at the work of two cognitive behaviour models. The first model was pioneered in 1955 by Albert Ellis, and the second was developed in the early 1960s by Aaron Beck.

Albert Ellis (1913–2007)

Albert Ellis was responsible for pioneering cognitive behaviour therapy (CBT) in the 1950s; since then, his own individual approach, now called rational emotive behaviour therapy (REBT), has become one of the most popular cognitive models. Ellis, who was trained in psychoanalysis, became disillusioned with what he perceived to be its limitations. As a result of his scepticism and his doubts about 'the efficacy of classical analytic techniques', he found himself trying out different methods, many of which he found unsatisfactory too (Ellis, 1991: 7). Ellis, who was born in Pittsburgh, Pennsylvania, was President of the Albert Ellis Institute in New York. Until his 90s, and despite numerous health problems, he conducted regular workshops in rational emotive behaviour therapy at the Institute. His background training included studies in accounting, clinical psychology, family and marriage counselling and, of course, psychoanalysis. Classical psychoanalysis is an in-depth and time-consuming form of therapy, not suited (or available) to many clients, and Ellis was concerned to establish a more egalitarian and pragmatic approach, which would address the needs of a wider range of people seeking help (Ellis, 1991).

Albert Ellis held many posts throughout his career, including Consultant in Clinical Psychology to the New York Board of Education and Vice President of the American Academy of Psychotherapists. He also wrote numerous books and articles and served as consulting or associate editor of many professional journals.

Development of the approach

During the 1950s Ellis became interested in behavioural learning theory. He noted that psychoanalysis and learning theory have a great deal in common, since both emphasise the importance of conditioning in early life (Ellis, 1991). However, he concluded that action as well as insight is necessary if people are to address the difficulties that stem from childhood and the early conditioning that determines so many problematic responses in adult life. In addition, Ellis identified the central place of negative thinking in the perpetuation of emotional disturbance, and he was especially interested in the type of negative thinking which reinforces early disturbing and traumatic experiences. Clients, he believed, often cling to outdated feelings of anger and guilt, which impede psychological growth, and are, in any case, no longer applicable to the present situation. Outdated or negative thinking is often the direct result of information that has been conveyed to clients at an early stage by parents or other important people at that time. In Ellis' view, language is the key to the perpetuation of emotional problems, since it is through the use of language and 'the symbol-producing facility that goes with language' that clients enforce their fears and anxieties stemming from early life (Ellis, 1991: 14). To compound the problem even further, people frequently denigrate themselves and their efforts, demand perfection from themselves and others and become 'illogically upset' over the frustrations of ordinary life (Ellis, 1991: 71).

Other influences

The importance of both language and thinking is stressed throughout Ellis' writing. References to philosophy and literature are also frequent and, indeed, these two subjects have informed and helped to define many aspects of his work. Ellis was especially interested in the Stoic philosophers, including Epictetus, who believed that people become disturbed, not by events themselves but by personal interpretations of those events.

Development of the title

Ellis changed the title of his approach several times from its inception in the 1950s. The original title (rational psychotherapy) did not do full justice to the layers underpinning the theory, since it failed to incorporate the three components – cognitive, emotional and behavioural – of human experience. Ellis also wanted to differentiate between his own model and other purely cognitive approaches that were emerging in the 1950s. In 1959, two years after he abandoned psychoanalysis, he founded the Institute for Rational Emotive Therapy, now the Albert Ellis Institute. In 1993 Ellis changed the title again, this time to Rational emotive behaviour therapy (Ellis, 2005).

The theory of rational emotive behaviour therapy

Ellis believed that many human problems are generated from three important sources. These include thinking, emotional and

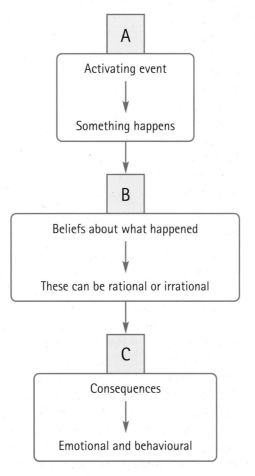

Figure 8.2 The ABC model (adapted from Ellis, 1991:176)

behavioural sources, but he placed special emphasis on the significance of 'cognition', or thinking, in the perpetuation of psychological disturbance (Ellis, 1991: 106). Ellis referred to a number of philosophers to support his thesis, and suggested that human beings create their own disturbed feelings, which they either consciously or unconsciously generate. If we accept this is the case then it follows, according to Ellis (1991), that people have within themselves the resources and willpower necessary to effect lasting and healthy change. Ellis further described the sequence of events that lead to psychological disturbance through the use of an ABC model (see Figure 8.2).

In the first instance, people start with goals in life, and these are usually constructive and positive. What tends to happen, however, is that problems and difficulties are encountered at various stages, which interfere with a person's desire for success and comfort. After this, people construct their own largely negative beliefs, or interpretations, of these events and these beliefs lead to certain emotional and behavioural consequences. According to Ellis, people are liable to believe that unless they do well in all aspects of everyday life they are 'worthless' or 'no good', attitudes which inevitably lead to feelings of failure and guilt (Ellis, 1991: 28).

CASE STUDY

The ABC model

Bill, who was in his 50s, had a very good relationship with his next-door neighbour, Roy, who was about the same age. Bill applied to his doctor for counselling help because he suffered from increasing depression, linked to several significant changes in his life. His parents had died in the previous year, and he had just discovered that his daughter's marriage was breaking up. In addition to his depression, Bill suffered from severe loss of confidence, which, he said, had been prompted by his experience of early retirement and by feelings of panic about his age. During counselling Bill talked about an incident with his neighbour, Roy, which had caused him a great deal of anxiety and had knocked his confidence even further. Roy's eight-year-old grandson had come to stay for a holiday and, several days later, Bill's own grandson came to stay with him too. When Bill suggested to his neighbour that they should plan some activities together, Roy responded by saying that while he would be happy to share some time as a group, he would also like to reserve most outings with his grandson and members of his own family. Bill ruminated at length about this response, which he took as a personal rejection of himself and the friendship he offered. Afterwards he became even more depressed and withdrawn, and for several weeks avoided his neighbour. The rational emotive therapy model, see Figure 8.3, shows in diagram form this sequence of events.

CASE STUDY Cont...

Comment: Ellis' ABC model of personality and emotional disturbance highlights the relationship between thinking and emotion. In Ellis' view, (Ellis, 1991) it is not what happens at point A that causes emotional disturbance or distress. People form their own inferences and beliefs at point B, and reinforce them through the use of negative and 'catastrophising' self-talk and rumination. It is this internal soliloquy which then leads to the emotional and behavioural reactions that occur at point C. Bill's action in avoiding his neighbour led to a worsening situation, since eventually Roy stopped making social overtures in the mistaken belief that Bill had lost interest. This had the effect of deepening Bill's depression and general loss of confidence. In counselling, he was helped to see how his own thinking had contributed to his problems overall. The counsellor explained the ABC model of rational emotive behaviour therapy to Bill. It should be added, however, that there were other factors in this client's life that contributed to his depression, and these were also addressed in counselling.

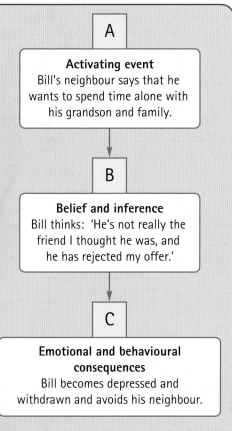

A

Activating event
Bill's neighbour says that he wants to spend time alone with his grandson and family.

B

Belief and inference
Bill thinks: 'He's not really the friend I thought he was, and he has rejected my offer.'

C

Emotional and behavioural consequences
Bill becomes depressed and withdrawn and avoids his neighbour.

Figure 8.3 Irrational thinking and emotional disturbance

Figure 8.4 shows how Bill might have chosen to respond to the activating event described.

Rational and irrational thinking

Ellis (1995) took the view that people have a basic tendency to be irrational as well as rational in their thinking. Irrational thinking is seen as a fundamental cause of psychological disturbance. It is developed early in life and is due, in part, to biological tendencies, but it is also the result of social learning and the emotional investment we all have in our own particular beliefs. Rational emotive behaviour therapy aims to help clients to develop more rational, less punitive, ways of thinking, and this means encouraging them to consider

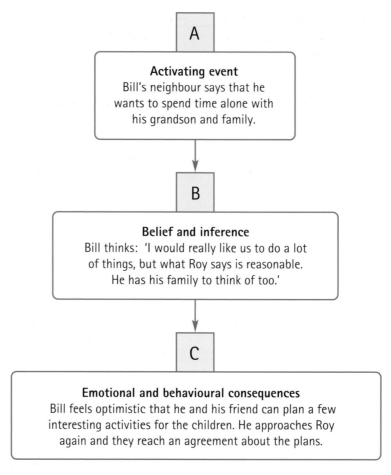

Figure 8.4 Changing irrational beliefs

the ways in which their irrational thinking of the past has contributed to numerous problems. Clients are also encouraged to work towards long-term, rather than short-term, change so that the ordinary (and less ordinary) difficulties of life are dealt with more effectively as time goes on.

Some irrational beliefs

According to Ellis (1991), most people subscribe to a number of irrational or illogical beliefs, which lead to many of the problems experienced by clients. These beliefs, which are seldom questioned by anyone, tend to be passed from one generation to another so that they become accepted wisdom. Ellis referred to these beliefs as 'superstitions and prejudices' (Ellis, 1991: 60) and he went on to say that, in his opinion, they can only be changed through a radical shift in individual and societal outlook. The following are some of the irrational beliefs he described:

- I should be loved and approved of by everyone.
- In order to be a worthwhile person, I need to be good at everything.
- Bad people, including myself, should be severely punished.
- If things are not the way I want them to be, it's a disaster.
- I have no real control over my problems, which are caused by external factors.
- I need to keep on reminding myself of the awful things that may happen.
- It's easier to avoid than to face problems and responsibilities.
- I always need someone stronger to take care of me.
- I can't change my behaviour because of my awful past.
- I should always become emotionally engaged in other people's problems.

(Adapted from Ellis, 1991)

> **EXERCISE**
>
> ## Irrational beliefs
>
> Working with a partner, look at the above list of irrational beliefs and say how many of them you subscribe to, or may have subscribed to at certain times of your life. Discuss these with your partner, paying special attention to any beliefs you have in common. Consider the origins of such beliefs and say how you think you may have acquired your own.

Shoulds and musts

Throughout his writing on the subject of rational emotive behaviour therapy, Ellis often referred to the shoulds and musts that are frequently used by clients who seek to impose demands on themselves and others. People, for example, express the view that they must be good at certain things or that other people must always be nice to them. If these 'musts' are not realised, life is seen as intolerable, awful or not worth living. These misleading and disturbance-producing shoulds and musts are irrational according to Ellis (1995); and in rational emotive behaviour therapy, they are regarded as primary causes of emotional problems. Ellis also used the terms 'catastrophise' or 'awfulise' to describe those forms of irrational thinking which tend to cause disturbed or neurotic behaviour (Ellis, 1991: 60–88). Ellis believed that once people accept their own or other people's irrational beliefs, they are likely to produce additional anxieties or disturbances. Thus people become very anxious about their anxiety, depressed about their depression, or self-loathing about their anger towards others.

Helping clients to change

In rational emotive behaviour therapyclients are taught the ABC model at an early stage. Clients are also encouraged to look at the 'activating event' and the 'emotional disturbance' they have experienced. Afterwards, attention is directed to the 'beliefs' and inferences that have created such a powerful influence in the production of emotional disturbance. It is possible to teach this model effectively and quickly and most clients, apart from those who are seriously ill or confused, are able to grasp it. Clients are also encouraged to identify and dispute their 'musts' and any other irrational beliefs they entertain.

This is a highly active and direct approach, which incorporates elements of teaching, persuasion, debate and even humour within its repertoire. Ellis was, in fact, notable among psychotherapists and counsellors for his support of humour as a therapeutic tool. It is not something we tend to associate with therapists who, as a group, have tended to avoid it. There are various reasons for this reluctance to engage in humour, and it has to be said that humour is, indeed, often inappropriate in the therapeutic context. However, as Strean (1995) indicates, Freud admired humour and freely appreciated it in his friends and in his patients. Ellis, too, appreciated it, and he recommended the use of humour as a way of helping clients to diffuse their own seriousness and to separate themselves from stuffy outmoded beliefs (Ellis, 1995). It goes without saying that humour should never be used against clients in therapy. It also needs to be sensitively timed and appropriate to the situation. The following is an example of the way humour was used with one client who had a compulsion to check, at very frequent intervals, all the cups in the kitchen cupboard.

CLIENT: What we talked about last time did work quite well. Instead of checking the cups when I got home from shopping, I went out into the garden instead and did some work there. I felt a lot better about doing that. I think it's getting better, but I still feel like counting something.

COUNSELLOR: The saucepans and cutlery maybe?

CLIENT: Oh, God, no [laughs]. Well, I am beginning to look more closely at the way I think about this checking, and I can see how I have actually been thinking the worst . . . that if I don't count the cups, everything will go wrong and I'll be out of control. I actually can laugh at myself now and I think that's real progress.

Homework and other tasks

Clients may be given homework tasks to do, and they are frequently asked to read self-help books on the subject of rational emotive behaviour therapy. Homework may include self-monitoring and recording of negative thoughts and self-sabotaging beliefs, as well as exercises in critical thinking and questioning. Written work is sometimes included in homework exercises, and this might take the form of writing down and disputing personal beliefs that may have caused problems in the past. Imagery is another technique used in this approach, and clients are sometimes asked to 'imagine' themselves responding in positive ways to situations that have been problematic for them in the past.

Role play, which is used extensively in assertiveness training and behaviour therapy, is incorporated into the Ellis model. A client could, for example, role play some feared or threatening future event such as public speaking, a job interview, or an appointment to ask for a change of conditions at work. 'Modelling' is also used, but in this approach its application is not restricted to counselling sessions. It may be extended to models of positive behaviour which clients may have observed in others. Many clients are familiar with favourite characters in literature who display the kinds of personal qualities they would like to develop.

Ellis believed that distraction was a way of helping clients to deal with anxiety and depression. In simple terms, this means encouraging them to learn relaxation procedures, yoga or meditation, but it also means teaching them how to dispute the irrational beliefs that cause problems for them. Semantic correction is another interesting rational emotive behaviour technique, which is used with clients who over-generalise, or make sweeping statements (Ellis, 1995). The following is an example:

CLIENT: People always let me down, always. Then I get depressed and fed up.

COUNSELLOR: Absolutely always let you down?

CLIENT: Well no, but quite often.

COUNSELLOR: Try changing what you first said around a bit.

CLIENT: In what way?

COUNSELLOR: Instead of the statement you made, change it to this: I allow myself to become depressed and fed up when other people let me down.

CLIENT: Like the ABC we discussed? Yes, but it takes time to change things around like that.

COUNSELLOR: That's why all the practice is important.

Dealing with shame

In Ellis' view feelings of shame, guilt or inadequacy are responsible for many of the problems that prompt people to seek help in therapy (Ellis, 1991). In order to help clients deal with these feelings, he devised 'shame-attacking' exercises. People who are fearful of exposing personal weakness, or those who are inhibited about expressing themselves, are encouraged to take risks and engage in some form of activity that will prove to them their fears are exaggerated. A client might, for example, be asked to become more gregarious socially, in dress, behaviour or manner. The purpose behind this approach is to show clients that they need not feel ashamed, nor will anything awful happen to them if they take more risks.

Contracts and commitment

Rational emotive behaviour therapy can be used as a brief therapy, but it is also suited to longer-term counselling when necessary. A primary focus of the model is to help clients understand the connection between thinking and emotional disturbance, which means they also need to understand the purpose of the exercises they are asked to do. Commitment to completion of assignments is important too, and any tasks clients do should be discussed in later counselling sessions. The behavioural focus in rational emotive behaviour therapy requires that clients receive 'positive reinforcement' for any progress they make. A working contract is always established at the beginning of therapy, the terms of which are detailed and specific.

The therapeutic relationship

We have seen that rational emotive behaviour therapy is an active, directive and teaching approach to counselling. These characteristics set it apart from many of the other models discussed in this book. However, the actual relationship between counsellor and client is just as important in this approach, as it is in any other. Dryden (1999) suggests that flexibility is an essential attitude on the counsellor's part. What works with one client may not necessarily work for another, so counsellors need to be open to the needs of individual clients. The counselling relationship is an egalitarian one, although equality may not be obvious at the beginning of therapy, when clients are disadvantaged because of the problems which preoccupy them. Once therapy is established however, counsellors are frequently willing to disclose information that is seen as helpful or encouraging for clients. This might include details of problems similar to those experienced by the client.

The Rogerian concept of empathy is problematic in rational emotive behaviour therapy, where attitudes of detachment and understanding are valued highly. Counsellors need to be separate from the irrational views clients express, and this means refusing to collude with, or support, these views when they are articulated. The concept of 'transference' is also viewed differently in this approach. Indeed, the idea that the counsellor should encourage a client's irrational dependence is anathema, and contrary to all the basic principles of rational emotive behaviour therapy. 'Debate' has a central place in the model and is meant to encourage openness and honesty between client and counsellor. In a document published on the internet, Ellis (2005) highlighted the point that REBT therapists give all clients unconditional positive regard, no matter what these clients have done or what mistakes they have made. He added that therapists also teach their clients to accept themselves totally, in spite of the shame and guilt that they may experience because of their failings. Unconditional positive regard is, as shown in Unit 5, a Rogerian concept, but it is one that Ellis was concerned to emphasise in his own approach to clients.

We have seen that humour is frequently used, and this goes along with an atmosphere of informality meant to encourage creative and less rigid attitudes in clients generally. On the other hand, there are clients who prefer a more formal approach and those wishes are centrally accommodated in the model. 'Logic' and 'persuasion' are valuable skills, which are also used extensively in rational emotive behaviour therapy.

Group work

Rational emotive behaviour therapy is often conducted in a group setting. Although resistant to the idea of group therapy initially, Ellis later came to regard it as an 'excellent medium' for helping clients (Ellis, 1991: 113). All the advantages of groupwork apply to rational emotive behaviour therapy, but there is an added bonus in the sense that more people are available to dispute their own and other people's irrational beliefs and statements. Therapy can take place in small groups or large groups, although Ellis himself favoured the large group setting, which he saw as more lively with more interesting material available for discussion (Ellis, 1991).

Another significant aspect of rational emotive behaviour therapy group work is that all the members are taught the principles of the approach. This means that individual participants can (with the guidance of the group leader) take turns in the role of facilitator or therapist, an experience that is empowering for them. Some members of the group may also attend individual therapy sessions; when this is the case, the group can supply the extra support often needed to consolidate the progress made in the individual setting.

Clients who benefit from this approach

Clients who lack assertiveness, or those who experience problems in relation to negative thinking and depression, are likely to benefit from a rational emotive behaviour approach in either an individual therapy, or a group work setting. Those who need specific interventions, such as family or marital therapy, may also be helped by therapists who are trained to use the model. Rational emotive behaviour therapy is accessible and fairly easy to understand, which means that the majority of clients (or at least those with the types of problems already mentioned) can benefit from it. The principles of the approach can be applied to education and child therapy as well, and this flexibility of application is one of its main assets.

Corey (2007) makes the point that the focus on learning and teaching, which is central to rational emotive behaviour therapy, ensures that many clients regard it in a positive light and untainted with associations of mental illness. In addition, there are many clients who welcome the stress on action under the direction of the therapist. Tasks like homework and role play may motivate those clients who would normally find it difficult to move into action without some support, initially at least. Putting ideas into action can inspire a real sense of achievement, though clients need to be committed and reinforced for all the gains they make. Rational emotive behaviour therapy can also be viewed as a self-help approach, since it advocates reading, listening to tapes, attendance at lectures and workshops, and generally becoming independent in the search for improvement and change. This aspect of the model helps to give confidence to those clients who use it. Clients are further encouraged to view themselves as capable of making change, regardless of any past traumas they may have suffered.

Some limitations

Clients who wish to conduct an in-depth study of childhood events and attendant traumas are unlikely to seek rational emotive behaviour therapy in order to do so. This is because the approach tends to minimise the past, although this does not imply that Ellis regarded the past as irrelevant in any way. On the contrary Ellis, who trained in Freudian psychoanalysis, was aware of the influence of past events, but be came to believe that little progress could be make through dwelling on them (Ellis, 1991).

To Ellis' own surprise, the REBT methods he devised produced quicker and more lasting results than those gained through deep analysis. However, critics of rational emotive behaviour therapy stress the point that fast methods can produce fast results, which may, in the end, be fairly transitory. The active, directive and action-based nature of the approach may not appeal to some clients and, indeed, there are probably a few who could feel quite threatened by it. If certain irrational beliefs are too vigorously disputed early in therapy, clients may vote with their feet and leave. On the other hand, as Weinrach (1995) has suggested, this type of situation can be avoided by the therapist's attention to the client's subjective experience of the problem. This requires empathy on the part of the therapist or counsellor and an attitude of respect for the client, whose difficulties feel unique to him or her.

Aaron T. Beck (1921–)

Like Ellis, Aaron Beck started his professional career as a psychoanalyst. Like Ellis, too, Beck experienced doubts about the effectiveness of psychoanalysis in dealing with psychological problems. In particular, he was sceptical about the usefulness of the classical model in dealing with forms of mental illness, including depression (Beck, A., 1977). Both Beck and Ellis developed their respective theories almost simultaneously, but there are some differences of stress and focus in their individual approaches. However, there are many similarities, too, since both are primarily concerned with cognition and with clients' maladaptive thought processes, as well as the situations and contexts that prompt these. In addition, both Ellis and Beck developed models of therapy that are practical and directive with an emphasis on working closely with clients to identify faulty thinking and to change it. Both also included the practice of behavioural exercises to empower clients and to facilitate progress in therapy.

Beck's cognitive therapy

Much of Beck's seminal work was carried out during the 1960s, when his research and clinical work led to the development of cognitive therapy as a treatment for depression. In fact, Beck's cognitive therapy evolved mainly from a detailed and systematic investigation of the thoughts and beliefs (cognitions) of his anxious and depressed patients. His research showed him that depressed and anxious people are preoccupied with thoughts that exacerbate or heighten their negative mood (Beck, A., 1977). These persistent and preoccupying thoughts are often so automatic that people are unaware of their insidious influence. A depressed person might, for example, respond to a perceived slight by instantly thinking: 'She doesn't like me, so I'm not worth much'. A central focus of cognitive therapy is to help clients identify the automatic thoughts that tend to emerge, especially when they are anxious or under stress.

In her book, *Cognitive Behaviour Therapy: Basics and Beyond*, Beck's daughter, Judith, offers a succinct definition of cognitive therapy and the theory underpinning it. She proposes that 'dysfunctional thinking is common to all psychological disturbance' and suggests that when clients in therapy are taught to change their dysfunctional thinking to more realistic and adaptive assessments, they will improve emotionally and behaviourally as a result (Beck, J. S., 2011: 3).

It follows from this definition and records of the early work carried out by Aaron Beck (1977) that a central principle of his cognitive therapy is, indeed, the idea that faulty thinking is the root of many psychological problems. Beck's educational model of therapy aims to effect lasting change in the way clients think about themselves and other people. Through modification of negative beliefs, clients are empowered to see themselves and others more realistically and with fewer negative connotations. The following case study is an example.

CASE STUDY

Automatic thoughts

Vicky wanted to learn to drive for her work, but was convinced she wouldn't be able to because she suffered from nerves. Vicky confided in her counsellor, adding that each time she imagined herself driving she was overwhelmed by negative thoughts. The counsellor asked her to describe this experience.

COUNSELLOR: Tell me what you're thinking when you have that experience.

VICKY: I immediately think I can't do it … I haven't got the nerve.

COUNSELLOR: And then what happens?

VICKY: I feel really down. I physically slump.

COUNSELLOR: So your thoughts about not being able to do it lead to you feeling emotionally and physically drained.

VICKY: Yes, every time.

COUNSELLOR: Let's look at the way you think about driving. Is there any evidence that you couldn't learn to drive?

VICKY: Well I'm no good with mechanical things.

COUNSELLOR: You can't do anything that involves mechanical skill.

VICKY: I can use a computer, the usual things, the lawn mower and I can even do a flat pack (laughs).

COUNSELLOR: What was the hardest thing about learning to assemble a flat pack?

VICKY: Time and patience.

COUNSELLOR: But you did it. What is the evidence that you can't harness those qualities again to learn to drive?

VICKY: It's just hard to get rid of thoughts that I can't do it.

COUNSELLOR: What if you work on changing those thoughts that sabotage you when you contemplate learning to drive?

VICKY: If I could change the thoughts, I know I would feel better. I would like to work on that.

Comment: This is a short example of an exchange between a cognitive counsellor and a client. The counsellor in this case worked with Vicky and encouraged her to identify and record the type of automatic thoughts that intruded when she considered learning to drive. The counsellor also continued to emphasise Vicky's positive experiences (the things she had actually learned to do), in order to counter her tendency to distorted and negative thinking. She was also taught to remind herself that when she experiences automatic negative thoughts, it didn't mean they were true. In addition, Vicky was given homework and reading assignments to help her to focus on her goals.

Anxiety-inducing thoughts

Anxiety-inducing thoughts are so automatic and subtle that clients are (initially at least) unaware of their negative and damaging effects on mood and feelings. According to Bourne (1995), automatic thoughts often appear in 'telegraphic form' so that an image, or one short word, often triggers other associations, memories or thoughts (Bourne, 1995: 174). An example of this is the way Vicky tells herself she 'can't do it', the repetition of which is likely to evoke other negative associations stretching back to childhood. Later on in counselling, Vicky was able to identify some of the associations that were evoked by the words. These negative childhood associations included being repeatedly told by over-anxious parents that she couldn't do certain things, because they were too difficult for her.

It is precisely because automatic thoughts, along with their associations, occur so rapidly that they tend to go unchallenged or unquestioned. Automatic thoughts can also generate panic so that certain physiological symptoms arise to compound the original problem. These physical symptoms including shallow breathing, increased heart rate, tightness in the chest and sweating are incompatible with clear and reasoned thinking. A basic tenet of cognitive therapy is that automatic thoughts are learned bad habits that can be changed. We know that it is possible for people to change other unhealthy habits of behaviour, including smoking, for example. Changing unhealthy thinking habits is also possible, though it's not always easy, but clients can be helped to achieve this though practice and with help from cognitive therapy.

Core beliefs or schema

The two terms 'core beliefs' and 'schema' are often used interchangeably in cognitive therapy, but there are differences. Core beliefs are beliefs about the self, which stem from early childhood, whereas the word 'schema' refers more specifically to 'cognitive structures', which contain the core beliefs (Beck, J. S., 2011: 228). Core beliefs can be positive or negative; while most people have sufficient positive core beliefs to maintain personal equilibrium, negative beliefs can emerge during periods of anxiety or stress. These core beliefs, which are deeply embedded, are so fundamental and unchallenged that they are regarded as true, even when the evidence points otherwise. They tend to be concerned with the world and familial attitudes to it and are carried forward from one generation to another. In common with many other approaches – including the psychodynamic, transactional analysis and behaviourism – cognitive therapy stresses the importance of early childhood experience and recognises that many later problems are due to childhood difficulties. Many of these early experiences give rise to distorted or erroneous thinking. In addition, these negative experiences, combined with emotional attitudes transmitted by parents, predispose many people to emotional problems, including depression. Some examples of core beliefs include:

- I'm a failure if I don't have a partner.
- I'm no good at practical tasks.
- Things never turn out right for me.

We can see at once that these examples of negative core beliefs have much in common with the irrational beliefs described by Albert Ellis in rational emotive behaviour therapy.

Judith Beck (2011) points out that in addition to the core beliefs held, people also tend to discount any information to the contrary and, instead, 'focus selectively' on information that confirms them (Beck, J. S., 2011: 32). A central focus of cognitive therapy is to encourage clients to consider how they have acquired their deeply held beliefs and then to show them how these can be changed. The counsellor's intervention in the case study outlined above was to show the client (Vicky) that she had accomplished practical tasks before; therefore, her belief that she was incapable of learning new skills was erroneous. People often start from a position of negative beliefs about their own level of competence, and they are often surprised when core beliefs are challenged, or strengthened, by contradictory evidence. Free (1999) makes the point that many beliefs (collective and individual) have changed throughout history: it is perfectly possible, therefore, for clients to modify long-held personal beliefs that hinder them in the present. A distinction between core beliefs and automatic thoughts should be made here, since automatic thoughts are the images or words that accompany core beliefs, and are specific to any given situation (Beck, J. S., 2011). A person may, for example, have the negative core belief 'I'm no good', which is then followed (after some minor mistake or failure) by the automatic thought 'stupid' or 'incompetent'. An immediate reaction to this process is emotional, behavioural and physiological, as we saw in the case study example of Vicky.

EXERCISE

Core beliefs

In this exercise you are asked to identify any core beliefs that stem from your childhood. Did you believe these to be absolutely true as a child and, if so, do you still believe them to be true? Work with a partner and discuss the most common childhood beliefs and how you were both personally affected by them. Discuss how individual and collective beliefs change over time.

Logical errors

'Logical errors' is a term that describes a tendency, often seen in depressed people, to think in a distorted or erroneous way (Beck, A. 1977). This mode of cognition can also be described as forms of extreme or arbitrary thinking that usually involve exaggeration. Logical errors also tend to disregard reality. A depressed person may, for example, draw a conclusion that has no real bearing on the situation. For example, 'I just know I won't do well in the exam because I failed that subject at school', exemplifies this form of distorted thinking. Selective abstraction is yet another aspect of illogical thinking, and involves emphasising a single element of the environment, while ignoring everything else; for example, 'I missed the bus this morning, so nothing will go right.' Overgeneralisation is another form of primitive thinking, which Judith Beck describes as a tendency to 'make a sweeping negative conclusion', which is then applied to every situation (Beck, J.S., 2011: 182). This general rule is usually derived from one isolated incident, such as, for example, 'I can't do anything right'. Sometimes events are magnified, thereby getting the general scale of things out of proportion. The statement 'If I fail my driving test this time, I'm hopeless' is an example of magnification of the actual situation. By the same token a situation may be minimised, also distorting reality; for example, 'I don't care about exams anyway, they don't mean much.' 'Personalisation' is another trait highlighted by Judith Beck, and describes a tendency (often seen in depressed people) to take everything personally, even though there is no real reason to make this kind of connection (Beck, J. S., 2011:182).

The therapeutic relationship

Judith Beck highlights the importance of establishing a good relationship from the outset with clients. This she sees as a prerequisite for a 'positive alliance' and can be accomplished through the use of good counselling skills, a variety of styles, joint decision-making, especially in regard to treatment plans, feedback, and open communication. This approach is designed with a view to helping clients solve their difficulties and overcome their problems (Beck, J. S., 2011: 18).

Throughout counselling sessions it is essential to check with clients that they understand the process taking place, they agree with it, and they are given the opportunity to correct any inaccuracies or misunderstandings that may emerge. Cognitive behaviour therapy is a highly structured approach, which also incorporates a teaching and educational dimension. In addition, it is directive with an emphasis on activity as an aid to client empowerment. Activities include homework and other assignments, role play, rehearsal, social skills and assertiveness training, and challenging negative self-statements. Techniques derived from behaviourism are used in cognitive therapy, too, including positive reinforcement and systematic desensitisation, described earlier in this unit. Clients' full participation is essential; this includes asking them to state which problems they wish to address during individual sessions. Clients need to know what to expect during therapy, and this understanding can be achieved through clear communication and feedback.

Brief cognitive therapy

One of the advantages of cognitive behaviour therapy is that it is adaptable enough to meet the needs of individual clients. Both REBT and Beck's cognitive therapy are often used as time-limited or short-term approaches, encompassing a specific number of sessions. This number can vary, but is usually six to ten weeks in duration. Curwen et al. define brief therapy as an approach in which 'maximum benefits' can be achieved, with the advantage of low cost to clients. They also make the point that 'purchasers' of psychotherapy, whether individual clients or organisations like the NHS, expect value for money (Curwen et al., 2000: 2). In addition to being less expensive, brief therapy has other advantages for clients, especially those who cannot afford the investment and time needed for more extended therapy. When people encounter difficulties, especially emotional or psychological difficulties, they tend to want fairly quick results. In fact, cognitive therapy has always tended to be brief and this is something that Ellis (1995) highlights. Beck, too, suggests that practitioners of cognitive therapy can use techniques in a medical or similar setting 'without conducting a full therapy session' (Beck, J. S., 2011: 3). This highlights the adaptability and versatility of cognitive therapy, and confirms that cognitive therapists place client needs at the forefront of their philosophy.

In recent times the demand for time-limited helping approaches has increased. This increase is not just the result of financial constraints, but is also linked to greater uptake of therapy and the need for quick (and verifiable) results.

KEY TERM

Brief therapy: Counselling which often takes place over six to eight weeks, or it may even be less. Brief therapy is characterised by clarity of focus and by the client's motivation in achieving results in the time allocated.

George Kelly (1905–1966)

George Kelly, who unlike Ellis and Beck, did not have a background in psychoanalysis, contributed in his own very individual way to the field of cognitive therapy. Kelly, who was born in Kansas, studied psychology and spent many years engaged in clinical work, then later became Professor of Psychology at the University of Maryland where he continued for 20 years. In 1955 he wrote and published his major work in two volumes, entitled *The Psychology of Personal Constructs*.

Kelly was not limited to one discipline but was qualified in a diverse range of subjects, including maths, education and physics. In the development of his theory of personal constructs, Kelly abandoned all other former theories of personality, including those intrinsic to both the Freudian and behavioural approaches. According to Ewen (1993), Kelly preferred to 'leave all familiar landmarks behind' including the concepts of ego, motivation, drives, reinforcement and even the unconscious (Ewen, 1993: 344).

It is clear, therefore, that in formulating his psychology of personal constructs Kelly wanted to start with a blank sheet, with the clear and specific aim of helping people to overcome interpersonal problems (Kelly, 1955).

Personal constructs

According to Kelly's theory of personal constructs, we all build mental theories about the environment in which we live, constantly testing these hypotheses against reality as we go along, and modifying them depending on how accurate they turn out to be. We do this in order to make sense of the world, to exercise some control over our environment and to make it more predictable. Although we may not always be accurate in the way we construe reality, it is, nevertheless, our own individual and creative interpretation which, as Ewen (1993) points out, 'gives events their meaning and determines our subsequent behaviour' (Ewen, 1993: 345).

There are some similarities between Kelly's theory of personal constructs and Beck's theory of schema or core beliefs, since both represent very personal attitudes that are firmly held and can be either positive or negative. A person's core beliefs or constructs cannot be accurately judged by other people to be positive or negative, however, since each person's experience is entirely unique and experiential. In counselling, therefore, the therapist's task is to understand the client's individual experience (which requires empathetic listening) and the ways in which these experiences have been formed. From Kelly's perspective, it is pointless to impose our own constructs on other people, though the goal of therapy is to help clients experiment with new core constructs, in order to detach from old and dysfunctional ones (Kelly, 1963).

Although much of Kelly's scientific theory and the terminology he uses is complex, the strength of his contribution lies in his emphasis on the importance of subjective cognition and the central role of empathy in understanding other people's experiences. In addition, his theory upholds the idea of personal uniqueness, along with the concomitant need to respect this. Criticisms have been levelled against Kelly's approach, including the view that he neglects attention to other human characteristics such as love and hate, sexuality, aggression, hope and despair. In addition, Ewen (1993) points out that Kelly paid no attention to experiences of infancy and childhood, thereby leaving himself open to charges of oversimplification by members of the psychoanalytic and behavioural communities. In response to these perceived deficits, some researchers, including Bannister (1985), have sought to redress the balance by directing attention to human emotions and theories of personality and away from purely isolated cognitive issues.

EXERCISE

Interpreting events

Working in pairs, discuss the ways in which groups of people often give different accounts of the same event. What are the factors that predispose people to interpret things so differently? Can you relate your discussion to Kelly's theory of personal constructs?

Mindfulness-based cognitive therapy (MBCT)

Within the past decade, the practice of mindfulness as an aid to mental health has become increasingly popular. Mindfulness, however, has a long and impressive lineage stemming from Eastern medicine, stretching back into antiquity. Within recent times, Western psychological medicine has begun to recognise its importance and has incorporated its concepts into the cognitive behavioural model of therapy. The development of mindfulness-based cognitive therapy has been applied to the treatment of depression, in particular, but its scope is gradually extending to encompass all aspects of psychological and emotional difficulties.

Professor Mark Williams of Oxford University is a researcher and pioneer in the field of mindfulness and is co-founder, along with colleagues, of mindfulness-based cognitive therapy, or MBCT. Williams and his colleagues have studied depression, anxiety and stress over a period of 30 years and have established that it is possible to tackle these problems through the practice of mindfulness as part of daily life. Moreover, they have designed a series of practices, which can be used by anyone, and they stress the effectiveness of these (as shown in clinical trials), particularly in alleviating depression (Williams and Penman, 2011).

Mindfulness practice is relatively simple, and can be used to prevent everyday feelings of stress and anxiety escalating out of control. It is based on self-observation, carried out without judgment or censure. There is an emphasis on compassion for self, especially when depression or anxieties strike. At its simplest level it means focusing attention on breathing, so that all negative self-talk recedes into the background. We are aware, initially, of the negative monologue inside our heads, but mindfulness teaches that we can stand back from it and listen without criticism. In some respects, the deep breathing exercise described here is reminiscent of the exercise described earlier in this unit, but it also goes beyond this. Williams and Penman (2011:6) describe it as a 'method of mental training', the practice of which does not take a long time and can be achieved by anyone.

One way of defining mindfulness is to say that it is the very opposite of mindlessness. When we do something in a mindless way we sleep-walk through the process, whereas doing it mindfully implies a conscious awareness of every step and paying attention in the present. We can fulfil everyday tasks in this way; for example, brushing our teeth or getting dressed. This type of practice anchors us to the present (the here and now) so that thoughts of the past and the future do not intrude. Paying attention to the present enables clients to deal with anxieties and emotions, which ordinarily might overwhelm them. They can be taught that instead of trying to decipher the meaning of stressful or anxious thoughts, they should simply observe them without criticism or comment. In this way, clients can learn that thoughts do not define us, but are constantly changing. This is where attention to breathing is important, because it draws attention back to the present and away from the past, which no longer exists, and the future, which has not yet arrived. Deep breathing is not the only method of drawing attention back to the present, however. Attention to any of the senses will act in a similar way. One client described her experience in the following way:

CASE STUDY

CLIENT   I was anxious and worried about getting the results of my scan. Just before I left for the hospital, I went out to the back garden to take clothes off the line. The scent of the rose bushes suddenly stopped me in my tracks. The perfume was all around me. I stood still, taking in the aroma and feeling my feet planted solidly on the ground. The experience simply took me over so that I felt rooted (like the roses bushes) in the ground. Anxieties about the scan results receded. I didn't have to think about it now while I stood there in the garden.

Comment: In this example, the client's sense of smell and her attention to her own feet planted firmly on the ground served as anchors and calmed her down.

Williams and Penman make a distinction between what they refer to as 'Doing mode' and 'Being mode'. When in Doing mode we tend to be on 'autopilot', where we end up performing tasks without clear awareness of what we are doing. Being mode, on the other hand, implies full consciousness of what we are doing (Williams and Penman, 2011: 34). A central aim of mindfulness therapy is to encourage clients to avoid being sidetracked by autopilot so that they become more fully alive and aware in the present. This does not mean telling them to avoid difficulties, especially difficult feelings. On the contrary, it means encouraging clients to allow these feelings to emerge and to acknowledge them, but with compassion and interest. This more compassionate and non-judgmental approach gradually diminishes the power of such feelings to overwhelm clients.

In order to help clients through MBCT, it is important to teach them its concepts and to emphasise the research that underpins its effectiveness. When clients understand that it is possible, through neuroscience and brain imaging, to see positive changes in the human brain brought about by the practice of mindfulness, they are usually impressed. Practice is an important element of the approach, and a series of daily exercises is usually recommended over a period of eight weeks. In the UK the National Institute for Health and Clinical Excellence (NICE, 2008) has (in its guidelines for depression) recommended MBCT for people with a history of three or more episodes of depression (Williams and Penman, 2011).

Solution-focused brief therapy

We have seen that Ellis' REBT and Beck's cognitive therapy are approaches that highlight the place of cognition in the development and continuation of personal problems. Another more recent development, called solution-focused brief therapy (SFBT), picks up the theme of cognition, or thinking in the context of psychotherapy. However, the difference here is that SFBT also encourages clients to think in terms of mental wellbeing, and finding solutions to the difficulties they experience. It is true, of course, that all forms of therapy are meant to empower clients in this way, but a key element of SFBT is that it emphasises health, rather than psychopathology, and encourages a focus on encouraging this more positive goal.

SFBT was developed and pioneered by Steve de Shazer (1998) and his colleagues who worked at the Brief Family Centre in Milwaukee, USA from the mid-1980s. Another important seminal figure in the approach was an American psychiatrist called Milton H. Erickson, who died in 1980. O'Hanlon and Weiner-Davis (2003) describe Erickson's unique and often creative approach to helping clients to find solutions to their problems. These methods were ostensibly eccentric, but seemed to work well, not least because they focused on clients' competence and individual strengths.

Though SFBT continues to grow and evolve, its underlying assumptions remain constant. O'Hanlon and Weiner-Davis identify a number of these assumptions, including the following:

1 'Change is constant'. Since the whole universe is in the process of ongoing change it is fair to say that clients' problems are not static, but are changing too (O'Hanlon & Weiner-Davis, 2003: 35). In SFBT, therefore, the counsellor steers the focus away from how the client's problems have been

or are, and towards the way in which they are changing. Often clients don't see the change until they are invited to consider it.

2 It is not necessary to gather extensive information about a problem in order to resolve it. Practitioners of SFBT believe that counsellors can spend too much time seeking information about problems, when they should be spending time on solutions.

3 It is not necessary to know what caused a problem in order to resolve it. Even if a client 'knows' why she drinks too much, for example, it won't automatically alleviate the problem. In SFBT the central aim is to overcome the problem by looking at solutions rather than causes.

4 In SFBT a small initial change can be seen as a catalyst for other bigger changes. Often clients get depressed because it all seems too much. Initial changes can also be very fast. SFBT practitioners believe in the possibility of rapid change leading to solutions. In addition, practitioners believe that the counsellor's conviction will ultimately affect the client's perception of what is possible in a short space of time.

5 Clients are the experts, they have the resources and they define their own goals. SFBT acknowledges that all clients are unique and know their own situations better than anyone else. In SFBT, solutions should be formulated to meet these unique needs, rather than the dictates of a particular set of theories.

O'Hanlon and Weiner-Davis (2003)

Skills used in solution-focused brief therapy

The way in which language is used by the counsellor is especially significant in SFBT. One aspect of this is the practice of matching the client's language. If, for example, a client describes an argument with a partner as a 'barney', the counsellor would use this term to mirror what has been said. To use another term would distort what has actually been said. Solution talk is always encouraged: though the client may be prompted to talk in terms of problems, the counsellor will seek to concentrate on solutions and will encourage the client to do the same. The counsellor will always ask open questions designed to encourage positive ways of considering change. The following are some examples:

1 What progress have you made since last time?
2 What are your coping strategies?
3 How will you know when you have reached that goal?
4 What positive things have been happening since?

During their first session, rapport is established between client and counsellor. After this, there is a fairly rapid focus on positive solutions and establishing goals. During subsequent sessions, positive change is assessed and the details are established. Any positive change that has taken place is acknowledged and reinforced by the counsellor's response to the client.

EXERCISE

The miracle question

In SFBT the focus is always on looking at the solution aspect of each client's situation. This solution principle underlies a technique called the 'miracle question', which is central to this approach. Working individually, think of a difficulty that you currently have. Then answer the following question, which is based on de Shazer's original technique (de Shazer, 1988):

Suppose that one night when you went to sleep, there was a miracle and your problem was solved. When you woke up in the morning, how would you know it was solved and what would be different?

Comment: The answer to this question should give you some idea of what your future would be like without the problem. In SFBT terms, this vision of a problem-free future should act as a catalyst to help you achieve it. Discuss your response to the exercise with members of your training group, saying how effective or otherwise you believe it to be.

Cognitive behaviour therapy today

The profile of cognitive behaviour therapy (CBT) has steadily increased in the UK and, indeed, worldwide. The enhanced prominence of CBT as a therapy of choice in the UK is linked to the Improving Access to Psychological Therapies (IAPT) initiative, which was launched in 2008. According to this initiative, access to 'evidence-based psychological therapies' will be available by 2015 for at least 15 per cent of the adult population (Department of Health, 2012). The National Institute for Health and Clinical Excellence (NICE) backed this proposed programme in 2008 and suggested that CBT should be recommended for a range of psychological problems, including depression, anxiety and panic disorder.

Another reason for the expansion of CBT as a preferred approach to helping clients, with anxiety and depression in particular, is its evidence-based status within counselling and psychotherapy generally. Much research has been carried out in relation to CBT, and results indicate its effectiveness for a range of psychological problems (Cooper, 2008). In addition, the Royal College of Psychiatrists stress on its website (2013) that CBT has been shown to help with many problems, including stress, phobias, depression and anxiety. Numerous research projects are detailed on the internet which highlight the effectiveness of CBT for a wide range of psychological problems; and increasing numbers of practitioners, including doctors, nurses and health visitors within the NHS are being trained to use it.

The research-based effectiveness of CBT (which is by no means confined to the UK) has surprised many practitioners, who have been trained in, and use, other approaches to helping clients. Some, including Yalom (2004), have expressed reservations about the effectiveness of CBT in the long term. His basic concern is that any gains that clients make in the short-term with CBT may not be maintained once they leave therapy. In Yalom's view, 'chronic distress requires far longer therapy' (Yalom, 2004: 224). He also points to the fact that clients frequently make quick gains at the start of therapy, a phenomenon that does not mean their problems are satisfactorily resolved. Another critic, psychoanalyst Darian Leader, expressed his view in the *Guardian* newspaper, describing CBT as 'a quick fix for the soul', whose aim is to get rid of symptoms (Leader, 2008:1). He contrasts this objective with other psychotherapeutic approaches that seek to understand what a client's symptoms could actually be saying.

Other writers, including Moloney and Kelly (2008), acknowledge that aspects of CBT may be helpful, but highlight environmental factors (including social and economic deprivation), which frequently contribute to psychological distress. Ignoring these factors is, in their view, one way of saying that they really don't matter. Furthermore, encouraging clients to adjust their thinking in such circumstances is misleading for clients and therapists alike. Proctor (2008) refers to the fact that CBT 'invests much authority in therapists', who are believed to know what is best for their clients, with little thought given to the dangers of such assumptions (Proctor, 2008: 253).

In relation to issues of power and control in CBT, it is worth remembering that Aaron Beck and Albert Ellis, the original pioneers of CBT, both began as psychoanalysts and later became disillusioned with psychoanalysis. Both were concerned to develop a form of therapy that was more located in clients' actual experiences, and did not require subscribing to Freudian theories about the past and its influence on the present. In addition, both Ellis and Beck wanted to develop a form of therapy that could be delivered in a shorter time span than psychoanalysis, and they envisaged CBT as a collaborative endeavour between client and therapist. To those who allege that CBT is authoritarian or controlling, Ellis pointed out that 'virtually all psychotherapies' can be described in this way (Ellis, 1991: 364). This is because all therapists, on account of their experience and training in a particular field, are, in fact, always in some kind of authority. Neither Ellis nor Beck envisaged CBT as a static theoretical approach to therapy; instead, they saw it as dynamic and evolving in a way that would meet the changing needs of clients.

Already there is evidence that CBT is changing to meet the diverse needs of clients. Many of these changes are linked to research, for as Palmer (2008) suggests, CBT is a 'pragmatic approach' that is not weighed down by dogma or rigid adherence to one particular set of skills (Palmer, 2008: 6).

These changes include incorporating aspects of other theoretical approaches to counselling within CBT, including person-centred empathy, elements of Gestalt counselling and aspects of object relations theory.

Not everyone is happy with this developing eclecticism and some, including Loewenthal and House (2008), suggest that there is the possibility of 'opportunistic exploitation' of other theoretical approaches, aspects of which are 'bolted on' to CBT (Loewenthal and House, 2008: 292). In their view, a corollary of this add-on approach is that it exposes CBT, with its strong scientific claims, to the opposite charge of being unscientific.

CBT and the internet

One area in which CBT has superseded all psychotherapeutic approaches is its seamless transferability to the internet. Online counselling is now well established, and when we consider that people use the internet for so many other purposes today, it is easy to see how this transition has come about. CBT is delivered online in two main ways: the first mode of delivery is via self-help programmes, which guide users step by step through them. The second method is when CBT is delivered, in real time, by a therapist working online. Research carried out at Bristol University and described by Kessler (2009) in the medical journal the *Lancet* concludes that CBT is effective for depression when delivered by a therapist online in this way. The researchers infer from these results that online counselling could be used in future to broaden access to CBT generally. Increasingly, counselling support is delivered online via email or Skype, depending on the needs of clients; fees may be cheaper than conventional counselling and are usually paid by subscription.

One criticism of online counselling is the absence of a therapeutic relationship when it is delivered in this way. However, an important point to remember is that clients do, in fact, have a relationship with a counsellor when using the internet for help. It is just that the counsellor is not face to face in the same room, and therefore not as immediately present as in the traditional counselling context, but this may suit some clients, especially those who cannot access help in other ways. Additionally, there are clients who prefer the comfort and seclusion of their own homes, while others value the anonymity certain forms of online counselling provide. As well as this, online counselling is often available over large geographical areas so clients are offered a wider choice of therapists. There is flexibility, too, in terms of timing, though this aspect needs to be negotiated between therapist and client, just as it would be in conventional counselling. Clients with certain problems, disability or social phobia, for example, or those who live in isolated or remote areas, may feel more secure when receiving help online. The difficulty here is that problems of isolation and loneliness may be compounded, if online help is used without any progression to social interaction or other forms of support.

One positive development in relation to online counselling is the provision of specialist training for counsellors already trained in traditional counselling methods. This means that the practice of online therapy has moved forward considerably, and some aspects of it that initially caused concern are now being addressed. These include ethical issues relating to the protection of client confidentiality and online identity, as well as proof of counsellor training and accreditation. There are some client issues (including suicidal feelings or violent impulses), which online counsellors consider incompatible with their particular mode of delivery. Like counsellors everywhere, online providers are obliged by law to report threats of violence to the relevant authorities. This may be easier said than done if client and counsellor are distanced geographically.

SUMMARY

Cognitive behavioural approaches to counselling were the subject of this unit. In the first instance, the foundations of behaviourism and the experiments underpinning it were considered. The contributions of Pavlov, Watson, Thorndike, Skinner, Wolpe and Bandura were highlighted and placed in the context of therapeutic practice and their relevance to cognitive behaviour therapy.

The primary focus of this unit was, however, the work of two pioneering cognitive therapists: Albert Ellis and Aaron Beck. The development of Ellis' rational emotive behaviour therapy was described, along with the factors which influenced his work. The ABC model was outlined in some detail, in addition to the nature of the counsellor–client relationship. The theories and work of Aaron Beck were similarly described, and examples of techniques and procedures used in both rational emotive therapy and cognitive behaviour therapy were discussed.

We also considered the use of both brief cognitive behaviour therapy and solution-focused therapy. Mindfulness-based cognitive therapy was included, and a summarised overview of online counselling, along with its benefits for certain clients was discussed. Finally, in this unit we looked at some of the research findings relating to cognitive behavioural therapy, highlighting its increasing prominence as the therapy of choice in health care and other settings.

References

Avery, B. (1969) *Principles of Psychotherapy*. London: Thorsons Publishing Ltd.

Bandura, A. (1977) *A Social Learning Theory*. Englewood Cliffs, NJ: Prentice Hall.

Bannister, D. (1985) (ed.) *Issues and Approaches in Personal Construct Theory*. Orlando, FL: Academic Press.

Beck, A. (1977) *Cognitive Therapy of Depression*. New York: The Guilford Press.

Beck, J. S. (2011) *Cognitive Behaviour Therapy: Basics and Beyond*. New York: The Guilford Press.

Bourne, E.J. (1995) *The Anxiety and Phobia Workbook*. California: New Harbinger Publications Inc.

Cooper, M. (2008) *Essential Research Findings in Counselling and Psychotherapy*. London: Sage Publications.

Corey, G. (2007) *Theory and Practice of Counselling and Psychotherapy*. Pacific Grove, CA: Brooks/Cole.

Curwen, B, Palmer, S. & Ruddell, P. (2000) *Brief Cognitive Behaviour Therapy*. London: Sage Publications.

Department of Health (DH). (2012) 'Improving Access to Psychological Therapies (IAPT). (online) *No Health without Mental Health: A Government-Funded National Project to Improve Mental Health and Wellbeing*. November 2012. Available at: www. iapt.nhs.uk/silo. Accessed July 2013.

de Shazer, S. (1985) *Keys to Solutions in Brief Therapy*. New York: W. W. Norton & Co.

Dryden, W. (1999) *Rational Emotive Behavioural Counselling in Action*. (2nd ed) London: Sage Publications.

Ellis, A. (2005) 'The Essence of Rational Emotive Behaviour Therapy: A Comprehensive Approach to Treatment' (online). New York: The Albert Ellis Institute. Available at: http//www. rebtnetwork.org/library.html. Accessed 12th July 2013.

Ellis, A. (1995) 'Fundamentals of Rational Emotive Behaviour Therapy for the 1990s', in Dryden, W. (ed) (1995) *Rational Emotive Behaviour Therapy: A Reader*. London: Sage Publications.

Ellis, A. (1991) *Reason and Emotion in Psychotherapy*. New York: Citadel Press.

Ewen, R.B. (1993) *An Introduction to Theories of Personality* (4th edn). Mahwar, NJ: Lawrence Erlbaum Associates.

Eysenck, H.J. (1960) 'The Effects of Psychotherapy', in Eysenck, H. J. (ed.) *Handbook of Abnormal Psychology*. New York: Basic Books.

Free, M.L. (1999) *Cognitive Therapy in Groups: Guidelines and Resources for Practice*. Chichester: John Wiley & Sons Ltd.

Kelly, G.A. (1955) *The Psychology of Personal Constructs: Vol. 1: A Theory of Personality. Vol. 2: Clinical Diagnosis and Psychotherapy*. New York: W.W. Norton.

Kessler, D. (2009) 'Therapist–delivered Internet Psychotherapy for Depression', in *The Lancet* (online), Vol. 374, No. 9690, pp 628-634, 22 Aug. Available at: www.thelancet.com/journals/lancet/article. Accessed 18th July 2013.

Leader, D. (2008) 'A Quick Fix for the Soul', in the *Guardian*, G2 (online) 9th September. Available at: www.theguardian.com/science/2008/sept09/psychology.humanbehaviour. Accessed 15th July 2013.

Loewenthal, D. & House, R. (2008) 'Contesting Therapy Paradigms about What it means to be Human', in Loewenthal, D. & House, R. (eds.) (2008) *Against and for CBT: Towards a Constructive Dialogue*. Ross-on-Wye: PCCS Books.

Moloney, P. & Kelly, P. (2008) 'Beck Never Lived in Birmingham', in Loewenthal, D. & House, R. (eds.) (2008) *Against and For CBT: Towards a Constructive Dialogue*. Ross-on-Wye: PCCS Books.

O'Hanlon, B. & Weiner-Davis, M. (2003) *In Search of Solutions: A New Direction in Psychotherapy*. New York: W. W. Norton & Co.

National Institute for Health and Clinical Excellence: Commissioning Guide-Implementing Nice Guidance (2008) (online) 'Cognitive Behavioural Therapy for the Management of Common Mental Health Problems', p.17. Available at: www.nice.org.uk/media/878/abtcommissioningguide.pdf Accessed July 2013.

Palmer, S. (2008) 'Polemics and Cognitive Behaviour Therapy', in Loewenthal, D. & House, R. (eds.) (2008) *Against and For CBT: Towards a Constructive Dialogue*. Ross-on-Wye: PCCS Books.

Pavlov, I. (1927) *Conditioned Reflexes: An Investigation of the Physiological Activity of the Cerebral Cortex*. G.V. Anrep (ed.) London: Oxford University Press (online). Available at: www. psychcentral.com/classics/Pavlov/lecture 12. Accessed July 2013.

Proctor, G. (2008) 'CBT: The Obscuring of Power in the Name of Science' in Loewenthal, D. & House, R. (eds.) (2008) *Against and For CBT: Towards a Constructive Dialogue*. Ross-on-Wye: PCCS Books.

Royal College of Psychiatrists (2013) 'Cognitive Behaviour Therapy' (online), in *Mental Health Website*. Available at: www.rcpsyche.ac.uk. Accessed July 2013.

de Shazer, (1988) *Clues: Investigating Solutions in Brief Therapy*. New York: Norton.

Skinner, B. F. (1988) *Beyond Freedom and Dignity*. London: Penguin Books.

Strean, H. (1995) *The Use of Humour in Psychotherapy*. New Jersey: Jason Aronson.

Thorndike, E. L. (1911) *Animal Intelligence: Experimental Studies*. New York. The Macmillan Company.

Watson, J. B. & Rayner, R. (1920) 'Conditioned Emotional Reactions'. *Journal of Experimental Psychology*, 3, 1, 1–14 (online). Available at: www. psychclassics.yorku.ca/watson/emotion.htm. Accessed July 2013.

Williams, M. & Penman, D. (2011) *Mindfulness: A Practical Guide to Finding Peace in a Frantic World*. London: Piatkus.

Wolpe, J. (1958) *Psychotherapy by Reciprocal Inhibition*. Stanford, CA: Stanford University Press.

Weinrach, G. (1995) 'Rational Emotive Behaviour Therapy: A Tough-Minded Therapy for a Tender Profession', in Dryden (ed.) *Rational Emotive Behaviour Therapy: A Reader*. London: Sage Publications.

Yalom, I.D. (2004) *The Gift of Therapy: Reflections on Being a Therapist*. London: Piatkus.

Further reading

Beck, J.S. (2011) *Cognitive Behaviour Therapy: Basics and Beyond* (2nd edn). New York: The Guilford Press.

Bohlmeijer, E. & Hulsbergen, M. (2013) *Live A Beginner's Guide to Mindfulness: in the Moment.* Maiden head: Open University Press.

Dryden, W. & Neenan, M. (2004) *Rational Emotive Behavioural Counselling in Action* (3rd edn). London: Sage Publications.

Garrett, V. (2010) *Effective Short-Term Counselling within the Primary Care Setting: Psychodynamic and Cognitive-Behavioural Approaches.* London: Karnac Books.

Neenan, M. & Dryden, W. (2006) *Cognitive Therapy in a Nutshell.* London: Sage Publications.

Sheldon, B. (2011) *Cognitive Behaviour Therapy: Research and Practice in Health and Social Care* (2nd edn). London: Routledge.

Thomas, M. & Drake, M. (2012) *Cognitive Behaviour Therapy Case Studies.* London: Sage Publications.

Van Bilsen, H. *Cognitive Behaviour Therapy in the Real World: Back to Basics.* London: Karnac Books.

Wills, F. & Sanders, D. (2013) *Cognitive Behaviour Therapy: Foundations for Practice* (3rd edn). London: Sage Publications.

Resources

Websites

www.beckinstitute.org

Information about Aaron Beck and the work of the Beck Institute.

www.babcp.com

The British Association for Behavioural and Cognitive Psychotherapies (BABCP).

www.rebtnetwork.org

Describes the work of Albert Ellis as well as the theory and practice of Rational Emotive Behaviour Therapy (REBT).

www.solutionfocused.org.uk

Information about Solution-Focused Therapy.

www.iapt.nhs.uk

Information about the Improving Access to Psychological Therapies (IAPS) programme.

www.moodgym.anu.edu.au

This is a self-help programme which teaches CBT skills to people with anxiety or depression.

Journals

Behavioural and Cognitive Psychotherapy

This is the journal of the British Association for Behavioural and Cognitive Psychotherapies.

The Cognitive Behaviour Therapist

This is the online journal for cognitive behaviour therapists.

9

Ethical
considerations

◆ Introduction

In this last chapter we consider a range of ethical considerations, which can be grouped under the heading of 'Fitness to Practice' as set out by the BACP (2013, page 7). These include the importance of adequate training for counsellors, the requirement for ongoing supervision and personal development, and issues relating to the therapeutic relationship between counsellor and client.

The word 'ethics' refers to the study of right and wrong behaviour, and in the counselling context this has special relevance. This is because of the close nature of the therapeutic relationship and the possibility of abuse that exists within it. Indeed, the actual counsellor–client relationship is perhaps the most important topic in this section, and many of the other issues, such as confidentiality, are impossible to separate from it. The subject of confidentiality will be discussed in this chapter, its limitations identified, and some examples will be given to highlight the difficulties it could present. Client–counsellor good practice, counsellor limitations and knowing when to refer will also be discussed. Finally, in this chapter we shall also discuss two very important dimensions of counselling: diversity of client groups and feminist counselling.

KEY TERM

Confidentiality: In the context of counselling, the word 'confidentiality' means ensuring that what is told in 'confidence' by a client is not repeated to anyone else, apart from certain exceptional circumstances.

Confidentiality

Confidentiality is one of the most important aspects of the counselling relationship. It is also a subject that generates a great deal of interest and discussion when it is raised in training groups. This is because it is a topic about which most people have very firm views. It is often seen as an absolute right for clients who, after all, trust counsellors with some of their most intimate thoughts, feelings and desires. The information clients disclose in counselling may never have been spoken to anyone before and, indeed, it often takes clients a very long time to summon up the courage to approach helpers in the first place. For this reason, clients need to have confidence in the professional integrity of helpers and in their ability to keep private anything they discuss.

Clients may take some time to arrive at a state of complete trust in counselling. One indication of this initial reticence and caution is the way in which clients often focus quite extensively on secondary issues before they feel secure enough to reveal themselves fully. This could be seen as a way of testing the counsellor, in order to ascertain just how unshockable, non-judgmental and discreet he or she is likely to be. Clients who do not get these assurances may retreat from counselling, but once trust has been established, they should feel sufficiently confident to disclose more about themselves. The following are some general guidelines relating to confidentiality.

1 Confidentiality is a subject that needs to be addressed as early as possible in counselling, although in crisis situations this may not be immediately feasible.
2 Even in crisis situations the issue of confidentiality should be addressed at some stage.
3 An atmosphere of trust is just as important as an explicit statement of confidentiality.

Some limitations

Some clients address the issue of confidentiality straight away; when this happens, the counsellor has an ideal opportunity to discuss the concept and clarify any limitations that may have to be stated. Those clients who do not address the subject of confidentiality may be reluctant to do so for fear of questioning the counsellor's professionalism. When this is the case, it is important not to assume that such clients are disinterested, or unaware of the issue. They may simply be waiting for the counsellor to provide the necessary information; if it is not provided, they may lose faith very quickly. Sometimes absolute confidentiality cannot be guaranteed in counselling, and when this is the case, clients should be aware of the limitations to it. The current BACP *Ethical Framework for Good Practice in Counselling and Psychotherapy* addresses the subject of confidentiality and stresses that client information should be protected, except in 'exceptional circumstances' (BACP, 2013: 6). Exceptional circumstances include urgent and serious situations, such as threats of harm to self, or others, by a client. In addition, confidential information about clients may be pooled in situations where helpers work closely together, but even here clients must be informed about (and agree to) this practice. There are certain situations where clients reveal information which, because of the guidelines stated by a particular counselling agency or organisation, cannot remain confidential. These usually include some of the following situations in which a client:

- threatens to injure another person or group of people
- discloses information about abuse of children
- expresses suicidal tendencies
- develops severe mental illness.

In describing the provision of good standards of care and practice, the BACP (2013) also highlights the importance of supervision when counsellors are faced with conflicting responsibilities. These conflicting responsibilities sometimes concern clients and other people, or society in general, who might be affected by them. Consultation through supervision is a mandatory part of good counselling practice, but it is especially important in situations where client confidentiality is questioned.

Perhaps the most important point to make about limitations to absolute confidentiality is that counsellors should be fully aware of guidelines pertaining to it within their organisations. Counsellors who are thus informed are in a better position to deal with emergencies as they arise. Occasionally aspects of confidentiality are far from clear cut, even where guidelines have been stated; in these instances, supervision can help the counsellor to get a clearer picture of what needs to be done. Later in this chapter, we shall look at supervision in more detail. It should be added here, though, that clients should be told about supervision, too, and given an assurance that their identity will not be revealed through it. When absolute confidentiality cannot be guaranteed to clients, they should be told this as soon as possible in the counselling process. The following case study highlights this point.

CASE STUDY

Confidentiality

Andrea, who was 24, received counselling over a period of six weeks because she was depressed. The counsellor who helped her was a trained psychiatric nurse, who had also completed a counselling skills course. Andrea had been referred by her doctor, who had prescribed antidepressants for her. However, he felt that she would benefit more from psychological support and Andrea agreed with this. During the first session, the counsellor talked about confidentiality and added that she could not guarantee this absolutely if Andrea became severely depressed, or suicidal. If either of these two situations arose then, as her counsellor, she would need to speak to Andrea's doctor about it. Andrea seemed to be reassured by this and, in fact, during a later session with the counsellor she admitted to having suicidal thoughts.

ANDREA: I think I began to feel worse after the recent rows with my boyfriend. There have been times when I wished it was just all over.

COUNSELLOR: These feelings of wishing it was all over . . . tell me about them.

ANDREA: Well, . . . I have felt like killing myself at times . . .

COUNSELLOR: Strongly enough to make a plan?

ANDREA: Yes I had a plan. I thought of driving my car along the motorway and crashing it.

COUNSELLOR: And that feeling . . . is it still with you?

ANDREA: Not so much . . . but yes, sometimes.

COUNSELLOR: You remember how we talked about confidentiality . . . about how I would need to speak to your doctor . . . it might be that your medication needs changing, or adjusting.

ANDREA: Yes, I do remember. That's all right. I don't know if these tablets are the right ones for me, anyway. I don't know if they have done me any good.

You can see from this example that clients can experience great relief when they know their problems are monitored and taken seriously in the way the counsellor demonstrated. The issue of confidentiality had been openly discussed at the outset, which meant that further discussion flowed naturally from there. In situations where 'absolute' confidentiality is guaranteed to clients, counsellors must be prepared to respect such assurances. Whatever the arrangement between client and counsellor, however, discussion is essential if misunderstanding and confusion are to be avoided.

EXERCISE

Confidentiality

Working in groups of three to four, discuss your individual areas of work, highlighting any special rules regarding confidentiality. Ask one person in the group to write these down under individual headings, for example:

- social work
- nursing
- teaching
- Citizens Advice Bureau (CAB)
- Samaritans
- Childline
- Cruse
- Women's Aid
- Alcohol Concern
- care of the elderly
- HIV and AIDS counselling
- drugs counselling.

Some of you will probably be involved in other areas of work apart from those listed above. The aim of the exercise is to generate a discussion about the issue of confidentiality generally, and to consider the ways in which guidelines differ among professions and organisations.

Talking about clients

In student training groups, there are frequent discussions about problems encountered in professional work. The usual practice is to refer to clients indirectly and never by name. It is difficult to see how ideas and issues can be shared without these discussions, but there is a case for saying that every casual reference to clients, however indirect, is bound to devalue the integrity of the counsellor–client relationship to some extent, at least. There is the added possibility that a member of the group will identify some of the details under discussion and, in doing so, recognise the person discussed. This may be a remote possibility, but nevertheless it does exist. This is not to suggest that clients are damaged by indirect discussion about problems and issues that could, after all, belong to anyone. However, we all need to be circumspect when talking about work, because even though clients have no knowledge of these discussions, the effects of the way the counsellors treat them behind their backs do become manifest during counselling. Weinberg (1996: 68) highlights this phenomenon and points to the possibility of the therapeutic 'alliance' being weakened as a result of this indirect loss of confidence. In other words, clients do pick up unconsciously transmitted messages during counselling, and when these attitudes convey casual attitudes about confidentiality, real trust will never develop.

The client's responsibility

Another aspect of confidentiality concerns the client's obligation (if any) towards maintaining it. Some therapists, including Weinberg (1996), take the view that clients do have responsibilities in this regard. As far as Weinberg is concerned, the issues should be discussed early in the first session with the client. When clients find the request for confidentiality difficult in some respect, then the difficulties are explored and discussed too. There are probably quite a few clients who would, in fact, experience anxiety if requested to make a pledge of confidentiality in counselling. These include people who have been traumatised in childhood, as a result of keeping 'secrets' relating to sexual or other forms of abuse. Clients in this position would certainly need to be given the opportunity to voice their anxieties about any request for confidentiality; if such a request is made, the reasons for it should be comprehensively explained. In spite of potential difficulties, however, confidentiality on the client's part could be considered important for the following reasons:

1 When clients discuss their sessions freely with other people, the beneficial effects of counselling are often negated. This is because others tend to offer conflicting opinions and even advice, which may prove confusing for the client.

2 Facts are very often distorted when they are discussed outside counselling.

3 Other people may feel the need to tell the client what to say in counselling. Clients who lack basic confidence may well lose sight of their thoughts, feelings and opinions, as a result of such pressure. This goes against the whole ethos of counselling, since a basic aim of therapy is to help clients identify their own needs and to become more autonomous generally.

4 Discussions which take place outside counselling tend to weaken the client–counsellor relationship. This is an important point to consider, since the quality of the relationship is, as Rogers points out, central to effective counselling (Rogers, 2003).

5 A client may choose a confidant, or confidantes, who will support his or her reluctance to change. When this happens, counselling may prove to be a waste of time.

6 If a client knows that he will talk to relatives or friends about counselling, he may become more inhibited about what he actually says in sessions.

Moreover, once other people are included, however indirectly, in the client's therapy, they are given the right to monitor progress and comment accordingly (Weinberg, 1996).

All the above points do not, of course, mean that clients should be encouraged to be totally silent about receiving counselling. Clients need to feel free to be open about this, just as they need to feel free to be honest about any other aspects of their lives. Counselling should not be something clients have to hide, but detailed accounts of what is discussed in sessions are probably best avoided. Clients often know this instinctively anyway, but when outside discussions do become an issue in counselling, helpers need to address this as they would address other significant aspects of the client's behaviour. The following is an example:

CASE STUDY

CLIENT: I talked to my friend Angie about some of the things I said last week. She said I should never have mentioned the abortion . . . that it's better to keep some things quiet . . . now I don't know.

COUNSELLOR: You don't know what to think now that your friend has given her opinion . . .?

CLIENT: I suppose it's made me worried about anyone else finding out . . .

COUNSELLOR: Perhaps you are worried about confidentiality . . .

CLIENT: I don't know . . . yes maybe.

COUNSELLOR: What you say to me here is confidential . . . what you told me last week is confidential.

CLIENT: Yes, I know. It's just that Angie made me feel I shouldn't have said it.

COUNSELLOR: This is something which obviously worries you. And Angie . . . her views matter to you a lot?

CLIENT: Well sometimes . . . though she does irritate me . . . I just wish she would keep her opinions to herself at times.

COUNSELLOR: And your own view . . . about what you said last week . . . are you regretful that you mentioned it?

CLIENT: No [slowly] No I'm not. I've never told anyone before . . . it was a great relief, even though Angie doesn't approve [laughs].

COUNSELLOR: Maybe we could look at why you ask for her approval . . . why you don't trust your own judgment more.

The example just given illustrates another point, which is that clients sometimes seek further assurances of confidentiality, apart from the one given early in counselling. In instances like this, clients should be given the assurances they need, though the underlying reasons for repeated pledges of confidentiality need to be discussed. This is because clients who lack trust in this important area may well lack trust in any relationship. For these clients, the development of trust is crucial, and over a period of time they need to learn to express trust, in order to foster and promote it.

EXERCISE

Developing trust

Working individually, think of a time in your life when you confided in another person. What were your feelings beforehand about revealing personal information? What were your feelings afterwards, when you realised you had given another person important information about yourself? Write down the feelings you experienced, and then discuss these with other members of the training group. It is not necessary to discuss the nature of the problem you disclosed, but you should focus on your reactions to the disclosure itself.

The counselling relationship

People are usually affected by some degree of emotional stress when they first seek counselling. This fact alone makes it imperative that they receive the best possible help, with the lowest possible risk of exacerbating any of the problems they already have. The difficulties clients experience may have been with them for a very long time. These include problems of depression, faulty relationships, marital problems, anxiety, phobias, difficulties at school or university – to name just a few. One of the factors that prompt people to seek help through counselling is the realisation that it might be impossible to continue to cope alone. When people feel helpless, they frequently look for someone who is 'expert' in a particular field. Though trained counsellors do not regard themselves as experts in this way, they nevertheless need to be aware that vulnerable people may have such a perception of them.

The majority of clients have a basic trust in a counsellor's ability to help them deal with the problems they experience. In fact, it is probably true that many clients overestimate any helper's prowess, and may actually ascribe to a counsellor exaggerated or magical powers which are, of course, unrealistic. It is important that clients do, in fact, trust the counsellors who help them, but excessive expectations can work against clients unless counsellors are aware that they do exist. When there is this awareness on the counsellor's part, then it becomes possible to help clients become more autonomous and self-directed over a period of time. Such a position of autonomy cannot, of course, be achieved until clients are given the opportunity to explore their problems and to consider what it is they need to do in order to effect change. The following example illustrates some of these points.

CASE STUDY

Mr Black

Mr Black was aged 68 when his wife died. Apart from the grief he suffered, he was also distressed by the many new and unfamiliar tasks he now had to perform. Mr Black's wife had been his best friend, as well as a loving partner; and their relationship was a traditional one, in the sense that both had clearly defined roles throughout their marriage. Mrs Black had taken care of the home and children, while Mr Black had gone out to work, earned the money and generally looked after all the financial aspects of their lives together. When Mr Black retired this pattern continued, and after his wife's death he found himself unable to cope with the basic tasks of shopping for food and cooking. The tasks his wife once fulfilled now seemed incredibly daunting to him. In a fairly short space of time he became depressed and neglected to care for himself generally.

Through his GP, Mr Black was persuaded to attend a day centre one day a week, where he received counselling help from a carer who was trained to give this kind of support. Mr Black's initial response was to abdicate personal responsibility for his diet and other practical aspects of his care. Over a period of time, however, he was encouraged to discuss the problem he now experienced and to consider ways in which he might become more independent and self-reliant generally. Mr Black confided that he always liked the idea of cooking, but his wife had opposed this ambition and always seemed to be threatened by it. With the help and encouragement of the carer who worked with him, Mr Black attended basic cookery classes, and after a while became proficient in many of the skills he had previously lacked. This gave him the confidence to tackle other practical problems. His depression lessened as he acquired new skills and became more independent.

Comment: Mr Black's case study highlights the point made earlier concerning the vulnerability of clients, and the tendency they often have to place all their expectations and trust in the person who is designated to help them. The carer who helped Mr Black did not encourage him to become dependent on her, although she accepted some measure of dependence in the initial stage of their relationship, since this is what he needed at the time. Having reviewed his life, however, and the current problems affecting him, Mr Black was then encouraged to identify his personal resources and to develop these in ways which would enable him to become more independent and confident about his own ability to cope. If the carer had encouraged his dependence (in many ways, an easier option for her) she would have acted unfairly towards the client, even though this is probably what he would have liked her to do initially.

Transference and the counselling relationship

The subject of transference is one we considered in some detail in Chapters 3 and 4, in the context of psychodynamic counselling. However, transference and its twin concept countertransference are not unique to psychodynamic theory, and the concepts have also been discussed in connection with other theoretical approaches described in this book. Because of their significance within the counselling relationship, transference and counter-transference also deserve extended consideration in this section, dealing specifically with the subject of the counselling relationship. We know that transference refers to the client's emotional response to the counsellor (or to any other helper) and that it is based on much earlier relationships, especially those formed in childhood with parents and other important people in the client's life. Transference, therefore, is by definition unrealistic, since it stems from outdated information that people carry with them and apply to others who help them (as parents might have done) in times of emotional upheaval or distress. When people are distressed they are, of course, vulnerable and this vulnerability makes them open to abuse, however unintended.

Unconscious feelings

Unconscious transference feelings can be positive or negative, distrustful, idealising, loving, erotic, envious or antagonistic. Though these (and many other possible responses) may not be obvious at the beginning of counselling, they tend to emerge once the client–counsellor relationship is established. In other words, clients may respond to helpers in totally realistic ways to start with, but later on they may respond in ways that are inappropriate or out of date. When Freud first wrote about psychoanalysis, he described it as 'the true vehicle of therapeutic influence' (Freud, 1909: 84). He also added that the less transference is suspected by a therapist, the more likely it is to operate in a powerful way (Freud, 1909).

The counsellor's response

One reason for highlighting these unconscious transference feelings is to show how important it is to be aware of their emergence in counselling. It is also important to realise that transference feelings are, as we have already indicated, unrealistic and inappropriate. This may be easier said than done, however, and it often takes another person to help us see this more clearly. Regular supervision is essential as an aid to monitoring both transference and countertransference feelings; without this facility, counsellors are quite likely to make serious mistakes in respect of their own feelings and those of their clients. The word 'countertransference' describes the counsellor's emotional response to the client's transference. A counsellor who is, for example, cast in the role of critical parent, may well be drawn into responding in the way that a critical parent would respond. This type of unconscious role play situation may continue unproductively and indefinitely, unless and until it is identified and changed either through spontaneous insight, or with the aid of supervision.

Lack of objectivity

The point to make here is that clients do not benefit when a counsellor's judgment is clouded because of countertransference feelings and residual complexes, stemming from unresolved problems of his or her own past. Any distorted view of the client–counsellor relationship will inevitably get in the way of objectivity when working with clients and their problems. When counsellors experience countertransference feelings towards clients, they need to be able to 'contain' these, rather than acting on them in a way that clients act on their transference feelings.

Apart from regular supervision, counsellors also need to develop habits of self-scrutiny if they are to identify those roles which are often unconsciously forced on them by clients. In addition, counsellor awareness of both transference and countertransference feelings can prove to be an invaluable asset to therapy, especially when it provides information about the client's emotional problems. However, it is important to remember that not all responses to clients come under the heading of countertransference. Counsellors frequently perceive their clients as they really are, and often the responses elicited by clients in counselling are similar to those elicited in any other situation or relationship. On the other hand, it is often difficult to differentiate between what is real in our responses to clients, and what is countertransferential. The following are some indications of countertransference reactions that may be experienced by counsellors:

- strong sexual or loving feelings towards the client
- inexplicable feelings of anxiety or depression
- feelings of over-protectiveness towards the client
- feelings of guilt in relation to the client
- extreme tiredness or drowsiness
- feelings of anger towards the client
- loss of interest in the client
- inability to make proper interventions when necessary
- dreaming about clients, or thinking about them outside sessions.

Unit 3 contained a more detailed account of countertransference and its related phenomenon, projective identification, with several examples of the way in which every imaginable feeling may present itself in these forms.

One way in which counsellors can monitor their own countertransference feelings is to ask the following questions in relation to clients:

1 Do I experience any strong feelings at the moment which seem inappropriate or out of place?
2 Are my interventions geared to the client's needs, or do they stem from my own needs?

It is not, of course, always possible to answer these questions, which is why regular supervision is needed for all counselling practitioners. Later in this chapter, we shall look at supervision in more detail.

EXERCISE

Countertransference responses

This is an extension of an exercise on countertransference (entitled 'Student self-assessment') given in Chapter 3. In this current exercise, however, you are asked to be more specific about personal responses. The list of possible responses given in this section should encourage you to approach the exercise at a deeper level of honesty and self-awareness.

Spend about 15 minutes thinking about your experience of working with clients in counselling. Are there any personal responses that you can identify from the list outlined here? If you do identify personal responses, are you aware of what prompted them? Discuss common countertransference with other members of your group.

The possibility of exploitation

Any discussion about exploitation in counselling tends to focus on the more obvious forms, including those relating to the sexual and financial abuse of clients. It is unfortunately true that these do occasionally occur, but there are other less obvious forms, which counsellors can, either knowingly or unknowingly, inflict on clients. It is fairly easy to see how sexual involvement with clients can arise, especially when we consider the heightened emotions clients often experience in relation to counsellors, as well as the imbalance of power that exists within the relationship. Such responses may be seductive and irresistible to helpers who currently experience problems in their own lives, especially if they are relationship problems, or problems of loneliness. Once again, this emphasises the point that counsellors need to know how to take care of their own needs without involving vulnerable clients. In Chapter 1 we looked at the subject of personal therapy, and discussed its inclusion or non-inclusion within counsellor training programmes. Whether or not it is part of training, however, it should certainly be undertaken later on when, and if, personal problems arise. Some of the other possible areas of abuse within counselling and therapy include the following:

- failure on the counsellor's part to undertake adequate supervision
- arriving late for sessions, or leaving early
- encouraging clients to become dependent
- being unclear or inconsistent about financial arrangements if these apply
- premature termination of counselling, and lack of consultation with clients
- failure to maintain confidentiality, or failure to inform clients if there is a conflict of interest in relation to confidentiality.

Contracts

In order to provide explicit and clear guidelines for clients, it is necessary to establish contracts with them. Establishment of a contract, preferably in writing, ensures that both client and counsellor understand the nature of the commitment between them and what it entails. In Chapter 3 we considered the subject of contracts, with special reference to their significance in a psychodynamic framework. However, contracts are an essential component of all approaches to counselling and should be made at an early stage. In the first instance, it is useful to clarify certain points with clients, especially those relating to the nature of counselling itself. Many clients believe that counselling includes advice, for example, while others may expect to receive friendship or a more intimate relationship. Clients need to know the exact nature of the counselling relationship, and they also need to know that the person to whom they have come for help is, in fact, a qualified counsellor. When contracts are made confusion is less likely to arise, especially when objectives and desired outcomes are also clarified and priorities discussed. The following are important aspects of counselling, which clients should be informed about from the outset:

- confidentiality and its limitations
- details regarding frequency and length of sessions and where these will take place
- financial terms if these apply, and how payments should be made
- arrangements concerning missed appointments
- details about holidays
- information about the counsellor's qualifications, accreditation, supervision and training
- information about the counsellor's approach and any specific procedures likely to be used
- details about regular reviews of progress between client and counsellor

- discussion about ending counselling and how this will be managed
- details about record-keeping by the counsellor and the client's right to see these
- information about making a complaint, and procedures for clients to follow if they wish to do this.

This may seem like a daunting and lengthy list of requirements for a counselling contract, but the more clients are informed about the process the more they are likely to 'own' it and to participate fully in a way that will empower them. When contracts are written, clients need time to study them and to ask any questions they may have about content. Clients are often baffled about the differences between counselling and psychotherapy, for example, and some may be concerned about the nature of the counselling process (especially if a specific model is being offered) and what to expect. Another important point to clarify for clients is that counselling is a joint commitment between client and counsellor, based on talking and listening, and not something that is 'done' to clients. A surprising number of people suspect counsellors of seeking to change (largely passive) clients who remain inactive throughout the process. Counsellors are aware of how inaccurate this is, but people with no prior experience of therapy may not be. This is why it merits some discussion with new clients so that they are motivated to joint participation and personal change.

KEY TERM

Contract: In counselling a contract is an agreement made between two people, the counsellor and the client. It may be verbal or written and is made before counselling starts. A contract encompasses all aspects of therapy, including confidentiality, times, dates, fees and commitment of both counsellor and client to the process.

EXERCISE

Making contracts

Working in pairs, look at the list of contract details included in this section and discuss any concerns you think clients may have about them. Are there any other details you would add to the list? Members of a training group may have differing views about contracts, depending on their experience or individual areas of work. What are the factors which emerge as the most important in relation to client–counsellor contracts?

Ending counselling

We have noted that the main objective in counselling is to help clients become more independent, self-reliant and capable of dealing with any present or future problems. This means, in effect, that the counselling relationship, unlike many other relationships, is meant to end. Termination of therapy is, therefore, always implicitly present. Endings can be difficult for all of us, however, and clients in counselling are no exception in this respect. Many people experience a variety of conflicts about endings in general, and this is especially true of those people who have been traumatised by separations in the past. The ending of any relationship is obviously much more difficult for someone who has lost a parent in early life, for example, or indeed for anyone who has been bereaved in later life too. Each new ending in an individual's life tends to reactivate memories of previous separations, endings or losses. Clients need to be able to talk about these experiences and what they mean to them; counsellors can help by encouraging expression of all these feelings.

Looking ahead

When contracts are established at the beginning of counselling, clients should be aware of the number of sessions they will attend. When the number of sessions is limited to a very few, and in many organisations and agencies this is currently the case, clients may also be very motivated to make whatever changes are necessary to help them deal more effectively with any difficulties they have experienced. A good beginning is often the key to a satisfactory ending in counselling, which is further reason for explicit contracting and clear goals from the outset.

Often a client's newly acquired confidence becomes obvious towards the last stage of counselling, and this may show itself in different ways. One way in which this new confidence is visible is in the client's attitude to counselling itself. What was once an important focus in the client's life is now placed in perspective and becomes secondary to other relationships and interests. Clients may also find it more difficult to think of subject matter during sessions. For those clients with a history of very specific problems, such as phobias or addictions, for example, there should be clear identifiable gains, which indicate a readiness to cope independently of counselling. Feelings about ending counselling may also surface in dreams. The following case study describes one client's experience of this.

CASE STUDY

Endings

A client called Terry received counselling over a period of eight sessions. Terry, who was 25, had been accused of assault by a colleague at work. Although he was acquitted of the charge, he suffered panic attacks and agoraphobia as a result of his ordeal. During counselling he was able to explore all the angry feelings he felt about the accusation, and he was later able to discuss the development of his other symptoms. The exploration of his feelings was a great relief to Terry, because the nature of the accusation made against him meant that he was extremely reluctant initially to acknowledge his anger to anyone. He felt that if he admitted to feelings of anger, this would be taken as proof of his guilt in relation to the incident with his colleague.

Over a period of time, Terry came to see that his feelings were a part of the ordeal he had been through; once he had acknowledged and expressed them, his panic attacks diminished in frequency and his reluctance to go out decreased too. Terry had formed a good relationship with the counsellor (a man), who worked as a volunteer helper at his local health centre. He had specifically asked to see a man, because he felt inhibited about relating the incident to a woman. A contact had been agreed between client and counsellor when they first met, so Terry was aware of the number of sessions there would be.

Towards the end of his counselling, Terry had a dream in which he was leaving school, but was unable to tell the teacher that he wanted to go. He related this dream to the counsellor and together they discussed it. Terry felt that the teacher in the dream would be hurt if he stated his intention to go. As a result of discussing the dream, the issue of endings and what they meant, Terry was able to place the dream in context, and to identify the counsellor as the teacher in it.

Other indications

The end of counselling, like the end of any close relationship, involves some degree of mourning. However, it should also involve internalisation of the process itself by the client so that the experience of counselling becomes a useful guide for more productive ways of dealing with any difficulties that may arise later on. Following a successful experience of counselling, clients may continue their own internal dialogue, similar to that conducted with the counsellor. In addition to the factors mentioned earlier, readiness to end counselling may also be indicated in other significant ways. The client is likely to feel more independent, for example, and as a result of this independence will see the counsellor as a 'real' person, rather than an object or a transference figure. Increased understanding of 'self' is another aspect of client development, and often clients will demonstrate more assertive attitudes as a result of this.

From the counsellor's point of view, this change is often 'felt' in the sense that the client's transference is no longer experienced and the counsellor becomes more relaxed. When client and counsellor actually do separate, they do so as equals who have worked together towards a goal (Solomon, 1992).

Additionally, they may both have a sense of sadness that the relationship has ended, although clients are sometimes offered the opportunity to attend another session in the future, in order to discuss progress.

> ### EXERCISE
>
> ## Looking at endings
> Working individually, make a list of all significant endings you have experienced in your life. These might include the end of some of the following:
>
> - school holidays
> - summer
> - childhood
> - college or university
> - friendship
> - working life
> - single life
> - childbearing years
> - an intimate relationship.
>
> Can you identify the range of feelings you had on any of these occasions? Discuss these, and any other thoughts you have about endings, with other members of the group.

Referral

Clients receive counselling in a wide variety of contexts, some of which have been discussed in this book. In addition, clients may be helped by people who work in a variety of helping occupations, many of whom would not describe themselves as counsellors. On the other hand, there is an increasing tendency for helpers and carers to undertake counselling skills training, and this trend (though welcome) can cause some confusion for those people seeking assistance with personal or psychological problems. One of the difficulties that helpers may have, as a result of these trends, is to determine the limits of their own capabilities in providing the right support for clients. An important aspect of training, therefore, is identification of specific problem areas that might require other forms of help or support. Obviously, helpers differ in terms of professional training and background, and it is these differences which necessitate discussion of the subject so that proper guidelines for referring clients can be defined. Some helpers may not, for example, have the specific skills needed to deal with clients in crisis, or those with severe depression, or other forms of psychological illness. We all need to know what our own limitations are; the first step is to look for these and then acknowledge them. The next step is to know 'how' to refer clients so that they receive the appropriate help when they need it.

In its *Ethical Framework*, BACP stresses that routine referrals to other services or agencies 'should be discussed with the client in advance' (BACP, 2013). It adds that the client's consent should be obtained before making the referral; in addition, client consent should be obtained in relation to any information that will be disclosed in the process of referral. It is also important to ensure, as far as possible, that the referral is appropriate for the particular client, and that it is likely to be of benefit to that client.

Referral may be difficult for clients for a number of reasons: some may have experienced rejection in the past, while others may come to believe that they (or their problems) are just too formidable for anyone to cope with. On the other hand, if referral is left too late, clients will not receive the kind of support or specialised help they need. This last point emphasises the importance of good communication with clients from the outset, so that the possibility of referral is identified early on. Clients should be given the opportunity to discuss their feelings about the prospect of referral too. If they are not given this chance to express feelings, they may experience resentment or anger in relation to the whole process.

Reasons for referral

At every stage of the counselling process, however, helpers need to ask themselves what is the best course of action for specific clients. The reasons for referral are obviously very varied. A counsellor or client may, for example, be in the process of moving away from the area, in which case referral might be necessary if the client is to receive ongoing help. Certain clients may require psychiatric support, or other specialised health services. There are clients whose problems are specific to certain areas, for example, adoption, recovery after surgery, disability or language difficulties, and they may well benefit from contact with a helper, specially trained in one of those areas. Whatever the circumstances, and regardless of the problem, it is essential that clients are given the opportunity to participate in any decisions made about them. The counsellor's task is to inform clients about any specialised services that are available to them; it is then up to the client to accept or decline.

Occasionally, clients may ask to see either a male or female counsellor. This request is usually made for very good reasons and counsellors should respect them. A woman who has been physically abused, for example, may feel more comfortable with a female counsellor, while a man who has sexual problems may well feel more at ease with a male counsellor. Sometimes clients who receive individual counselling are given the chance to participate in group work too. This necessitates referral of a different kind, since the client is not being asked to forfeit one kind of support for another. Another reason for referral is indicated when the particular theoretical approach another counsellor uses is considered more appropriate for an individual client's needs. Financial constraints may also have a bearing on the kind of help available to a client; someone who cannot afford the services of a particular helper may benefit from referral to a voluntary agency, for example.

The following is a list of factors that could impinge on your ability to help certain clients:

- lack of experience in specific areas; for example, severe mental illness such as psychosis or dementia
- insufficient time to offer the client
- your theoretical orientation and training may not be right for the client
- lack of the kind of information the client needs
- your relationship with the client is difficult or compromised
- client may receive appropriate help nearer their home.

EXERCISE

Referral

Working in groups of two to three, make a list of the reasons for referring clients to other people, or agencies. Do these reasons vary for different members of the group? Discuss the counselling skills necessary for successful referral, and indicate how early or late in the counselling process you would do it.

Resources for referral

Preparation is probably one of the most important aspects of referral. All helpers, including those whose work is part of other occupational responsibilities, need to be well informed about all the resources available to them within the community and, indeed, beyond. The names, addresses and telephone numbers of other professional workers who might be in a position to help clients with specific needs should be kept on record. Good liaison and consultation with other professionals is essential too. However, ongoing personal development and training is also needed for counsellors who wish to remain in touch with new developments in all the helping and allied professions. Continuing education has the added advantage of keeping counsellors in contact with as many people as possible, either locally or nationally, who may be able to help clients. Subscribing to professional journals and periodicals is also helpful and informative, since they can provide vital information about changes and trends in the helping professions generally.

Clients in crisis

In Chapter 1 we noted that clients often seek help when they experience a crisis. We also noted that each person's interpretation of crisis is quite subjective, which makes it difficult to list the experiences that may fall into that category. However, it is not just the client's response to a perceived crisis that we are concerned with here. The counsellor's response to the person in crisis is important in this context, and there are certainly a number of grave situations that are familiar to most experienced practitioners. These include those circumstances in which clients threaten suicide or violence towards other people. We have already considered the issue of confidentiality in relation to such expressed intentions, and the point has been made that many agencies have very specific guidelines about them. Apart from the practical steps counsellors can initiate, however, the emotional impact on them needs to be considered too. In this respect, discussion and preparation are vitally important, since issues discussed openly in this way tend to be less threatening when they are actually encountered. Suicide and violence are not subjects people readily talk about, but we need to address them in order to identify our own feelings in relation to them. We could start by looking at the following points:

1 Some people take the view that as far as suicide is concerned, there is no ultimate preventative
2 Others take the view that clients who say they feel suicidal are, in fact, asking for positive intervention from helpers.

Helping clients in crisis

The above two points are likely to generate a great deal of discussion in any training group, and you need to be clear about your own responses in relation to them. The view taken here is that clients should be offered whatever support and help we can possibly give. Clients who reveal themselves in this way are, in fact, seeking the reassurance that someone else cares sufficiently to intervene. It should be added that intervention does not necessarily mean dramatic action; what is usually needed is identification of all the client's feelings and plans so that a realistic assessment of risk can be made. When this is done, clients are frequently relieved to be taken seriously. Afterwards, practical steps can be implemented to lessen the suicide risk. These steps may include consultation with the client's doctor so that medication can be prescribed or adjusted, though none of this can be done without the client's permission. Helpers are sometimes reluctant to address the subject of suicide openly, on the grounds that to do so would encourage the client's action. This is an entirely mistaken belief and one with immense potential for causing harm to clients. More often than not, people are very relieved to articulate their worst fears and impulses in the presence (or hearing, as in telephone counselling) of someone who is supportive and calm. In order to determine the extent to which a person is serious about suicide, it is useful to establish the following:

1 Has the person made a plan?
2 Is the plan specific?

3 Does the person have the means to follow through a plan?
4 Is there a past history of deliberate self-harm?

Without looking closely at these factors, it is difficult to establish the level of risk to those clients who may refer to suicide in oblique terms only. Counsellors and other helpers should be aware of other factors that may accentuate the risk of suicide. These factors include:

- feelings of depression or hopelessness
- alcohol or drug abuse
- recent trouble with the law
- family history of alcohol or drug abuse
- mental illness (e.g. schizophrenia) or family history of mental illness
- suicide of another family member
- conflict about sexual orientation
- violence or sexual abuse
- being bullied
- loneliness, isolation or loss of an intimate relationship
- terminal illness or chronic pain.

One of the most effective ways of helping clients in crisis situations is to prepare through participation in suicide prevention courses. These courses, which are usually of short duration, are becoming more readily available and are meant for anyone (including counsellors) who work in a helping capacity. Their strength lies in that they inspire confidence in anyone facing a potential suicide crisis, and this is especially relevant for those people who were previously apprehensive about coping.

When helping clients in crisis, counsellors need to be prepared to look at the underlying causes. Suicidal feelings are often precipitated by a number of accumulating factors and these factors need to be identified and discussed with clients. Once this is done, clients tend to experience relief of pressure, and with ongoing support and therapy they may be able to deal with their problems. Counselling can be continued with those clients who are referred for specialist help, and often it is this combined approach which proves most beneficial for them.

Threats of violence

Sometimes clients express violent feelings or impulses towards other people. In these circumstances, helpers need to assess the degree of actual danger involved and act accordingly. This is much easier said than done, since all of us have probably experienced antagonistic and negative emotions occasionally, as a result of conflict with others. Most people hide these feelings, for fear they will cause unnecessary alarm or upset. However, clients in counselling may express their negative feelings more readily, especially when they know they will not be judged for doing so. On rare occasions, though, clients may be serious in the threats they make, and, in these instances, helpers need to adhere to the guidelines set down by the agencies in which they work. Clients who threaten violence to others, like those who threaten violence to themselves, may in fact wish to be stopped. It is unlikely that they would verbalise their impulses if they did not expect some intervention. However, counsellors, in common with other responsible citizens, have a duty to safeguard vulnerable people who might be at risk of violence. Support through supervision is probably the most effective way for helpers to deal with problematic issues of this kind. The guidelines for confidentiality and its limitations (described earlier in this chapter) are important in relation to any threats of harm to self or others expressed by clients in counselling.

Other crisis situations

Suicide and threats of violence are not the only forms of crisis which counsellors and other helpers may hear about from clients. Others include:

- sudden death
- rape and assault
- accident and injury
- discovery of child abuse
- acute illness
- diagnosis of terminal illness
- unexpected break-up of a relationship
- burglary or loss of belongings
- sudden financial problems
- loss of a job.

EXERCISE

Responses to crisis

Working in groups of three or four, discuss how people in crisis might respond to their new and unfamiliar situation. Make a list of the feelings that the crisis may generate, and then suggest ways in which clients can best be supported in counselling. Afterwards, consider how counsellors who work with clients in crisis can themselves be supported in their work.

Supervision

Throughout this book we have emphasised the central place of supervision for counsellors. In Chapter 1 we discussed the role of supervised counselling practice in training, and quoted the BACP *Ethical Framework* in relation to this. Some of the issues just discussed, especially those relating to crisis and its management, should highlight even further the need for regular support of this kind. Many professional agencies make their own arrangements for supervision, and helpers who work in these settings are aware of the benefits of professional assistance and backing. Here are some further considerations in relation to supervision.

What supervision means

The word 'supervision' refers to the practice of giving support, guidance and feedback to counsellors who work with clients. It is, in fact, mandatory for anyone who works with clients in psychotherapy or counselling context, including trainees. The British Association for Counselling and Psychotherapy (BACP) is clear on the subject of supervision, and it is important that you read its *Ethical Framework* (2013), which specifies the requirements for trained practitioners and for students.

Supervision is not, of course, an entirely new idea for it has been in existence for a very long time. Freud and his followers supported each other in a similar way. Supervision has been used ever since, though not just by therapists and counsellors. Helpers in a variety of other roles, including nursing and social work, recognise the place of supervision in maintaining good practice with patients and clients. Supervision is essential for counsellors and helpers, because it affords the opportunity to discuss all aspects of work with someone who has received specialist training in this area.

Support for counsellors

Supervision benefits counsellors for a number of reasons. It:

- provides a more objective view of the counsellor's work
- makes loss of confidence and 'burnout' less likely when it is regular
- gives the counsellor a clearer picture of transference–countertransference issues
- allows the counsellor to appraise the skills and approaches used with individual clients
- provides support, guidance, encouragement and differing perspectives
- affords time for reflection and thought
- can provide important information about the counsellor's work, since aspects of the relationship between client and counsellor are often mirrored in the supervisory relationship
- is rewarding for counsellors, both intellectually and emotionally
- can help counsellors to clarify and modify any negative emotions they may experience in relation to certain clients
- enables personal problems that counsellors have to be identified through supervision, although these are not directly dealt with by supervisors
- serves to identify the counsellor's own need for personal therapy
- enables counsellors to increase and develop their range of therapeutic techniques.

What supervision is not

Supervision is not the same as counselling, and the supervisor–counsellor relationship is quite different also. In the first place supervision is not therapy, although it can have therapeutic benefits. The supervisor's principal task is to improve the counsellor's relationship with his or her clients. This means that a supervisor is never directly involved in helping a counsellor to deal with personal problems, although evidence of these sometimes appears in the course of supervisory sessions. It may even be difficult to distinguish between the counsellor's personal problems and those of the client. One of the supervisor's duties is to help the counsellor differentiate between the two, and to recommend therapeutic support for the counsellor when necessary. Although supervisors do not give counselling, therefore, they nonetheless encourage counsellors to consider personal issues and to look at the way these impinge on their relationships with clients.

CASE STUDY

Jenny

Jenny worked as a student counsellor in a university. One of her clients, an 18-year-old student called Tamsin, had been dieting over a long period of time and had requested counselling when she realised that she had developed problems in relation to this. Jenny had also been overweight as a teenager, and this had caused her a great deal of anxiety and stress at the time. Because of her experience, Jenny felt deep empathy with her client, but sometimes this identification threatened to cloud the true nature of the counselling relationship.

On several occasions, Jenny was tempted to offer advice and to steer Tamsin towards certain courses of action. She also found herself worrying a great deal about her client outside counselling sessions. In supervision, Jenny was able to identify her countertransference feelings, and to separate her own memories and experience from the client's experience. Afterwards her relationship with Tamsin was much improved, and certainly less controlling than it had previously been.

Confidentiality and supervision

One point of similarity between the supervisory and counselling relationships is that both are confidential in nature. This means that supervision should be independent of other relationships that may be in conflict. One example of such a conflicting relationship is that between manager and employer. Employees are obviously accountable to managers for a variety of work-related reasons, and the nature of the manager–employee relationship may mean that true confidentiality cannot be guaranteed when supervision is also taking place. Another example of a relationship that could compromise the supervisory function is that of trainer and student. Teachers and trainers are required to assess their students, and this might inhibit those students who are concerned about receiving satisfactory grades. Some elements of teaching are certainly contained in supervision but it encompasses many skills; though its primary function is to protect clients through the provision of a safe and proficient counselling service.

Finding a supervisor

In Unit 1 we noted that students in placement need supervision as part of their overall training programme. Supervision in this context is known as training supervision, and is now an essential requirement of every training programme. Training establishments have, therefore, a duty to ensure that students have access to supervision. We know that supervision is not the same as counselling and that it requires a separate and specialist form of training. For students of counselling, the answer to finding a trained and competent supervisor lies in cooperating with trainers. Any suggestions you make for supervisory arrangements should be discussed and agreed with you.

How much and how often?

In its *Ethical Framework* (2013), the BACP states its supervision requirements for accredited courses; however, other courses may provide their own details in relation to frequency and number of supervisory sessions. These details should be worked out between the training establishment, the supervisor and the student or supervisee. When formalising a contract, it is also necessary to clarify any other relevant details, including those relating to student assessment and the degree of responsibility and accountability the supervisor has to the student's training establishment.

Forms of supervision

There are different forms of supervision, including the following:

1 Individual supervision, where there is one supervisee and one supervisor. This allows more time for the counsellor to present and discuss his or her work in a safe environment.
2 Group supervision, where a number of counsellors meet with one designated supervisor. This approach is more cost-effective than individual supervision, but a possible drawback is that less time is available for feedback to individual members of the group.
3 Peer group supervision, where a number of counsellors provide supervision for each other. This form is often used by trained and experienced counsellors; it is not recommended for student counsellors.
4 Co-supervision or peer supervision, where two counsellors provide supervision for one another, taking turns to do so and alternating the roles of supervisor and supervisee. This model is not suitable on its own for inexperienced or student counsellors, who may not feel confident enough to participate.
5 A combination of individual and group supervision is best for students and provides the right balance of support needed.

The relationship between supervisor and supervisee

It is obvious that the relationship between counsellor and supervisor needs to be based on trust and mutual respect if it is to work effectively. This means that supervisors should be prepared to discuss their qualifications, training and theoretical approach with their supervisees before work begins. As we have already indicated, all administrative and practical details of the supervisory contract should be openly discussed and agreed upon by both counsellor and supervisor.

EXERCISE

Experiences of supervision

Working in groups of three to four, discuss the benefits and disadvantages of the different methods of supervision described in this section. What experience of supervision do individual members of your group have?

Education and training

In Chapter 1 we discussed a range of issues relating to counsellor training, and most of these are common to many programmes, though individual programmes do still vary to some degree nationwide. The British Association for Counselling and Psychotherapy and other professional organisations are committed to continuing research and development in relation to both training and standards within the profession. This means that key elements in counsellor training programmes are quite likely to be deemed essential, or even mandatory, in the near future. These key elements, including supervision (which is already a requirement) and personal therapy, have been highlighted throughout this text. In addition, there is now greater emphasis on continuing professional development (CPD) for trained and accredited counsellors.

Continuing professional development

There is widespread recognition that counsellors must offer the best quality service to clients, and to do this they need to improve and update their knowledge and skills at regular intervals. Counsellors benefit personally from a commitment to training and development, because such a commitment keeps them in touch with the rapidly expanding discipline of counselling and with other practitioners, whose support and knowledge is invaluable. In its guidelines for maintaining competence practice, BACP (2013) states that counsellors should be involved in education if they are to keep in touch with the latest knowledge and developments in the profession. The following are examples of activities which support or enhance CPD:

- personal therapy
- courses on professional or related issues
- academic study and research
- seminars and conferences
- facilitating courses and workshops for others
- research and publication
- counselling-related committee work.

Research

Student counsellors are often less than enthusiastic when the subject of research is mentioned in group discussion. This response is understandable when we consider the many elements already included in counsellor training. As we have seen in Unit 1, these elements encompass theory, written work and assignments, skills training, supervised practice, supervision, personal therapy and ongoing self-development. This is a demanding (and increasingly expensive) commitment and, for this reason, students tend to regard research as a daunting extra, which can be deferred until later on when training is complete. It is easy to see why the introduction of another area of study into an already crowded syllabus is seen by many student counsellors as a demand too far.

And yet, the extensive list of training requirements is not the only reason for lack of student enthusiasm when the subject of research comes up in discussion. Another, and perhaps the core reason, is that students often fail to see the relevance of research to counselling. Research is viewed as an 'intellectual' activity, whereas counselling is categorised in the 'affective' or feeling domain. Students, as well as many qualified counsellors, sometimes say that they do not believe it is possible to measure the complex individual experiences of clients with the research tools currently used in other areas of science.

Consequently, one of the challenges for teachers and trainers is to convince students of the value of research, and to place it at the very heart of training so that it becomes normalised, less intimidating and better understood. As we have seen, evidence-based therapies, in particular CBT, are currently favoured in the Improving Access to Psychological Therapies (IAPT) initiative, and it is likely that this demand for evidence in counselling and psychotherapy will continue.

Research, therefore, should be an integral part of education and training, so that when students graduate they are predisposed to engage with it. The most effective way of inculcating an interest in research from the outset is through extensive and varied reading. When students see that research findings (many of them health and psychology related) dominate newspaper and magazine headlines, they can start to make the connection with their own discipline, and develop an interest in finding out more about it. At a very basic level, we need to know what works and what doesn't work, and this is as true in counselling and psychotherapy as it is in any other field. It is not just articles in newspapers and magazines that stimulate an interest in gaining new knowledge about therapy, however; books are essential too. There are numerous books available on the subject of research, a selection of which is included for further reading at the end of this chapter. But students should also be encouraged to read eclectically across a range of subject areas, including literature and philosophy, so that habits of reflection and enquiry are inculcated. This may seem like a tall order, and students are often reluctant to invest in extra books because of the expense involved. Libraries, however, are free, and the internet is an endless, though not always infallible, source of information. Journals and newspapers can be accessed in this way as well, and professional bodies such as the BACP regularly publish articles and research findings on a range of diverse subjects. When research is viewed as something that we can read about and is accessible, then it loses some of its off-putting esoteric status and becomes interesting and relevant to all of us. Once interest is in place, a desire to find out more is nurtured and this forms the basis for future research projects in areas of specific interest to individual counsellors and psychotherapists.

There are some obvious areas of mental and physical health that all students (and trained practitioners) should understand if they are to offer optimal support to clients. Keeping abreast of developments in these areas requires ongoing reading and research and, preferably, attendance at forums where they are discussed. The following areas should be relevant to counsellors and generate interest in study and research:

- mental health and illness
- physical illness and its psychological effects
- theories about the links between physical and mental illness
- environmental factors which impinge on health and wellbeing
- neuroscience and counselling.

Neuroscience, which is described in Medical News Today (2012) as the study of the brain and spinal cord and is included here because findings increasingly suggest that counselling engenders positive and lasting changes in the brain. Williams and Penman (2011) refer to this effect too and suggest that these changes in the brain include the regeneration and building of new neurons, a process called **neurogenesis**.

These effects have been detected through the procedure of **neuroimaging**, a medical procedure normally used for diagnostic purposes. Another term often used in relation to brain function is **neuroplasticity**, which describes the brain's ability to change in response to the environment and throughout a person's lifespan. In relation to counselling, this is a relatively new and exciting area of study, so it is important that student counsellors and trained practitioners keep in touch with its developments.

Undertaking an actual research project while in training is a substantial commitment and may not be feasible within a busy schedule. However, it is important to be aware of how it is done and to take an interest in it for future reference. In *Doing a Successful Research Project*, Brett Davies suggests that many students are inhibited about research, because they wrongly believe it 'involves complex methodological theories' when in fact it does not. He encourages students to have patience, plan carefully, aim for simplicity and to be realistic about what can actually be achieved (Davies, 2007: 9)

Cultural diversity and counselling

Though we live in a multicultural society, counselling and psychotherapy are still predominantly white, middle class, heterosexual and largely affluent professions. This situation may reflect the fact that the traditional client base for counselling and therapy has tended (historically) to be drawn from these groups as well. This situation has obtained, not because people of different races or ethnic minority groups do not have the same rights and needs for therapy. On the contrary, it is because, until recently, most training courses failed to address cross-cultural issues in their programmes for students. Often, as Sue Marshall suggests in her book *Difference and Discrimination in Psychotherapy and Counselling*, intercultural and cross-cultural therapy is still regarded as a 'specialist' or 'marginal area of interest' outside mainstream counselling or psychotherapy (Marshall, 2004: 64). In addition, the theories underlying counselling and psychotherapy fail to take account of the experiences of black people or those from diverse ethnic groups. Freudian theory and its derivative psychodynamic theory are, for example, formulated on the experiences of a particularly narrow group of people living in Europe in the nineteenth century. This is a criticism that counsellors working from a feminist perspective would also level against traditional psychodynamic theory, though as Marshall (2004) notes, the situation has been redressed to some extent by the feminist movement itself, and by later theorists.

One interesting and disturbing factor that Marshall notes is that people of different races (if they do have access to it) tend to leave counselling early. Furthermore, they are less likely to benefit from therapy, even when they are committed to it. An explanation proposed by Marshall is the fact that all models of psychotherapy and counselling are 'rooted in white Western values' (Marshall, 2004: 59). It is not surprising, therefore, that theories derived from a white middle-class context do not address the values and ideals of other groups outside that narrow band. This white Western bias stems, of course, from the wider society, so it is no surprise that its insidious influence has permeated therapy as well. Because it fails to take into account the validity of equally important and diverse views, it becomes accepted as the norm and, unless challenged, will continue to do so. However, within recent years there has been a decided focus on race as a factor in counselling and psychotherapy, and the BACP is committed to research and the implementation of good practice in the context of intercultural and cross-cultural counselling.

In addition, BACP is dedicated to equality of treatment in all areas and, along with The British Psychological Society, opposes any treatments or interventions (referred to as conversion or reparative) designed to change same-sex orientation. Included in this group are gay, lesbian, bisexual and all other 'non heterosexual orientations', which have in the past been subjected to prejudice and regarded as illnesses (British Psychological Society, 2013:1). This is an important step forward in terms of addressing a hitherto neglected area of counselling and psychotherapy. What is needed, though, is more emphasis on cultural competency and diversity training for all student (and qualified) practitioners within the helping professions to address the deficit that still exists. Without this level of training, counsellors are liable to fall into the trap of trying to reframe clients' views and behaviours so that they fit those of mainstream values and perspectives. Such an approach is not only stultifying for clients (who will probably abandon counselling because of it), but it is also limiting for practitioners who will learn nothing of the varied and culturally rich lives of other people.

It is not within the scope of this chapter to discuss all the important issues that need to be addressed in relation to cultural diversity and counselling. However, it is an ethical issue, which means that students and practitioners need to ensure adequate training in order to meet the needs of all clients. Increasingly, specialist courses are available, but diversity awareness is so fundamental to good practice that it should form a substantial part of all counsellor training programmes. It is important that counsellors of the future are culturally competent and able to offer the best possible help to meet the needs of all communities.

EXERCISE

Terms and what they mean

Working in small groups, look at the following list of terms and discuss their meanings and the relevance they may have in the counselling context:

- discrimination
- culture
- ethnicity
- heterosexism
- multiculturalism
- dominant group
- empowerment
- diversity
- stereotypes
- prejudice.

Feminism and counselling

It is interesting to note that almost all the psychotherapeutic approaches described in this chapter have originated from a male perspective and, from Freud onwards, have demonstrated an almost exclusively masculine viewpoint about women and their experiences. The writer Nancy Chodorow, commenting in 1989 on the history of feminist discourse, suggests that 'dominant ideologies' have shaped opinion, so that women's own voices have been 'ignored or silenced' (Chodorow, 1989:199). It is true that Melanie Klein addressed some aspects of female experience, though she did not focus on women's experiences of oppression, but instead wrote extensively about the early mother–child relationship, with little or no reference to the father. Adler, too, was interested in the experiences of women; in *Understanding Human Nature* (1927), he wrote about the problem of 'male dominance' and the difficulties it meant for women who were disadvantaged because of it (Adler, 1927: 106). Adler, though obviously not a female voice, was writing about discrimination in the early part of the twentieth century, which makes his prescient approach all the more remarkable.

It was not though until the early 1960s and 1970s (when the feminist movement began) that those aspects of ordinary women's lives became a sustained focus of discussion and debate. During this time feminists provided conditions, mainly through their writing and facilitation of consciousness-raising groups, for women to tell their own stories in their own words. It would be wrong to suggest, however, that few people protested about women's relative lack of power, or about their social and sexual subordination, before the second half of the twentieth century. As far back as 1792, Mary Wollstonecraft had written her treatise, entitled *A Vindication of the Rights of Women*, which argued for (among other things) women's right to education. That woman have a right to education is a fundamental aim of feminism today, but education here is defined in the widest possible sense and includes empowerment and the awareness of women's assigned roles in society and the social control traditionally used to enforce them.

In contrast to all other approaches, feminist counselling was not founded by one particular person but encompasses many strands and is derived from feminist philosophy, in general, and the women's movement of the 1960s, in particular. Those women, who collectively contributed to the movement, realised that the social, cultural and political context of their lives had to be recognised as factors in the cause of many of their problems. Before the emergence of feminism and feminist therapy, most women's problems were believed to stem from personal or innate inadequacies, usually located in the female psyche, or in women's refusal to conform to a predetermined and male view of how they should behave. Feminist counselling takes a different view and, instead of blaming women for their emotional or psychological distress, suggests that oppression and environmental causes are the basis of their concerns. In order to address these concerns, feminist counselling has developed its own unique approach to clients, which is based on a historical awareness of women's difficulties. It is also linked to specific values and attitudes, including respect for individual client experience and awareness of the environment in which they live. Clients are not expected to adjust to a particular situation (often toxic or abusive) but are supported in their efforts to identify personal strengths and to change the environment that has a negative impact on them. Feminist counsellors also acknowledge the power balance between themselves and their clients and endeavour to encourage equality with them. One way of achieving this is through counsellor self-disclosure and through educating clients about the therapy process itself. Although there are no specific techniques used, feminist counselling can be incorporated into a variety of other therapeutic approaches, with the proviso that the origins of the client's problems are reframed in the context of environmental causation, rather than personal ineptitude or weakness. Assertiveness training is often offered to clients to help them develop confidence in interpersonal relationships and social situations. Reading (or bibliotherapy) is also often recommended to address issues, including power imbalance between men and women, gender role stereotyping and societal pressure on women to look or dress a certain way.

A basic tenet of feminist theory is that the 'personal is political', a phrase that is not attributable to any one person, but encapsulates and describes the relationship between individual experience and the devaluation of women as a group within society generally. It emphasises, too, that individual change is most likely within the context of social change. This realisation helps women to see that they are not alone, but part of a larger community of others with similar experiences. In addition, it stresses the wider issues affecting women of different races as well as lesbian feminists, and upholds certain fundamental values including equality, respect and dignity. Sharing of personal experience is an important aspect of group counselling, in particular, and is especially pertinent in the context of women's groups, which also provide peer support, information sharing, role modelling, and opportunities for 'identifying commonalities' (Israeli and Santor, 2010:236). Other features of feminist counselling include the fact that it is a person-centred approach, whose goal is to help clients identify and acknowledge their own strengths. When clients are enabled to do this, they can then mobilise their own resources and support systems. Ideally, they may also be prompted to work towards social change, not just for themselves but for women, in general, and other disadvantaged groups within society. Finally, feminists understand that counsellors should be drawn from a diversity of backgrounds, classes, races, abilities and sexual orientations, if they are to provide the broad spectrum of support their clients deserve.

SUMMARY

In this chapter we considered a range of ethical issues in counselling. These include the subject of confidentiality and its central place in the therapeutic relationship. The limits of absolute confidentiality were discussed and examples given of situations in which it might not be guaranteed. Contracts in counselling were discussed, and the subject of 'endings' and its attendant difficulties were considered. Aspects of the counselling relationship were discussed, including the twin concepts of transference and countertransference. The subject of referral and reasons for it were detailed. Crisis situations and their effects on both client and counsellor were addressed in this section, and the need for regular supervision highlighted.

Although this chapter did not attempt to deal with the subject of research in detail, it does emphasise the increasing importance of developing an interest in it. We looked at ways in which students can be encouraged to view research as a fascinating and relevant component of training, as well as a prerequisite of future exploration.

A section on diversity in counselling and another on feminist counselling were included within this chapter entitled 'Ethical considerations'. This is because the word 'ethical' refers to that which is right or fair, and because counselling should, rightly and in fairness, be available to all members of society who wish to access it.

References

Adler, A. (1927) *Understanding Human Nature*. Oxford: Oneworld Publications.

British Association for Counselling and Psychotherapy (2013) *The Ethical Framework for Good Practice in Counselling and Psychotherapy* (online). Available at: http://www.bacp.co.uk/ethical _ framework. Accessed 4th August 2013.

British Psychological Society (2013) *Opposing Sexual Conversion Therapies* (online). Available at: http://www.bps.org.uk/news/opposing-sexual-conversion-therapies. Accessed 15th August 2013.

Chodorow, N.J. (1989) *Feminism and Psychoanalytic Theory*. New Haven: Yale University Press.

Davies, M.B. (2007) *Doing a Successful Research Project*. London: Palgrave Macmillan.

Freud, S. (1909) *Five Lectures on Psychoanalysis*. London: Penguin Books.

Israeli, A.L. & Santor, D.A. (2010) 'Reviewing Effective Components of Feminist Therapy'. *Counselling Psychology Quarterly*, 13, 3, 2000, 233–47 (online). Available at: http://www.darcyasantor.net/feminist % 20therapy. pdf. Accessed 20th August 2013.

Marshall, S. (2004) *Difference and Discrimination in Psychotherapy and Counselling*. London: Sage Publications.

Medical News Today (2012) 'What is Neuroscience?' (online). Available from: http://medicalnewstoday.com/articles 248680.php. Accessed 24th August 2013.

Solomon, I. (1992) *The Encyclopaedia of Evolving Techniques in Dynamic Psychotherapy*. New Jersey: Jason Aronson Inc.

Weinberg, G. (1996) *The Heart of Psychotherapy*. New York: St Martins Griffin.

Williams, M. & Penman, D. (2011) *Mindfulness: A Practical Guide to Finding Peace in a Frantic World*. London: Piatkus.

Wollstonecraft, M. (1792) *A Vindication of the Rights of Women*. Great Books Online. Available at: Bartleby at Columbia University. http://www.bartleby.com/144/. Accessed 27th August 2013.

Further reading

Bond, T. (2009) *Standards and Ethics for Counselling in Action* (3rd edn). London: Sage Publications.

Brown, L.S. & Brodsky, A.M. (1992) *Feminist Therapy: A Social and Individual Change Model* (online). Available at: http://www.sagepub.com/upm-data/37813_chapter2.pdf. Accessed 13th August 2013.

Chaplin, J. (1999) *Feminist Counselling in Action*. London: Sage Publications.

Copeland, S. (2005) *Counselling Supervision in Organisations: Professional and Ethical Dilemmas Explored*. London: Routledge.

Cooper, M. (2008) *Ethical Research Findings in Counselling and Psychotherapy*. London: Sage Publications.

Culley, S. (2004) *Integrative Counselling in Action* (2nd edn). London: Sage Publications.

Davies, M.B. (2007) *Doing a Successful Research Project*. London: Palgrave Macmillan.

Davyse, A. & Beddoe, L. (2010) *Best Practice in Professional Supervision*. London: Jessica Kingsley.

Hawkins, P. & Shohet, R. (2004) *Supervision in the Helping Professions*. Maidenhead: Open University Press.

Marshall, S. (2004) *Difference and Discrimination in Psychotherapy and Counselling*. London: Sage Publications.

McLeod, J. (2003) *Doing Counselling Research* (2nd edn). London: Sage Publications.

Oliver, P. (2003) *The Student's Guide to Research Ethics*. Maidenhead: Open University Press.

Page, S. & Wosket, V. (2001) *Supervising the Counsellor*. London: Routledge.

Rogers, C. (2003) *Client Centred Therapy*. London: Constable.

Wheeler, S. (2006) *Difference and Diversity in Counselling*. London: Palgrave.

Wright, E. (ed.) (1992) *Feminism and Psychoanalysis: A Critical Dictionary*. Oxford: Blackwell.

Resources

Websites

www.bacp.co.uk
British Association for Counselling and Psychotherapy.
www.eac.eu.com

European Association for Counselling.
www.irish-counselling.ie
Irish Association for Counselling and Psychotherapy.
www.bps.org.uk
British Psychological Society.
www.psychotherapy.org.uk
United Kingdom Council for Psychotherapy.
www.tandfonline.com
Taylor & Francis online journal of Feminist Family Therapy.
www.researdgate.net
Website of feminist family therapy.
www.ingentaconnect.com
This is a supervision research and practice network funded by the BACP.
www.counsellingsupervisiontraining.co.uk
Dedicated to counsellor training and supervision
http://ec.europa.eu/justice/discrimination.
The European Commission for justice and tackling discrimination. Outlines legislation and lists events, networks and courses.
www.uktrauma.org.uk
UK Trauma Group (services relating to trauma).
www.therapytoday.net
The online magazine for counsellors.

Journals

European Journal of Psychotherapy and Counselling
The Counselling Psychologist
Counselling and Psychotherapy Research
Cognitive Behaviour Therapy (Research)
Journal of Counselling and Development
Journal of Counselling Psychology
Journal of LGBT Issues in Counselling
Women and Therapy: A Feminist Quarterly
Journal of Gay and Lesbian Mental Health
Journal of Social Action in Counselling and Psychotherapy
Journal of Refugee Studies

Glossary

Abnormal psychology   The study of behaviour disturbance, including the causes, classification and description of abnormal types of behaviour.

Abreaction   A term used in psychodynamic theory to refer to the process of reliving, either in speech or action, a previously repressed experience. It also involves the release of the emotion associated with the experience.

Acquisition   The process whereby a conditioned stimulus begins to produce a conditioned response.

Actualising tendency   A propensity described by both Rogers and Maslow. It refers to the human urge to grow, develop and reach maximum potential.

Adaptation   The ability to function effectively in the environment. Adaptations are helpful changes which enable people to cope with others and with their surroundings.

Addiction   A pronounced physical or psychological dependence on, or need for, a particular substance or activity.

Adlerian   Referring to Adler, who was an early follower of Freud, and to the theories developed by him.

Affect   Refers to feelings and emotions.

Affective disorder   Mental disorder characterised by mood changes. Depression is one example, while extreme excitement (mania) is another.

Agoraphobia   An abnormal fear of being alone or in a public place where escape might be difficult. The term is derived from two Greek words: 'phobos' (fear) and 'agora' (marketplace).

Ambivalence   Conflict of feelings or emotions (love and hate) towards another person or object. There may be contradictory impulses as well, and often one of the ambivalent feelings is conscious, while the other is unconscious.

Anal stage   According to psychoanalytic theory, this is the second stage of psychosexual development. Gratification and conflict are experienced in relation to the expulsion and retention of faeces. Control of bodily function and socialisation of impulses are major tasks at this time.

Anima/animus   Jungian terms referring to unconscious opposite sex images. The anima is the unconscious female image in the male psyche, while the animus is the unconscious male image in the female psyche.

Anxiety   Feelings of dread associated with physical symptoms including raised pulse and sweating. According to Freud, anxiety is related to unconscious mental conflicts stemming from childhood.

Archetypes   Unconscious images or patterns of thought which, according to Jung, are inherited from our ancestors and are universally present in all of us.

Aversion therapy   The use of punishment to remove undesirable behaviour such as alcoholism. Once used as part of behaviour therapy, but is less popular now.

Basic needs   A term used by Maslow to describe a range of needs which all humans experience. Maslow arranged these needs in a hierarchy, and although it is often assumed that they are in a fixed order, he did not intend that it should be interpreted so rigidly.

Basic trust   A fundamental attitude derived from positive early experience. The term is used by both Erikson and Winnicott and refers to the feelings about self which are formed as a result of an infant's relationship with the primary caregiver.

Behaviourism   The scientific study of behaviour based on observable actions and reactions. The focus is on analysing the relationship between behaviour and the environment, and the way that stimuli provoke responses.

Behaviour therapy   A term first used by Skinner to describe a method of psychotherapy based on learning principles. This is also sometimes called 'behaviour modification'. Clients are taught, through a variety of techniques, to modify or change problem behaviour.

Belongingness need   A term used by Maslow (1954) to describe the human need to give and receive acceptance, affection and trust.

Biological determinism   Freudian concept which states that sexual and aggressive forces govern human experience and behaviour.

Bipolar disorder   This describes two emotional and alternating extremes of depression and mania, which a person may experience intermittently. The condition was formerly referred to as 'manic depression'.

Blind spots   A term often used to describe characteristics, behaviours or areas of personal experience which are (temporarily at least) outside our awareness.

Brief therapy	Counselling which often takes place over six to eight weeks, or it may even be shorter. Brief therapy is characterised by clarity of focus and by the client's motivation in achieving results in the time allocated.
Burn-out	The outcome of accumulated stress, characterised by physical, psychological and behavioural dysfunction.
Case history	Material or information recorded for the purpose of understanding a patient's (or client's) problems. Case histories are often used to help plan helping strategies or treatments, and they are sometimes used for research purposes too.
Castration complex	In Freudian theory, an unconscious fear of genital mutilation or loss, as punishment for sexual attraction to the opposite sex parent. The concept applies to both women and men, and should be interpreted in a symbolic rather than a literal way. Men may, for example, fear a loss of power or potency, while women may actually experience disempowerment because of their relative lack of status or opportunity in society.
Catastrophising	A term used by Albert Ellis to describe a tendency to dwell on negative events or possibilities. An over-emphasis on the worst possible scenario or outcome.
Catharsis	Release or elimination of repressed emotions, usually achieved through crying or verbal expression of anger or resentment. The word is translated from Greek and means 'to clean'. See also **Abreaction**.
Cathexis	A term used in Freudian theory to describe the attachment of emotional energy or libido to mental representations of other people (object Cathexis) or to aspects of oneself (ego or id Cathexis).
Censor	A Freudian term used to describe an unconscious mechanism used by the ego in the production of defence mechanisms. Also used to denote the mechanism whereby dream content is distorted to make it more acceptable to the ego.
Claustrophobia	An abnormal fear of enclosed spaces.
Client	In psychotherapeutic terms, the word 'client' has come to refer to someone who seeks help in counselling. The word 'patient' was traditionally used for anyone accessing psychological support, and some of the older books (those published before 1960) still feature it. In the process of moving away from a purely medical model of helping, however, both counselling and psychotherapy have adopted the term client, which is increasingly used in the hospital context too.

Clinical psychologist	A psychology graduate who specialises in the understanding, assessment and treatment of emotional or behavioural problems.
Cognition	The experience of thinking, reasoning, perceiving and remembering. Early behaviour therapy highlighted observable behaviour only, while cognitive behaviour therapy stresses that thinking affects how we feel and what we do.
Cognitive dissonance	Conflicts in attitude or thinking which lead to feelings of unease. These feelings then motivate the person to seek ways of achieving consistency.
Cognitive restructuring	The process of replacing stress-producing thoughts with more positive or constructive thoughts. Often taught as a therapeutic technique to clients in therapy.
Collective unconscious	A Jungian concept which postulates that all human beings have, at an unconscious level, shared memories, ideas and experiences, based on the knowledge acquired through time by our common ancestors.
Compensation	The development of personality traits designed to overcome other inadequacies or imperfections. In Freudian terms, a defence mechanism.
Complex	The word 'complex' is used in both Freudian and Adlerian theory. The Oedipus complex is a Freudian term, while the inferiority complex stems from the work of Adler. In both cases the term complex denotes a cluster of interrelated conscious and unconscious feelings and ideas, which affect a person's behaviour.
Condensation	The representation of several complex ideas in a single symbol. Used in Freudian theory to describe aspects of dream imagery.
Compulsion	An overwhelming drive to repeat certain actions or rituals. See also **Obsessive compulsive disorder**.
Confidentiality	In the context of counselling, the word 'confidentiality' means ensuring that what is told in 'confidence' by a client is not repeated to anyone else, apart from certain exceptional circumstances.
Contract	In counselling, a contract is an agreement made between two people, the counsellor and the client. It may be verbal or written and is made before counselling starts. A contract encompasses all aspects of therapy, including confidentiality, times, dates, fees and the commitment of both counsellor and client to the process.

Conversion reaction   Turning a psychological problem into a physical one so that anxiety is transformed into a tangible form.

Crisis intervention   The procedures used in an immediate response to any psychological emergency.

Counselling   The process of counselling is very different from the dictionary definition of advice giving. In therapeutic terms it refers to a form of confidential helping which values and seeks to elicit each client's innate internal resources, coping abilities and strengths. Counsellors may help clients with specific problems in the present, but they may also support clients with long-term problems stemming from the past too.

Death instinct   A concept introduced by Freud in 1920 to describe aggressive or destructive forces which are directed against 'self' rather than against others. Certain self-destructive forms of behaviour, drug-taking or alcoholism for example, could theoretically be prompted by the death instinct.

Defence mechanism   A method of coping with the threat of anxiety. A pattern of behaviour designed to obscure unpleasant emotions.

Delusion   A false belief or conviction which is firmly held and defended.

Denial   Defence mechanism often used in situations of extreme stress. For example, a person with terminal illness might simply deny the diagnosis in order to reduce intolerable anxiety.

Depression   A feeling of hopelessness, apathy or despair. A mood (or affective) disorder, see also **Affect**. May include physical symptoms, loss of self-esteem, sleep disturbance, loss of appetite and tiredness.

Depressive position   The second of Melanie Klein's developmental positions (age three months) characterised by a recognition that the object (mother) who was hated is also loved and is, in fact, a 'whole' object rather than just disjointed parts. This realisation is accompanied by depressive anxiety, feelings of guilt, concern and a desire to repair the (imagined) damage done to the object.

Developmental psychologist   A psychology graduate who specialises in the study of development throughout the lifespan. There is a special emphasis on the relationship between early and later behaviour, and on the experiences of childhood and adolescence.

Displacement   A defence mechanism whereby unacceptable motives or impulses are directed towards another target or object.

Dissociation	A lack of integration or connection between mental processes. Loss of contact with reality which may occur during sleep-walking, hypnosis, loss of memory, illness or severe stress.
Dreams	According to Freud, dreams originate in the unconscious, have psychological meaning and can be interpreted. In psychodynamic theory, dreams are said to have a manifest content and a latent content. The former refers to that which is remembered by the dreamer, while the latter refers to the deeper meaning which can only be accessed through interpretation.
Eclectic	An approach used in counselling and psychotherapy characterised by adherence to one preferred theoretical school, while using methods belonging to other schools when appropriate to the needs of individual clients.
Ego	The 'I' or conscious part of personality. In Freud's tripartite theory of personality, the Ego mediates between the impulses of the Id and the strict demands of the Superego.
Ego boundary	The imaginary line which separates 'self' from others. A person who lacks ego boundaries finds it difficult to maintain a separate identity from others.
Ego ideal	How each person would like to be. Often used interchangeably with the term superego. Refers to the parental and other influences which set guidelines for civilised behaviour.
Ego integrity	Refers to the last of Erikson's psychosocial stages (ego integrity versus despair). Indicates equanimity and acceptance of both life and death in old age.
Ego psychology	A branch of psychodynamic theory which stresses the positive, autonomous and creative functions of the ego. This is in contrast to strict Freudian theory, which limits ego function to the arbiter in disputes between the id and superego.
Electra complex	A Freudian term used to describe a constellation of impulses in girls, similar to the Oedipus complex in boys.
Endogenous	Originating from within the person; for example, endogenous depression.
Environment	All outside influences, including other people, which affect the individual.
Environmental determinism	The idea enshrined in behaviourism that people are influenced by external forces.

Esteem needs From Maslow's hierarchy, where the need for respect for oneself and others is described.

Eros Used by Freud to denote the life force or sexual instinct. See contrast with the death instinct or '*Thanatos*'.

Extravert Personality type described by Jung. Refers to people who are inclined to direct mental energy and interests outwards towards other people and events. The term was also used by Eysenck (1991) to describe the outgoing personality type.

False memories Memories recalled during therapy or hypnosis which may, in fact, be dreamlike creations prompted by suggestion (spoken or unspoken) from the therapist.

Family therapy A psychotherapeutic approach in which the whole family is involved so that common problems can be addressed.

Fantasy Daydreaming to fulfil a psychological need. A defence mechanism which may be used as a substitute for reality.

Fitness to practise This term is used by many professional bodies and by BACP in their *Ethical Framework for Good Practice in Counselling and Psychotherapy* (2013:7). It means that practitioners should have the required skills, knowledge, competence, and supervision to practise as counsellors.

Fixation In Freudian theory arrested development at an early stage of life. Failure to progress through the stages of psychosexual development; for example, oral fixation.

Flight into health Describes the way in which clients in therapy sometimes seem to recover rapidly. May be viewed as a defence against introspection or self-analysis.

Flooding A method used in behaviour therapy to treat clients with phobias. The person is encouraged to stay in the feared situation and to experience all the anxiety that involves.

Free association A procedure originated by Freud and used in many approaches to therapy. The client is encouraged to say whatever comes to mind in the hope that unconscious ideas and conflicts will surface.

Free floating anxiety Generalised anxiety of unknown cause or origin.

Freudian slip A mistake, either verbal or action-based, which indicates some underlying meaning. One example is the student who misses the bus on the way to sit an important exam.

Genital stage The last of Freud's psychosexual stages of development. It is characterised by an interest in forming sexual relationships.

Gestalt	The word 'gestalt', which is German, means a pattern, shape or configuration. In Gestalt therapy it applies to a person's whole or complete sensory experience which is seen as more important than the parts of that experience in deciding meaning. Gestalt psychology states that *the whole is greater than the sum of its parts*.
Ground	The background in our visual field. The term is used in Gestalt theory along with the word figure (figure and ground) to describe a whole or pattern, which is known as a gestalt.
Group dynamics	The study of the way in which group members interact.
Group polarisation	A tendency, present in groups, to make decisions which are more extreme than those made by individuals.
Group think	A tendency among group members to lose the ability to be objective and realistic in their evaluation of decisions.
Growth motive	Described by Maslow as a human motive to develop and grow, even when there is no obvious need to continue striving.
Halo effect	A belief in the total goodness of a person possessed of one outstanding quality.
Hallucination	A sensory perception which may be visual, auditory, olfactory or tactile. Experiences which are not present in reality, but are nevertheless believed to be real by the individual. Common in certain forms of illness, including psychosis. May also occur after bereavement when the hallucination is seen as evidence of the dead person's presence.
Hierarchy of needs	The order of importance which Maslow ascribes to human needs. Lower order needs must be fulfilled before higher order needs can be experienced.
Holistic	An approach which emphasises the connection between all areas of experience, including the physical, the emotional and the environmental.
Homeostasis	An organic tendency to maintain a constant state or optimum level of functioning. One example is the physiological mechanism which ensures a uniform body temperature. In Jungian theory, psychological homeostasis or automatic self-regulation also occurs, and is achieved when there is a balance between the conscious and unconscious aspects of the psyche.
Horney, Karen (1885–1952)	A German psychoanalyst who moved to America in 1932. Emphasised the role of cultural and environmental factors

in the development of mental problems, especially those affecting women.

Humanistic psychology   A psychological approach which emphasises subjective experience and the uniqueness of human beings. Sometimes referred to as the 'Third Force' in psychology, after psychoanalysis and behaviourism.

Hypnosis   The trance-like state resembling sleep. Artificially induced state during which a person's perception, voluntary actions and memory may be altered, and susceptibility to suggestion is heightened.

Hypnotherapy   The treatment of problems or illness through hypnosis.

I   The subjective experience of self similar to the word 'ego'. However, 'I' is a personal pronoun whereas the word ego is used as an objective description of the self.

Id   Refers to the primitive pleasure-seeking part of the personality described by Freud.

Ideal self   A Rogerian concept describing the kind of person one would really like to be. Conflict often arises between the 'ideal self' and the 'false self', especially when the former cannot be expressed or fully acknowledged.

Identification   A process of modelling personal behaviour on the behaviour of someone else. In extreme cases a person's identity may be totally merged with that of someone else. In psychoanalysis, primary identification refers to a relationship in which the mother is the object, whereas secondary identification refers to a relationship where the object is seen as having a separate identity. See also **Projective identification**.

Identity crisis   A term used by Erikson to describe the turmoil which accompanies certain developmental stages, especially in adolescence. Young adults are faced with the task of separating from parents and of finding a suitable place in society. Erikson also describes the tendency to form peer groups at this stage, so that individual identities become merged.

Illusion   A mistaken perception of reality.

Imago   A term used in psychoanalytic and Jungian theory to describe unconscious object representations. Similar to Jung's concept of the **Archetype**.

Incorporation   In Freudian theory this refers to a fantasy of having taken in or swallowed an external object or person.

Individuation	A Jungian term which refers to the process of psychic development and growth. A lifelong process which is particularly significant in middle age, when existential issues appear in sharp focus.
Inferiority complex	A term used by Adler to describe a constellation of ideas and feelings which arise in response to personal deficiency. The term is now more commonly used to denote feelings of worthlessness and inadequacy which often lead to lack of self-esteem or aggression.
Insight	In psychoanalytic terms, the capacity to understand mental processes, personal motives and the meaning of symbolic behaviour.
Instinct	Innate, unlearned, goal-directed behaviour arising from a biological source.
Intellectualisation	A defence mechanism which is used to ward off emotionally threatening material.
Internal reality	A person's own subjective experience of events.
Internalisation	The process of acquiring mental representations of people or objects in the external world. Often used in object relations theory to describe the way in which an infant builds up an inner world of images which are derived from relationships, especially the relationship with the mother. These representations are then used to form an image of 'self' which can be either good or bad, depending on the quality of early relationship experience.
Intrapsychic	Refers to mental activity and the processes which occur between the id, the ego and the superego.
Introjection	This is the process whereby objects (or other people) are internalised and become mental representations. The mental structure resulting from this is referred to as an *internal object* or an *introjected object*. These internal objects then form the subject's values, beliefs and attitudes and are the basis of the superego.
Introversion	A psychological type described by Freud. Refers to a human tendency to withdraw inwards, especially at times of stress. See also **Extraversion**.
Isolation	A defence mechanism used by people to separate thoughts from emotions. Experiences are deprived of affect or feeling and can be viewed in a wholly detached way.

James, William (1842–1910)	An American psychologist who wrote the two-volume book *Principles of Psychology* in 1890.
Latency	Freud's fourth stage of psychosexual development (age 6–12 years) during which sexual interests become dormant.
Law of effect	Refers to a law stating that any behaviour followed by reinforcement is strengthened. Responses which are not rewarded are less likely to be performed again.
Learned helplessness	A state of apathy or helplessness described by Seligman (1975), which develops when a person is unable to escape or avoid a situation in which there is discomfort or trauma.
Libido	In Freudian theory refers to a person's basic life instincts.
Longitudinal study	Research method used to study people over a period of time and taking measurements at different stages of development.
Lucid dreaming	Being aware that we are dreaming while the dream is actually in progress. This indicates that sleep may not always involve a total loss of consciousness.
Mania	An elevated expansive mood with increased levels of restlessness or irritability. There may also be a sense of grandiosity, flights of ideas and marked reduction in the need for sleep. Frequently accompanied by alternating periods of depression. See also **Bipolar disorder**.
Masochism	A desire for pain, humiliation or suffering inflicted by oneself or by others.
Maturation	The process of growing and becoming fully developed both mentally and physically.
Medical model	Sometimes called a biological model. An approach which states that mental illness and behaviour disorders are due to physical causes which should, therefore, be treated by medical means.
Meditation	An altered state of consciousness induced by intense concentration or the repetition of certain words or actions, and resulting in inner feelings of peace and tranquillity.
Mindfulness	A practice used to alleviate stress and anxiety by paying attention to the present moment. It is a way of stilling the mind and overcoming negative mental thoughts. Teaches self-observation with an emphasis on compassion for self.
Moral principle	Refers to the influence exerted by the superego whose purpose is to restrict free expression of id impulses. Guilt is

reduced when such impulses are restricted through the moral principle.

Multiple personality
A dissociative disorder in which a person appears to possess more than one identity, all acting and speaking in different ways.

Multidisciplinary approach
A team approach to working with clients. Counsellors working in the public sector frequently liaise with other professionals, including doctors and social workers.

Narcissism
A form of self-love in which there is an investment of energy or libido in oneself. In other words, the subject is preferred to the object. In Freudian theory the term 'primary narcissism' refers to the infantile love of self, which is then followed by 'secondary narcissism' when love of self is replaced by love of an introjected other person or object.

Need satisfying object
An object or other person valued for an ability to satisfy one's basic or instinctual needs, without any regard for the needs or personality of the object.

Negative therapeutic reaction
A term used in psychoanalysis to describe a negative response whereby a client's general condition worsens as a result of interpretation offered by the therapist.

Neo-Freudian
Description of a group of American theorists who re-interpreted Freudian theory and emphasised the influence of society and relationships on people and their behaviour. This group includes Eric Fromm, Karen Horney and Harry Stack Sullivan.

Neurosis
A pattern of behaviour, including fear and anxiety, with no organic basis. Possible psychological causes include past events or traumas, relationship and sexual difficulties.

Neuroscience
The study of the brain and spinal cord, usually associated with medicine, but increasingly relevant into other disciplines, including counselling.

Norm
Average, standard or common. A learned and accepted rule of society which dictates behaviour in various situations.

Object
In object relations theory the word 'object' refers to another person to whom emotional energy, including love and desire, is directed by the subject. An object may also be a part of a person, or a symbolic representation of either a person or part of a person. Additionally, an object may be external, or it may be an internal image derived from an actual external relationship.

Object Cathexis	Investment of emotional energy in another person. Contrast with **narcissism**.
Object constancy	The tendency to adhere to a specific lasting relationship with another person. In infancy, object constancy refers to the baby's preference for and strong bond with, the mother or primary caregiver.
Object, good	May be internal (as a mental representation) or external. An object perceived as reliable, dependable, trustworthy and loving.
Object permanence	The knowledge that objects exist even when they are hidden from view. Such knowledge is a result of the ability to form mental representations of external objects.
Object, transitional	A substitute for another person or for an important relationship. Winnicott uses the term to describe soft toys, dolls and pieces of cloth or blanket which children value because of the symbolic link to the mother. These objects are effective in helping children move gradually from dependence to independence.
Object, whole	The object or other person who is seen as separate and existing in their own right, with feelings and needs similar to those of the subject.
Observational learning	The process of observing and learning from the behaviour of others.
Obsessive compulsive disorder (OCD)	Persistent thoughts, ideas and impulses which are inappropriate and intrusive, and which lead to anxiety and a compulsion to do certain things. The goal of such compulsive behaviour is to prevent or reduce anxiety. Cleaning rituals and checking are examples of OCD.
Oedipus complex	This is a Freudian concept used to describe the phallic stage of psychosexual development (3–6 years) when a small boy is said to be sexually attracted to his mother. There is accompanying hostility towards the father who is seen as a rival. Fear of retaliation ensures that these incestuous desires are repressed, and the eventual outcome is identification with the father and the adoption of male sex-role behaviour by the son.
Omnipotence	A Freudian concept which indicates a belief that thought can alter the environment or events. At an early stage, infants are said to experience omnipotence of thought, and only later come to realise, through the frustration of everyday living, that reality prevails.

Operant conditioning	The process whereby an animal or person learns to respond to the environment in a way that produces a desired effect. In laboratory research, B.F. Skinner trained animals by immediately rewarding them for correct responses. He later applied the same concept to human learning.
Oral stage	In psychoanalytic theory, the first of Freud's stages of psychosexual development is characterised by an infant's pleasure in feeding and dependence on the mother.
Organismic self	The real inner life of the person which is present from birth and gravitates towards self-actualisation, integration and harmony.
Panic disorder	Sometimes referred to as panic attacks, and include frightening recurrent anxiety which appears without warning and is not associated with a specific phobia. The panic is accompanied by fast heart rate, sweating, shortness of breath, trembling, dizziness and sometimes nausea.
Paranoia	A mental disorder in which delusions of persecution or grandeur are common.
Paranoid–schizoid position	The first of Melanie Klein's positions which occupies the first three months of an infant's life. It is characterised by feelings of persecution and threats of annihilation, along with splitting of the ego into good and bad. In Klein's view, this precedes the depressive position and represents the infant's attempts to deal with destructive impulses which are projected onto the mother (object).
Paraphraxis	A term used to denote unconscious mental forces which prompt certain unintended actions or mistakes in speech. These errors are more commonly referred to as Freudian slips, and are seen as evidence of unconscious conflicts or wishes.
Persona	A Jungian term which translated means 'a mask', and describes the characteristics which people assume as part of their roles in everyday life.
Person-centred	This refers to an attitude which counsellors, or ideally anyone in the helping professions, should have. It means paying attention to the real person of the client and identifying their individual experiences and needs, which are quite separate from anyone else's.
Personal construct	A personality theory proposed by the American psychologist George Kelly (1905–1967), which suggests that people construe their own worlds. According to Kelly, we interpret things and

try to understand them, and to do this we employ personal constructs. These represent our own private logic and include deductions and conclusions which determine personality and guide behaviour. When events accord with our expectations we feel comfortable and our personal constructs are validated. If, however, we anticipate wrongly we are obliged to reconstrue, a process which causes discomfort and threat.

Personality
General patterns of behaviour and thought which are characteristic of an individual. Major theories have been forwarded by Freud, Adler, Jung, Klein, Sullivan, Horney and Erikson, though other writers have contributed to the field as well.

Personality disorder
Psychological disturbances in which personality traits or behaviour interfere with social functioning.

Phallic stage
The third of Freud's psychosexual stages of development, preceded by the oral and anal stages. Characterised by the **Oedipus complex**.

Phantasy
Refers to unconscious mental activity, and differs from **Fantasy** which takes place at a conscious level. The word is used in object relations theory to describe much of the psychic activity occurring in infancy.

Phobia
Irrational fear of a specific object or situation. An anxiety disorder which interferes with daily life. In psychodynamic theory, the phobic situation or object represents an unconscious fear or impulse which the person is unable to face.

Pleasure principle
In psychodynamic theory this is the operating principle of the id, which prompts people to seek immediate satisfaction of desires and needs.

Post-traumatic stress disorder (PTSD)
The development of symptoms following an extremely stressful experience or situation. It differs from other anxiety disorders because of its specific causation. The traumatic event is usually experienced through recurrent and intrusive recollections, images, thoughts or perceptions. Distressing dreams and nightmares also occur, and there is often persistent avoidance of anything associated with the trauma.

Primary process thinking
A Freudian concept used to describe a primitive form of thinking which is characteristic of early infancy. A very basic form of wishful thinking through which the infant can access images of a desired object (mother).

Projection	A defence mechanism stemming from psychoanalytic theory. It describes the way people often ascribe unacceptable desires or feelings to others instead of to themselves. The result is a reduction in guilt and discomfort. In Kleinan terms, projection has a different meaning, and refers to a normal developmental strategy used in early infancy. In this sense, impulses, including good and bad feelings, are projected by the infant on to the object (mother).
Projective identification	A Kleinian term which describes the way in which clients in therapy may force aspects of their internal world onto the therapist (see Units 3 and 4).
Psychiatrist	A medical doctor with specialist training in the treatment of mental or emotional disorders.
Psychoanalysis	This term refers to two aspects of Freud's work. First, it denotes his theory of human development and behaviour, and secondly it describes the related therapy which is used to help clients gain access to mental conflicts. Among the techniques used in psychoanalysis are *free association, interpretation,* and the analysis of *resistance* and *transference*.
Psychodrama	This refers to the exploration of emotions and situations through actions in a supportive therapeutic environment. When emotions are explored in this way feelings tend to surface quickly, and are re-experienced in a way which leads to new learning.
Psychodynamic	In the context of psychotherapy and counselling the word 'psychodynamic' refers to an approach which originates in Freudian theory. The term is derived from two words *psyche* (meaning mind) and *dynamic* (meaning active or alive) both of which are Greek in origin. Put together these two words describe the activity of the human mind, both conscious and unconscious.
Psychologist	A person who has obtained a degree in psychology. May also specialise in different areas of psychology including clinical, developmental, educational, industrial and abnormal psychology.
Psychopathology	The study of mental illness.
Psychosis	A severe mental illness in which a person loses contact with reality and is unable to manage daily living. May include delusions and hallucinations.
Psychosocial	This is a term used to describe Erikson's stages of human development. The first part of the word 'psych' refers to

the mind, while the second part 'social' refers to one's place within society and our relationships with others. Erikson's stages, therefore, describe mental and social development throughout the life span.

Psychosomatic disorder   Physical illness with a psychological cause.

Rationalisation   Freudian defence mechanism which offers false reasons for unacceptable behaviour. A person who steals might, for example, overcome feelings of guilt by saying that the people he steals from have too much money anyway.

Psychotherapy   The terms counselling and psychotherapy are often taken to denote the same process, and in many instances it is difficult to identify any appreciable differences between them. Traditionally psychotherapy training differed in length from that of counselling and tended to take longer. Psychotherapists use all the skills of counselling, but may have additional specific training, and may be concerned with life patterns relating to the past and its influence on the present.

Reaction formation   Another Freudian defence mechanism in which a person's views, impulses and behaviour are directly opposite to what she or he really feels.

Reality principle   Describes the operating principle of the ego in Freudian theory. The reality principle is acquired through development and experience, and is that part of personality which seeks to compromise between the unreasonable demands of the id, and the demands of the real world.

Regression   Returning to an earlier less mature stage of development when stressful conditions prevail. An example is the small child who reverts to baby language after the birth of a sibling.

Reinforcement   In classical conditioning, these are strengthening responses through a system of rewards. Rewards increase the likelihood that a person will behave in certain desired ways.

Reparation   A Freudian defence mechanism which involves a process of repair. Guilt is reduced when action is taken to atone for imagined damage to internal objects. One way of doing this is to recreate the object which has been destroyed in Phantasy. In Kleinian theory, reparation is a normal part of the developmental process and is used by the infant to resolve ambivalent feelings (of love and hate) towards the mother.

Repetition compulsion	A Freudian term which describes the tendency to repeat certain patterns of behaviour derived from early experience. Since much of this early experience is based on relationships with parents and other significant figures, later repetitions also tend to occur in the context of relationships.
Repression	A Freudian defence mechanism which involves pushing unacceptable emotions or feelings into the unconscious. This ensures that deeply distressing impulses or emotions do not cause anxiety.
Resistance	A word used in psychoanalytic literature to describe a person's opposition to the process of therapy. It is especially relevant in relation to interpretations offered by the therapist. These interpretations may be rejected for fear that unconscious material will surface and so have to be faced. Resistance may also be present when sessions are missed, or when clients arrive late or talk about totally irrelevant topics.
Rorschach test	A personality test devised by Swiss psychiatrist Hermann Rorschach (1844–1922). The test uses a series of ink blots which the subject is asked to interpret. Answers are meant to provide evidence of the subject's fantasy life and personality structure.
Sadism	A pathological need to obtain pleasure by inflicting pain on others (see also **Masochism**).
Safety need	From Maslow's hierarchy of needs: the human need to be safe from physical and psychological danger.
Schizophrenia	A severe mental illness characterised by hallucinations, delusions, disorganised behaviour, incoherent speech and withdrawal.
Script analysis	This is based on the idea that everyone has a life plan or 'script' which determines behaviour and life choices. Analysis of scripts brings these, largely unconscious, motivations into conscious awareness.
Secondary gain	Any advantage derived from an illness or condition, or positive side effects which accompany a negative event.
Secondary process thinking	In contrast to *primary process thinking*, this refers to logical and realistic thought processes (see also *primary process thinking*).
Self	The way in which a person experiences him or herself. This is in contrast to the concept of 'ego' which is a descriptive term used in psychoanalytic theory to refer objectively to a *part* of human personality (see also *ego*).

Self-actualisation

A Rogerian concept describing an innate tendency towards growth and self-realisation.

Self–concept

This is a person's view of self which is acquired in early childhood, and developed through life experience. It is reinforced by the reflected appraisals of other people, especially parents, and other important figures in a person's life.

Self-fulfilling prophecy

Ideas or beliefs about people which influence our attitudes towards them. These ideas and beliefs are then reinforced when people's responses fulfil our expectations.

Sibling rivalry

The competition for parental attention which occurs between children in the same family.

Social psychology

That branch of psychology which studies social interaction, including the thought processes and behaviour of individuals, pairs and groups.

Solution focused brief therapy (SFBT)

This is a form of therapy pioneered by Steve de Shazer which focuses on finding solutions to problems, rather than dwelling on the past, and is described in Unit 8.

Stereotyping

Preconceived ideas, and expectations about certain groups of people, and about male and female behaviour and roles. Although some stereotypes may seem positive, they are always, in fact, negative. This is because individuals should be assessed on personal merit, rather than on judgments about the perceived attributes of their particular group.

Structural analysis

This refers to a theory of personality based on the study of specific ego states. These ego states are: Adult, Parent and Child.

Structural model

Regardless of the theoretical approach, counselling needs a framework in order to provide structure for the process. This framework begins with a contract between counsellor and client, but is more extensive than this and includes consideration of the various stages of counselling and the skills and processes which are relevant to them.

Sublimation

A defence mechanism which involves the conversion of instinctual impulses into socially acceptable activities.

Stack Sullivan, Harry (1892–1949)

An American psychiatrist who emphasised the importance of social factors in the development of personality.

Superego

In the Freudian tripartite structure of personality, the superego is the component which guides ethical and moral behaviour.

Thanatos	The Greek god of death. The term was used by Freud to describe the aggressive instinctual forces which, in his view, motivated human beings towards destructive behaviour and death.
Theoretical approach	Each model of helping is informed by a set of theories about human development and personality. These theories underpin the skills and techniques used by practitioners of the model, and they also determine the kind of training needed to qualify in that approach.
Thorndike, Edward Lee (1874–1949)	An American behavioural psychologist, famous for his studies in animal learning and his research in educational psychology. He established that mental abilities are independent so that, for example, a person who is good at verbal skills might lack an aptitude for maths.
Token economy	A procedure used in behaviour modification for rewarding desired behaviour with tokens which can be exchanged for privileges. These tokens include snacks, gifts, access to television or trips. Sometimes used in institutions, including hospitals.
Transaction	This refers to communication between two or more people in any social situation. Communication can be verbal or non-verbal. Berne used the term 'strokes' to denote the exchanges that people engage in socially (Berne, 1964, p.14).
Transactional analysis	This refers to the analysis of a person's communications style or 'transactions' which is carried out with the aid of diagrams so that the specific ego states involved are identified.
Transference	In psychodynamic theory this refers to the process of directing feelings, attitudes and conflicts experienced in childhood to people in the present (see Units 3 and 4).
Transpersonal psychology	An approach to therapy that focuses on experiences which go beyond the purely personal. It is similar in some ways to existential therapy, but is different in that it emphasises the spiritual component of human experience in a way that the existential approach avoids.
Trust versus mistrust	The first of Erikson's psychosocial stages which corresponds roughly to Freud's oral stage of development. When early experience is positive and supportive a child is likely to develop a sense of basic trust and confidence in self.
Unconditional positive regard	An attitude described by Carl Rogers in his client-centred approach to therapy. It refers to the way the client should be valued and accepted unconditionally by the counsellor.

Unconditional response   A term used in behavioural psychology to describe the automatic or unlearned response to a stimulus.

Unconditional stimulus   Another term used in behavioural psychology to describe the stimulus which elicits an automatic response with learning or conditioning.

Unconscious   That area of mental activity which, according to Freud, is outside immediate awareness. Contains feelings, memories and motives as well as sexual and aggressive impulses which, although hidden, nevertheless affect behaviour.

Unconscious motivation   As the term implies it refers to a process outside conscious awareness. However, some motives have both conscious and unconscious components and occasionally a motive is discernible in distorted or disguised form.

Wish fulfilment   A term used in Freudian theory to suggest that dreams may express unconscious wishes or desires. Clearly not all dreams could be described as wish fulfilment, since many of them are frightening or disturbing.

Working through   A term used in psychodynamic theory to describe the process whereby a client in therapy gains insight, becomes independent and prepares to change. This process also involves some degree of mourning for the past.

Index